Mexican Revolution

Genesis under Madero

Photograph Brown Brothers

Francisco I. Madero

Mexican
Revolution

Genesis under Madero

By Charles Curtis Cumberland

GREENWOOD PRESS, PUBLISHERS
WESTPORT, CONNECTICUT

The Library of Congress cataloged this book as follows:

Cumberland, Charles Curtis.
    Mexican Revolution, genesis under Madero. New York,
Greenwood Press ₍1969, °1952₎

    ix, 298 p. illus., map, ports. 23 cm.

    Bibliography: p. 261–278.

    1. Mexico—History—1910–1946. 2. Madero, Francisco Indalecio,
Pres. Mexico, 1873–1913.   ɪ. Title.

F1234.C975 1969   972.08′1   71–90495
SBN 8371-2126-4   MARC

Library of Congress   70 ₍4₎

Reprinted with the permission of the University of Texas
Press

Reprinted in 1969 by Greenwood Press, Inc.,
51 Riverside Avenue, Westport, Conn. 06880

Library of Congress catalog card number 71-90495
ISBN 0-8371-2126-4

Printed in the United States of America

10 9 8 7 6 5 4 3 2

Preface

THE MEXICAN REVOLUTION, which began in 1910 and is still in progress, has been one of the most important and ambitious sociopolitical experiments in modern history. The Revolution has developed in three distinct stages: the period which saw the overthrow of the dictatorship and attempts at modified reform, the longer era of bloodshed and devastation during which radical ideas were written into the constitution but during which little actual progress was made, and the much longer span during which the ideas have been put into practice. The present volume concerns itself with only the first stage of this development; later volumes will deal with the succeeding stages.

The task of research has been made easier through the kindness and helpfulness of a large number of persons in both Mexico and the United States. To José C. Valadés I owe a debt of gratitude which can never be repaid. I wish also to express my deep appreciation for the aid given me by Juan B. Iguínez, Arturo Arnaiz y Freg, Silvio Zavala, Roberto Ramos, Paul V. Murray, Emilio Madero, and a host of unnamed librarians in Mexico City who gave me valuable assistance in finding materials and made my working conditions as pleasant as possible. The staffs of the Library of the University of Texas, the Library of Congress, and the Archives of the United States were unstintingly co-operative and helpful.

For financial assistance which made much of the research and writing possible, I am indebted to the United States Department of State, the Faculty Research Committee at Princeton University, and the Research Council of Rutgers University.

CHARLES C. CUMBERLAND

New Brunswick, New Jersey
January 16, 1952

Concerning Footnotes

IN ORDER to conserve space, the footnotes in this work have been condensed in so far as possible. Short titles, abbreviations, and initials are used wherever such use leads to economy. For full bibliographical information on any items cited, see the Bibliography. The following cues on documentary collections are used throughout:

BN — Madero Archive, Biblioteca Nacional, Mexico City. A collection of documents concerning the period between January and August, 1911. Each BN reference is followed by a number, indicating the number of the document in the collection.

DP — Toribio Esquivel Obregón, *Democracia y personalismo*. This work, in both the text and the appendix, contains a large selection of documents concerning the peace negotiations and the revolutionary movement.

FR — *Papers Relating to the Foreign Relations of the United States*. The number immediately following the *FR* reference indicates the year of the volume.

LO — Documents published in *La Opinión* of Los Angeles, California. All documents appear in section 2 of the paper; the date immediately following the *LO* reference indicates the date of the paper. These documents, the originals of which are not now available for use by researchers, were edited and annotated by José C. Valadés, author of *El porfirismo* and other historical works.

LP — Same as above, for *La Prensa* of San Antonio, Texas.

MP — Francisco Vázquez Gómez, *Memorias políticas, (1909–1913)*. Dr. Vázquez Gómez, one of the principals in the Revolution, includes a large collection of his documents.

SP — *British Foreign and State Papers*. The dates following the *SP* reference indicate the date of the volume.

VC — A private collection of documents in the hands of José C. Valadés.

Contents

Illustrations

Mexican Revolution

Genesis under Madero

I

Background for Revolution

W<small>HEN IN</small> S<small>EPTEMBER</small>, 1910, Mexico played host to the embassies of the world at the magnificent spectacle celebrating a century of Mexican independence, the special delegates vied with one another in extolling the virtues and strength of the Díaz regime. General Porfirio Díaz was completing his seventh term as constitutional president of Mexico, having been the dictator of his country for thirty-four years,[1] and was then about to embark upon his eighth term. His nation was honored and respected; as a head of state Díaz had been phenomenally successful in stabilizing Mexico and bringing her material prosperity. The power and prestige of the aged dictator, who appeared to be hale and vigorous in spite of his eighty years, had never been greater; his government was believed to be impervious to attack, his power unassailable, his country assured of a peaceful future. And yet, within the space of eight months the Díaz government crumbled, the dictator and most of his chief advisors fled into exile, and a revolution of tremendous force began.

That the Díaz government was a dictatorship no one denied. Even its strongest supporters freely admitted that the Constitution of 1857 had been perverted, that the branches of government were nonexistent inasmuch as Díaz was the final arbiter in all questions, and that "democracy" was merely a term used indiscriminately. As Francisco Bulnes expressed it, the question was not whether Díaz was a dictator, since the Mexicans in the past had possessed neither liberty nor democracy, but whether he was a good or a bad dictator.[2] His task, on assuming control in 1876, had been to weld the Mexican people into a peaceful unit, to stabilize the government and pacify the country, and to bring material gain and prosperity to the nation. Each part of the

---

[1] Even though Manuel González was president for one term, 1880–84, Díaz still partially, but not completely, dictated policy.

[2] Francisco Bulnes, *El verdadero Díaz y la revolución*, 23–28.

3

task impinged on the other; failure in one would have meant almost inevitable failure in the other two.

The Mexico of 1876 was far from an integrated nation; innumerable factions had long contested for power, and the basic class structure which had existed during the colonial period had changed but little in the half-century since independence. At the top of the social structure, from the point of view of prestige and wealth, were the creoles,[3] who in turn were divided into three distinct groups.[4] Following the creoles were the mestizos,[5] again divided into a number of groups, and these were followed by the Indians.[6] Under the Díaz government, each class was to play its part, each group had its particular function; furthermore, all social classes acclaimed the dictatorship for the peace and stability which prevailed. With a consummate skill which approached intuition, Díaz recognized the desires and needs of each group and was able to meet those needs at least partially.

Of these groups the largest, and from the standpoint of national development the most important, was the mestizo. Constituting approximately half the population[7] and harboring a germ of strident nationalism, the mestizos were important to Díaz as a support to his regime; accordingly, it was the mestizos to whom he turned for his chief administrators and his principal political backing. Great numbers of military men, unemployed since peace, were attracted to the regime through financial benefits emanating from newly created agencies; large numbers of civilians were accommodated in the government through an expanded bureaucracy which, according to one estimate, by 1910 employed nearly 70 per cent of the mestizo middle class at an annual cost of seventy million pesos.[8] With rare exceptions, the chief ministers, the state governors, and the superior officers of the army were mestizos. This class in general had little to complain of and tended to support the Díaz government.

The creole groups, though having distinct, and sometimes conflict-

---

[3] Men of presumably pure European stock, unmixed with Indian; the term quite often indicated wealth and social position only.

[4] The new "creole," frequently of non-Spanish heritage, who emerged into a position of power from the War of Reform (1858–61) and the Maximilian period; the old creole of ancient Spanish lineage; and the clerical creole, adherent of extreme clericalism.

[5] Ethnically, people of Spanish and Indian blood; in practice, all who adopted mestizo mores.

[6] Andrés Molina Enríquez (*Los grandes problemas nacionales,* 196–270) discusses the social stratification in detail.   [7] *Ibid.,* 196–98.

[8] Bulnes, *El verdadero Díaz,* 42–43.

4

ing, interests, were agreed on at least one basic principle: they had a "perceptible orientation in the direction of their original countries, or at least toward the European continental grouping" which they considered as their common country. They were born in Mexico, but they looked toward Europe as a source of inspiration and as an ideal place in which to be educated and in which to live.[9] They were convinced that both the mestizos and the Indians, savage and bestial hordes who should never be allowed to take part in politics, were far beneath them. Further, they were convinced that approval by foreign powers was an absolute essential to successful and stable government in Mexico; the "idea that foreign interests should be above those of national life . . . was a current dogma," according to one contemporary critic.[10]

Whereas Díaz made his peace with the mestizos by giving them limited political participation, he gained the support of the creoles by catering to their economic interests. The old creoles, many of whom were *hacendados,*[11] asked nothing more than to be left alone to enjoy the fruits of their holdings. Believing in a minimum of government control over economic life, they had no desire to participate directly in politics; but by virtue of their large holdings they exercised an enormous influence on political developments.[12]

The clerical creoles—the Church hierarchy and those laymen who supported extreme clericalism—were principally interested in preventing strict enforcement of the anticlerical Laws of Reform.[13] When Díaz made it clear that he would not enforce the laws, even though the provisions remained on the statute books, he placated the clerical creoles; so long as such a condition prevailed, the hierarchy had no desire to participate in politics other than to give support to the dictator.

The new creoles, having come into prominence as a result of a political upheaval, were more inclined toward direct political action; Díaz satisfied their political urge by giving them positions of honor but little power—as diplomatic representatives, members of Congress, and occasionally as cabinet members of lesser rank—and then invited sup-

[9] Molina, *Los grandes problemas,* 294.　　　　[10] *Ibid.,* 305.
[11] Owners of haciendas, immense estates which were often self-contained units with many similarities to feudal baronies.
[12] Molina (*Los grandes problemas,* 69) insisted that the creoles actually determined economic policy.
[13] A body of "liberal" laws, the principal characteristic of which was anticlericalism, decreed by Juárez during and immediately after the War of Reform (1858–61) and included as amendments to the Constitution during the administration of Sebastián Lerdo de Tejada.

5

port from their class by granting special concessions which were quite lucrative. The new creoles becames the bankers, the financiers, the industrialists, and the concessionaires in the new economic program; many, like the old creoles, gained social prestige and economic advantage by acquiring haciendas. Their economic and social position secure under the dictatorship, the creoles as a whole had little cause to condemn the lack of political freedom, but they had real cause to support the regime.[14]

The third major element in Mexican society when Díaz seized control in 1876 was the Indian, constituting approximately 35 per cent of the total population. In spite of this numerical strength, the indigenous population was a negligible factor in the political sphere because of its submerged economic and social position. Díaz never considered it necessary to make any special concession to the Indians; in fact, from the beginning he tended to believe the creole doctrine that the Indian was a hindrance to progress and should be extirpated or kept in perpetual subjugation.[15] Aside from the rather dubious advantages accruing to the Indians through the division of the *ejidos*,[16] Díaz made no attempt to gain the support of this large segment of the public.

Within a relatively short time after coming to power, Díaz managed to obtain the active or tacit support of the great majority of the Mexican people of all classes by attempting to meet the special interests of each class. Through this practice, supplemented by a policy of harsh repression against revolutionaries and bandits, he brought peace to Mexico, the first peace the nation had known since the colonial period, and laid the foundation for an amazing material development.[17] Railway lines, which in 1876 had been negligible, totaled more than fifteen thousand miles in 1910. During the same period, exports and imports increased nearly tenfold, with a favorable balance of trade in most years. Smelting of precious and semiprecious metals increased fourfold, petroleum production became a major industry, textile mills were built by the hundreds, sugar mills sprang up in the southern states, and nu-

[14] For a critical analysis of the position of the creoles, see Molina, *Los grandes problemas*, passim.

[15] See Frank Tannenbaum, *Peace by Revolution*, 31 ff.

[16] Community lands held by Indian villages, dating from the precolonial and the colonial eras. Under the terms of the Ley Lerdo, passed in 1856, these lands were to be divided in fee simple among the villagers. See below, pp. 19–24.

[17] During the first fifty-five years of her national existence, Mexico was the victim of three major revolutions and approximately one hundred *coups d'état* and minor movements.

6

Background for Revolution

merous smaller but important industries began. The prosperity of the epoch was reflected in the favorable relationship between national debt and national income, and in the foreign-credit standing. Mexican bonds on foreign markets sold at a premium, the national debt declined until in the early 1900's it was the smallest in the country's history, revenues increased more than tenfold, and reserves accumulated annually. The domestic and foreign financial standing of the Mexican government, under the direction of the dictatorship, was very sound.[18]

These advances were made at the expense of constitutional government and were accompanied by monopoly and special privilege. Díaz, a skillful politician, insisted on outward conformity to the constitutional and legal structure, even though he governed dictatorially. When a major change was necessary for the convenience or the policy of the dictatorship, the constitution was amended by the proper process, but Díaz controlled the process. The courts were ostensibly independent, but in all important cases Díaz dictated the decision; the American ambassador to Mexico in 1910 characterized the courts as "lame, incompetent, and corrupt."[19] Even though freedom of the press was guaranteed by law, all opposition papers were in constant danger of suppression and the editors subject to imprisonment.[20] Elections, regularly held for all elective officials, were meaningless inasmuch as Díaz virtually appointed all officeholders.[21]

Despite the absence of constitutional government and the occasionally brutal destruction of political enemies, the Díaz dictatorship was not excessively harsh.[22] The dictator employed cajolery and political maneuvering to attain his ends; he used repressive measures only when all else failed. The slogan of his administration, *Pan y palo*,[23] is an al-

---

[18] Statistics concerning economic developments may be found in the following government publications of Mexico: Secretaría de Fomento, Colonización é Industria, *Anuario estadístico de la República Mexicana* and *Informes y documentos relativos a comercio interior y exterior;* and Ministerio de Fomento, Dirección General de Estadística, *Censo General de la República Mexicana.* Censuses were taken in 1895, 1900, and 1910.

[19] Henry Lane Wilson to State Department, October 31, 1910, *FR*, 1911, p. 353.

[20] Ireneo Paz (*Porfirio Díaz*, II, 53–59) lists the various repressive measures employed against newsmen in the late nineteenth century.

[21] Ernest Gruening, *Mexico and Its Heritage*, 59 ff.; Francisco I. Madero, *La sucesión presidencial en 1910*, 205–206.

[22] The most notorious case was the execution of a group of revolutionaries in Veracruz in 1879.

[23] Literally "Bread and Stick," meaning advantage for the co-operative and repression for the opposition.

7

most perfect description of his technique: the skillful employment of a mixture of favoritism and force. Men who attended to their own business and were not hypercritical of the government had nothing to fear: no secret police molested the average citizen, academic political discussions were tolerated and sometimes encouraged, political parties were seldom outlawed, and many opposition publications were allowed to continue if they did not become too violent.

On the other hand, men who gave unquestioning service to the dictator received rewards in the form of rich economic concessions or valuable political sinecures; they became governors, generals in command of military zones, or lesser officials—depending on their importance to the regime. Francisco Bulnes, a Díaz critic even though he served for many years as a Díaz-appointed senator, gives as an illustration of this policy the case of a man who, having fruitlessly sought a government position for many years, was appointed to a high-salaried job three days after his publication of a eulogy of the Díaz government.[24]

This policy had its weaknesses, of course, particularly in that it often placed in positions of responsibility and power men who were not qualified to fulfill the functions of the office or who were more solicitous of the dictator's position than he himself. As a consequence, many of the state governors were harsher in combating opposition than was the President, and many other officials were so corrupt that the administration itself was tainted. This system of favoritism led Díaz to distrust men whom he did not know personally, and encouraged him to depend on men of his own generation. Manuel Calero, whose enthusiasm for Díaz in 1900 had cooled by 1910 and hardened into bitter criticism by 1920, commented on Díaz' "horror of injecting new blood into the governmental organism. Not only did he retain in his cabinet a group of doddering mummies as respectable as they were useless, . . . but when he was presented with the necessity of making a change in the state governments he preferred . . . to disinter some political cadaver already forgotten in his grave."[25] Two of these "political cadavers" whom Díaz appointed to gubernatorial posts in the last years of his rule had a combined age of something over one hundred and sixty years.[26] While the rewards so distributed were a positive aid in supporting the

---

[24] *El verdadero Díaz,* 59.

[25] Manuel Calero y Sierra, *Un decenio de política mexicana,* 16.

[26] Policarpo Valenzuela, governor of Tabasco, and Alejandro Vázquez del Mercado, governor of Aguascalientes.

regime, the merits of such a system as a means of perpetuating the dictatorship are doubtful.

It was the economic advances and their by-products, however, that served as a stimulus for most of the support of, and much of the opposition to, the dictatorship. In view of the general financial condition of Mexico and her people when Díaz came to power—the government was heavily in debt and the people had little cash reserve for new investment—it was absolutely necessary to encourage a flow of foreign capital to Mexico if there was to be material development. From the beginning of his administration, Díaz deliberately fostered foreign investment on terms highly advantageous to the investor. The policy brought money to Mexico, but the zealous regard for the interests of the foreigner created another class in Mexican society and added to the already prejudicial social and economic stratification. The foreigner, particularly the American, was now considered the most important element in society, with much of the economic legislation framed to favor his group. The concessions made to foreigners, especially in the changes in the mining code, worked to the grave disadvantage of the nation, inasmuch as the government's proportion of income from the mines was lessened and speculation in mining properties was encouraged. The preference granted to foreigners was constantly humiliating to the nationals and was one of the most irritating facets of the dictatorship. On the other hand, often the robber was robbed, for the majority of foreigners who invested in Mexico were victimized by ignorance and sharp dealing, even though many of those who came to the country did amass fortunes.

The emphasis on industrialization had other evil effects as well, for with the development of monopolies the already clearly defined difference between rich and poor became even more marked. Mexico's economy was largely controlled by a small group of businessmen and financiers who completely dominated money and credit, controlled the most lucrative concessions, and soon became the "arbiters of the prosperity of the Mexicans."[27] For example, of the sixty-six financial, transportation, insurance, and industrial corporations listed in the 1908 report of the Banco Central Mexicano, thirty-six had common directors from a group of thirteen men; and nineteen of the corporations had more than one of the thirteen. One of the thirteen men was on the boards of nine banks, one railroad, one insurance company, and four

[27] Calero, *Un decenio de política mexicana,* 19.

9

industrial concerns.[28] This tight control by a small group led to many of the economic and social abuses of which the Díaz government was accused, and brought into being what a Díaz opponent called "mercantilism." "It was this 'mercantilism,' " he said, "which overwhelmed the nation, increased despotism, despoiled the people, implanted degrading speculation, and sustained infamous and depraved governors."[29] As the monopolists became more opulent, they were blinded by their own prosperity and became less able than ever to see the needs of the less fortunate. Their own prosperity, too, bolstered by the statistics of production, foreign trade, and finances, convinced them that Mexico as a nation was prosperous and that their own interests were synonymous with national interests.

In the last decade of the nineteenth century, a few men representing the new moneyed class banded together under Díaz' father-in-law, Manuel Romero Rubio, into a group which soon came to be called the Científicos.[30] Hardly a political party at its inception, the organization was nonetheless allied closely with a political party formed in 1892 and came to exercise all the functions of a party.[31] The group soon determined that the most effective means of guaranteeing a continuation of the economic system that had developed would be to control the government in so far as possible during Díaz' life and absolutely after his death. Until the formation of the Científicos, Díaz had maintained his early policy of meeting the demands of the mestizos; but as the Científicos grew in power, they successfully drew him away from the mestizos and convinced him of the necessity for supporting the creoles.[32] Looked upon by many in the nineties and in the early years of the new century as the hope for a regenerated Mexico, the Científicos came to be feared and hated, even by men who had previously been their ardent supporters. Manuel Calero, writing in 1903, could hardly find words graphic enough to sing their praises as loyal, honest, able, and

[28] Banco Central Mexicano, *Las sociedades anónimas de México, Año I, 1908,* passim.
[29] José R. del Castillo, *Historia de la revolución social de México. Primera etapa. La caída del General Díaz,* 28.
[30] *Ibid.,* 27.
[31] The Liberal Union was formed in that year to develop a program of economic and political liberalism, demanding greater political participation for the upper classes. The leaders of the Científicos were originally members.
[32] Andrés Molina Enríquez, *Esbozo de la historia de los primeros diez años de la revolución agraria en México,* IV, 15.

10

patriotic men.[33] Fifteen years later, Calero concluded that the Científicos were the "greatest rascals" in the nation.[34] A more bitter commentator summarized their characteristics as "insatiable cupidity, terrifying avarice, absolute baseness of sight, absolute lack of patriotism, . . . notorious amorality, and complete cynicism. . . . All that can be said against the artfulness, the falsity, the refined hypocrisy, the malevolence, and the absurd vanity of the leaders of *cientificismo* is pale in comparison to reality."[35]

Whether vicious cynics or progressive patriots, the Científicos and their partisans were the extreme proponents of control by the upper class. One of their spokesmen insisted that the dictatorship was a natural result of the inability of the Mexican people to govern themselves,[36] and that the form of government should be one which would protect the nation against the dangers of political action by illiterate masses.[37] In their formative years the Científicos contended that a limited democracy, in which suffrage would be restricted to the upper class, was a vital necessity; as the group increased in strength, and as the influence of the brilliant Minister of Hacienda José Ives Limantour became more marked, their attitude changed to such a degree that by 1909 they openly espoused a continuation of the dictatorship as a permanent form of government.[38] The change in attitude had developed primarily because of a struggle for power among the upper class, in which the Científicos were violently opposed by such men as Joaquín Baranda, General Bernardo Reyes, and Governor Teodoro Dehesa of Veracruz. The quarrel convinced the Científico leaders that anything short of a dictatorship would cause serious political upheavals, which in turn would mean interference with, or destruction of, the group's profitable concessions. Limantour and the other Científicos therefore devoted much of their efforts after 1901 to an attempt to guarantee that their own control would be absolute when Díaz died.

[33] Manuel Calero y Sierra, *El problema actual. La vice-presidencia de la República,* 7.
[34] Calero, *Un decenio de política mexicana,* 17.
[35] Castillo, *Revolución social,* 38.
[36] Calero, *El problema actual,* passim.
[37] Manuel Calero y Sierra, *Cuestiones electorales,* passim.
[38] Federico González Garza, "A nuestros adversarios, los sostenedores de la ilegalidad," *Anti-Reeleccionista,* August 19, 1909; Santiago J. Sierra, *Apuntes biográficos del C. Ramón Corral, candidato de la clase obrera a la vicepresidencia de la República en el próximo sexenio,* 19.

11

They fought to have Ramón Corral selected for the vice-presidency in 1904 and to retain him in that position in 1910; in both efforts they were immediately successful, but at the cost of stimulating public animosity because of Corral's unpopularity. Ostensibly, they gave unstinting support to Díaz and his policies; to the public they presented a solid front with the dictator. Actually, in private and among themselves, they objected strenuously to some of Díaz' actions, but concern for their own position kept them silent.[39]

The Científicos, particularly Limantour, took credit for much of Mexico's economic development. There is no doubt that Limantour's financial policies, which stabilized government finances, were largely responsible for continued peace, but some opponents insisted that the advantages then enjoyed by Mexico were not solely the result of the Díaz administration. Federico González Garza, later to become powerful in government circles, maintained heatedly that to "attribute to General Díaz and his government all the good which may be found . . . is a lie which is hammered into the minds of the majority" by a small group intent on sustaining an autocratic regime.[40] Be that as it may, so long as the national economy was sound, or appeared to be, no popular demand for the removal of the Científicos from government could be expected.

There were many evidences, tenuous to be sure, of economic instability after 1904, even in Limantour's own special province—banking. Adoption of the gold standard in 1905, followed by the 1907 money panic in the United States and an export price decline, brought shrinking national revenues, which necessitated further foreign borrowing, and at the same time placed a heavy strain on domestic financial institutions. The banks, although outwardly prosperous, demonstrated symptoms of instability which endangered the entire Mexican financial structure. Limantour himself recognized the symptoms and called a national conference of bankers early in 1908 for the purpose of studying the situation and proposing new laws to rectify the existing weaknesses.[41] The banks had obviously been indulging in speculation, lending enormous sums on poor security; institutions authorized to issue bank notes were particularly at fault, engaging in practices which

[39] Calero, *Un decenio de política mexicana,* 24.
[40] F. González Garza, "¿En donde está el mal? ¿Quién es culpable?" *Anti-Reeleccionista,* July 25, 1909.
[41] Secretaría de Hacienda, *Memoria de Hacienda,* 1907–1908, pp. 180 ff.

12

sometimes brought large returns but which were generally unsound. As a consequence of the conference and Limantour's recommendations, a new banking law to correct some of the dangerous policies and to encourage the establishment of investment and mortgage banks was passed in the summer of 1908.[42]

The new regulations, however, did not correct all the evils. Less than a year later the Banco Central Mexicano, the central reserve institution, was in a condition that approached the critical. The weakness of the bank was largely the responsibility of the government itself, which at various times had "suggested" to the bank that loans be made to administration friends.[43] When the public learned that the central bank had absorbed enough worthless paper to impair its capital, confidence in all credit and financial institutions was seriously undermined.

The weakness of the central reserve bank was not the only evidence of financial instability. The mortgage-bank field was completely dominated by two banks,[44] both of which had expanded much too rapidly for soundness,[45] and there was no system of agrarian mortgage banks which could meet the needs of the small rural proprietor. Díaz, in half-hearted recognition of such a need, established a commission to study the situation and make recommendations; but the commission's efforts proved completely sterile when the bankers blocked development of new and possibly competitive institutions. The plan to establish banks for the small rural proprietors was abandoned, and in its stead the government authorized a Caja de Préstamos para Obras de Irrigación y Fomento de Agricultura, designed primarily to finance the operations of haciendas.[46] Far from meeting agricultural needs, the new institution "became merely the instrument through which a coterie of officials and their friends exploited their particular enterprises and ended, as might have been foreseen, disastrously."[47] By 1910 the general financial situation in Mexico had become so critical that it was necessary for Limantour to make a special trip to the European money markets for the pur-

[42] For the revised law, see Banco Central Mexicano, *Las sociedades anónimas de México, Año I, 1908,* 7–30.
[43] Walter Flavius McCaleb, *Present and Past Banking in Mexico,* 188.
[44] The Banco Internacional é Hipotecario de México and the Banco Agrícola é Hipotecario de México.
[45] McCaleb, *Present and Past Banking in Mexico,* 189–90.
[46] For the law authorizing the Caja, see Banco Central Mexicano, *Las sociedades anónimas de México, Año I, 1908, xi–xxiii.*
[47] McCaleb, *Present and Past Banking in Mexico,* 193.

13

pose of refunding debts and negotiating new loans. The vaunted economic structure, so laboriously built by the Díaz administration, was approaching collapse.

As might be expected in such a financial situation, inflation was rampant during most of the latter part of the Díaz regime. The cost of most items, particularly the staples on which the mass of the population depended, increased enormously; there was not a corresponding increase in the wages of agricultural and industrial workers. The wage earners were therefore forced into a constantly deteriorating position. What was happening to corn, a basic part of the diet of 85 per cent of the population, indicates the trend.[48] Between 1893 and 1906 the value of corn per unit increased on the average by 50 per cent, and after 1906 the increase was more rapid.[49] Occasionally the government would sell corn at "much lower prices than those esablished by the speculators," to use Díaz' words, but these sales were temporary expedients only and were usually confined to the capital itself.[50] Somewhat the same trend was noted in other staples. Even more destructive of the well-being of the masses was the violent fluctuation in the price of staples from day to day and from place to place; a change of 400 per cent in a matter of days was not unusual. The government, in spite of the obvious need for price stabilization, did nothing permanently constructive. Its policies sometimes actually encouraged price increases by making special concessions to exporters of basic commodities. In August, 1902, such a concession was made to exporters of cotton in order to exempt those goods "from the burdens weighing on them when consumed at home."[51] At the same moment the price of cotton garments for workers was so high that many laborers wore little or no clothing.[52]

While basic commodity prices were on the increase, there was no ascertainable rise in salaries. In the early nineteenth century Baron Alexander von Humboldt had estimated the average daily wage to be ap-

[48] Molina, *Los grandes problemas,* 196–98.

[49] Secretaría de Fomento, Colonización é Industria, *Anuario estadístico de la República Mexicana,* for 1893 and 1906, gives the total production and the total value of corn for those years.

[50] Message of the President on Opening the Mexican Congress, April 1, 1902, *SP,* 1901–1902, p. 378.

[51] Message of the President on Opening the Mexican Congress, September 16, 1902, *ibid.,* 392.

[52] Clothing was so scarce, among rural workers particularly, that merchants in some towns did a thriving business in renting trousers by the day to men coming to market.

proximately twenty-five centavos; in 1891 the prevailing wage was between twenty-five and fifty centavos, with the average nearer the lower figure;[53] in 1908 the daily wage was almost exactly what it had been one hundred years earlier.[54] In sum total, the static wage and the increasing cost of commodities meant a drastic decline in real wages. One economist has estimated that a day's labor would buy only one-third as much in 1908 as it would in 1804.[55] Another writer asserts that the real daily wage was only one-fourth of what it had been a century before.[56] A more conservative estimate indicates that the laborer toiled nearly one and one-half times as long for a bushel of corn and four times as long for a kilogram of flour as did his nineteenth-century ancestor.[57] Even if the more conservative estimate is used, a comparison between the Mexican laborer and his contemporary counterpart in the United States reveals the startling fact that the real wage of the Mexican was about one-fifteenth as great in terms of wheat, one-twelfth in terms of corn, and one-nineteenth in terms of cheap textiles—and the American laborer was dissatisfied with his own low wage. Francisco Bulnes concluded that "the real daily wage . . . [was declining], and its direction was toward death by hunger."[58]

In the face of his rapidly deteriorating economic position, the laborer was helpless. Not only were there no labor laws to aid the worker but as Díaz became more closely allied with the creoles and their interests he became less sympathetic to the predicament of the mestizos and Indians, who composed the working class. A cheap labor supply being one of the principal assets which Mexico could offer to foreign investors and Mexican industrialists, and the general standard of work among the laborers being rather poor, the government never considered that protection of the laborer was either necessary or desirable.[59] In vain did some intellectuals demand an improvement of conditions; in vain did Wistano Luis Orozco, scholar and humanitarian, insist that the lower classes were the brothers of the remainder

[53] Secretaría de Fomento, Colonización é Industria, *Informes y documentos relativos a comercio interior y exterior,* for April and June, 1891, contains data concerning wages and hours in many sections of the Republic. The agricultural workers received the lowest wages.
[54] Jesús Silva Herzog, *Un ensayo sobre la revolución mexicana,* 22.
[55] *Ibid.*
[56] Bulnes, *El verdadero Díaz,* 398.
[57] Toribio Esquivel Obregón, *La influencia de España y los Estados Unidos sobre México,* 343–44.
[58] Bulnes, *El verdadero Díaz,* 398.
[59] Ricardo García Granados, *Por qué y como cayó Porfirio Díaz,* 16–19.

of society and had a right to demand improvement, "morally and physically."[60] The alliance between government and special privilege was too strong. Labor organizations were practically unknown before 1900; and even if the workers had been organized, they would have found it almost impossible to act in their own behalf. In most states and territories the laws forbade strikes; in the Federal District heavy fines and imprisonment could be imposed on any person attempting to use physical or moral force for the purpose of increasing salaries or wages.[61] Even in areas where no specific law applied to striking, various means were used, often with the aid of public officials, to defeat the aims of the workers.

But these industrially idyllic conditions, in which the laborer worked for a pittance without question, could not continue indefinitely. The syndicalist and anarchist concepts, though late in penetrating into Mexico, became known after the turn of the century through the work and writing of Spaniards and Mexicans, the most important of whom was the Mexican Ricardo Flores Magón. Accordingly, the workers, "better taught than before to look out for their own interests, resented . . . oppression and resolutely aspired to improve their condition."[62] Beginning in 1906, the laborers insisted that wages be raised and hours shortened; as a result of the industrialists' adamant refusal to meet these demands, a period of unrest developed. Although the strikes were defeated in most cases through government intercession, most industrial centers saw strife of varying intensity, and the workers were at last beginning to realize their potential strength, even though industrial labor constituted only a small proportion of the country's total labor force.

The first violent labor trouble occurred at Cananea, Sonora. There miners of the Green Consolidated Mining Company received higher wages and worked shorter hours than the average Mexican laborer; but many of them were familiar with the wage scale in the United States, and they knew that Americans working for the company were receiving more money for the same work. Even though the legal code of Sonora forbade labor organizations, early in 1906 a group organized and continued to hold surreptitious meetings during the spring.[63] Under the leadership of Manuel Dieguez and Esteban Calderón Baca,

---

[60] Wistano Luis Orozco, *Legislación y jurisprudencia sobre terrenos baldíos,* II, 829.

[61] Marjorie Ruth Clark, *Organized Labor in Mexico,* 10.

[62] García Granados, *Por qué y como cayó Porfirio Díaz,* 12.

[63] Jesús Romero Flores, *Anales históricos de la revolución mexicana,* I, 55.

and encouraged by the propaganda of Ricardo Flores Magón, on May 30 the miners demanded a number of changes.[64] The demands included a minimum daily wage of five pesos, an eight-hour day, a system of promotions, and equal pay for equal work with American employees; the miners also demanded that at least three-fourths of the workers be Mexicans.[65] When the company absolutely refused to consider the demands, two thousand men struck on June 1, 1906.

That night the strikers went to the company offices to invite the office personnel, most of whom were Americans, to join the protest; as they approached the offices, they were fired upon by the Americans, who feared mob action. Although the demonstrators were unarmed, the attack provoked the strikers into riots and destruction. After a large number of buildings had been burned, the local officials asked the state goverr aid, and the American consul requested the United States to send troops to protect American property.[66] By June 3, Cananea was free of riots, martial law had been declared by the state governor, and armed Americans patrolled the streets.[67] On the following day many workers began returning to their jobs under the same conditions which had existed before the strike; but large numbers of the strikers had fled to the hills and returned tardily, if at all.[68] Over twenty persons were killed during the strike; and a like number, including Dieguez and Calderón Baca, were sent to the miasmic federal prison of San Juan de Ulloa, convicted of arson and murder. Public reaction to the strike and the means employed to defeat it was severely critical, but among government officials the episode seemed to have no effect other than to harden the determination to prevent any growth of labor organizations.

Shortly after the Cananea strike, Ricardo Flores Magón published while in exile in the United States a revolutionary program under the title of the Plan del Partido Liberal, advocating an armed revolt against Díaz and proposing far-reaching social reform. Among the host of provisions concerning labor were demands for shorter hours and

---

[64] Agustín Casasola (ed.), *Historia gráfica de la revolución mexicana*, I, 63. Governor Rafael Izábel of Sonora, writing to the Minister of Gobernación, June 28, 1906 (*Diario oficial*, 801–808), gives an account of the strike as seen through the eyes of state officials. Both Dieguez and Calderón Baca, miners at the time, later became generals in the Carranza army.

[65] Romero, *Anales históricos*, I, 56.

[66] *Ibid.*, 58.

[67] Casasola, *Historia gráfica*, I, 63.

[68] Clark, *Organized Labor in Mexico*, 10.

more pay, a minimum wage, safe and sanitary working conditions, and educational opportunities for laborers and their families.[69] Under the aegis of the Partido Liberal a short-lived rebellion began in Veracruz in September, 1906, in an area which was the center of the textile industry and had long been a region of independent liberalism.[70] Encouraged by the Flores Magón demands and spurred on by the September rebellion, the textile workers of Veracruz, Tlaxcala, and Puebla organized the Círculo de Obreros Libres and were ready to contest the strength of the mill owners when in late December management issued new restrictive regulations concerning working conditions and payment of wages.[71]

First in Puebla and Tlaxcala, and then in Veracruz, the workers struck and asked Díaz to act as arbiter in their demands for higher wages, shorter hours, abolition of the *tiendas de raya,* and safer working conditions.[72] Díaz accepted the request to settle the issue and let it be known that the final decision would be favorable to the workers; but when he made his judgment public, it was found that he supported the mill owners on almost every count. No changes in either hours or wages were made, wages were still subject to fines imposed by management for infraction of the rules, each worker still was required to retain his workbook,[73] strikes were prohibited, and any publications which the workers wished to circulate among themselves needed prior approval by the local political chief.[74]

In a tumultuous meeting on the night of January 7, 1907, the men of the Río Blanco mill in Veracruz flatly refused to accept the President's decision; they felt that they had been cheated through dishonest representation. Infuriated by the terms of the judgment, and probably aroused by Magonistas in the region, the strikers with wanton abandon attacked the mills, the owners' homes, the stores, and their own company-owned houses in an orgy of rapine and pillage. Federal troops, sent to the region as soon as the riots began, broke the strike by

[69] See Plan del Partido Liberal, Articles 21–34, in Francisco Naranjo, *Diccionario biográfico revolucionario,* 253–56.

[70] See C. D. Padua, *Movimiento revolucionario en Vera Cruz,* passim.

[71] Clark, *Organized Labor in Mexico,* 12; Casasola, *Historia gráfica,* I, 83.

[72] Casasola, *Historia gráfica,* I, 83. A *tienda de raya* was a company store in which the workers were forced to buy by virtue of the type of payment they received. The high prices in these stores often cheated the men of from 10 to 12 per cent of their wages.

[73] In which the employer recorded any criticisms or commendations of the quality of the man's work, and without which no man could obtain employment.

[74] Clark, *Organized Labor in Mexico,* 13.

killing an undetermined number of men in the streets and executing an additional two hundred or more before firing squads.[75] Díaz, having fallen completely under the influence of the industrialists, was paying for past favors and continued support. While many thinking men were horrified by the brutality displayed toward the workers, the remaining years of the Díaz regime were not disturbed by serious strikes, even though obvious discontent existed among the working class.

The poor condition in which the industrial worker found himself had its counterpart, perhaps exaggerated to a degree, in the situation of the vast number of Indians whose primary source of livelihood was the land. The rural inhabitants, largely Indian, had been at the mercy of the Spaniard and the creole during the colonial epoch and continued in that state after independence. But many Indian villages had been allowed to retain the community holdings which were in their possession prior to the Conquest, and many more had been granted land by the Spanish crown. These areas, generally called *ejidos* though actually divided into five distinct classifications, served as a guarantee of partial independence for members of the community, but in the immediate postindependence period considerable difference of opinion arose among liberals over the question of the Indian and his relation to the land. Some, arguing that the Indian did not have a European concept of ownership, insisted that the village *ejidos* be left undisturbed; others, convinced that communal holding was evidence of backwardness and was not conducive to progress, favored a distribution of village land among the inhabitants of the village, with the individuals holding the parcels in fee simple. It was this last contention which prevailed when the triumphant liberals, after defeating Santa Anna and his conservative supporters in the Revolution of Ayutla, drafted the Constitution of 1857. The Ley Lerdo, which had been passed the previous year and which prohibited civil or religious corporations from owning real property not directly necessary for the functioning of the corporations, was written into the constitution. The village lands were therefore open to distribution among the members of the communities.

In the meantime the haciendas, enormous holdings of land often poorly and incompletely cultivated, were becoming increasingly important as an institution—economic, social, and political—in the rural

---

[75] On the strike, see *ibid.,* 11–13; Casasola, *Historia gráfica,* I, 83–85; Romero, *Anales históricos,* I, 60–73.

19

areas. Many haciendas dated from the colonial period, but with the application of the Ley Lerdo and the Reform Laws effectuated a few years later, and with the confiscation, during both the War of Reform and the French Intervention, of much of the property belonging to the losing factions, the hacienda system was extended and a new hacienda class developed.[76] This new group of *hacendados* were in the main new creoles, with an affinity for the Díaz regime and supported by Díaz. Whoever owned the haciendas—new creoles, old creoles, mestizos, or foreigners—the work in the main was done by Indians attached to the hacienda itself, men who worked for very small wages and who sometimes had the privilege of cultivating a tiny parcel of land on which they could grow a small amount of corn or beans. At best it was a meager existence, and at worst it approached slavery.

In addition to *hacendados,* Indian agricultural laborers, and Indians who had access to community lands, there had long been another group whose fortunes depended on agriculture. These were small independent proprietors, normally called "rancheros," who by a variety of means had come into possession of plots ranging from a few hectares to as much as a hundred hectares.[77] Small in number but increasing after the period of the Reform and the Maximilian interlude, the rancheros were principally mestizos who did their own work with occasional assistance at harvesttime. Their methods were often crude and not too productive, but their limited lands were fully cultivated.

It was on this foundation that the Díaz land system developed, and it was in the agrarian field that the Díaz government recorded one of its greatest failures. In a nation which depended heavily on agriculture, the Díaz government made no attempt to improve agricultural production through education or experimentation.[78] Although much of the country was arid or semiarid and needed irrigation planning on a national scale, the government did practically nothing. It did not attempt to relieve the critical food shortage by encouraging increased production of cereals or other items consumed by the masses; although statistics indicate an annual increase in agricultural production, the increase was largely in items for export and gave little aid to the mass

[76] The Ley Lerdo was designed to force the Church to sell its lands; among the Laws of Reform was a confiscatory decree.

[77] A metric land measure, equivalent to approximately 2.47 acres.

[78] In 1895, of a population of 12,491,573 the census listed 2,838,222 as either agriculturalists or peons and 167,161 as engaged in commerce.

Background for Revolution

of the population. These were errors of omission; much more serious were the errors of commission in land legislation.

Díaz was not completely responsible for the development which robbed the villages of their land and forced the major portion of the Indian population into economic slavery; previous legal and constitutional provisions had set the pattern. The first interpretations of the constitutional provision had stipulated that the *suertes,* or *terrenos de común repartimiento*—agricultural lands attached to the villages at the time of the Conquest—were not subject to parceling, and as long as that interpretation prevailed many villages in the heart of the agricultural districts would retain their independence.[79] By successive decrees in 1889 and 1890, however, Díaz brought all village lands within the categories to be parceled, and from that time forward the laws were more stringently applied. The new owner, unaccustomed to thinking in terms of private ownership and not given proper protection by the government, was easily victimized by unscrupulous officials and by individuals who legally or illegally gained control of the land. In the final analysis, the Indian villager too often found that as a result of the distribution he no longer had access to any land of his own and was forced to seek employment at the nearest hacienda.

Not all the Indian villages, however, lost their land through the instrumentality of the distribution law; many were victimized outright by a variety of other means. In some cases grasping government officials, charged with the responsibility of parceling the land and dispensing justice to the villagers, merely sold all village property to a company or an individual; such sales were irregular and illegal, of course, but the despoliation was effectuated nevertheless.[80] In many cases the village was destroyed when an outsider gained control of the water supply and forced the village to sell.[81] But the most disastrous practice, in so far as the loss of village lands was concerned, resulted from a series of surveying laws passed in 1863, 1883, and 1894.[82] Under these laws, each more advantageous than the last to the surveying companies and demanding fewer responsibilities from them, national lands were surveyed by individuals and companies and the sur-

[79] Helen Phipps, *Some Aspects of the Agrarian Question in Mexico,* 112.
[80] *Ibid.,* 114.
[81] Eyler Newton Simpson, *The Ejido—Mexico's Way Out,* 30–31.
[82] Only one of these laws, the last, was passed during Díaz' administration; but it was the most destructive.

21

veyors allowed to gain control of enormous amounts of land.[83] Under the 1894 law any parcel to which a legal title could not be produced could be declared *terrenos baldíos,* or untilled national lands, and any individual could file a claim to purchase the property at a set cash price. Legally, the occupant had first choice in case of a denunciation; but in practice if the occupant was a small landowner or a village, the cash was almost impossible to obtain. Those with cash resources accordingly were able to take full advantage of a legal technicality.[84] In many instances the village could not produce evidence of legal title, even though the village had been occupying the property for many generations; often the rancheros found that their titles were defective as a result of the complex legal structure which had been built around the land question since the beginning of Spanish domination.[85] Through the operation of the laws, and through official or quasi-official chicanery, enormous quantities of land came under the control of a small group of men or companies. One estimate indicates that over two and one-quarter million acres of good land, representing the means of livelihood of tens of thousands of Indians, passed from the Indian communities to the *hacendados;* this was in addition to the untold millions of acres of bona fide national lands which were alienated.[86]

A combination of the above forces and practices meant disaster to the Indian village, and tremendous growth to the haciendas. The free agricultural village—one in which the majority of the residents had access to sufficient lands to make a living—was disappearing, and concentration of land ownership was intensifying. Between 1881 and 1889, 14 per cent of the arable land was concentrated in twenty-nine companies or individuals; by 1894, more than 20 per cent was controlled by fewer than fifty holders; and by 1910, less than 1 per cent of the families owned or controlled about 85 per cent of the land.[87] While the villages comprised 51 per cent of the rural population, they

[83] The definitive work on land legislation, particularly concerning national land, up to 1895 is Wistano Luis Orozco, *Legislación y jurisprudencia sobre terrenos baldíos.* For a short account of the laws and their use, see Simpson, *The Ejido—Mexico's Way Out,* 27–29.

[84] For details, see Molina, *Los grandes problemas,* 124–60.

[85] *Ibid.,* 113–14.

[86] Phipps, *Some Aspects of the Agrarian Question in Mexico,* 115.

[87] Angel Carvajal, *Al margen de las resoluciones presidenciales sobre la cuestión agraria,* 22, 23; Tannenbaum, *Peace by Revolution,* 143.

had only a very small proportion of the land, and most of them were dependent on nearby haciendas.[88] Only in the seven mountain states surrounding the Valley of Mexico did the free villages outnumber the hacienda villages[89]—those enclosed by and dependent on the hacienda —and in those states a war of despoliation was fought until the final days of the Díaz regime. In the other states, particularly the northern, the Indian villages had lost all self-direction in the majority of cases, with a high of over 80 per cent of the village populations of San Luis Potosí and Guanajuato being completely dependent on haciendas.[90] Even those still remaining free suffered from a lack of land, from poor land, and from partial domination by neighboring plantation owners.

Despite the enforcement of the laws dividing the village lands,[91] and despite the process of despoliation, some villages were able to retain an uneasy independence which was threatened by an agricultural economy geared to the heavy producer. Law and practice favored the hacienda. Agricultural credit was extended on favorable terms to the *hacendado* only, the small farmers and villages paid far more than their share of taxes, export and import duties and regulations favored big operators, clear titles were difficult and expensive to obtain, and irrigation projects were constructed for the haciendas, not the villages or small farmers.[92]

Had the land acquired by the haciendas been profitably used, and had the villagers now forced to work for the haciendas been properly treated, the situation would not have been so disastrous. But the haciendas were not economically successful: they left too much arable land uncultivated, and they were not so productive, proportionally, as the smaller holdings.[93] The rapid development of the hacienda system

[88] Frank Tannenbaum, *The Mexican Agrarian Revolution*, 53; Simpson, *The Ejido—Mexico's Way Out*, 35–36.

[89] Tannenbaum, *Peace by Revolution*, 194.

[90] Tannenbaum, *The Mexican Agrarian Revolution*, Appendix B, Table V.

[91] In the fiscal year 1907–1908, for example, approximately 174,000 acres of village land were parceled. See Secretaría de Estado y del Despacho de Fomento, Colonización é Industria de la República Mexicana, *Memoria presentada al Congreso de la Unión*, 11.

[92] McCaleb, *Present and Past Banking in Mexico*, 191–93; Molina, *Los grandes problemas*, 95, 124–60. Special concessions were granted to large exporters since it was both politically prudent and fiscally advantageous to encourage foreign trade. See Message of the President on Opening the Mexican Congress, September 16, 1902, *SP*, 1901–1902, pp. 381–94.

[93] See Molina, *Los grandes problemas*, 81–111, concerning weakness of haciendas.

23

under Díaz constituted a burden on, and a retrogression of, the agricultural economy, rather than, as its proponents insisted, an improvement.

More damaging, perhaps, to the peace and security of the Díaz regime than the improper use of the land was the treatment accorded the workers. The great landowners, who normally did not live on the haciendas except for short periods during the year and who left the administration of the property to resident managers, looked upon their laborers as slaves or chattels, fit only to take orders without question.[94] The men were bound to the haciendas through debt peonage, they were subject to the whims and fancies of the *hacendado* and his manager, and the only justice they knew was that dispensed by the landowner or his representative, since national or state law seldom penetrated to the hacienda.[95] Outright slavery was practiced in some isolated areas; in others a type of feudalism existed.[96] On virtually all plantations the worker had no rights, little recreation, a minimum of freedom, and a bare existence.

A few farsighted men recognized the dangers inherent in the situation and favored land reform as a means for improving the condition of all the lower classes. Wistano Luis Orozco as early as 1895 pointed out that the government was shirking a grave responsibility and insisted that elevation of the masses was a "strict moral dictate" and a "principle of the clearest utility." He advocated dividing public lands among the poor and providing a means whereby "the unused and enormous excess of private holdings could also be divided."[97] A few years later Andrés Molina Enríquez wrote a penetrating analysis of the agrarian problem and insisted on reform.[98] Others, too, pointed out that land reform was essential, but the Díaz government, firmly committed to the fortunes of the upper class and suspicious of the lower, refused to listen.

Díaz' attitude toward rural and industrial labor is indicative of his loss of political perception. In contrast to his remarkable acumen in recognizing the paramount interest of each important group and in

[94] Congreso Constitucional, Cámara de Diputados, *Diario de los debates,* December 3, 1913, p. 3.

[95] According to some bitter critics, the fancies of some of the *hacendados* extended to the medieval practice of "first night."

[96] The henequen plantations of Yucatán were notorious for the bestial treatment accorded the workers, who were often held in actual slavery.

[97] Orozco, *Legislación y jurisprudencia sobre terrenos baldíos,* I, 827–28.

[98] *Los grandes problemas nacionales,* written in 1909.

24

catering to those interests before 1900, after the turn of the century he was no longer able to see the forces or to adjust his policies accordingly. Labor was rapidly becoming a factor to consider in national politics, and yet Díaz and his advisors could think of nothing more constructive than suppression. When confronted with somewhat the same condition in 1876 with respect to bandits,[99] Díaz had adroitly obtained the support of a sufficient number to counterbalance those who were recalcitrant. To labor he made no concession at all, and after 1900 labor constituted a greater potential force than had the bandits in 1876.

Not only were the laborers themselves numerous enough to consider but labor had its spokesmen who refused to be quieted by threats or by imprisonment. Even though the effectiveness of newspapers as a propaganda medium may well be doubted, since only about 14 per cent of the population could read and write,[100] a large number of pro-labor papers of limited circulation were published after 1900. In its appeal to the intellectual class to work in behalf of the laboring man, *Regeneración*, published by Ricardo Flores Magón and a small group following his lead, was probably the most outstanding.[101] In addition to *Regeneración* and others which supported labor but were not directed to the worker, a number of frankly proletariat weeklies were published between 1900 and 1910. Some twenty-five of these papers, all selling for one centavo, and all of four sheets, were registered publications and appeared regularly as critics of the government or some facet of current policy. *El Diablo Bromista* was, according to its masthead, a "Weekly for the working class, the whip for evil *bourgeoisie*." *El Chile Piquín* was "dedicated exclusively to the proletariat," and *Pero Grullo* was to bring "some instructions to the humble classes." *El Papagayo* defended labor; *El Chango* was the "organ of the working class with political aspirations"; *Don Cucufate* was an "administrator of justice"; and *La Banda Negra*, also aimed at the workers, was "completely anticlerical." *La Chintatlahua* was an "unconditional defender of the worker, whip for tyrants, and bugaboo of the *bourgeoisie*."

Most of these publications, and a variety of similar weeklies, demonstrated a marked affinity for socialism, anarchism, and syndicalism;

---

[99] The situations are analogous only in that both groups constituted a danger or source of strength, depending on the manner of treatment.

[100] According to the 1895 census, of a population of 12,491,573 persons 1,782,822 could read and write and an additional 323,336 could read.

[101] Over a period of ten years *Regeneración* was published successively in Mexico, in St. Louis, in El Paso, and in Los Angeles. In spite of its limited circulation, it was widely known in both the United States and Mexico.

many showed an underlying but subtle anticlericalism. Frankly oppositionist, they nevertheless were careful not to criticize people or specific actions; they depended on satire, generalities, and apocryphal stories to condemn Díaz' policies. Díaz, afflicted as he now was with political and social myopia, failed to see the implications of the propaganda thus subtly injected into the labor picture. So secure was he in his beliefs, or so blind, that he did not consider the publications important enough to warrant his attention. He and his advisors were never cognizant of the approaching social revolution.

Díaz was also unconcerned with the nationalism which had been developing rapidly in the latter part of the nineteenth century. The constant condescension displayed by the President and his government to everything Mexican, and the near adulation for everything foreign, were irritating to the younger generation. The foreigner was treated with the deference of an invited guest, the mining laws governing concessions and subsoil rights were reframed to conform with foreign concepts and practices, enormous areas of land were sold or practically given to foreigners, and foreigners were regularly favored in Mexican courts.[102] Since citizens of the United States were the most numerous among the foreigners, one bitter critic summed it up by saying that the regime "destroyed national honor in the face of Yankee demands."[103] Díaz was not alone in his preference for foreigners; most of the social elite were prejudiced in favor of foreign goods, foreign literature, and foreign ideas. Industrial concerns, whether under the control of Mexicans or aliens, regularly paid higher wages to foreign employees than to natives; the policy was probably justified by the foreigners' greater technical skill, but it did not endear the government or the industrialists to the laborers. All those who were proud to be Mexicans resented the rank favoritism which seemed to be common.

Even the upper classes were mixed in their support of the government after 1900. Díaz, consistently refusing to allow widespread political participation to the social and economic plutocracy, destroyed the public spirit of the class and weakened it as a bulwark of the regime. To be sure, the moneyed groups gave unstinting praise to Díaz' government,[104] but they were without organization and without leader-

---

[102] A popular charge in Mexico was that only generals, bullfighters, and foreigners were assured of favorable court decisions.
[103] Castillo, *Revolución social*, 28.
[104] For example, see Cadena, Marín y Compañía, *Voto de confianza del comercio de la República al Sr. Gral. Porfirio Díaz.* A pandering eulogy of every-

ship other than that formed by the government. In his anxiety to protect himself against the political ambitions of this group, Díaz had enervated a potentially powerful support.

Without quite realizing what had happened, Díaz gradually lost the active support of most elements in Mexican society. Many mestizos were alienated by his gradual orientation toward creoles and foreigners, as well as by the treatment accorded labor and small proprietors. The proprietors, allied with the labor leaders, became a solid core of opposition before the end of the regime. The Indians, while not openly hostile except in rare instances, generally were becoming more and more restive as a result of agrarian developments which either threatened their independent existence or left them destitute. Members of the upper class not directly connected with the regime were either not allowed to render public service or were driven into partial opposition by the government's bland assumption that all able men served the government and that all who questioned the policies were either knaves or fools.[105] Added to the insult was the economic injury which seemed to be impending; the rather precarious economic situation after 1905 forced many men who previously had been staunch Díaz supporters to question the safety of Mexican economy under Díaz' continued administration. The group whose economic interests were in danger did not always actively oppose the administration; but when the revolution came, the plutocracy gave Díaz little help.[106]

Díaz still had strong support, particularly among those who profited directly, or hoped to profit, from his government. More important to the future of the nation, and more widespread, than the support to Díaz himself was the belief in his philosophy of government. Many of those who turned against the Díaz administration, or who no longer supported it, did so because they detected weaknesses in his government rather than because they opposed the principles upon which he acted. These men, including many of the great *hacendados* and financiers, were quite willing to see Díaz removed from office, even though they looked with horror upon fundamental changes in the govern-

---

thing Díaz had ever done, the vote of confidence was signed by over three thousand individuals or firms in 1909, supporting Díaz' re-election.

[105] Federico González Garza (in "Falsa noción del prestigio en política," *Anti-Reeleccionista,* July 18, 1909) insisted that this assumption was one of the prejudices most damaging to Mexico.

[106] Among this group were Rafael Hernández, Ernesto Madero, Luis Terrazas, and Tomás Braniff.

mental or social structure. They were the men who made possible a successful revolution against Díaz, but at the same time their attitude would make it difficult for a reform government to function. As a class they foresaw a revolution, but they did not foresee the nature of the struggle; they believed it would take place after Díaz' death and would be nothing more than a quarrel over political power among the upper class. They did not recognize the symptoms of a social revolution developing in Morelos, for example, where "ragged plebeians, with their thin veneer of rudimentary civilization, were acting like savage gluttons of human carrion" during the 1908 gubernatorial election.[107] They were unconcerned with the needs of the masses, and being unconcerned they were ignorant of the potential of those masses. They were concerned only with their own interests, which at the moment seemed to demand that Díaz not be given strong support.

The loss of support to the regime was so gradual that it was almost imperceptible, with most observers agreeing that Díaz was never stronger than in the first decade of the new century. Only a few intractable malcontents spoke in terms of overthrowing the government after the abortive 1879 movement in Veracruz, and those who did hope to foster revolution remained in exile. When Ricardo Flores Magón, after years of bitter denunciation, organized a series of revolutionary movements against Díaz between 1906 and 1910, the general public was not even aware of the fact because of the ease with which the rebellions were suppressed.[108] A more dangerous rebellion in Yucatán, under the leadership of Maximiliano Bonilla, attracted little more attention and was defeated quickly by combined state and federal forces.[109]

The utter failure of either Flores Magón or Bonilla to attract sufficient adherents to make the revolutions effective convinced the government and the public that Díaz was still the popular favorite, secure in his position. But the malcontents were not searching for a leader such as Flores Magón, an avowed anarchist, or Bonilla, an unknown from Valladolid. Any anti-Díaz movement would have to appeal to the laborers, the mechanics, the rancheros, many *hacendados,* many

[107] Bulnes, *El verdadero Díaz,* 405.

[108] For a discussion of these attempts, see Charles C. Cumberland, "Precursors of the Mexican Revolution of 1910," *Hispanic American Historical Review,* XXII, 344–56.

[109] For a fairly full but biased account of the Yucatán revolt, see Carlos R. Menéndez, *La primera chispa de la revolución mexicana.*

financiers, the intellectuals, the businessmen, and the politically ambitious but politically frustrated. The leader of such a movement would have to be a man from a respected family, would have to be well educated, would have to be relatively unknown politically, would have to have liberal leanings but ties with the conservative groups, and, above all else, would have to have courage and sufficient color to stimulate the imagination of the people. With such a leader a revolutionary movement could go far. He was found in the person of Francisco Indalecio Madero, a young *hacendado* from Coahuila.

II

Madero: Education and Political Development

FRANCISCO I. MADERO was born in Parras, Coahuila, on October 30, 1873, the first child of a marital union representing two of the greatest creole landowning families in northern Mexico.[1] His family had never evinced any particular interest in politics; his grandfather had served a term as governor of Coahuila when Manuel González was president, but thereafter all members of the Madero family had devoted their entire efforts to ranching, farming, and commerce.[2] None of the Maderos or their immediate connections suffered under the Díaz administration; their business prospered and they became rich. Don Evaristo Madero, Francisco's grandfather, was a personal friend of many of Díaz' principal advisors and was on especially close terms with Minister of Hacienda José Ives Limantour.

In view of the Maderos' stake in the continued peace which the Díaz administration seemed to guarantee, it appears strange that Francisco Madero should emerge as the catalyst of a profound social and political revolution. But Madero represented a combination of the new forces in Mexico: nationalism, humanitarianism, intellectualism, and national progress. He more nearly represented the mestizo than the creole.

As a youth Madero lived the life of a normal hacienda heir. He was tutored privately while still quite young, attended a Jesuit school in Saltillo for one year, and spent a year at a Catholic school in Baltimore. In October, 1887, he and his younger brother Gustavo sailed for France, where they attended school in Versailles and in Paris for five

[1] Francisco I. Madero, "Mis memorias," *Anales del Museo Nacional de Arqueología, Historia y Etnografía*, 9.
[2] Luis Lara Pardo, *Madero. Esbozo político*, 64; Madero to Don E. Madero, December 20, 1908, *LO*, February 11, 1934, p. 2.

30

Madero: Political Development

years, studying commercial and economic courses.[3] Unlike most creoles, who became immersed in European culture patterns and looked with disdain on Mexican institutions, Madero used his European experiences as a basis for comparison, which showed him the need for improving Mexican conditions through Mexican efforts. French customs and French political institutions, particularly the spirit of equality and the democratic republican form of government, made a strong impression and convinced him that Mexico could and should attain the same level of development.[4] In France he also met students and businessmen from Colombia, Chile, Uruguay, and Argentina; his conversations with them led him to believe, erroneously to be sure, that all those countries had made greater democratic progress than had Mexico.[5] Proud of being a Mexican, he condemned the system of government and the undemocratic spirit which had prevented his country from fulfilling its heritage.[6] With his many Mexican friends in Paris he was wont to discuss the shortcomings of the Mexican political structure and the Díaz dictatorship, the evils of which were becoming apparent to him in spite of his youth. In his frequent discussions of contemporary political institutions in the western European countries, with which he was becoming familiar through travel, Madero always came to the same conclusion: his beloved Mexico suffered when compared with western Europe.

With their commercial course completed in June, 1892, he and Gustavo returned immediately to Mexico, where they spent the remainder of the summer before departing again for the United States. At the University of California in Berkeley they diligently applied themselves to the study of agriculture as practiced in the northern country, for they wished to incorporate as much American practice as possible into the management of the Coahuila haciendas.[7] On their return to Mexico in the summer of 1893, the young men discovered that a severe drought made any constructive work virtually impossible, but there was much to learn about the condition of the land and the

[3] See Madero, "Mis memorias," *Anales del Museo Nacional,* 9–12, for his education.
[4] *Ibid.,* 11–14.
[5] He probably did not fully realize what conditions were in many of those countries. Certainly neither Colombia nor Uruguay gave any sign of real democracy before 1900.
[6] José Vasconcelos, *Breve historia de México,* 525–26. Vasconcelos was one of Madero's close personal friends.
[7] Madero, "Mis memorias," *Anales del Museo Nacional,* 15.

people. Young Francisco and Gustavo, by now his older brother's almost inseparable companion, spent long hours in the saddle visiting all parts of the vast holdings and becoming thoroughly acquainted with economic and social conditions in the region.[8]

It was during these months that Madero really saw his country as it would be viewed through the eyes of a foreigner. His business—for he had been made manager of a portion of the hacienda—took him often to Saltillo, to Torreón, to San Pedro, and to other population centers. In those areas it was borne home to him, nakedly and bitterly, that economic and political liberty was completely denied the mass of the population. The inferiority he had felt in France, as a youth, was now magnified as he inspected conditions through the eyes of manhood. For the time being, however, there was little he could do except attempt to improve conditions on the Madero haciendas, and for the next few years he devoted himself almost exclusively to the cultivation of his acres and the management of his portion of the estate. In 1894, after the drought had broken, he and his father introduced the best type of American cotton, which produced a much greater yield than the native varieties and brought large profits to the enterprise.[9] On his own section he introduced new techniques and agricultural products which earned for him the respect of his neighbors.

In addition to his interest in the material improvement on the hacienda, Madero developed a deep interest in the welfare of the families who worked for him. At all times he was generous with his time and, if need be, with his money in giving aid to the unfortunate.[10] His interest in the lower class was made manifest in other ways as well, particularly in the field of education; he aided in establishing the Escuela Comercial in San Pedro and periodically donated large sums to the institution to keep it solvent.[11] Further, he personally paid the fees for a number of promising students; to others he gave money during their years in school and aid in finding employment after the completion of their studies.[12]

Firmly convinced that only through education would a progressive Mexico be born, Madero developed a passion for public schools and educational facilities. At every opportunity, during the early years of

[8] Gabriel Ferrer, *Vida de Francisco I. Madero,* 16.
[9] Madero, "Mis memorias," *Anales del Museo Nacional,* 15.
[10] Alfonso Taracena, *Madero. Vida del hombre y del político,* 24.
[11] Casasola, *Historia gráfica,* I, 96.
[12] Ferrer, *Vida de Francisco I. Madero,* 19.

the century, he supported and encouraged public training for all children of school age, but it was a losing fight. The ruling oligarchy, believing universal education to be useless or even dangerous, was firmly opposed to teaching the lower classes.[13] Undismayed by official lethargy and opposition, Francisco did what he could as a private citizen, building schools and paying for the food, clothing, and teachers for children of school age on his own hacienda.[14] But this was scratching the surface only. Because he believed firmly in his principles, he took every opportunity to foster public education, even using the elevation of Enrique Creel to the governorship of the neighboring state of Chihuahua as an excuse for writing a congratulatory letter which was in large part a plea to improve the state's school system.[15] In his first flight into politics Madero included educational reform as one of his five planks.[16]

During these years on the hacienda, when every day he was confronted with concrete evidence of the Mexican government's failure to weld the people into a nation, Madero's awareness of the social and economic ills was developing. While the members of his family, in their generally more enlightened actions, were far from representative of the *hacendado* class in its attitude toward the men on the haciendas, Francisco was more liberal than his family. Gustavo took somewhat the same interest in the workers' welfare, probably as the result of long and close association with his elder brother.

In part the explanation for Madero's advance in ideas lies in his character. He was a gentle and emotional man in whom humanitarianism and national pride combined to make him recognize existing evils and desire to eradicate them. More important, however, was his conversion to spiritism while in France. During the last years of his sojourn abroad he had read widely concerning the doctrine, but only after his return to Mexico did he become engrossed in the subject. As a leader of spiritism in Mexico, on one occasion he thus summed up his beliefs: "Spiritism invites a more elevated conception of Divinity, and an admission of the immutability of divine law; as a consequence [it also invites] a recognition that the sufferings of humanity are caused by its own imperfections and are not the result of divine ire."[17] At a later time he said:

[13] Federal law called for compulsory education but was not enforced.
[14] Taracena, *Madero,* 25.
[15] Madero to E. C. Creel, October 12, 1907, *LO,* February 18, 1934, p. 1.
[16] Madero, "Mis memorias," *Anales del Museo Nacional,* 27.
[17] Address to Spiritist Congress, VC.

33

This is the great work which spiritism pursues, and in which we invite you to join us: the liberation of humanity by means of school and science, so that once free and with an ordered intelligence, it can understand the revelations of spiritism [and so that] it can free itself forever from the domination of bestial instincts, from the domination of materialism.[18]

Since the policies of the Científicos and other members of the plutocracy were generally materialistic, those policies were an anathema to Madero.

Through his spiritistic experiences he also came to believe that all actions should be morally correct in order to bring the greatest benefits. To his father he once said:

The philosophical study which I have made has brought me to the conviction that in this world we have been created to work for its progress; if we think only of ourselves and desire progress for ourselves alone, disregarding the rest of humanity, our egoism will isolate us from that humanity . . . and it is certain that not only will we do nothing for it but neither will we do anything for ourselves.[19]

The study and practice of spiritism meant to Madero a deep awareness of the responsibility of society for its members, the duty of every individual to do the best he can to improve society. The development of a philosophy and a moral code was the result. This philosophy explains his determination to reform the Mexican political situation, even in the face of family opposition and official persecution. Conscience and self-esteem were of prime importance to him. To his father he wrote: "Fortune means nothing; . . . [since] I have come to identify my life with a noble and elevated cause, no other tranquillity exists except that of conscience, and that I will obtain only by complying with my duty."[20] Madero believed, too, that independence of spirit and strength of will are vital in order to obtain the most from life and to comply with duty to family, nation, and mankind. Not only should each man be the master of his own will but every decision should be the result of mature deliberation, free from influences which have no bearing on the subject; Madero was not an exponent of opportunism.[21]

---

[18] Address to Spiritist Congress, April, 1908, VC.
[19] Madero to Don F. Madero, December 20, 1908, *LO,* February 11, 1934, p. 1.
[20] Madero to Don F. Madero, January 8, 1909, *ibid.,* 2.
[21] Madero to Evaristo Madero, August 24, 1906, *ibid.,* February 4, 1934, p. 2.

Furthermore, vacillation and indecision would bring defeat, he said to his father when the family objected to his political activities.[22]

His philosophical studies and his observation of conditions in Mexico engendered a passionate conviction that it was the duty of every Mexican to take an active part in the rehabilitation of the homeland. A man's highest duty was to fight for the well-being of his country, and Madero felt impelled to take part in any activity which would foster improvement.[23] Patriotism demanded that every man do his part in the struggle, even at the risk of danger to his person or family.[24] The future of the country and of humanity depended on comprehensive action by all members of society. Not only was it necessary for those who were economically fortunate, the *gente decente,* to take an active part in government but all segments of society would have to become contributing parts in order to bring the greatest benefit to the whole, the nation.

Madero was firmly convinced that Mexico's only hope of salvation lay in the practice of democracy; a continuation of the nondemocratic policies of the Díaz government would bring ruin, and Mexico would never occupy the elevated position to which she was entitled.[25] His belief in democracy was strong—so strong that he would support only those candidates who had been nominated through democratic processes; so strong that he supported men whom he did not like or trust, but who had been designated by a presumably democratic convention.[26] But his belief in democracy did not go to extremes. He knew that the masses of the Mexican people did not at the moment have the capacity to practice an idealistic democracy; he knew that the majority of the Indians had neither the training nor the experience to take an active part in politics.[27] He did believe, firmly, however, that they could be taught the advantages, beauties, rights, and responsibilities of a democratic society. For this reason he was insistent upon public and universal education.

In consonance with his general attitude concerning the rights and responsibilities of man, Madero believed that work was a right and a

[22] Madero to Don F. Madero, December 20, 1908, *ibid., February 11, 1934,* p. 1.   [23] Madero to M. G. de Madero, December 20, 1908, *ibid.,* 2.
[24] Madero to M. G. de Madero, December 22, 1908, *ibid.*
[25] Madero to Don F. Madero, January 20, 1909, *ibid.*
[26] Madero to Don F. Madero, December 20, 1908, *ibid.,* 1; Madero, "Mis memorias," *Anales del Museo Nacional,* 21–23.
[27] Madero to J. I. Limantour, November 18, 1909, *LO, February 18, 1934,* p. 2.

35

duty, that there was dignity, not degradation, in physical labor.[28] His attitude toward labor was based largely on the concept that any man would be happy with freedom and an opportunity to make a decent living, through his own efforts, for himself and his family.[29] He resented the armed attack on the Río Blanco strikers, and he encouraged the newspapermen who were attempting to expose the chicanery involved.[30] On his own properties he was careful to see that the men and their families worked under good conditions and that they had adequate, though not pretentious, housing. After his definite move into national politics, he studied the labor problem to some extent, but his fundamental ideas, based on the nobility of work, changed but little. It was always apparent that he did not want to give anyone anything except an opportunity.

Madero's experience with his own family had a strong bearing on many of his actions after he came into national prominence. The family, including a host of brothers, sisters, uncles, and cousins, was large and extraordinarily co-operative, functioning as a unit, with the interests of one being the interests of all. Francisco gave credit for the perpetuation of this spirit to his grandfather Evaristo and paid particular tribute to his uncle Ernesto, whose astuteness and effort kept the various family financial interests from going into bankruptcy.[31] In addition to the interdependence, there was a genuine and strong affection, especially among the brothers and sisters of the future president, which permeated all family relationships. As was to be expected, Francisco had a deep respect for his father and grandfather, being anxious at all times to have their approbation of his actions. He looked upon Don Evaristo as the patriarch of the family, the guide who would lead them out of all difficulties, the example which all of them should try to emulate.[32] In spite of the desire for the approval of the elder members, Francisco did not always conform to their wishes when there seemed to be a fundamental difference of ideals. This independence of spirit was especially marked when, over the strong objections of his father and grandfather, he entered politics. With the younger members of the

[28] Casasola, *Historia gráfica,* I, 96.
[29] Madero to Don E. Madero, September 19, 1908, *LO,* February 4, 1934, p. 8.
[30] Madero to F. de P. Sentíes, January 19, 1907, *LP,* November 26, 1933, p. 1.
[31] Madero to Don E. Madero, September 19, 1908, *LO,* February 4, 1934, p. 8. The family enterprises included plantations, ranches, vineyards, wineries, steel mills, and banks.
[32] Madero to Don E. Madero, December 20, 1908, *ibid.,* February 11, 1934, p. 1; and September 19, 1908, *ibid.,* February 4, 1934, p. 8.

family, Madero was always affectionate, diplomatic, and understanding, qualities which created a strong bond between him and his brothers. His dependence on his family after he came to the presidency should not be surprising in view of the close family associations and the recognized abilities of the group. He believed he could trust their honesty and their ability, even when there was a difference in political philosophy between them, as was the case with his uncle Ernesto Madero and his cousin Rafael Hernández, both of whom had typical creole attitudes, and both of whom served in Madero's cabinet. Conversely, it should not be surprising that some of his brothers, including Gustavo, Raúl, and Emilio, seconded his actions when he rose in arms in late 1910. Even though they might have had some misgivings concerning the revolutionary plans and program, they loyally supported their elder brother.

Successful political leaders rarely spring into prominence fully developed, and dictatorships seldom collapse of their own weight; Madero and his revolution which overthrew Díaz are not exceptions. The elements which were finally responsible for the fall of Díaz were present on the Mexican scene long before 1910, but welding these elements into a striking force which, in spite of appearances of spontaneity, could defeat a well-established dictatorship was a task covering a number of years. Because he was overshadowed by older, better-known politicians before 1910, Madero's victory in the revolution was startling, and he appeared to be nothing more than a nominal leader who happened to be on the scene at the moment when a spontaneous indignation destroyed the dictatorship. But Madero became the leader of a successful revolutionary movement through arduous application and not alone by fortuitous circumstance.

By 1904, when Madero began his political career, the fundamental characteristics which he was to display as a national political figure had become fixed; he had developed certain basic concepts and ideals, which never changed. His decisions and activities were all consistent with a clear pattern; any changes afterward were changes in degree rather than in kind. As early as 1900 he had seriously considered a venture into politics with some relatives and friends, but the group limited their activities to academic discussions of Mexico's needs until a series of events blasted Madero out of his apathy and compelled him to take an active political stand.[33]

[33] Madero, "Mis memorias," *Anales del Museo Nacional,* 18.

The first of these was an attack by administration forces on an op-position organization in San Luis Potosí in January, 1902. The political club Ponciano Arriaga, organized in 1900 under the leadership of Camilo Arriaga, grandson of the famous liberal for whom the club was named, had held its first national convention in San Luis in 1901.[34] Al-though the meeting had been unmolested by government officials, some of the participants had been sent to prison on various charges in the following April.[35] Undaunted by this evidence of official ill-will, how-ever, the group had decided to continue, and the second national con-vention was held in January, 1902. At that meeting Heriberto Barrón, who had received an invitation to attend by posing as a liberal but who actually was an emissary of Governor Bernardo Reyes of Nuevo León, led an attack which completely disrupted the meeting and resulted in the arrest of most of the convention members.[36]

Inasmuch as Arriaga was a close personal friend, the attack affected Madero deeply and convinced him that nothing was to be gained by merely hoping for an official change in policy.[37] Nevertheless, the inci-dent had only a transitory effect; Madero resented the dictatorial per-secution, but it did not move him or his friends to act. To attempt any real reform would be at best an arduous and perhaps dangerous task and would mean the interruption of a pleasant and profitable way of life—this seemed to be the general reaction among the family and friends of the young *hacendado,* a position which at the moment he himself shared. The "criminal indifference"[38] to political conditions on the part of the *hacendados* and intelligentsia was further undermined on April 2, 1903, when an unjustified and shocking attack was made upon a peacefully parading opposition group in Monterrey by troops under the command of General Bernardo Reyes. In the "veritable orgy of blood"[39] a large number of people were killed or wounded; among the demonstrators and witnesses to the attack were many of Madero's friends and relatives.[40] The shooting, according to Madero, made it

[34] Casasola, *Historia gráfica,* I, 66.
[35] J. Flores Magón to L. Rivera, January 14, 1924, VC.
[36] Casasola, *Historia gráfica,* I, 66–67.
[37] Madero, *La sucesión presidencial en 1910,* 8.
[38] *Ibid.,* 9.
[39] [Pedro Lamicq], *Madero, por uno de sus íntimos,* 14.
[40] Madero, *La sucesión presidencial en 1910,* 9.

Photograph Culver Service

Porfirio Díaz, a tired old man

Photograph Underwood & Underwood

General Bernardo Reyes

clearly evident that the central government was determined to crush with a hand of iron, or even to suffocate in blood, any democratic movement. I say "the central government" [*el gobierno del Centro*] because it knew everything that happened in Monterrey, perhaps even giving prior permission for the action, and finally it absolved him [Reyes] whom the public accused of the horrible crime.[41]

The combination of conditions and events was more than Madero could accept, and he felt compelled to begin a true reform movement. At that time he had no thought of the national government, however, for he believed it impossible to displace Díaz or to convince him that representative government was either desirable or necessary. Accordingly, Madero determined to concentrate on the state and local level, where he hoped to be able to make some advances in the municipal elections in San Pedro in 1904 and the gubernatorial campaign in Coahuila in 1905.[42] Since he was not a resident of Nuevo León, Madero could do nothing directly concerning the conditions there, but he believed that a defeat of the official candidates in Coahuila would constitute a defeat for Reyes, since the general's influence in Madero's home state was strong. There was still hope that Díaz' retirement or death, either of which was expected momentarily because of his advanced age, would bring a solution to the national political problem and a reaction in favor of democracy.[43] This optimism was shattered in June, 1904, when the office of the vice-presidency was reinstituted and the presidential term lengthened to six years by constitutional amendment; the amendment was immediately followed by the designation of Ramón Corral as the official candidate, and within a month Corral had been elected to the new post.[44]

The amendment and the subsequent "election" put the situation in an entirely different light, for it was now clear that the death or retirement of Díaz would not bring democratic government. Díaz and the Científicos had demonstrated their intention of maintaining the dictatorship indefinitely, for now in the event of the President's death the government would be handed over to a successor already well established in an official position. A severe blow had been dealt the hopes of

---

[41] *Ibid.,* 9–10.
[42] Madero, "Mis memorias," *Anales del Museo Nacional,* 18, 26.
[43] Madero, *La sucesión presidencial en 1910,* 6.
[44] F. R. McCreery to State Department, June 20, 1904, *FR,* 1904, p. 491; P. Clayton to State Department, December 8, 1904, *ibid.,* 493.

the northern reformers.[45] The short time elapsing between the announcement of the amendment and the elections had precluded any effective counteraction, and it therefore now became doubly important to make a serious bid in the local campaigns. With the firm intention of transferring national politics to the local level, Madero and his friends entered the electoral lists in late 1904.

Madero, having no political ambitions and no desire to be a candidate himself in the municipal elections, prevailed upon an *hacendado*[46] of good reputation, and a friend of the Madero family, to accept the nomination for municipal president and head a slate of civic-minded men. A mild reform platform, including free elections, better schools, and public sanitation, was drafted and presented to the public.[47] During the primary voting there were a number of unpleasant episodes, but in general the balloting was peaceful and the reformers had high hopes of success. At the last moment, however, the Díaz-supported governor of Coahuila interfered and made certain that the officially designated candidates were victorious.[48] Madero's first venture into politics had resulted in defeat, but he had gained valuable experience which was soon put to test in the more important gubernatorial election.

As the state campaign began, it appeared as though the two strongest candidates would be Miguel Cárdenas, the incumbent and presumably the Díaz-approved candidate, and Frumencio Fuentes, an independent. But Frumencio, the choice of Ramón Corral and Andrés Garza Galán, could hardly be considered truly independent.[49] Far from desiring to be an opposition candidate, Frumencio hoped that he could persuade Díaz, through his friendship with Corral and by posing as a popular selection, to substitute his name for that of Cárdenas on the official list. To Madero and his immediate group. the prospect of Frumencio was no more attractive than that of Cárdenas, and therefore the founding of the Club Democrático Benito Juárez in October, 1904, was directed as much at Frumencio as at Cárdenas.[50]

[45] Madero, *La sucesión presidencial en 1910,* 7.
[46] Francisco Rivas.
[47] Madero, "Mis memorias," *Anales del Museo Nacional,* 27–28.
[48] *Ibid.,* 29–30.
[49] Garza Galán was political "boss" of Coahuila. Although he and Cárdenas were bitter enemies, both stood high in Díaz' favor. Díaz often gave support to men of opposing interests as a means of preventing one man from gaining too much power.
[50] Madero, *La sucesión presidencial en 1910,* 11; and "Mis memorias," *Anales del Museo Nacional,* 18.

40

Madero: Political Development

Madero, who took a major role in organizing the opposition and was largely responsible for financing *El Demócrata*, the party organ,[51] was elected the first president of the club.[52] In order to prevent undue criticism and to negate the charge of radicalism, Madero needed both the support of a respected personage and the tacit, if not active, approval of his family. In order to achieve both these ends he invited a kinsman, Jaime Gurza, to aid in directing the campaign.[53] Since Gurza was well known and respected both in Coahuila, of which state he was a native, and in Mexico City, where he was engaged in business, his adherence to the new party gave weight to Madero's contention that this was a program of needed reform and not of radical revolution. Madero's immediate family were not particularly pleased with the prospect of having Francisco in political opposition to the Díaz government, since their continued prosperity was dependent on at least cordial relations with the central government. Gustavo, at Madero's request, persuaded Don Francisco and Don Evaristo not to offer any serious objection to the formation of an opposition group; accordingly, both Gustavo and Alfonso, another younger brother, were active during the succeeding campaign.[54] Because of official intervention the group was only relatively successful in its endeavors to organize branch clubs in all the centers of the state,[55] but by late 1904 enough had been accomplished to warrant holding a convention, "following the American custom," to nominate candidates and to draft a platform.[56]

In the meantime the organization sponsoring Frumencio Fuentes was flourishing in restricted areas, particularly in Torreón, and he was making a strong bid for independent support. Both Madero and Frumencio realized that it would be disastrous to split the independent ranks, for such an event would guarantee Cárdenas' re-election. Negotiations between the two groups contrived a working agreement, by the terms of which the convention was to be held on May 21, 1905, the delegates were to be chosen from the various clubs, and each delegate was to have a weighted vote based on the total population of the area represented, not on the actual club membership.[57] These decisions were

[51] Madero, "Mis memorias," *Anales del Museo Nacional,* 19.
[52] [Lamicq], *Madero, por uno de sus íntimos,* 14.
[53] Taracena, *Madero,* 39. Gurza ultimately served in Madero's cabinet.
[54] *Ibid.,* 39; Madero, "Mis memorias," *Anales del Museo Nacional,* 19.
[55] Madero, "Mis memorias," *Anales del Museo Nacional,* 20.
[56] Madero, *La sucesión presidencial en 1910,* 11.
[57] Madero, "Mis memorias," *Anales del Museo Nacional,* 20; Madero to E. Vázquez Gómez, July 20, 1909, *LO,* January 7, 1934, p. 1.

reached easily, but consideration of a place for the meeting brought out some real differences. Since Torreón and San Pedro were the centers of strength for the respective contenders, the site that was agreeable to one was unacceptable to the other. Frumencio then suggested Mexico City, reasoning that the capital would be a safe place since Miguel Cárdenas could not intervene. Madero opposed holding the convention outside the state, especially in Mexico City. The selection of the metropolis would make it appear that the independents were asking permission of the central government to carry on their campaign; it would appear that the party leaders did not have the courage to demand their political rights in their own state. Furthermore, since going to Mexico would constitute an open bid for support from Ramón Corral, Madero objected because he was convinced that such a bid would give tacit approval of the policies of the dictatorship. He summed up his stand by saying:

To go to Mexico is to kneel before the despot, to kiss the hand that oppresses us, to recognize the right of the dictator to mix in our internal affairs, to sanction the custom of asking for a change in government when we have the right to change [that government], and, finally, to give the *coup de grâce* to the sovereignty of our state. We should not and we cannot do so.[58]

In spite of the strong stand taken by Madero, the central committee representing both groups voted him down and chose Mexico City.[59] Approximately one hundred representatives from the independent Coahuila political clubs gathered in the national capital for the convention,[60] where Madero was outguessed and outmaneuvered at every point by Frumencio Fuentes' clever and politically experienced supporters. Madero's candidate for the nomination, a man of integrity but without political experience, could do little to help himself.[61] During the proceedings the sponsors of Frumencio, by shrewd political maneuvering and through the judicious application of subtle pressures, steered the convention to select him as the candidate to represent the political independents.[62] One of the prime factors in the defeat suffered by Madero was the prior agreement concerning the method of repre-

[58] Madero to Comité Central, in Taracena, *Madero,* 41–44.
[59] Madero, "Mis memorias," *Anales del Museo Nacional,* 20.
[60] Madero, *La sucesión presidencial en 1910,* 12.
[61] Madero, "Mis memorias," *Anales del Museo Nacional,* 21.
[62] Taracena, *Madero,* 45.

42

sentation and voting. Frumencio, whose support was primarily from Torreón, represented the more populous sections and therefore was able to muster a larger number of votes even though Madero's candidate probably represented a larger number of persons organized into political clubs. Madero was to remember this lesson in political procedure and to insist on club rather than area representation in the convention of 1910.[63]

Even though Madero did not approve of the choice, and in spite of his conviction that Frumencio's election would be of little benefit to the state, he campaigned actively in the candidate's behalf. To do otherwise would have been inconsistent with his principles, and he still hoped to force Frumencio into depending on the popular vote in the state. Madero meant to accomplish this by making the campaign so frankly oppositionist that Díaz would look on the Coahuila candidate as a political enemy. If Díaz could be convinced that Frumencio was an oppositionist, and if Coahuila could elect the independent candidate in spite of official disapproval, then Frumencio would be forced into a position of depending on the electorate.[64] Madero also worked for the election of a group of independent deputies who would serve to keep the governor in line after the election.[65]

During the summer of 1905 the bitterness of the campaign increased with each passing day, and, following the pattern of the times, political persecutions became more and more commonplace. Meetings were broken up, arrests were made, and vague rumors of official intervention permeated the atmosphere. The independent group continued its activities, however, and it appeared as though the election would be nationally significant until Frumencio lost his nerve and all but withdrew from the contest. Frumencio, unlike Madero, still hoped to obtain the official blessing of the dictator through the influence of Corral; when the campaign was well under way, he approached Díaz in an effort to obtain his public support. At first Díaz temporized, but soon definitely notified Frumencio that Miguel Cárdenas would receive the government's blessing.[66] The information threw the candidate into a panic; he was prevailed upon to continue only with the understanding that he himself would engage in no active campaigning, and that his party would publish nothing which might be construed as hostile to the administration. These concessions almost guaranteed his defeat.

[63] Madero to E. Vázquez Gómez, July 20, 1909, *LO*, January 7, 1934, p. 1.
[64] Madero, "Mis memorias," *Anales del Museo Nacional*, 21.
[65] *Ibid.*, 22.   [66] *Ibid.*, 23.

Even so, on election day there was a great amount of activity at the polls. Madero was extremely busy, advising the voters of their rights and insisting that the officials allow the voters an opportunity to cast their ballots, but his efforts were useless. The polls were all but closed to the opposition, and it was officially announced that Miguel Cárdenas had won an overwhelming victory.[67] Immediately after the election an order was issued for Madero's arrest, but strong public reaction, coupled with the importance of the Madero name, convinced the central government that his arrest would be a political error, and Mexico City therefore ordered the local officials to take no further action.[68]

Madero's first reaction to the defeat was to bend all his efforts toward organizing a national party to combat the government at every turn; but when he broached the subject to a number of liberals in different areas, he received little encouragement. After carefully considering the political situation, he concluded that any attempt to draw together a cohesive national party in 1905, to campaign for the presidential election of 1910, would be sheer folly, since the organization would probably disintegrate long before the election.[69] He considered the defeat to be no more than a temporary setback, however, and decided to devote himself to the aid of independent movements. The needs of Ricardo Flores Magón, who had been forced to leave Mexico,[70] soon attracted his attention, and in 1905 he sent the Liberal party leader a small financial contribution to assist in the publication of *Regeneración* in the United States.[71]

Assistance to men of the caliber of Flores Magón, however, was only a small part of the program which Madero outlined for himself. Much more important, in view of his desire to lay plans for the next presidential campaign, was to cement friendships with recognized opponents of the Díaz regime. From 1906 to 1909 he corresponded freely with a number of newspapermen whose policies were well known; Paulino Martínez, Francisco de P. Sentíes, Fernando Iglesias Calderón, and Victoriano Agüeros especially were the recipients of many letters concerning the general political and economic condition of the nation. Martínez, the most implacable and the least diplomatic of the opposi-

---

[67] [Lamicq], *Madero, por uno de sus íntimos*, 15.
[68] *Ibid.*, 16.
[69] Taracena, *Madero*, 51.
[70] R. Flores Magón to H. Weinberger, May 9, 1921, VC.
[71] Taracena, *Madero*, 45. Madero later criticized Flores Magón for his activities, but in 1905 he believed Magón's writings to be an expression of the desires of the majority.

tion newspapermen, had suffered innumerable arrests because of his editorial policy, but the incarcerations had no dampening effect on his enthusiasm for the contest against the government. Since the greater part of Martínez' time was being spent either in prison or in repairing the damage of confiscation, Madero believed his efforts to be largely wasted and, while sending funds for the editor's relief in 1906, suggested caution rather than frontal attack.[72]

Essentially Madero was a cautious man who did not favor useless attacks against overwhelming odds; before engaging in any activity, he wanted assurance that there was at least some chance of success. He decried actions by the liberals which would lead to suffering without permanent or real amelioration of existing conditions. He therefore advised Martínez, on a later occasion, to change the form of his accusations and to tone down the general tenor of his remarks in order to minimize the dangers of arrest.[73] He particularly advised against attacking the lesser officials by name, since the *jefes políticos* and the minor officials were exceedingly prone to resent and prevent criticism. His general attitude was well summarized in one letter to Martínez:

> If you want to fight against the present despotic government, you should wait for the next presidential campaign because it is almost certain that if Díaz intends to have himself re-elected there will be a strong movement all over the country against that re-election, and that will be an opportune moment to make a vigorous attempt to recover our rights. . . . In that campaign you and two or three other valiant newspapermen will not be the only ones exposed to the blows of the enemy; . . . we will be a phalanx of fighters.[74]

Madero wished each man to feel it his duty to avoid persecutions when sacrifice was futile, to save himself in order to make his weight felt at the proper time.[75] And that the proper moment would come there was never any doubt, for Madero intended to make that opportunity; as early as 1906 he was determined to "throw off the yoke of the Tuxtepecan tyranny" in the succeeding presidential election.[76] On the other hand, at that early date he firmly believed that opposition to the government should be within the limits of the law;[77] on that basis

---

[72] Madero to P. Martínez, May 19, 1906, *LO,* January 21, 1934, p. 1.
[73] Madero to P. Martínez, July 5, 1906, *ibid.*
[74] Madero to P. Martínez, May 19, 1906, *ibid.*   [75] *Ibid.*
[76] Madero to E. Madero, August 4, 1906, *ibid.,* February 4, 1934, p. 2. The "Tuxtepecan tyranny" refers to the plan under which Díaz came to power.
[77] Madero to unidentified person, undated, in Taracena, *Madero,* 63.

45

he condemned the Liberal party revolution of 1906, even while recognizing the distinct possibility of an imminent revolutionary outbreak of wide proportions.[78] To Madero revolution then was not only impracticable; it endangered the success of any reform movement, since it would give Díaz an excuse to indulge in severely repressive measures.[79] The nation desired a change in government, but not at the expense of a bloody fight; Madero therefore discouraged his friends from taking any part in the abortive movement fostered by the Partido Liberal.

In his campaign to attract men to his political viewpoint, Madero made use of every event which would cast aspersion on the governmental policy. He castigated Díaz for the action against the strikers at Río Blanco and volunteered to finance a minute study of the event;[80] the publication of the results could have been used in his campaign to discredit the administration, but the investigation was never made. He attacked the government for leasing Magdalena Bay to the United States, for he feared a loss of Mexican sovereignty if the leases were consummated.[81] Even though he felt no particular antipathy toward the American government and had a deep respect for the political institutions of the northern neighbor, he feared that the lease might pave the way for a like request from Japan; and in case of war between Japan and the United States, Mexico would inevitably be drawn into the conflict.[82] Madero was so incensed over the situation that he momentarily threw caution to the winds and drafted a violent protest condemning the government in harsh and pointed terms, but mature deliberation showed the futility of such a proclamation, and he was easily persuaded by some of his friends to withhold publication of the manifesto.[83]

By early 1908, little had been done toward the formation of a strong party of opposition; the elections were still two years in the future, Díaz was approaching the age of eighty, and it was difficult to prophesy the nature of his actions or of public reaction to any attempt at strong party organization. Both government and opposition politicians were generally uneasy about the attitude of the aged dictator and his ability

[78] Madero to E. Madero, August 4, 1906, *LO,* February 4, 1934, p. 2.
[79] Madero to Don E. Madero, undated, in Taracena, *Madero,* 53.
[80] Madero to Sentíes, January 19, 1907, *LP,* November 26, 1934, p. 1.
[81] Madero to F. Iglesias C., undated, in Taracena, *Madero,* 67–69.
[82] Madero to R. Hernández, undated, *ibid.,* 70–71.
[83] Madero to V. Agüeros, undated, *ibid.,* 79–83.

to maintain himself as the head of government. It was under these conditions that the minor bombshell of the Creelman interview burst upon the public.

In spite of almost daily requests by the Mexican press, Díaz steadfastly refused to make any statement concerning his plans; finally on February 17, 1908, he clarified his position through James Creelman of *Pearson's Magazine*. It was not until March 3, when *El Imparcial* published a translation of Creelman's article, that the Mexican public was enlightened, and then Díaz absolutely declined to comment further on his earlier interview with the American journalist. While the thoughts expressed to Creelman were and are clear enough, the objectives of the dictator were not, and are not, so obvious. Basically, Díaz stated that he was a firm believer in democratic principles and had been careful to preserve the form and theory of democracy during his terms in office. He recognized the dangers inherent in repeated terms in office, for the officeholder had a tendency to "regard it as personal property"[84] after many terms; but he justified his past actions on the ground that his retention of the presidency was a necessity for the country's development and a duty which the public expected of him. Now, however, after thirty years of faithful service, he felt he could retire with the assurance that Mexico would continue in the path of progress. He could then devote his remaining years to guiding the next president, whomever the Mexican people might choose; he wished to foster a truly representative government. He explained the absence of an opposition party in the past by saying that since his friends constituted such a vast majority his few opponents did not wish to identify themselves with a small minority. Now, however, he would welcome and support the formation of active political parties which would participate in the forthcoming elections. "Regardless of the feelings and opinions of my friends and supporters," he avowed, "I am determined to retire at the end of my present term, and I will not accept reelection. I will then be eighty years old."[85]

The explosive nature of the interview was not immediately apparent. The statements were seemingly quite straightforward and sincere; there was no evident dissimulation, even though it was clear that a large portion, particularly concerning the gentleness of his rule, had

[84] Díaz' statement to Creelman, in *El Imparcial*, March 3, 1908.
[85] *Ibid*.

been made with tongue in cheek. But the conditions under which the interview had been granted gave food for thought, for Díaz had talked to a foreigner instead of to a Mexican. Those who knew Díaz well, and who had felt the weight of his power, feared that the statement was a trap specifically designed to bring into the open those who were in opposition. Both opposition and adherent groups, however, were in a dilemma; the stakes were high, and an error in judgment would be disastrous. If Díaz were sincere, there would be an opportunity, one which would come but once, to form an opposition party under the unofficial aegis of the powerful dictator. At the same time, it would be mandatory for the administration hangers-on to select as a new candidate one whom they could manage and who would continue the pattern of patronage established by Díaz. If, on the other hand, the interview had been purely for foreign consumption or for the purpose of giving a false sense of security to active or potential enemies of the regime, any overt action taken in response to the "magnanimous" attitude of the dictator would lead to sure destruction.

Díaz' exact intention is still open to question, but on the basis of his later actions certain valid conclusions may be drawn. In all probability he did not intend to step down at the end of that period of office. He had been led to believe, by the men around him, that the populace would refuse to accept his retirement. Therefore, the declaration of intention was nothing more than an empty gesture designed to satisfy the more loquacious and vindictive of his enemies and to prove to the world the democratic nature of his government. It was a gift which would cost the giver nothing. There is no evidence to show that Díaz ever realized the opposition's strength or that he properly gauged the dissatisfaction of his people. Regardless of his motivation, however, the interview was a cataclysmic error of judgment.

For a few months all was quiet. Madero was suspicious and cautious; he merely did nothing. The Científicos, uncertain of their ground, began organizing a protest. The administration anti-Científicos, largely supporters of Bernardo Reyes, watched developments closely but took no action. Díaz, too, waited—waited for a mass protest which never materialized. He refused to amplify his pronouncement and consistently denied to the Mexican press the privilege of firsthand information concerning his attitude. Finally, on May 30, 1908, the suspense was broken by Díaz himself when he allowed Limantour, Ramón Corral, and Olegario Molina to "convince" him of the necessity of accepting another presidential term.[86] Since the dictator had spoken, there was no longer any question in the minds of the administration group concerning the presidency; it was now a question of the all-important vice-presidency, for few believed that Díaz would live to see the end of his next term. The decision by Díaz also simplified the situation for the opposition, since they now knew more nearly where they stood and were in a better position to plan their campaign.

Renewed attacks by the Magonistas in June, 1908, were symptomatic of the general unrest, even though they were viewed coldly by the majority.[87] Madero was genuinely disturbed by the outlook; a strong sense of impending disaster conditioned his thinking and his actions. The incidence of dissatisfaction was ascending, and some change was inevitable; the nature of that change would largely determine the success or failure of Mexico as a nation. A continuation of the Díaz regime, or of a government in consonance with the practices of the Díaz administration, would result in the country's complete enervation—the dissipation of its strength, its energies, its vitality, and its patriotism— leaving it prey to any foraging foreign power. The alternative to such a dreary outlook was equally disastrous: recurrence of revolution as an instrument of politics. Madero hoped that there was a third course of action, one which would be more attractive to him personally and which at the same time would bring benefits to the nation: the institution of a democratic government supported by freely elected legislative assemblies and guaranteed by regular rotation of offices.[88] He strongly deprecated fighting the government through ill-founded utterances, exaggerated accounts, or direct frontal assault, since the times were not propitious for such methods but were conducive to the formation of a strong opposition.[89] The Coahuila campaign in 1905 had shown the impossibility of developing an effective party within one state; only in concert with other states might any concrete advance be made. Madero therefore favored the organization of a Partido Democrático as soon as sufficient groundwork had been completed to assure its success;[90] the party platform could be developed after the party was functioning. Madero was nevertheless convinced of the necessity of

[86] Alfonso Taracena, *En el vértigo de la revolución mexicana,* 23.
[87] Taracena, *Madero,* 73.
[88] Madero to Agüeros, undated, in Taracena, *Madero,* 79–83.
[89] Madero to P. Martínez, September 17, 1908, *LO,* January 21, 1934, p. 1.
[90] Madero to Agüeros, undated, in Taracena, *Madero,* 85–89.

undertaking a propaganda campaign, before organizing a national party, to mold public opinion toward the acceptance of the concept of a successful opposition party.[91]

In the meantime a gubernatorial campaign in Coahuila gave Madero an opportunity to form a local party which could serve as the nucleus for a national party. It was not his object to win the state campaign, for he believed a victory would be fruitless inasmuch as the central government could force its will on the state officials, but to set the stage for the presidential election.[92] The local campaign would serve only as a focal point and propagandizing medium to encourage other states to take like steps, and this would ultimately result in a national party. The people of Coahuila objected to the general scheme, believing that the major efforts should be devoted to the state campaign, but on this point Madero was insistent.[93]

Madero's choice for the place of meeting of the various components of the opposition was Mexico City, in spite of some obvious objections to that site.[94] Because of the pall of servility which hung over the capital, and the large number of government employees whose very existence depended on Díaz, Mexico City seemed a poor choice for the formation of an opposition party, but advantages were also evident. A political party having Mexico City as its birthplace would command greater respect than a party originating in one of the states; there would be greater freedom in the capital than in other sections, for it was certain that none of the state governments would allow frankly oppositionist meetings; and Mexico City was far more convenient as a convention site than any other city in Mexico.[95] In view of these factors Madero insisted that Mexico City should be the meeting place.

While he was perfecting his plans for the national organization, rumors of the founding of another party in the capital reached him. Since he knew nothing of the new group and could obtain no information about its personalities or its aims, he feared that it was a preventive move by the administration to block his own plans, and subsequent events proved his suspicions to be well founded. During the latter part of 1908, Madero did little to bring his plans to a head inasmuch as he

[91] Madero to Sentíes, October 10, 1908, *LO,* November 26, 1933, p. 1.
[92] Madero to Agüeros, undated, in Taracena, *Madero,* 91–93.
[93] Madero to Sentíes, undated, *ibid.,* 77–79.
[94] Madero to Agüeros, undated, *ibid.,* 88–89.
[95] Madero to Sentíes, undated, *ibid.,* 77–79.

was convinced that public opinion had not yet been properly molded.[96] Francisco de P. Sentíes tacitly agreed with him regarding the advantages of postponing action; and Madero was mildly enthusiastic when Sentíes and Juan Sánchez Azcona, a friend of his student days, proposed the establishment of a newspaper[97] to act as a propagandizing medium in the preparation of public opinion. It was somewhat of a shock to Madero, therefore, when he read in a Mexico City newspaper that the Centro Organizador del Partido Democrático had been organized at a meeting sponsored by Sentíes, Sánchez Azcona, and Heriberto Barrón.[98] The fact that the party had begun without his knowledge was not the most surprising and disturbing factor; it was Barrón's association with the group which was disappointing and suspicious. Barrón, who had been responsible for the attack on the Club Ponciano Arriaga in 1902, was a well-known Porfirista and Reyista, and Madero was convinced that he would do what he could to destroy the original purpose of the party.[99] It was disheartening to see men of the caliber of Sentíes, Sánchez Azcona, and Benito Juárez Maza associating with Barrón, for it was contrary to logic; the only explanation was that in some manner Barrón had either completely deceived the others or had been able, through shrewd politics, to interject himself into a situation in which he was not wanted. But the election of Barrón to the position of secretary of the Centro Organizador seemed to belie the latter interpretation. Madero was so distressed that he wrote Sentíes three long letters during the course of one day, in each of which he questioned the propriety of allowing Barrón to occupy a position of importance and confidence on the directive council.[100] He feared the reaction of the states, since he felt that most of the outlying organizations would look on Barrón's secretaryship as merely another indication that Reyes and Díaz were maneuvering to maintain control of the nation's political destinies.[101] Madero's confidence in Sentíes was seriously undermined; he felt that the calling of the meeting in Mexico without his having been given prior notice indicated a desire to eliminate him from any

[96] Madero to Sentíes, October 10, November 4, and December 3, 1908, *LP*, November 26, 1933, p. 2.
[97] To be called *México Nuevo*.
[98] Madero to Sentíes, December 3 and 19, 1908, *LP*, November 26, 1933, p. 2.
[99] *Ibid.*
[100] These letters, written December 19, 1908, may be found in *LP*, November 26, 1933, p. 2.
[101] Madero to Sentíes, December 19, 1908, *ibid.*

51

participation. And yet—and this was the crowning blow—he was asked for money to aid in the publication of the new paper. He flatly refused to make any contribution until he was more conversant with the aims and ideals of the organization and could assure himself of the party's independent character.[102]

Within a few days he was partially mollified by Sentíes' assurance that Barrón exercised no important influence and that Sentíes and Sánchez Azcona were in complete control of the organization. Nevertheless, Madero was dissatisfied; he not only insisted on the removal of Barrón from office but also made clear his determination to keep free of any organization which had Rodolfo Reyes, son of the general, among its members.[103] In order to advise himself more adequately concerning the purposes of the Centro, Madero then wrote Fernando Iglesias Calderón for his opinion; the answer confirmed Madero's worst fears:

> My opinion concerning this so-called "Democratic party" is that it is a group of scheming Reyistas, protecting themselves with the names of some deceived independents—among whom I include our friend Sentíes, and among whom they are trying desperately to make you and me figure . . . in an effort to present General Reyes as the man designated by Public Opinion for the presidency.[104]

With this independent and valued judgment as a strong support for his own suspicions, Madero began to think seriously of forming another party, even while trying to convince Sentíes of the futility of attempting to work with Barrón.[105] But his admonitions were in vain. By mid-January it was clear that the C.O.D.P.D. was purely and simply an instrument by which certain administration leaders were furthering their own ends. A large number of deputies to Congress were included in its membership, and this, coupled with the lack of a strong stand on the question of re-election, created a complete lack of confidence in its aims. The most eloquent evidence of that lack of confidence was the name which popular parlance attached to the organization; with characteristic Mexican humor the C.O.D.P.D. was referred to as "Con

---

[102] Madero to Sentíes, December 19, 1908, *ibid*. This is the third in the series of that date.
[103] Madero to Sentíes, December 25, 1908, *ibid*.
[104] F. Iglesias C. to Madero, undated, in Taracena, *Madero*, 155–59, in reply to Madero's letter dated December 31, 1908, *ibid*., 153–55.
[105] E.g., Madero to Sentíes, January 8, 1909, *LP*, November 26, 1933, p. 8.

Orden de Porfirio Díaz."[106] When Ignacio Mariscal, the Minister of Foreign Relations, presided over the meeting on February 5, 1909, all doubt as to the auspices of the party was dispelled.[107] Madero even feared that Juan Sánchez Azcona had gone over to the Reyes camp.[108]

Under those conditions there was little Madero could do but denounce Sentíes and begin the formation of another party more in accord with his own ideas. He had already established relationships with a number of independents, both inside and outside the C.O.D.P.D., whom he hoped to interest in the new party. Among these were Emilio Vázquez Gómez, Toribio Esquivel Obregón, and Heriberto Frías, all of whom figured prominently in the ensuing presidential campaign. With the open rupture with the so-called Democratic party, Madero began the painfully slow process of building his own party, depending to a large degree on the three men named.[109]

Madero's development as a politician between the first hesitant and tentative venture into the political field in 1905 and the full-scale declaration of war on the Díaz regime in 1909 has some interesting and important characteristics. Although he is generally regarded as a visionary, Madero gave evidence of realism and sound political judgment during those years. The realization that Mexico could not support an opposition party over a period of years, during which nothing could be done to stimulate enthusiasm and maintain it at a high pitch, indicates not only a realistic approach to an important political problem but also an understanding of one of the basic characteristics of the Mexican people. There were cogent reasons for believing that a party could not exist for a four-year period; after the first shock of crusading zeal had worn off, there would have been little to feed a militant party. There were to be no important intervening national elections, and as a consequence the only core around which the party could operate would have been the rather ephemeral opposition to the government. Under those conditions the failure of the party would have been inevitable, particularly since repressive measures by Díaz could have been expected.

After thirty years of dictatorship, a period devoid of opportunity for political organization, it would have been foolhardy to believe that a strong political party could materialize from nothing. While dissatis-

---

[106] Roque Estrada, *La revolución y Francisco I. Madero,* 40.
[107] *Ibid.,* 41.
[108] Madero to Sentíes, January 20, 1909, *LP,* November 26, 1933, p. 8.
[109] Madero to T. Esquivel O., February 23, 1909, *LO,* January 28, 1934, p. 1.

faction with the Díaz government was evident, more than discontent was needed as motivation for bringing a major undertaking to a successful conclusion. The task required painstaking organization, which in turn depended upon public confidence. It was that confidence which Madero was anxious to instill in the hearts of all those who were potential opponents of the Díaz administration. This anxiety was the basis for his cautious approach to the question of organizing a political party, and for his opposition, in the early stages of the campaign, to supporting any individual for the presidency. During those years, he was developing the political ideas which he put into effect shortly after his decision to form his own party, and which he expounded in his literary magnum opus, *La sucesión presidencial en 1910.*

Díaz and his cabinet, 1910

Justino Fernández, *Justice*; General Manuel González Cosío, *War and Marine*; Ramón Corral, *Vice-President*; José Ives Limantour, *Treasury*; Díaz; Olegario Molina, *Fomento*; Enrique C. Creel, *Foreign Relations*; Justo Sierra, *Public Instruction*; and Leandro Fernández, *Communications and Public Works*

Awaiting Madero's crossing into Mexico
Standing, center: José Garibaldi (in topcoat), Mariano Hernández,
Eduardo Hay, and Raúl Madero

III
The Book and the Parties

"To the heroes of our country; To the independent newspapermen; To all good Mexicans"[1]—so reads the dedication of one of the most important documents in the history of Mexico: important for its influence, not for its sagacity or depth of wisdom; interesting for what it omitted rather than for what it said. Only on rare occasions does a literary work, the product of one man's thinking and labor, change the course of a nation; more rarely still does a mediocre publication have that effect.

La sucesión presidencial en 1910 presents an interesting paradox. That the work was mediocre by any standard—literary, philosophical, or factual—cannot be denied, but its influence was infinitely more startling and powerful than that of most great literary productions. The publication of a work of equivalent worth in any other country, under almost any conditions, would have created hardly a ripple on the national scene; and yet Madero's work was one of the major contributory causes of the growth of the tidal wave which engulfed the Díaz administration and swept it from power. Not only is the publication interesting in itself because of its tremendous effect, but the situation surrounding its writing and distribution uncovers some facets of Madero's character which give an insight into the soul of a man who would not be denied the completion of a task which he deemed of fundamental importance to Mexico.

Exactly when Madero began the task of writing is not certain, but the germination of the idea probably began shortly after the unsuccessful Coahuila gubernatorial campaign. As early as 1907 he began to arrange his business and financial affairs to leave himself free for politics when the proper moment arrived.[2] The actual drafting of the text was

[1] Madero, *La sucesión presidencial en 1910*, 1.
[2] Taracena, *Madero*, 112.

55

done primarily in October, 1908.[3] Shortly thereafter a local press in Parras, Coahuila, began the printing, even though Madero's original intent had been to commission Victoriano Agüeros, editor of *El Tiempo,* to complete that task.[4] During the latter months of the year Madero piqued the curiosity of some of his friends by making casual reference to a book he was writing, but in none of his correspondence did he elucidate, and he always asked that the information be treated as confidential.

By early December, 1908, about half the work had been printed, and Madero had hopes that it would be ready for publication by January 1, 1909.[5] Since he believed his book would be a powerful influence in forming public opinion, he opposed the actions taken by Francisco de P. Sentíes and Sánchez Azcona in the latter part of 1908. When the Centro Organizador del Partido Democrático showed its Reyista sympathies in late December, he hoped to counteract Barrón's influence by the circulation of *La sucesión presidencial en 1910;* publication date was therefore set for January 15, 1909.[6]

Writing the book proved to be less difficult than getting family permission for its publication. Even though Madero was thirty-five years old, his respect for the elder members of his family forced him to obtain their blessing before he would venture into the political struggle. In addition, the Madero family had been suffering severe financial difficulties since the economic recession of 1907, and negotiations for a loan were in process in late 1908 and early 1909. His father, convinced that any political participation by Francisco would prejudice family fortunes, opposed his son's publishing a work which attacked the administration.[7] Faced with these stern and unyielding objections, Madero began campaigning to change the stand taken by his parents and his grandfather; by steady and unremitting pressure he hoped to wear down their resistance. He reminded his mother of each citizen's high duty to take an active part in public affairs and implied that she should have been proud of a son willing to make the necessary personal sacrifices.[8] He requested his father to hurry the completion of the financial trans-

[3] Madero, *La sucesión presidencial en 1910,* 75.
[4] Taracena, *Madero,* 112–13.
[5] Madero to Sentíes, December 3, 1908, *LP,* November 26, 1933, p. 2.
[6] Madero to Don F. Madero, December 20, 1908, *LO,* February 11, 1934, p. 1; Madero to Don E. Madero, December 20, 1908, *ibid.*
[7] Madero to Don F. Madero, December 20, 1908, *ibid.*
[8] Madero to M. G. de Madero, December 20, 1908, *ibid.,* p. 2.

56

actions in order to clear the field for political activities.[9] He reminded his grandfather of his own part in a political struggle of an earlier time and then used a flattering tone to minimize the patriarch's resistance.[10] In late December he sent copies of the newly printed work to his father and grandfather, asking for comments on the general thesis and the organization. He assured his parents that he intended to take no action until the family finances had been bolstered, but again he begged them to make every effort to complete the transactions.[11] At the same time he fell back on the use of genteel blackmail; because a number of people knew of the book's existence and knew its general thesis, he said, there would be greater danger in not publishing it than in putting it into circulation, since rumors were exaggerating the virulence of the material. It was therefore necessary, according to the insistent Madero, to complete the financial transactions as soon as possible and begin the circulation of *La sucesión presidencial* at once.[12] He had committed himself to a course of action in national politics, and he had no desire to debate the wisdom of his decision; the only point at issue was the time at which his activities would begin.[13]

At this juncture the validity of Madero's claim to authorship was questioned, and since that doubt became widespread the situation needs some clarification. Don Evaristo did not believe Madero to have been the writer inasmuch as he doubted his grandson's ability to express himself with such clarity and precision.[14] Before the outbreak of the revolution it was common gossip that Madero had paid someone to do the work while he took the credit.[15] Rafael Hernández was proclaimed as the ghost writer by some, while others would have given credit to Sentíes or Roque Estrada, but there can be no doubt concerning the real identity of the writer.[16] Not only did Madero insist to his grandfather that he had indeed done all the writing without assistance, but there is no reason for a contrary belief.[17] The precision and clarity

[9] Madero to Don F. Madero, December 20, 1908, *ibid.,* p. 1.
[10] Madero to Don E. Madero, December 20, 1908, *ibid.*
[11] Madero to M. G. de Madero, December 22, 1908, *ibid.,* p. 2; Madero to Don F. Madero, December 26, 1908, *ibid.*
[12] Madero to M. G. de Madero, December 22, 1908, *ibid.*
[13] Madero to Don F. Madero, December 26, 1908, *ibid.*
[14] Don E. Madero to Madero, January 5, 1909, *ibid.,* p. 1.
[15] Henry Baerlein, *Mexico, the Land of Unrest,* 220.
[16] Taracena, *Madero,* 114–15.
[17] Madero to Don E. Madero, January 7, 1909, *LO,* February 11, 1934, p. 1.

of which Don Evaristo spoke were not so outstanding as the grandfather seemed to think, and the style and the use of words bear a striking resemblance to Madero's other writings, particularly some of his longer letters and his memoirs. It was ridiculous to assign the authorship to Roque Estrada, for by Estrada's own statement he did not know Madero until after the book was on the market; and since Estrada was a bitter enemy before Madero's fall, he certainly would have taken credit if by so doing he could have discredited his erstwhile chief.[18] Whether Don Evaristo's doubts were the basis of the rumors which later circulated, or whether the rumors were the results of attempts to belittle Madero, is not clear, but the nature and vehemence of the attack on the Díaz regime were surprising to his friends and family and could easily have given rise to doubts.

In the latter part of December and early January the elder Maderos were inspecting Francisco's work. After generally castigating Madero for his participation in politics, Don Evaristo took him to task for publishing his work, particularly questioning the wisdom of circulating it under existing conditions. The government, he feared, would consider the work as inspired by the elder members of the Madero family, in which case there would be serious repercussions on the family interests. Nevertheless, by making some pointed criticisms concerning the material, Don Evaristo indicated at least partial sympathy with the ideas presented.[19] Madero's father had no concrete objections to the book or its phraseology, but he was reluctant to give his blessing. As the days passed and still the permission did not come, Madero became impatient and nervous. The opposition movement had begun, yet he felt "detained in the midst" of his career; a "powerful force" prevented his taking positive action or circulating his book. He needed his father's moral support, and without it he was certain that defeat would be inevitable. He begged Don Francisco to consider all aspects of the problem and then to give his blessing to the undertaking. Finally, on January 22, Don Francisco succumbed to the repeated pleas and sent his son a telegram in which Madero was tendered the desired support from both his parents.[20] Within a matter of days the publication of *La sucesión presidencial en 1910* was announced and copies were be-

[18] Estrada, *La revolución y Francisco I. Madero*, 55.

[19] Don E. Madero to Madero, January 2, 1909, *LO*, February 25, 1934, p. 1; and January 5, 1909, *ibid.*, February 11, 1934, p. 1.

[20] Madero to Don F. Madero, December 26, 1908, and January 20 and 23, 1909, *ibid.*, p. 2.

ing sent to various parts of the country. Madero had the audacity, or perhaps the sincerity, to send a copy to Díaz, asking him to read it carefully and to reflect on the subject presented and the conclusions drawn.[21]

The effect of the book was startling, even though the importance of the work was not immediately discernible. Roque Estrada has given a good description of his reaction, and since Estrada was Madero's enemy at the time of writing, the effect which the work had on him is important and indicative of the general influence.

Estrada was a disillusioned and bitter young man in 1909 when he read *La sucesión presidencial en 1910*. Having been in prison once for his attacks on the Díaz regime, and anxious to ally himself with an opposition group, he had attended a number of the meetings of the Partido Democrático, only to become disgusted when he ascertained the pronounced sympathy for Reyes. He was therefore searching for an alliance which could hold his interest and which would follow a political pattern in line with his anti-Díaz beliefs. His studied opinion of Madero's writing was that it was shallow and ill organized but sincere and courageous. He was convinced of the deep feeling and infinite good will of the author, even though the ideas expressed were somewhat hazy; because the author was a rich *hacendado* and not a professional politician, his work was in a class of its own as an expression of hope for the nation. Estrada, in Mexico City at the time, was anxious to meet Madero, and from this meeting grew the close association which lasted until after the successful conclusion of the revolution against Díaz.[22]

Innumerable others were affected in the same manner. Within a short time the first edition of three thousand copies was sold, and new editions followed. Men who had never before heard of Madero became interested in the man who had had the courage to criticize the regime, and they were willing to join his political party during the course of the year. The Díaz supporters laughed at the pretensions of the little man from the north and looked at his book as a subject for jest, but the malcontents slowly gathered.

What, then, did this book contain that it should have become so important in the history of Mexico? There was nothing new or startling, either in the information or in the interpretation. It was merely a

[21] Madero to Porfirio Díaz, February 2, 1909, *LO,* February 18, 1934, p. 1.
[22] Estrada, *La revolución y Francisco I. Madero,* 56, 72–73.

rather dry and somewhat inaccurate presentation of the national political history of Mexico, with the primary emphasis on the evils of dictatorial rule. Almost purely political in character, it hardly mentioned the social or economic ills; but there was much emphasis on the need for freedom of suffrage, nonre-election of high public officials, and rotations in office. Madero did not overlook the social needs, but he believed there would be time enough to attack such problems after the political situation had improved.[23]

The outstanding features of *La sucesión presidencial en 1910* were its courage and sincerity. While Madero treated Díaz himself, as a personality, with kindness, not only was there harsh criticism of the Díaz administration but the Díaz myth as well was attacked with fury. Madero decried the tendency to surround every action of the dictator with an aura of uniqueness and greatness and contended that the country's pacification was merely an instrument for retention of power, not the outcome of an innate love of peace. He accused Díaz of having fomented disturbances in order to gain political dominance; of having been responsible for the corrupt administration of Manuel González in order to make his own return to office more palatable; and of having used any means which came to hand, regardless of the moral implications, to maintain his power.[24] In spite of the obvious distaste with which Madero viewed the dictatorship, he was careful to condemn revolution as a means for bringing about change; his acceptance of the use of force to correct political abuses was a later development.[25]

A careful reading of *La sucesión presidencial en 1910* shows Madero to have been a student of history, but not a careful or an analytical student. Many of his conclusions are open to serious criticism, and often he fell into the error of confusing cause and effect. No deep intellectual powers are evident, nor does the picture of an original thinker emerge. The most interesting feature is the separation of Díaz the man from Díaz the administrator; Madero was not attacking a man, but rather was castigating a system of government which allowed one man to harm the country so fundamentally by falling into errors of judgment. Consequently, the book presents the rather curious paradox of praise on the one hand and unleavened criticism on the other. Madero had no quarrel with Díaz; the quarrel was with the Díaz

[23] Madero to Sentíes, December 25, 1908, *LP*, November 26, 1933, p. 2.
[24] Madero, *La sucesión presidencial en 1910*, 84–85, 118, 119, 127–37. Madero cites many examples on this last point.
[25] *Ibid.*, 56–57.

government, and the ills of that government stemmed from the fallacies of the system rather than the weaknesses of the man. Even though this book was no major contribution to political philosophy, it revealed the author as a man of integrity and honesty and conviction. It was this man of feeling and of ideals who appealed to the politically discontented; therein lay the primary strength of the book.

With his publication on the market, Madero was free to devote his energies to organizing a party which would more nearly reflect true independence than did the Partido Democrático. He did not hope to elect a full slate of candidates, but he was convinced that in either victory or defeat an opposition party of independent affiliations could serve Mexico well. It would act to awaken the public and would enhance the growth of true democracy, curbing the growth of absolutism.[26] There was little hope of electing an independent president, but there was some chance of frightening Díaz into allowing relatively free elections for the vice-president, governors, municipal presidents, and deputies to Congress. Free elections for all positions save that of president would be a compromise, to be sure, but Madero held that it would be a notable stride forward and could be interpreted as a victory. Therefore, even though Madero himself had no ambitions to hold office, in late February he left for Mexico City to put his plans into effect.[27]

After he arrived he immediately began trying to gather a group, but he had difficulty in seeing the men he most wanted in the organization. Fernando Iglesias Calderón, who had previously evinced interest, consistently refused to talk to him concerning the project. Manuel Vásquez Tagle, whom Madero hoped to enlist, was lukewarm but willing to talk.[28] Others reacted in similar fashion, giving a variety of reasons or excuses. The newspapers refused to publish manifestos drawn up by Madero and Toribio Esquivel Obregón; even Juan Sánchez Azcona's paper, *México Nuevo,* was now so obviously Reyista that no aid could be expected from that source. One by one the earlier adherents lost interest. An important younger member was forced by his father to abstain from political activity; Iglesias Calderón definitely refused to participate because he thought the nascent organization too mild for his political tastes; Vásquez Tagle withdrew in discourage-

---

[26] Madero to Sentíes, December 28, 1908, *LP,* November 26, 1933, p. 8.
[27] Madero to Sentíes, January 8 and 24, 1909, *ibid.;* Madero to H. Frías, February 24, 1909, *LO,* January 21, 1934, p. 2.
[28] Madero to Esquivel, March 17, 1909, *LO,* January 21, 1934, p. 1.

ment; Alberto García Granados refused to act because he believed nothing could be done for reform. By late March the embryonic party was moribund, with only Madero, Patricio Leyva, and Esquivel showing any positive interest.[29] Not only was there apathy on the part of those whom Madero had hoped would be the mainstays, but the servants of the government were indulging in a round of mildly repressive measures, the best example of which was Enrique Creel's action when he closed the offices of the independent *Correo de Chihuahua,* imprisoned its editor, and urged the national government to take strong action against militant opposition newsmen.[30]

In spite of these hindrances, however, Madero continued his work and attracted a number of able men. During the course of the preceding year, Emilio and Francisco Vázquez Gómez had indicated some desire to form an opposition party, in spite of Francisco's position as personal physician to many government officials. Emilio especially was interested. In April he became closely associated with Madero and in the following month he clarified his own position on political reform, particularly pointing to the need for an orderly rotation of government officials through the use of a free ballot and within the existing legal framework. His desire was for an orderly and peaceful campaign, essentially moderate in design and aspiration.[31] While Emilio Vázquez could not speak for all the men who later were immersed in the party activities, he did reflect the thinking of the majority of those then interested.

Shortly after Vázquez made his statement, a few of the interested men met and launched, on May 19, 1909, the Club Central Antirreeleccionista with a provisional directorate consisting of Emilio Vázquez Gómez as president and Madero and Filomeno Mata as secretaries. About forty-five men, including Luis Cabrera, Alfredo Robles Domínguez, Paulino Martínez, José Vasconcelos, Patricio Leyva, and Francisco de P. Sentíes, attended the meeting.[32] Sentíes had become thoroughly disgusted with the Partido Democrático as a result of its Reyista proclivities and forsook his membership in that organization, since the policies of the Antirreeleccionistas were more to his liking. At the first

[29] Madero to Esquivel, March 25, 1909, *ibid.,* January 28, 1934, p. 1.
[30] *El Diario del Hogar,* May 11, 1909, p. 1; Creel to Corral, April 18, 1909, *LP,* October 3, 1937, p. 1.
[31] E. Vázquez Gómez to Director of *El Diario del Hogar,* May 11, 1909, *El Diario del Hogar,* May 14, 1909, p. 1.
[32] "Primera sesión del 'Club Central Antirreeleccionista,' celebrada el día 19 de mayo de 1909," *Documentos de la revolución mexicana,* 22–23.

meeting the general aims and purposes of the organization were discussed, but no basic decisions were made other than that there was no need to draft a specific platform; a committee was finally appointed to draft a set of principles for consideration at a subsequent session.[33]

At the following meeting, on May 22, the committee reported, and the group adopted a program in basic agreement with Madero's principles. In the final form, the statement of purposes included a commentary on the necessity for democratic action to prevent the indefinite election of officials, the value of exercising all political rights, and the need for accepting "effective suffrage and no re-election" as the basic tenets which would satisfy the demands of the country and guarantee the success of the party. In addition to these broad principles, the organization decided to undertake a propaganda campaign to educate the public concerning its political rights and to promote political meetings in all sections of the nation, with the ultimate objective of forming a national Partido Antirreeleccionista with local governing boards.[34] There was some difference of opinion concerning co-operation with other parties; but Madero argued that such action would be advantageous so long as there was adherence to the fundamental principles established by the Antire-electionists, and his argument prevailed.[35] After reaching these decisions, the organization was officially christened the Centro Antirreeleccionista de México.

At succeeding meetings a public manifesto was drafted and a permanent directive council was elected to serve one year. Emilio Vázquez Gómez was elected president, the choice probably dictated by the mildness of his philosophy and the official connections of his brother Francisco, both of which would tend to prevent persecution. Madero and Toribio Esquivel Obregón were selected to be the vice-presidents, and the four secretaries were Filomeno Mata, José Vasconcelos, Félix F. Palavicini, and Paulino Martínez.[36] The manifesto, approved on May 29 but not made public until two weeks later,[37] largely reflected the political thinking of Madero inasmuch as he was a member of both the Committee for Manifesto and the Committee on Rules and Regulations.[38] In a fashion rather mild, but forceful for all its mildness, the ills

[33] *El Diario del Hogar,* May 29, 1909, p. 1.
[34] *Ibid.,* May 25, 1909, p. 1.
[35] Estrada, *La revolución y Francisco I. Madero,* 85; *El Diario del Hogar,* May 25, 1909, p. 1.
[36] *El Diario del Hogar,* June 1, 1909, p. 1.
[37] *Ibid.,* June 16, 1909, p. 1. It was also circulated in handbill form.
[38] *Ibid.,* May 29, 1909, p. 1.

of the nation were ascribed to the dictatorial regime. The deplorable condition of the courts, in which justice was tempered by position, prestige, and power of the litigants, was declared to be an outgrowth of thirty years of personal government. The party decried the inferior business positions which the Mexicans occupied with respect to the foreigners, even in those companies, such as the railroads, which were directly under government control. It was critical, too, of the lack of public instruction. Other serious ills were noted: emigration of Mexican workers to foreign lands where they could expect greater opportunities for liberty and economic betterment, costly and useless wars against the Yaquis and Mayos,[39] dangerous concessions to foreigners, and the deliberate destruction of public spirit. The Díaz government was charged with the responsibility for having fostered all these dangerous and unhealthy symptoms of a decaying nation. The major emphasis, however, was not on the developments of the past, but on the danger of a continuation of the same pattern for the future; there was a likelihood of a complete degeneration into anarchy or decadence. In addition to the charges made, and in spite of the frequent protestations of peaceful intent, a veiled threat ran through the document: the "suffering" public would not "resign" itself to the loss of its rights, and the "national volition" would be the "supreme arbiter."[40]

The manifesto was a subtle mixture of threat and supplication. The harshness of its charges against Díaz was partially counteracted by frequent reference to the moderation with which Díaz had used his extensive powers; there was a studied and fairly successful attempt to make it appear that the attack was being made on the institution of personal power and not on Díaz himself. The influence of the milder and more diplomatic thinking of Emilio Vázquez Gómez is evident, for the phraseology was less direct than that used by Madero himself in his book. There was little in the manifesto which would give the government cause for persecution, and yet there was much which would stimulate thought and oppositionist activity; the document was carefully designed to offend few and attract many.

With the publication of the manifesto, the Centro was on a pre-

---

[39] The Yaquis and Mayos of Sonora (not to be confused with the Mayas of Yucatán) were in almost constant war with the government as a result of despoliation of their tribal lands by the whites. A more enlightened and co-operative policy would probably have prevented the costly outbreaks.

[40] The manifesto may be found in *El Diario del Hogar,* June 16, 1909, p. 1, or in Estrada, *La revolución y Francisco I. Madero,* 86–93.

sumably firm and permanent foundation, so that both time and energies could be devoted to the dispersion of the twin doctrines of effective suffrage and no re-election. Madero and Palavicini began a speaking tour on June 18, while others made use of their time in encouraging the formation of branch clubs in the immediate environs of Mexico City.[41] There was particular success among the workers in the capital, for the Club Antirreeleccionista de Obreros Benito Juárez rapidly became important both in numbers and in activities.[42] Similar activities in Jalisco, Coahuila, Nuevo León, and Puebla, coupled with the special work being done in Mexico City and in the places visited by Madero, were setting the stage for a full-scale campaign against the re-election of Díaz.

In the meantime there were other developments which were of grave importance to the success of the Antire-electionists: the Re-electionists, too, were making their plans. As early as the preceding December they had, under the unofficial tutelage of Ramón Corral, advanced far enough with their plans to name a tentative convention date and to set in motion the machine for selecting delegates. Governor Enrique Creel of Chihuahua, who was friendly to Corral, took the lead in circularizing the other state governors and proposing a plan for their consideration. Creel was not the actual leader of the Re-electionists, however; he merely acted as the agent through whom Corral's suggestions were executed,[43] for the Vice-President wished to make it appear that a large segment of the population demanded the retention of the incumbents.

At least one powerful personage in Mexico did not favor the re-election of Corral: Bernardo Reyes himself desired the presidency. He had never had the courage to flout openly the power of the dictator, but his ambitions had become more pronounced with the years and now he hoped to displace Corral as the official candidate for the vice-presidency. Generally supported by the anti-Científico element among the Díaz protagonists, Reyes was in a strong position to demand accession to his desires, but he preferred to remain on good terms with the government while exercising his wiles to improve his position. Afraid to oppose Corral, who had the support of Díaz, he notified the Vice-President that he would back him for the re-election and then

[41] Casasola, *Historia gráfica*, I, 112.

[42] Estrada, *La revolución y Francisco I. Madero*, 104–105.

[43] Creel to Corral, December 29, 1908, and January 17, 1909, *LP*, October 3, 1937, p. 1.

reiterated this pledge a few days later by appointing a delegate to the Re-electionist convention and instructing the delegate to take his directions from Corral.[44] On the other hand, Reyes was one of the three governors who refused to give Creel full co-operation in planning for the convention, evidently hoping to convey to the public that he considered himself eligible for the vice-presidency.[45] These opposing hopes and fears were responsible for the double-dealing of which Reyes was undoubtedly guilty. As was to be expected, however, at the Re-electionist convention which met on March 25, the nomination of Díaz and Corral was duly confirmed after six days of meaningless oratory filled with obsequities to the President and the Vice-President.[46] There is a note of grim humor in Creel's hearty congratulations to Corral on the success of the convention, as though there had been some doubt about the outcome.[47]

Nevertheless, Reyes could not yet be completely discounted as a force in politics. He denied any interest in the vice-presidential position, but managed to make the statement in such a way as to create doubt about his sincerity; and on May 5, placards postulating the Díaz-Reyes combination appeared as if by magic in Mexico City.[48] He gave outward evidence of a desire to co-operate with Díaz, but he nevertheless asked Corral for a résumé of the press reports in Mexico City concerning the strength of Reyista feeling. Corral was not deceived about the intent behind the request; he did not answer Reyes' question directly but told him quite frankly that any Reyista activity would be cause for more grief than satisfaction to the northern general.[49]

In all this early maneuvering Díaz took no public part, but there were indications of the weight of his influence. The Partido Democrático, patently Reyista by May, made no public commitment on candidates, evidently because the leaders had been told by Díaz not to do so. The Reyes supporters were in a dilemma, not knowing what steps to take or what to expect from the President, and the confusion

[44] Reyes to Corral, March 3, 1909, *ibid.,* January 23, 1938, p. 1; and March 6, 1909, *LO,* October 17, 1937, p. 1.

[45] Creel to Corral, March 7, 1909, *LP,* October 3, 1937, p. 1.

[46] Casasola, *Historia gráfica,* I, 109.

[47] Creel to Corral, April 7, 1909, *LP,* October 3, 1937, p. 1.

[48] *El Diario del Hogar,* May 6, 1909, p. 1.

[49] Reyes to Corral, May 21, 1909, *LO,* October 17, 1937, p. 1; Corral to Reyes, May 25, 1909, *ibid.*

and uncertainty gave birth to some curious bits of political philosophy. Juan Sánchez Azcona delved into political theory and decided that any stipulation against re-election was in itself undemocratic, since it prevented the voters from making a completely free choice in the election of officials. He further recommended concentrating on the vice-presidential campaign and discarding any discussion of Díaz' re-election, since Díaz was going to continue in the presidential chair regardless of what was done or said by other groups. Sánchez Azcona, however, recognized the dangers inherent in continued occupation of the presidency by the same man and proposed a constitutional amendment to rectify the situation. His recommendation was to forbid the election to the presidency of any man over sixty-five years of age on the supposition that a younger man would not have the power or prestige to perpetuate his control over the administration. This provision, said the editor, would automatically eliminate the danger of a long dictatorship.[50] As Madero pointed out in reply, the age of the incumbent was inconsequential, for a younger man could consolidate his position, once in office, and could continue in control, by making constitutional changes if necessary, exactly as Díaz had done. After all, Díaz had been forty-six when he took over the presidency. In addition, restricting the right to hold office on the basis of age would be undemocratic and could conceivably preclude making use of the services of an outstanding man.[51]

The most interesting proposal, however, and the one most indicative of Reyista despair, came from Heriberto Barrón. In order to meet the delicate problem posed by the rival candidacies of Corral and Reyes, Barrón proposed a constitutional amendment providing for two vice-presidents, the candidate receiving the majority of the votes being designated first vice-president and the other the second vice-president. The first vice-president would succeed to the presidency in the event of the president's death or resignation during the term, and the second vice-president would thereupon ascend to the vice-presidential office. Barrón, who took it for granted that Reyes and Corral would be the only candidates, favored the scheme as a balance-of-power mechanism; regardless of which became first vice-president and then succeeded to the presidency, he would be checked in any personalistic or dictatorial

[50] *México Nuevo,* May 18, 1909, p. 1.
[51] Madero, "No-Reelección," *El Diario del Hogar,* May 20, 1909, p. 1.

plans by the other, who would have strong backing and powerful resources at his command. Another great advantage to such a system, according to Barrón, would be to guarantee to everyone an opportunity to cast his ballot for the candidate of his choice.[52] The assumption was, of course, that everyone in the nation wanted either Reyes or Corral to be in line for the presidential succession. Obviously, the proposal bordered on the ridiculous, since two of the basic assumptions were incorrect. There was certainly no reason to believe that all voters in Mexico wanted either Corral or Reyes and that a choice between them would be a free choice; Madero and his companions believed that the election of either one would be an unadulterated disaster.[53] But Barrón had overlooked a more basic factor: Reyes and Corral could never become allies in sharing the government. The adherents of the two men had almost diametrically opposite points of view with respect to government and the personnel in official positions. Reyes was anti-Científico and could be expected to evict that group if he had the opportunity. Corral, on the other hand, was Científico to the core, anxious to retain the ascendancy of his confreres. With Reyes as president and Corral as vice-president, or vice versa, administration would have been mired in petty politics; at best an armed truce could be expected, and open warfare might have resulted. Perhaps Barrón realized all this, but was so anxious to discover some means by which Reyes could be included in the administration that he was willing to face the consequences.

By early summer of 1909, Mexico was teeming with political activity on a scale which had not been known for years. While many small and unimportant political groups were functioning throughout the nation, basically the struggle developed into a three-way fight among the adherents of Corral, those of Reyes, and the Antire-electionist group, which had not yet selected a candidate. That Corral had no intention of allowing a free campaign is clearly evidenced by events in Jalisco in the latter part of May. On May 22 a group of Reyes supporters went to Guadalajara to speak on behalf of their candidate, but they had hardly left Mexico before Rosendo Pineda, a Corral henchman and probably the most powerful politician in Mexico save Díaz and Corral, "recommended" to Governor Ahumada that "the greatest possible difficulties" be placed in their path to guarantee the failure of the

[52] *El Diario del Hogar,* May 22, 1909, p. 1.
[53] Madero to Sentíes, January 8, 1909, *LP,* November 26, 1933, p. 8.

mission. Ahumada did as he was instructed, and the desired result followed.[54]

In the shifting political scene the position of Díaz was still unclarified. The publication of the antiadministration manifesto of the Antireelectionists had not been challenged by the government, and there was no evidence of positive action by Díaz to prevent the formation of political clubs. The President's failure to act encouraged the opponents of the regime, while it also served the same purpose for the opponents of Corral. The more optimistic among the opposition saw signs of a rosy future and were almost on the point of believing in the sincerity of the Creelman interview. Since later events proved them mistaken, some reason must be found for Díaz' inaction at this time. In the first place, there is absolutely no indication that Díaz or any of his immediate advisors considered the eventuality of a strong Antire-electionist movement as a threat to the administration's equanimity. Corral did mention rumors he had heard concerning the Maderos' distribution of arms to the men on their haciendas, but he justifiably discounted the stories as figments of overtaxed imaginations.[55]

There was no reason to believe that Madero would be able to develop an opposition party; or, more accurately, the administration leaders could see no threat of such a development. The Antireelectionists were looked upon with tolerance and not a little humor; their propaganda, though noisy and irritating, was considered to lack force. It pleased Díaz and the Científicos to allow such manifestations of democracy and civic spirit. Therefore, the only question of importance to Díaz was the relative positions of Corral and Reyes, and it was consequently Reyes, rather than Madero, who was suspect. Díaz, moreover, throughout his career had been very successful in playing one force against another to prevent the rapid growth of either, and now he played the same game. Corral and the Científicos were becoming arrogant, and the time had come to take their measure—not to destroy them, but to check their ambitions. At the same time, by allowing Reyes to go unchecked Díaz could, in case of need, effectively remove him from the scene, since it was almost certain that, given sufficient freedom, he or his followers would become indiscreet. Thus the campaign was allowed to develop without the aid or the interference of President Díaz.

[54] M. Ahumada to Corral, May 24, 1909, *LO,* September 26, 1937, p. 1. In this message the Jalisco governor quoted the Pinedo telegram.
[55] Corral to Reyes, May 25, 1909, *ibid.,* October 17, 1937, p .1.

IV

The Preconvention Campaign

WITH THE CENTRAL CLUB in Mexico now operating, the organization was ready for an expansion which could be carried out only through active propagandizing by members from the Mexico City center. Even though Madero was one of the vice-presidents, he had been given no official functions so that he might be left free to carry on the work of conversion by traveling to the outlying cities and states and encouraging the foundation of branch clubs.[1] The decision to name Madero as the agent of the Antire-electionists was not one which was dictated solely by the leadership he had shown in the organizing movement; there were other reasons of equal or greater importance. It was extremely difficult to persuade anyone of real ability and political standing to engage in opposition speaking, for it was generally believed that such activities would be both useless and dangerous.[2] Such a belief narrowed the field and made the choice fairly easy; even though Madero was a comparative newcomer in politics and had never occupied a political post, he had the courage to undertake the task, and through *La sucesión presidencial en 1910* his name was relatively well known. An even more important factor made his selection mandatory: he was the only man of independent means in the group, and as yet the party was unable to finance an extended trip from its own coffers. The other men who might have been qualified speakers, such as Emilio Vázquez Gómez, José Vasconcelos, and Filomeno Mata, were professional men whose very existence depended on their jobs; they had neither the time nor the money to devote themselves completely to politics.

One might think that the selection of Madero as the principal exponent of the party doctrines was a move of desperation since, aside from his enthusiasm and money, he seemed to have little to offer.

---

[1] José Vasconcelos, *Ulises criollo,* 365.   [2] *Ibid.,* 366.

Preconvention Campaign

Small in stature and unprepossessing in general appearance, with a heavy growth of beard covering a small chin, at first sight he gave little evidence of great strength of character or of will. His face, however, had a strong redeeming feature in a broad, high forehead set off with startlingly bright, restless, and intelligent eyes. Few of the attributes of an orator were his, for he lacked stage presence, ease of expression, and polish of phraseology; his voice was high and had a tendency to crack under emotion or strain. But with all these weaknesses, he was an effective speaker if his popularity and the results of his speaking campaigns are any criteria. What he lacked as an orator or as a commanding figure was more than compensated by his complete sincerity, his courage, his enthusiasm, and his almost fanatical belief in the essential justice of his cause. He was able to communicate something of his determination, his conviction of the need for a political change, and his faith in the ultimate success of his ideas to the discontented but hesitant people who crowded the halls and plazas to hear him speak. By sheer force of will, rather than by strength of oratory, he lifted the mantle of lethargy which covered the country.

Since Veracruz had a long tradition of opposition and liberalism and had been the seat of the 1879 movement against Díaz, Madero and his advisors decided that the port city would be a fertile area in which to introduce the Antire-electionist code. Madero invited Félix F. Palavicini to accompany him and to speak in behalf of the party principles, his idea being that Palavicini would complement Madero's own contributions by a different approach and by more accomplished oratory.[3] On June 18, 1909, a departure in Mexican politics was inaugurated, for on that day Madero and Palavicini left Mexico City on a frankly oppositionist speaking tour, the first of its kind since the beginning of the Díaz regime.[4] For the past thirty years no one had dared to take such liberties or to flout the power of the dictator in such an open manner; the very fact that it was being undertaken was of sufficient import to encourage many who wished to attack the government but were afraid to do so.

Madero reached Veracruz to find "some two thousand persons in the station and its environs when the awaited train arrived," even though there had been little advance publicity.[5] He immediately an-

---

[3] Félix F. Palavicini, *Mi vida revolucionaria,* 27.
[4] During all his campaigning Madero was accompanied by his wife and his secretary.
[5] *El Dictamen* (Veracruz), June 19, 1909, p. 1.

71

nounced to the assembled group that an open meeting would be held on Sunday, June 20, to organize an Antire-electionist club; and on the following day he issued a formal invitation to the public to take part in a demonstration which was to be the first step in allowing "the public [to] recover its rights, the municipalities their liberties, and the states their sovereignty."[6] As a result of the two invitations, a large crowd gathered at the Dehesa Theater to hear a reading of the May 29 manifesto and addresses by Madero and Palavicini. Madero, stressing the political aspects of the reform movement, emphasized the necessity for changing the practices of the administration and the need for a rotation of personnel in government offices; Palavicini spoke of the nation's social and economic ills.[7] Both presentations were well received, heavy applause being accorded each speaker. They were followed by a business meeting in which a provisional directive council, with Editor José Hinojosa of *El Dictamen* as president, was selected.[8]

Encouraged by the reception at Veracruz, Madero decided to continue his journey through the states of Yucatán, Campeche, Tamaulipas, and Nuevo León, even though his grandfather attempted to dissuade him from this course of action.[9] Don Evaristo again reminded Madero of his duty to his family, particularly in view of the continuing financial difficulties, but Madero turned a deaf ear, listening instead to the dictates of his conscience, and continued to Yucatán.[10] The landing at Progreso was not auspicious; in spite of the advance notice, there were only six persons at the water front to meet the travelers. The fact that among the six were three who were outstanding in their opposition to Díaz did little to alleviate Madero's acute disappointment, and on the trip from Progreso to Mérida both he and Palavicini were downcast.[11] Their surprise and pleasure on arriving at Mérida to find an immense and cheering crowd was therefore all the greater.[12] In a strongly worded statement issued shortly after his arrival, Madero pointed out that the "yoke of despotism" under which Mexico had

[6] Palavicini, *Mi vida revolucionaria,* 28. Madero and Palavicini issued the "Invitación al Pueblo," June 19, 1909.
[7] *Ibid.,* 29–30.
[8] *El Diario del Hogar,* June 25, 1909, p. 1.
[9] Palavicini, *Mi vida revolucionaria,* 32.
[10] Don E. Madero to Madero, June 21, 1909, *LO,* February 25, 1934, p. 1.
[11] The three were Delio Moreno Cantón, José María Pino Suárez, and Carlos R. Menéndez.—Palavicini, *Mi vida revolucionaria,* 35–36.
[12] *Ibid.,* 36.

suffered for thirty years had been borne with "singular impatience" by the people of Yucatán, and that it was time to "cast off the yoke" and to regain the liberties to which they were entitled.[13] Under existing conditions in the state, this came dangerously near an invitation to rebellion, but the local officials chose to overlook the implication and placed no obstacles in the path of the organizers. Under a blazing midday sun thousands of people, obviously enthusiastic, gathered to hear the emissaries of the new party and to establish a club of their own under the leadership of José María Pino Suárez.[14]

Moving on to Campeche after the conclusion of the Mérida demonstration, Madero was disappointed at the lethargy and lack of interest, even though a club was established and an organization begun.[15] Palavicini was later told that the principal reason for the lack of enthusiasm was a fear on the part of the local populace that Madero and Palavicini were agents of the government sent to uncover malcontents. After leaving Campeche, the organizers held a rather torpid meeting in Progreso; but little was accomplished, and a rather discouraged group embarked for Tampico.[16]

During the short stay in the peninsular region, Madero consistently spoke in terms of political evils, political necessities, political action, and political reform. Only on rare occasions did he mention social or economic problems. The failure to discuss the need for social and economic reform, however, was not a reflection of a failure to consider such problems; he merely believed political reform to be the first step, with the social and economic to follow. That he was fully aware of these needs is clearly indicated by his reaction to conditions in Yucatán, for in spite of his having been entertained by *hacendados* intent on showing him the best side of Yucatán hacienda life, Madero was convinced that the area was ripe for social revolution.[17]

In Tampico, the next stop after Progreso, the same lack of success as in Campeche and Progreso was in store, but the failure was the result of opposition rather than apathy. Madero arrived on the morning of July 8, but either by accident or by design the ship entered the harbor at six in the morning instead of the scheduled eight o'clock, and

[13] Madero and Palavicini, "Invitación al Pueblo," June 26, 1909, *ibid.*, 37.
[14] [Lamicq], *Madero, por uno de sus íntimos,* 21.
[15] *Ibid.;* Palavicini, *Mi vida revolucionaria,* 39.
[16] Palavicini, *Mi vida revolucionaria,* 39, 40.
[17] *Ibid.,* 41.

the plans which had been made for an impressive welcome to Tamaulipas were not carried out.[18] Madero requested permission from the local authorities to hold a meeting, but the petition was denied; he appealed to the governor for permission, but from that worthy no answer was forthcoming. He had difficulty in finding a shop to print a public manifesto, since the printers feared reprisals.[19] A meeting was held without official intervention, but the grip of the local officials on the public was too strong to allow freedom of expression and only a few people attended the conclave. In view of the situation no attempt was made to form a political club.[20]

The day after the dreary conference in Tampico, Madero and his small entourage entrained for Monterrey, the last stop on the campaigning circuit. Here on the afternoon of July 11 the Antire-electionists achieved the success which had been denied them in Campeche and Tampico, despite the fact that Monterrey was Bernardo Reyes' capital.[21] The time and place did not seem auspicious for a successful political demonstration, for that same morning veiled but deliberate intervention sponsored by Ramón Corral had broken up a rally of the Reyista Partido Democrático.[22] The events of the morning seemed to augur ill for Madero's afternoon meeting, but with characteristic determination he refused to be intimidated by threats of persecution. Surprisingly enough, there was no attempt, either overt or covert, to interfere with the Antire-electionists, and the party emissaries held a completely satisfactory demonstration in the main plaza. In introducing the guests, the spokesman for the host organization took the opportunity to stress the fact that the local Antire-electionists had not as yet chosen a candidate and were supporting no particular person; they were supporting principles, not men. The crowd of approximately three thousand clamored its approval of the policy stated and of the speeches made by Madero and Palavicini. When the speeches were concluded, the more enthusiastic members of the local organization carried Madero from the plaza on their shoulders.[23]

The interference with the Reyistas and the complete freedom in

---

[18] *México Nuevo,* July 10, 1909, p. 5. Palavicini believed the early arrival to have been the result of government orders. The fact that the ship went through quarantine at such an early hour lends credence to the charge.

[19] *Ibid.;* Palavicini, *Mi vida revolucionaria,* 41.

[20] [Lamicq], *Madero, por uno de sus íntimos,* 22.

[21] Reyes was then "resting" at Galeana; see below, p. 83.

[22] Palavicini, *Mi vida revolucionaria,* 42.

[23] *El Diario del Hogar,* July 13, 1909, p. 1.

which the Antire-electionists held their meeting were indicative of Corral's attitude concerning the relative strength and potential danger posed by Madero and Reyes. Reyes, a threat to Corral's position and to the government itself, was blocked in his efforts to gain adherents; but Madero, who seemed to present no danger to the established regime, went unmolested.

With the meeting in Monterrey concluded, the first propaganda tour came to an end. Palavicini returned to Mexico City to continue his work there, while Madero and his wife went to their home in San Pedro, Coahuila, to rest after the month of campaigning.[24] Madero was anxious to return to his own state, for the gubernatorial contest, in which he was vitally interested, was in full swing. All in all, the tour just completed had been more successful than there had been reason to believe it would be. Madero had learned much, all of which convinced him more than ever that his fundamental assumption was correct: Mexico was ready for a change. He was now certain that the public was determined to "conquer its rights" and that it would obtain them.[25] His disrespect for Corral and his fear that Corral's accession to the presidency would be an unalloyed disaster were strengthened, for many of the ills he had observed could be traced directly to Corral and his friends.[26] The trip had served as a stimulus, even though there had been minor reverses in Campeche and Tampico. With this taste of success to whet his appetite, Madero could and did overcome major obstacles as the campaign progressed.

For the next few months Madero's travels were restricted to his own state. He sponsored a meeting in Torreón in the latter part of July; although the city was considered to be rather strongly Reyista, the meeting was signally successful. In his address he made a careful distinction between Reyes and Reyistas, castigating the former but appealing to the latter, since he believed there were many potential Antire-electionists among those who supported Reyes only because they believed there was no other strong opposition to Díaz. Madero was greatly encouraged when many of the Reyistas applauded his position.[27]

A large part of the summer was devoted to the state political campaign; for despite the fact that the local campaign was incidental to the broader plans for a national party, Madero was intensely concerned

[24] Palavicini, *Mi vida revolucionaria,* 42.
[25] Madero to Don E. Madero, July 20, 1909, *LO,* February 25, 1934, p. 1.
[26] Palavicini, *Mi vida revolucionaria,* 41.
[27] Madero to G. Madero, July 26, 1909, *LO,* February 11, 1934, p. 8.

over the outcome of the elections. The Antire-electionists were supporting Venustiano Carranza for governor, although Madero was suspicious of his sincerity. He believed him to be a supporter and henchman of Reyes; but since the association had not been proved, Madero
was willing to support him against Miguel Cárdenas, again the official
candidate. While giving Carranza his aid, Madero kept a careful eye
on him nonetheless.[28]

In spite of his interest in the local campaign, Madero continued to
maintain heavy correspondence with the Centro in Mexico City and
made his contributions to the national cause. He wrote steadily for *El
Demócrata* and *El Renacimiento,* both in Coahuila, and sent occasional articles to *El Anti-Reeleccionista* in Mexico City.[29] More important than these literary contributions was his financial aid to candidates
and publications. He subsidized *El Demócrata* of San Pedro and *La
Hoja Suelta* of Torreón and regularly contributed funds to the official
organ of the party in Mexico.[30] In addition, he solicited money for
the publication among his friends and relatives, collecting a sum sufficient to launch and maintain *El Anti-Reeleccionista* as a daily paper.[31]
Most of the money came from his relatives in the San Pedro area; by
mid-August they alone had given over twelve thousand pesos.[32]

Partly as a stimulus for the state elections, but primarily in the interest of the national campaign, in early August, Madero made a swing
around his own state to aid in the establishment of political clubs. He
visited Ciudad Porfirio Díaz (now Piedras Negras), Saltillo, and some
of the smaller communities, at each of which he left the nucleus of a
party group. He held another successful meeting in Torreón, where
about a thousand people, all ardent Antire-electionists, attended.[33] In
addition to the clubs which he was instrumental in establishing, there

[28] Madero to H. Frías, July 27, 1909, *ibid.,* January 21, 1934, p. 2; Madero to
E. Vázquez Gómez, July 26, 1909, *ibid.,* January 7, 1934, p. 1.
[29] Madero to E. Vázquez Gómez, July 20, 1909, *ibid.,* January 7, 1934, p. 1.
[30] Madero to G. Madero, July 26, 1909, *ibid.,* February 11, 1934, p. 8; Madero
to E. Vázquez Gómez, July 26, 1909, *ibid.,* January 7, 1934, p. 1.
[31] See following from Madero: to Don E. Madero, July 20, 1909, *ibid.,* February 25, 1934, p. 1; to G. Madero, July 26, 1909, *ibid.,* February 11, 1934, p. 8;
to Manuel Madero, July 28, 1909, *ibid.;* to E. Vázquez Gómez, July 26, 1909,
ibid., January 7, 1934, p. 1. Also, Don E. Madero to Madero, July 22, 1909,
ibid., February 25, 1934, p. 1.
[32] Madero to Esquivel, August 15, 1909, *ibid.,* January 28, 1934, p. 1; Madero
to M. Vásquez Tagle, August 23, 1909, *ibid.,* p. 2.
[33] Madero to E. Vázquez Gómez, August 2, 1909, *ibid.,* January 7, 1934, p. 2.

were other groups organizing in Coahuila and in the surrounding states; it appeared that every hamlet in the area would have its political organization before the summer's end.[34]

Because he believed that a single state working alone could do nothing for its own political advancement, Madero was intensely interested in the elections in other states. Puebla, Morelos, Yucatán, and Sinaloa were all attempting to rid themselves of the Porfirian governors. Sinaloa, particularly, was the scene of important political activity, and Madero volunteered to aid the independent candidates by appearing personally in their behalf if the campaign directors thought it would be useful.[35] Before he could free himself from local commitments, however it had become obvious that nothing could be done to stem the tide ˜cial imposition, and Madero did not make the trip. As was to be expected, the candidate favored by the central government, Diego Redo, was the victor.[36] But here again, as in the case of Coahuila, Madero was primarily interested in the permanent gains which might come from increased interest in the national Antire-electionist party, and he therefore used the campaign against Redo as a mechanism for attacking Reyes.[37] To the other states carrying on the fight against the administration he gave his encouragement, but his efforts were unavailing and the official candidate in each was elected.

In one other field Madero made a notable contribution during the summer. He had long accepted the principle of a party convention for the nomination of candidates; and in drafting the proposed convention rules and regulations which he and Esquivel Obregón had been instructed to present to the Centro, he was careful to avoid the mistakes of 1905. He insisted on setting a convention date at the earliest possible time and giving its place, date, and importance immediate and widespread publicity. He demanded proportional representation of delegates to the convention, with the basis of such representation being the number of active club members and not the total population on which the club drew; the failure to include such a provision in the Coahuila convention four years earlier had proved costly for the independents. Further to insure an honest representation, Madero recommended

---

[34] Madero to G. Madero, July 26, 1909, *ibid.*, February 11, 1934, p. 8; Madero to E. Vázquez Gómez, August 2, 1909, *ibid.*, January 7, 1934, p. 2.
[35] Madero to Frías, July 27, 1909, *ibid.*, January 21, 1934, p. 2.
[36] Casasola, *Historia gráfica*, I, 118.
[37] See particularly Madero to Frías, July 27, 1909, *LO,* January 21, 1934, p. 2.

printing a standard credential form to be used by the delegates. Using these basic ideas as a framework, he and Esquivel drafted a set of proposals which, in the main, were accepted by the Centro.[38]

Before the end of the summer, Madero made a final attack on Reyes. Addressing himself to *los reyistas de buena fé* he severely criticized the elderly general while again making a distinction between Reyes and the Reyistas. The events of the past few months had given ample evidence of the honesty and sincerity of some of the Reyes adherents; some were virtually exiled to Yucatán and other frontier outposts because they had given him support.[39] At least one man died because he had spoken in behalf of the general.[40] But this faith, Madero insisted, was not justified; for not only had Reyes been dictatorial in his government of Nuevo León for twenty years but he had said and done nothing which could be construed as an attack on the Díaz government, and he had given no evidence of the moral courage necessary to accept the leadership in a political party. Madero reiterated that a choice between Reyes and Corral would be barren; as long as there were other qualified men who could be chosen in open convention there was little reason to support Reyes for the vice-presidency. In his general plea to Reyes' supporters, Madero made no attempt to appeal to those who were supporting the General in order to secure positions or keep those already held; for this group he had only contempt, but to those who sincerely believed that Reyes would make a good president he issued an appeal which he hoped would convert them to his cause. With this parting shot at Reyes, Madero practically ceased his work for the party during the summer of 1909. Shortly thereafter he became seriously ill and for some months was incapacitated.[41]

In the meantime important events were transpiring in other sections of the country, for the government was liquidating the Reyes threat while the Antire-electionists were improving their position in central Mexico. Emilio Vázquez Gómez acted as the spearhead of the Mexico City Centro in developing allied political clubs in the capital and in

[38] Madero to E. Vázquez Gómez, July 20 and 26, 1909, *ibid.,* January 7, 1934, p. 1. The rules governing the convention were published in *El Diario del Hogar,* December 15, 1909, p. 1.

[39] Ahumada to Corral, June 1, 1909, *LO,* September 26, 1937, p. 1.

[40] Lt. Gutiérrez Verduzco; he had been transferred to Quintana Roo, where he died while on campaign.—*México Nuevo,* July 24, 1909, p. 1.

[41] Madero, "A los reyistas de buena fé," *El Diario del Hogar,* August 10, 1909, p. 1; *México Nuevo,* August 5, 1909, p. 7; *El Diario del Hogar,* October 3, 1909, p. 1.

the outlying regions. Guadalajara, a center of Reyista sympathy in spite of the activities of Corralista Governor Miguel Ahumada, was visited by Roque Estrada, Paulino Martínez, and Toribio Esquivel Obregón, who were able to interest a number of influential men in giving support to the Antire-electionists.[42] The immediate results were not too encouraging, but within the next few months Guadalajara became of real importance to Madero.

In Mexico City itself the Centro was busily engaged in adopting a set of principles to act as a guide for the party organization. The result of these labors was to apply only to the Centro; but the members hoped that the plan drafted would be applicable to other areas, and that the general rules and regulations for party membership and election of party officials would be acceptable to all local clubs. Membership was in two categories, active and passive, only the active members being obliged to pay membership dues. Active members were enrolled only if sponsored by two other members in good standing. They took part in public demonstrations, disseminated propaganda, and encouraged others to vote. In return for these duties and responsibilities, the active members alone determined party policy and held office in the organization; all officers were elected to their positions for one year only and were not eligible for re-election. The passive members paid no dues, were expected only to vote and to take part in public demonstrations, and could not hold party office; they became members merely by requesting that their names be added to the list.[43] Within this framework the Mexico City Centro operated in 1909 and 1910.

Of more importance than the organization of small political clubs, however, was the establishment of a party newspaper during the early summer. If the party was to make any impression on the public, it must have the support of a good newspaper, one upon which it could depend for publicity. Both *El Diario del Hogar* under Filomeno Mata and *La Voz de Juárez* under Paulino Martínez were sympathetic, but they could not be completely utilized by the new party since they were predominantly commercial newspapers. Consequently, in early June the weekly *El Anti-Reeleccionista* was launched on its short and eventful career with José Vasconcelos as the first director. As the party grew, it soon became obvious that there was a distinct need for a daily if full advantage were to be taken of the opportunities, and one of Madero's

---

[42] Estrada, *La revolución y Francisco I. Madero,* 106; Ahumada to Corral, June 1, 1909, *LO,* September 26, 1937, p. 1.

[43] Regulations published in *El Diario del Hogar,* July 2, 1909, p. 1.

first actions after his return to San Pedro from Monterrey in mid-July was to raise money for financing the enterprise until it could become self-sustaining. With Gustavo's aid and that of other members of the family, by late July Madero had collected enough money to begin sending regular contributions to Mexico, and within a short time the shift from a weekly to a daily was made.[44]

As long as *El Anti-Reeleccionista* was a small weekly newspaper, the work could be done on a volunteer basis without compensation, but with the shift to a daily a full-time staff was required. Since Vasconcelos was inexperienced and Madero had been generally pleased with Palavicini's comportment, Palavicini was chosen as the first full-time managing editor.[45] Emilio Vázquez Gómez, as president of the Centro, outlined the position and function of the party for the editor's benefit, stressing the need for a peaceful campaign and the importance of a free and effective suffrage. He was careful to point out, however, that the party was not necessarily one of ultraliberal political and economic views, and all independent thinkers, liberal or conservative, were invited to join.[46] Emilio Vázquez was more interested in attracting members to the party than he was in establishing a party program.

With the conversion of the newspaper to a daily, the Antire-electionists had an organ to support their policies and act as their propaganda medium. In an effort to establish the paper on a permanent basis, a corporation was formed for the sale of stock.[47] When Madero pointed out that "those who come to power have poor memories and frequently forget their promises,"[48] it was decided to retain the name *El Anti-Reeleccionista* regardless of the outcome of the election. From a campaign daily, the paper was converted to a permanent party instrument. But the Díaz administration willed otherwise, and within less than two months the publication offices were closed and the staff arrested. Before detailing this action, it is necessary to trace the fortunes of the other political movements within the country, for the elimination of Reyes as a political threat was in part responsible for the fate of *El Anti-Reeleccionista*.

[44] Palavicini, *Mi vida revolucionaria*, 45, 46; Vasconcelos, *Ulises criollo*, 366.
[45] Palavicini, *Mi vida revolucionaria*, 48–49; Vasconcelos, *Ulises criollo*, 367; Madero to E. Vázquez Gómez, July 26, 1909, *LO*, January 7, 1934, p. 1.
[46] E. Vázquez Gómez to Palavicini, August 9, 1909, *El Diario del Hogar*, August 13, 1909, p. 2.
[47] Madero to Vásquez Tagle, August 23, 1909, *LO*, January 28, 1934, p. 2.
[48] Madero to E. Vázquez Gómez, August 2, 1909, *ibid.*, January 7, 1934, p. 2.

Preconvention Campaign

General Bernardo Reyes, who hoped to be designated as the official candidate in lieu of Ramón Corral, was in an admirable position to elicit support from the independents had he chosen to make a strong bid. Because Díaz distrusted Reyes, he had no desire to elevate the General to the vice-presidency, but he feared Reyes' potential power to such an extent that he dared not risk an open break and therefore had retained Reyes as the governor of Nuevo León for a period of twenty years. Reyes' popularity was an unknown quantity, making it dangerous for Díaz to make a public pronouncement against him; an open condemnation might easily bring on a revolution. The only way to attack Reyes, then, was to allow him complete freedom, but at the same time to put every possible obstacle in his path without making it obvious that the government was blocking his campaign. To Ramón Corral, Reyes' bitter enemy, fell the task of co-ordinating the campaign of attrition.

Reyes was particularly popular among the younger army officers, having instituted a number of reforms which were advantageous to the lower ranks. Corral felt it was essential to suffocate any attempt by this group to give active support to the General. When a group of lieutenants and captains stationed in Mexico City formed a political club to stimulate the Reyes campaign in late May, 1909, therefore, action against them was swift and sure, but not too drastic. They were transferred to duty in Yucatán, Quintana Roo, Sonora, and Sinaloa, all of which were more or less isolated and at sufficient distance from Mexico City to preclude the creation of difficulties by the malcontents.[49]

Newspaper reaction varied with the political complexion of the directing staffs; *El País,* a Catholic daily which generally supported the government, attacked the officers who were backing Reyes on the ground that their action had all the appearances of a military junta formed to dictate policies to the government.[50] Filomena Mata and *El Diario del Hogar,* on the other hand, just as vigorously upheld the officers and loudly condemned as arbitrary the government's move in sending them to outlying posts.[51] As some of the "exiles" passed through Guadalajara, their train was met by an admiring and vociferous crowd which, indicating their approval of Reyes and disapproval

[49] *El Diario del Hogar,* June 1, 1909, p. 1.
[50] *El País,* May 31, 1909, p. 1.
[51] *El Diario del Hogar,* June 1 ,1909, p. 1.

81

of Corral, created an *escandalito* and were dispersed by the police only after a number of serious altercations.[52] Even though Governor Ahumada minimized the importance of the incident, the frightening overtones indicated the need for caution in handling the Reyes problem and showed the necessity for curtailing Reyes' popularity. Ahumada had another disturbing bit of information to pass on, information which made eliminating Reyes more than ever essential. Up to that time the General had not made his position clear, for he had made no public pronouncement of his candidacy. But Ahumada had received information from a local Reyista who was in communication with the Nuevo León governor that Reyes would accept the nomination for the vice-presidency. When he reported, Ahumada had not yet ascertained the truth of the statement; but since it would be of "grave importance" if it were true, he was doing everything he could to "obtain proof by some means."[53]

Within two weeks another episode in Guadalajara showed Reyes' growing strength in Jalisco. When a group of Re-electionists visited the city to popularize the Díaz-Corral candidacy, they were met at the station by a large crowd of Reyistas who were determined to prevent the rally. As the disturbance became violent, the police were forced to intervene; and before the incipient riot was quieted, some forty men, most of whom were soon released because they were students, were taken into custody. Continuing violence during the remainder of the month culminated in the wholesale expulsion from the schools of students active in Reyes' behalf. Ahumada's action seemed to have a quieting effect for the moment, but he could not get at the root of the trouble. He was frankly at a loss and begged Corral to give him instructions.[54]

Reyes, in the meantime, was doing little or nothing in his own behalf. He had strong support in Mexico City in the Partido Democrático and the Partido Nacionalista Democrático, both of which had ramifications in other parts of the country, with the Partido Democrático forming a branch in Guadalajara in early May and the P.N.D. having co-operating groups in Veracruz and other states. The principal strength of both groups, nevertheless, remained in Mexico City and its environs.[55] In addition to these larger organizations, there were other,

---

[52] Ahumada to Corral, June 1, 1909, *LO,* September 26, 1937, p. 1.
[53] *Ibid.*   [54] Ahumada to Corral, June 14, 22, and 29, 1909, *ibid.,* 1, 2.
[55] Estrada, *La revolución y Francisco I. Madero,* 96, 97; *El Diario del Hogar,* May 2, 1909, p. 7.

smaller groups, most of which were connected with one another and with the major Reyista parties through common membership but acted independently, campaigning in Reyes' behalf. During May and June Reyes' leading supporters made vain efforts to obtain direct and positive commitments from him concerning his acceptance of a nomination, but he consistently refused to clarify his position. Finally, on July 6, 1909, the Club Central Reyista 1910 demanded a clear and unequivocal answer, with an explanation of his reasons if he decided not to run.[56]

Reyes, in the meantime, had gone to his estate at Galeana, in the southern part of the state, to "rest," which made it appear, in the existing political situation, as if he were preparing for direct action against the government. His reply to the Mexico City club seemed to belie that intention, for he said categorically that he was unconditionally supporting Corral in view of Díaz' support of his vice-president.[57] This terse statement, followed by an enlarged exposition[58] of the reasons for his decision, brought a temporary halt to propaganda in his behalf; but the lull was short lived, and on the very day that Reyes wrote his lengthy explanation (ten days after his first refusal) there was a serious clash in Guadalajara between his supporters and those of Corral. On the morning of July 24 a group of Re-electionists arrived in the city to hold a rally, but from the beginning it was a fiasco. The train arrived with large *vivas* for Reyes and *mueras* for Corral painted on its sides, the result of Reyista ingenuity, and the party debarked with the jeers of the assembled Reyistas ringing in their ears. The planned ceremonious parade through the streets was abandoned, the speakers retiring instead to their hotel to wait for the police to disperse the heckling crowd. For many hours during the day the officials struggled to establish order, while the mob hurled stones at the hotel and epithets at the Corralistas. The crowd was finally scattered, but the *gritos* for Reyes persisted.[59]

Disregarding the inauspicious beginning and depending on the power of the authorities to prevent a recurrence, the Re-electionists determined to hold a meeting the following morning in the Degollado

[56] Club Central Reyista 1910 to Reyes, July 6, 1909. The letter, signed by officials of the club, was published in *México Nuevo*, July 17, 1909, p. 1.

[57] Estrada, *La revolución y Francisco I. Madero*, 111–12.

[58] The fuller statement, dated July 25, appeared in *México Nuevo*, July 29, 1909, p. 1.

[59] Taracena, *En el vértigo de la revolución mexicana*, 45.

83

Theater. The result was calamitous. As soon as the rally began, an outbreak of hostilities disrupted the meeting; then the disturbance spread, wave on wave, throughout the city. Viciousness begat viciousness, and an uneasy order was restored only after a large number of demonstrators had been injured, some of them mortally. After this display of public hostility, the chastened Re-electionists returned to Mexico City on the next train, convinced at last that Guadalajara was firmly in the Reyes camp.[60]

The administration's reaction was prompt and to the point; Reyes must be halted before he became the focal point of a revolution, and the best means of accomplishing that end would be to place a guard over him. Within a few days General Gerónimo Treviño, an old and powerful opponent of Reyes, was recalled from retirement and given command of the Third Military Zone, including the state of Nuevo León.[61] Treviño watched Reyes' every move from that point on, as Reyes well knew. The Nuevo León governor was henceforth known as *el atrincherado de Galeana* because he refused to stir from his hacienda.

Reyes made no public comment on Treviño's appointment, nor did he take any action which might be construed as adverse to the interests of the government. He was extremely quiet—so quiet, in fact, that when Monterrey was swept by a disastrous flood in late August he made no attempt to return immediately to his stricken capital city, leaving himself open to severe criticism. When General Treviño took over the administration of relief for the flood victims, it was generally conceded that Reyes was afraid to come out of the hills and attend to his duties, though the newspapers were not quite that blunt in their accusations. Ten days after the inundation Reyes quietly appeared in Monterrey, after an absence of two months, to be met with stolid silence by the citizenry, in contrast to the pomp and circumstance which had accompanied his previous returns.[62] His popularity had dissipated.

Even though his return brought a renewal of the political tension which had been evident in Monterrey before the flood, it was soon rumored that Reyes intended to resign as governor.[63] By the end of the month Treviño, castigating the governor for maladministration and charging him with misuse of funds, took it for granted that Reyes was

[60] *El Diario del Hogar,* July 27, 1909, p. 1.
[61] *México Nuevo,* July 31, 1909, p. 1.
[62] *El Diario del Hogar,* September 3, 1909, and September 10, 1909, p. 3. Reyes returned to Monterrey on September 6; the flood occurred on August 29.
[63] *Ibid.,* September 10, 1909, p. 3.

to retire and asked for a new governor who would give his unqualified support to the government and to General Díaz. Although Reyes continued as governor of Nuevo León, still enjoyed a powerful following in Jalisco and Nuevo León, and retained the support of the Mexico City group, he was no longer a threat to the government.[64] In late October he arrived in Mexico City, apparently having been summoned by Díaz, and within a few days he was designated to go to Europe on a government mission, a kind of political exile.[65] He did not have the courage to maintain a struggle against Díaz; that it was a lack of courage, and not principle, which prevented his taking the lead is obvious from his later actions. At any rate, when he quit the country the Reyes bubble burst, leaving the field open for Corral, particularly in the northern states. There were rumors of impending military action in Reyes' behalf in early December, but nothing happened, and it was generally conceded that Reyes as a political force was through.[66]

With the gradual decline of Reyes' popularity, his supporters tended to split into three groups. Some continued to believe in Reyes and looked for him to take a strong position vis-à-vis Corral and the administration, but they were a definite minority. Others shifted their loyalty to Teodoro A. Dehesa, popular governor of Veracruz, who was a Porfirista but an anti-Científico; and the remainder gradually drifted into the Antire-electionist camp.[67] With the waning of Reyes' cause and the waxing of the Antire-electionist strength, the administration turned its attention to the Madero organization, and on September 30, 1909, the offices of *El Anti-Reeleccionista* were raided, the staff arrested, and the doors barred; the party organ was now dead after less than two months' existence as a daily. Two of the principal staff members, Félix Palavicini and José Vasconcelos, had been warned of the impending raid and escaped arrest, but their activities were curtailed since they were forced into hiding for some weeks. The ostensible reason for closing *El Anti-Reeleccionista* was that treasonable statements had been made in an article appearing in the September 22 issue, in which the Taft-Díaz conversations concerning Bahía Magdalena were

---

[64] Treviño to Corral, September 30 and October 20, 1909, *LO,* October 10, 1937, p. 1; Ahumada to Corral, October 14, 1909, *ibid.,* September 26, 1937, p. 2. See *El Diario del Hogar,* October 28, 1909, for a manifesto of October 23 issued by the Mexico City group.
[65] *El Diario del Hogar,* October 28, 1909, p. 1.
[66] Treviño to Corral, November 5, 1909, *LO,* October 10, 1937, p. 1; F. A. Beltrán to Corral, December 1, 1909, *ibid.,* November 7, 1937, p. 1.
[67] Taracena, *En el vértigo de la revolución mexicana,* 48.

discussed; the article was unsigned.[68] Some people, including Emilio Vázquez Gómez, either believed or feigned to believe that the closing of *El Anti-Reeleccionista* was the result of a mistaken idea on the part of the government that the paper was a tool of the Reyistas. Vázquez Gómez even saw fit to publish a manifesto[69] denying any connection with Reyismo, apparently hoping to prevent further persecution.

Following the closing of the paper, there was a general disintegration of opposition to the government. Madero, ill with a serious attack of fever, could do nothing to stimulate flagging interest in his own party, which appeared to be falling apart. Delio Moreno Cantón, the independent candidate for governor in Yucatán, and most of his advisors were imprisoned by order of the governor, and the Reyista organization in Mexico City had degenerated to political nullity but satisfied itself by issuing innocuous manifestos concerning municipal elections. Within the ranks of the Antire-electionists there was ample evidence of the subversion of their basic principles and of a general loss of enthusiasm for the cause, with Roque Estrada proposing General Treviño and Esquivel Obregón as candidates for the presidency and vice-presidency, an obvious effort to placate Díaz.[70] Emilio Vázquez Gómez, president of the Antire-electionist Centro in Mexico City, strayed even farther from the fold in proposing the re-election of Díaz; by sheer sophistry, Vázquez attempted to prove that only through the re-election of Díaz could the concept of no re-election be introduced.[71]

At no other time in his career did Madero give better proof of his leadership and his determination than in the dark months of November and December. He arrived in Mexico City late in October, still a sick and weak man, en route to the health resort of Tehuacán, Puebla.[72] He stayed in the capital city only a few days, giving what help he could in drawing up the final plans for the party convention,[73] and then resumed his journey to Tehuacán, where he wrote long letters of encouragement to the men who were falling away from the party. Vasconcelos had become disgusted and said that he would do nothing

[68] *El Diario del Hogar,* October 1, 1909, p. 1; Palavicini, *Mi vida revolucionaria,* 61.
[69] In *El Diario del Hogar,* October 1, 1909, p. 2.
[70] *Ibid.,* October 3, 1909, p. 1; October 10, 1909, p. 1; October 17, 1909, p. 1; October 28, 1909; and November 18, 1909, p. 2.
[71] E. Vázquez Gómez to Agüeros, November 19, 1909, *ibid.,* January 13, 1910, p. 1.
[72] *Ibid.,* October 20, 1909, p. 2.
[73] Taracena, *En el vértigo de la revolución mexicana,* 49.

more unless there was a revolution, and to him Madero insisted that the party still had a good chance of success if the members had the courage to combat the government on a legal basis.[74] Madero did not promise an easy way, however; after asking Vasconcelos to stay with the party, he wrote: "Nevertheless, if you decide to continue at our side, remember this: the obstacles to this point cannot be compared to those which we shall have to overcome. The dangers we have run are as nothing to those which await us."[75]

In addition to writing to his friends, Madero attempted to induce the government to alter its policy and give greater freedom to legitimate political efforts. Realizing the futility of approaching either Díaz or Corral, he asked Minister of Hacienda José Ives Limantour, an old friend of the family in whom Madero had confidence, to consider the question. He referred briefly to the reasons behind the Antireelectionist movement, pointed out instances of repression, and asked the Minister of Hacienda to use his influence to prevent recurrences. He also mentioned the dangers inherent in repression, for, he said,

we have a right to hope that since we are working loyally, so will the Díaz government treat us. We have confided in the patriotism of General Díaz and those who surround him . . . because if the public is not left free to exercise its rights at this time, and has no hopes of exercising them during the administration of Corral, the idea of conquering those rights by force will be seriously entertained in the heart of every Mexican who is anxious for liberty.[76]

This was strong and almost threatening language, and so was another passage which mentioned the "ill which comes from trying to suffocate democratic movements by force."[77] Limantour gave a noncommittal answer, gently chiding Madero for a difference in the interpretation or "appreciation of many acts and the manner of presenting the truth," and refused to intervene in behalf of Delio Moreno Cantón, popular candidate for governor of Yucatán, on the ground that the case was in the hands of the judiciary and out of his own province.[78] Limantour had made it plain that Madero was to receive no

---

[74] Vasconcelos, *Ulises criollo,* 387; Madero to Vasconcelos, November 13, 1909, in Taracena, *Madero,* 195.

[75] Madero to Vasconcelos, November 13, 1909, in Taracena, *Madero,* 195.

[76] Madero to Limantour, November 18, 1909, *LO,* February 18, 1934, p. 2.

[77] *Ibid.*

[78] Limantour to Madero, November 25, 1909, *ibid.*

promise concerning future freedom of action, and that he and his party would have obstacles to overcome if they persisted in their efforts to elect top officials.

To add to the misery of official repression and general apathy, Madero was forced to contend with further efforts by his family to dissuade him from his course. Since a case involving one of the Madero family holdings was then pending, Madero's political activities were threatening the family with ruin. Don Evaristo Madero had already warned his grandson that if an armed revolution resulted from the political discontent engendered by the Antire-electionists, he himself would be the first to defend the government in spite of his seventy-eight years. He now reiterated his demand that Madero cease his political dabbling, since, as he said, "you are far from knowing the country in which we live."[79] Madero's father, too, begged him to return to private life; after reviewing the various financial complexities and stressing his need of his son's aid, Don Francisco then said that Francisco's mother was seriously ill and "it is, then, a sacred duty for you not to aggravate her illness and cause her irreparable harm. In order to do this, it is necessary for you to get out of politics."[80]

For Madero the outlook in all directions was bleak. The Mexico City Centro was almost dead and had done nothing constructive for many weeks. Many independents in Puebla, Yucatán, Sinaloa, Coahuila, and other states were languishing in prison for the part they had taken in local campaigns. The party newspaper was closed, with all the expensive machinery, which had been procured at the cost of tremendous effort, under lock and key. Toribio Esquivel Obregón, one of the vice-presidents and presumably the leader of the party in Guanajuato, was completely inactive.[81] Emilio Vázquez Gómez had openly espoused the re-election of Díaz, and others were attempting to placate the administration. Many of the younger men were discouraged and disillusioned, while Félix Palavicini was free on bond but unable to take part in political ventures even if he had desired to do so, which is doubtful.[82] The family besought Madero to let the movement die, particularly since it

[79] Don E. Madero to Madero, September 29 and November 22, 1909, *ibid.*, February 25, 1934, p. 2.
[80] Don F. Madero to Madero, November 29, 1909, *ibid.*
[81] For Esquivel Obregón's attitudes and reactions, see Esquivel to Madero, March 15, 1910, *ibid.*, January 28, 1934, p. 2.
[82] Palavicini, *Mi vida revolucionaria,* 69; Taracena, *En el vértigo de la revolución mexicana,* 50.

88

was moribund and its revival would be difficult.[83] The combination of these factors, coupled with the long illness from which he was only now recuperating, should have been enough to discourage any man, but his indomitable will and his faith would not let him be discouraged. It was quite evident, from the manner in which the party had lost strength, that Madero was indispensable even though he never said or hinted as much in any of his correspondence. But if the party was to regain strength and increase its importance, the burden was on his shoulders. It was a burden which he gladly took up as soon as his health permitted.

Even before he left Tehuacán he was full of plans: a trip to Oaxaca to gain adherents there, a joint meeting in Mexico City with the Partido Democrático, another swing around the country to instill courage and enthusiasm, a renewal of propaganda from the Centro—these and other things were needed to put the party on an operating basis once more.[84] His journey to Oaxaca was not unusually fruitful, principally because Díaz had been more careful to preserve the interests and liberties of the people in his own state than he had in others. In Oaxaca, Madero was greeted with no public demonstration, nor, according to the governor's report, was he even moderately successful in his attempt to establish an Antire-electionist club.[85] Undismayed by the rebuff, he returned to Mexico City to put his other plans into execution; and from that time forward gradual but important increase in the strength and prestige of his party could be discerned.

Shortly after his return to the capital, a final decision was made regarding the procedures to be established for the nominating convention. April 15, 1910, was set as the meeting date; a method was adopted for the selection of a directive council for the convention and a campaign committee; and the rules and regulations concerning delegates were widely published.[86] While the finishing touches were being put on the manifesto announcing the convention, Madero also arranged to speak to the Partido Nacionalista Democrático, one of the stronger Reyista organizations, which was now without a candidate.

[83] Don F. Madero to Madero, November 29, 1909, *LO,* February 25, 1934, p. 2.
[84] Madero to Esquivel, December 2, 1909, *ibid.,* January 28, 1934, p. 2.
[85] Governor E. Pimentel to Corral, December 4, 1909, *LP,* January 2, 1938, p. 7.
[86] The manifesto was published in *El Diario del Hogar,* December 15, 1909, p. 1, and in other independent papers at about the same date.

Both Madero and Roque Estrada spoke; both were received with general approval. As a result of a suggestion made by Madero at this meeting, there was a joint meeting of the principal members of the two political organizations three days later, at which time the P.N.D. showed a marked desire to co-operate with the Antire-electionists. The P.N.D. speakers, as well as Madero and his men, were critical of Corral and stressed the evil influence which he had exerted on the government.[87]

Almost immediately after this meeting Madero began his long-delayed political tour through the western states, choosing Roque Estrada as his companion because the young *tapatío*[88] lawyer had given bountiful proof of his abilities as an orator and because Palavicini was no longer available.[89] The first stop was Querétaro, where, even though a local club was organized, Madero met with indifferent success.[90] From Querétaro the party moved to Guadalajara. Here, largely because Jalisco had been the center of a type of Reyismo which was a manifestation of antiadministration feeling rather than a pro-Reyes sympathy, an entirely different atmosphere prevailed.[91] In contrast to the apathy of Querétaro, Guadalajara was enthusiastic. In Querétaro there had been no attempt at official intervention, but Madero had hardly arrived in Guadalajara before he was warned against holding a political rally.[92] Since a great crowd gathered to greet him, and the crowd was obviously expecting a political demonstration, Madero disregarded the official warning by holding an impromptu session in a hotel lobby. The lobby of a hotel, however, was obviously too small for an effective demonstration, and Madero immediately applied for permission to use the Degollado Theater on the following day.[93] But the management of the Degollado refused to rent the theater to Madero, as did all the owners of the larger theaters in the city; they obviously feared official repercussions if they helped Madero compound a felony. Finally, after an exhaustive search, he found a small theater on the city's edge, which he could use if he paid a month's rent in advance.

[87] *El Diario del Hogar,* December 17 and 21, 1909, p. 1.
[88] That is, a native of Guadalajara.
[89] Taracena, *En el vértigo de la revolución mexicana,* 50; *El Diario del Hogar,* December 17, 1909, p. 1; Madero to Esquivel, December 2, 1909, *LO,* January 28, 1934, p. 2.
[90] *El Diario del Hogar,* December 26, 1909, p. 2; Taracena, *En el vértigo de la revolución mexicana,* 50. Taracena gives the date of December 23, but newspapers said December 24.
[91] Ahumada to Corral, October 14, 1909, *LO,* September 26, 1937, p. 2.
[92] Madero to E. Vázquez Gómez, January 28, 1910, *ibid.,* January 7, 1934, p. 1.
[93] *El Diario del Hogar,* December 26, 1909, p. 2.

He had little choice; payment was made.[94] As soon as Madero had rented the theater, he notified the local authorities that he intended to hold a rally there; the *jefe político* refused to grant permission, and when Madero insisted on his rights he was referred to Governor Ahumada. Ahumada had already warned Madero that he would be held responsible for any disturbance resulting from a demonstration, to which Madero replied that he was perfectly willing to take that risk. He had a legal right to hold a meeting and did not intend to deviate from his plans merely because of threats and intimidation.[95] Willing to co-operate, nevertheless, he made an appointment to see the Governor on Sunday morning to discuss the situation, but Ahumada failed to appear.[96] Madero was then confronted with two alternatives: he could either defy the local officials and complete his plans—for it was obvious that he would never receive official sanction—or he could quit the city without holding the demonstration. Such an alternative was no alternative at all; he had come to the city for a specific purpose and he was determined to proceed unless restrained by force.[97]

Circumstances made the decision easy. While Madero had been waiting for the Governor, a large crowd had gathered to witness the outcome in the duel between Madero and Ahumada; and when Madero left the gubernatorial office without having seen his protagonist, the crowd shouted for a speech. Taking advantage of a fortuitous condition which the government had helped create, from a hotel balcony Madero and his group addressed a sympathetic crowd of some six thousand. The listeners were enthusiastic, interested, and orderly; when the speakers had concluded, the crowd scattered quietly.[98] Even though a company of police arrived during one of the addresses, they made no attempt to interrupt the proceedings, nor was any action later taken against any of the participants.[99]

The events in Guadalajara encouraged Madero. The public had clearly demonstrated its interest in the movement for an independent candidate and its determination to hear opposition candidates regardless of official intimidation. To be sure, Ahumada had not been as firm as he either could have been or was expected to be, but there were cer-

---

[94] Madero to E. Vázquez Gómez, January 28, 1910, *LO,* January 7, 1934, p. 1.
[95] *Ibid.*
[96] *El Diario del Hogar,* December 28, 1909, p. 3.
[97] Madero to E. Vázquez Gómez, January 28, 1910, *LO,* January 7, 1934, p. 1.
[98] *El Diario del Hogar,* December 28, 1909, p. 3.
[99] Madero to E. Vázquez Gómez, January 28, 1910, *LO,* January 7, 1934, p. 1.

tainly threats and attempts to prevent Madero from fulfilling his mission. It was only a combination of a determination on the part of Madero and insistence by the populace which had foiled the local government. The entire episode showed that much could be done if firm leadership were exercised; it was also a vindication of everything Madero had been saying for months past.

Madero's experiences in Colima, to which town he went immediately from Jalisco, reaffirmed the convictions which had been strengthened in Guadalajara. In Colima the authorities took no overt action to prevent a demonstration, but they attempted intimidation by the judicious distribution of police at strategic points around the plaza in which the rally was held. In spite of the presence of the police with their threatening gestures, over a thousand persons were on hand to hear Madero and Estrada when they delivered their addresses on December 28.[100] An early sailing of the vessel which was to take them from Manzanillo to Mazatlán left insufficient time to complete the organization of an Antire-electionist club; so Madero and his companions contented themselves with the formation of a directive council to carry on the work they had started.[101]

From Colima the group continued to Sinaloa, holding meetings in Mazatlán, Culiacán, and Angostura. Nothing of outstanding interest, other than a series of successful meetings, transpired in any of these cities. In each, the officials tried to prevent the demonstrations by making it difficult to find places to speak, but in each there was sufficient interest among people of power and prestige to overcome these machinations. In each an Antire-electionist club was organized.[102] One of the most important results of the journey through the state was the cementing of firm friendships among the younger and more liberal men; Manuel Bonilla of Culiacán was probably the most important convert.

Whereas only quasi repression had been experienced in Jalisco, Colima, and Sinaloa, Madero was subjected to real and dangerous persecution when he reached Sonora, the home state of Ramón Corral. In Alamos, Madero and his party were refused rooms in the hotel where he had made advance reservations, and it was necessary to stay in a private home. The *jefe político* then refused to grant permission for a meeting, prohibiting gatherings of more than two people to discuss political questions. In vain Madero wired Díaz requesting authority to

[100] *El Diario del Hogar,* December 31, 1909, p. 2.
[101] Madero to E. Vázquez Gómez, January 28, 1910, *LO,* January 7, 1934, p. 1.
[102] *Ibid.*

exercise his rights; in vain, too, was a similar request by a group of citizens headed by Benjamín G. Hill. Finally resorting to subterfuge, Madero prevailed upon one of his adherents to give a private dance to which were invited only people of independent political thought, and he was able to address this restricted gathering in an informal manner.[103] Although the method was far from satisfactory, it was better than complete surrender to the dictates of the local officials.

As Madero and his party left Alamos for Hermosillo, they were followed by a group of twenty *rurales,* presaging an attempt to imprison him.[104] In Hermosillo the Alamos experience was repeated with variations; Madero, again confronted with the difficulty of securing personal accommodations, spurned the evident signs of repression and notified the local authorities that he intended to hold a rally on January 12. Surprisingly enough, there was no official denial of the right to speak; but when the crowd began to gather, numerous methods of intervention were practiced. The police attempted to disperse the crowd, free drinks were offered to all, thugs and bullies circulated through the crowd insulting speakers and audience, and other hirelings began throwing overripe fruit. It being impossible to hold a meeting under such conditions, Madero, seeing that he and Estrada would be arrested in case of any disturbance, decided to postpone the meeting until the next day.[105] On the following day, however, he saw the futility of attempting to lead a demonstration and so he passed on to Nogales and out of the state.

The journey through Sonora was almost barren of results because of official intervention. Though there was no political advance, the few days in Sonora had given Madero an opportunity to demonstrate that political freedom was nonexistent in the state. He also had made powerful friends. One of the most constant of these was Benjamín G. Hill, who showed his concern for Madero by accompanying him from Alamos to Nogales because he had heard a rumor (the veracity of which was never established) that the governor had ordered that Madero be either arrested or killed while in the state.[106] Another fruitful connection which Madero established in Sonora was with José María Maytorena, who was closely allied with the Antire-electionist and Madero cause until Madero's death. In addition to making these and

---

[103] *El Diario del Hogar,* January 9 and 11, 1910, p. 2.
[104] *Ibid.,* January 14, 1910, p. 1.
[105] *Ibid.* This is a later dispatch.
[106] Taracena, *Madero,* 229.

other important friendships, Madero was also learning a lesson—the more popular his cause, the more intensive the interference—and he had received proof of the type of government which could probably be expected were Corral to become president. Although it is not clear from the evidence, it is logical to assume that Madero was by then considering the necessity of a revolution.

After leaving Sonora, Madero traveled by way of the United States to Ciudad Juárez in Chihuahua, where he arrived on January 18, 1910.[107] His rapid trip through the state was not an outstanding success, although some interest was shown in Ciudad Juárez, Chihuahua, Parral, and Jiménez. His strongest supporter in the state was Abraham González. Governor Enrique Creel looked on Madero with tolerance and contempt, choosing to believe that curiosity rather than interest brought the crowds to hear him.[108] The accuracy of Creel's observations may be judged from the fact that Chihuahua was the center of armed revolt before the end of the year.

During his entire trip Madero had stressed only one point, a point which he hammered home at every meeting and in every conversation: the need for an orderly change in government officials through the exercise of the constitutional right of casting the ballot. There was no mention of economic or social needs except on such rare occasions as that when he spoke to the Yaquis of Sonora and wept[109] at the tales of slavery and woe which had befallen them. His prime interest at this stage was to arouse interest in the selection of an independent candidate who would assure the victory of the principle of effective suffrage and rotation in office. At no time did he mention himself as a possible candidate; he still regarded himself as the leader of the party and the guardian of the rights and privileges of the citizens, exactly as he had earlier in Coahuila.

In spite of Madero's reticence in advancing his own candidacy, a survey of the field for likely candidates showed that the choice was practically limited to the one man who had built the party and carried its doctrines to all corners of the nation—Madero himself. No other individual had given evidence of sufficient courage and constancy to make an active campaign against the ever increasing pressures being applied by the central government, and by popular acclaim Madero was certain to be nominated for the leading position. To whom should

[107] Taracena, *En el vértigo de la revolución mexicana,* 54.
[108] Creel to Corral, January 25, 1910, *LP,* October 3, 1937, p. 7.
[109] In Navojoa, January 8, 1910.

go the credit for first proposing Madero's name is not clear, but on January 21, 1910, Abraham González reported that the Club Antirreeleccionista Benito Juárez de Chihuahua had, by secret ballot, overwhelmingly indicated its belief in Madero as the best candidate.[110] During the same month the Antire-electionists of Puebla indicated a like frame of mind, and others soon followed.[111] Madero had become the leading candidate by default.

While Madero returned to San Pedro in late January for a short rest before continuing through the central states, Roque Estrada went to Guanajuato, at Madero's request, to consult Toribio Esquivel Obregón concerning the formation of an Antire-electionist club in that state.[112] Esquivel, even though he was vice-president of the Centro and one of the organizers of the party, had apparently lost heart for the fight and for months had done nothing constructive for the party. His only contribution had been a sharp exchange of letters with the Centro over Emilio Vázquez Gómez' pronounced re-electionist proclivities.[113] To Madero it appeared that Esquivel intended to take no action and was using weak excuses—pressure of business, illness, and the like—to keep himself aloof from any party activities.[114] It was Estrada's mission to see Esquivel, obtain a direct commitment regarding his future plans, and attempt to persuade him to sponsor a meeting in the city of Guanajuato.[115]

There is a wide discrepancy between Estrada's report of the projected interview and Esquivel's report of the same incident, although both agree on one item: they did not see each other. According to Estrada, on arriving in Guanajuato he immediately called at Esquivel's home, but neither then nor at subsequent times during the next two days did he find the Guanajuato leader, even though frequent appointments were made. Estrada left Guanajuato only when prior speaking commitments demanded his appearance in Mexico.[116] Esquivel, on the other hand, reported that despite an important business engagement he had stayed at home in order to see Estrada, that he had made frequent attempts to discover his whereabouts, and that he was sorely disappointed and a little disgusted because Estrada had failed to keep the

[110] A. González to Madero, January 21, 1910, in Taracena, *Madero,* 234–35.
[111] E. Arenas to Madero, March 1, 1910, *LO,* March 11, 1934, p. 2.
[112] Estrada, *La revolución y Francisco I. Madero,* 168.
[113] Esquivel to Madero, March 15, 1910, *LO,* January 28, 1934, p. 2.
[114] Estrada, *La revolución y Francisco I. Madero,* 169.
[115] *Ibid.*   [116] *Ibid.*

Mexican Revolution

appointment.[117] In the light of Esquivel's general attitude and his subsequent actions, it is safe to assume that Estrada's report showed a greater respect for the truth than did Esquivel's. This was the first of a series of differences between Madero and Esquivel which served to start an ever widening breach. Esquivel's refusal to co-operate with Madero probably cost him the vice-presidential nomination.

The Antire-electionists were also plagued with other difficulties during February and March. Emilio Vázquez Gómez was adamant in his insistence that it would be correct and proper to support the re-election of Díaz, but others could not see the logic of the argument. Estrada complained that Vázquez Gómez refused to publish an article Estrada had written for the new party newspaper, *El Constitucional,* on the ground that Díaz was attacked too viciously. Estrada charged that Emilio's "excessive prudence" was wrecking the party, making it impossible for the more progressive party members to give any aid to the party paper. As a consequence of the dissension, the Centro was not so active as it should have been, the most vociferous groups in the capital being those recently organized clubs consisting principally of laborers.[118]

In the northern and central states the Antire-electionist cause suffered a decline in strength and popularity, largely because nothing was done to organize opinion. In February, General Treviño reported that Nuevo León, Coahuila, and Tamaulipas showed no inclination to oppose the re-election of Díaz, and then said: "We should, now that there is absolutely no fear [of defeat], take up democratic practices as much as possible."[119] The earlier strength of the Antire-electionists in those states had dissipated.

There was therefore still much work to be done, and the task devolved on Madero as it had in the past. During February he made frequent trips to Mexico City to confer with Emilio Vázquez Gómez, Roque Estrada, and Filomeno Mata, in an attempt to formulate policies for carrying on the campaign.[120] One result of these conferences was a decision that Madero would travel through Durango, Zacatecas, Aguascalientes, and Guanajuato in an effort to stimulate interest; but when the subject was broached to Esquivel Obregón, he opposed any meeting in Guanajuato. Even while he spoke of the strength of the Antire-electionist sentiment in the state, he objected to any propagan-

[117] Esquivel to Madero, March 15, 1910, *LO,* January 28, 1934, p. 2.
[118] Estrada to Madero, February 17, 1910, *ibid.,* January 7, 1934, p. 2.
[119] Treviño to Corral, February 6, 1910, *ibid.,* October 10, 1937, p. 1.
[120] Taracena, *En el vértigo de la revolución mexicana,* 55.

96

dizing tour on the basis that it would be dangerous for the laborers who by and large made up the mass of those interested in the party; he believed that they would be subjected to all types of persecution. Furthermore, Esquivel had serious misgivings about an attempt to elect a president and vice-president in the forthcoming elections. In lieu of attempting to elect the president, which he was convinced would be prevented by a combination of repression and official juggling of election figures, he proposed a concentration of efforts on the congressional elections.[121] In proposing the change in campaign plans, Esquivel overlooked one extremely important item: any attempt to attain a majority in either house of Congress would meet with the same type of government reaction as would an attempt to elect the president. Since Esquivel could hardly have been so naïve as to believe otherwise, the sincerity of his proposal is doubtful.

In spite of Esquivel's advice, Madero began his tour in March. The first meeting was held in Torreón,[122] and then the group continued to Durango, where Estrada joined them for the remainder of the trip. In Durango, Madero made a serious blunder in discussing the Laws of Reform, leaving the impression that he was in complete sympathy with Díaz' policy toward the Church and generally approved the entire Díaz program. Some ill feeling resulted; but later speakers enlarged upon and more fully explained Madero's attitude, and the ruffled feelings were somewhat smoothed. Nevertheless, from that time forward Madero was more careful in his phraseology when speaking on controversial subjects.[123]

The next stop was Zacatecas, where he was met by an enthusiastic crowd, predominantly students, but was denied the right to hold a rally.[124] Governor Francisco de P. Zarate attached no importance to Madero or the Antire-electionists, but justified his action in banning the meeting on the ground that a public gathering for political purposes would serve no end save to disturb public order.[125] Such was the general attitude of the Díaz governors toward political activity.

In Aguascalientes, Madero was taken to task for allowing Emilio Vázquez Gómez to remain in the party while advocating Díaz' re-election. Madero did not comment on the validity of Emilio's opinions,

---

[121] Esquivel to Madero, March 15, 1910, *LO,* January 28, 1934, p. 2.
[122] Taracena, *En el vértigo de la revolución mexicana,* 56.
[123] Estrada, *La revolución y Francisco I. Madero,* 179, 180.
[124] *Ibid.,* 180.
[125] F. de P. Zarate to Corral, March 24, 1910, *LP,* January 2, 1938, p. 1.

but he insisted that Emilio was one of the group's most constant members, giving more aid and being of greater service than some of the more radical members.[126] He had cause later to change his opinion.

From Aguascalientes the group moved to San Luis Potosí, where they found Dr. Rafael Cepeda, who had issued the public manifesto announcing the demonstration, in prison as a consequence of the wording of the announcement. Despite some official intimidation, an open-air meeting was held, a club formed, and Cepeda elected president even though he was still in jail.[127]

On April 1, 1910, Madero arrived in León, Guanajuato, where an open break almost occurred between him and Esquivel. Roque Estrada's timely intervention prevented an irreparable rupture, but Esquivel refused to co-operate in holding a rally.[128] A relatively small group at the demonstration reacted favorably to Madero's presentation, but the meeting was cut short when Madero was ordered, by a police officer, to desist. He was apparently not particularly anxious to continue after his altercation with Esquivel. Nevertheless, an Antireelectionist club was formed, with Esquivel named honorary president.[129] One more stop was made in Guanajuato, and here the reaction was much more encouraging than it had been in León, with an enthusiastic crowd forming an active organization.[130] Estrada also made a side trip to Guadalajara, but the police intervened and forced the speaker to leave on the first train for Mexico. Ahumada considered Estrada's words "subversive and seditious."[131]

The preconvention campaign now drew to a close, for within little more than a week after Estrada's forceful eviction from Guadalajara the convention was held. One of the most revealing commentaries on Madero's position in the development of the democratic concept and his role in the Antire-electionist movement was the manner in which affiliated clubs were formed wherever he went. José Hinojosa in Veracruz, Moreno Cantón and Pino Suárez in Yucatán, Rafael Cepeda in San Luis Potosí, Heriberto Frías in Mazatlán, Manuel Bonilla in Culiacán, Maytorena and Hill in Sonora, Ugarte in Guanajuato, Alberto

---

[126] Estrada, *La revolución y Francisco I. Madero,* 181. Madero had long believed in the possibility of some compromise with Díaz as a last resort but did not openly espouse such a cause in late April. See Chapter 5.
[127] *Ibid.,* 181–82.
[128] Taracena, *En el vértigo de la revolución mexicana,* 56.
[129] Estrada, *La revolución y Francisco I. Madero,* 184.
[130] *Ibid.,* 185.
[131] Ahumada to Corral, April 7, 1910, *LO,* September 26, 1937, p. 2.

Preconvention Campaign

Fuentes D. in Aguascalientes, and many lesser lights in all the states were adherents of the Antire-electionist idea; but they had done practically nothing toward the formation of active political organizations previous to Madero's arrival in each of these areas. In almost every instance he was able to destroy, by means of his own example, the fear and hesitation in the hearts of the local populace. Not all the clubs formed maintained themselves in active status; for as soon as Madero left there was a tendency to revert to inaction. But most of the clubs organized did remain active, and when the convention met on April 15, almost every state was represented by one or more delegates from active Antire-electionist groups.

Largely in recognition of his services, on the eve of the convention it was generally conceded that Madero would be the presidential choice; there was literally no one else who could command the respect of the independents so well as he, nor was there any other independent so well known. In the long and eventful months since he had left the capital on his initial speaking tour, he had visited fifteen states and had spoken hundreds of times. Though most of the emphasis in his tours had been on speaking to large gatherings in cities, he had lost no opportunity to stop at any pueblo or community where he could gather a few people together to extol the virtues of a free and democratic society. He was probably more widely known through personal contact than any other man in Mexico.

While it was easy to foretell the convention's choice for the presidential nomination, the selection of a running mate was not so simple. During the course of the past few months various men, including Fernando Iglesias Calderón, José María Pino Suárez, Emilio Vázquez Gómez, Toribio Esquivel Obregón, and General Gerónimo Treviño, had been discussed as potential candidates.[132] A prime consideration, however, was Madero's own preference for the candidate, for it was essential to have at his side a man who not only would co-operate with him but would also attract a large number of adherents to the party. Esquivel Obregón had practically eliminated himself, Emilio Vázquez Gómez was out of the picture because too many independents refused to countenance his re-election thesis, Pino Suárez was relatively unknown outside of Yucatán, and General Treviño had too many links with the Díaz government and was too old. The final choice of a candidate lay with Madero, for some of the clubs had already indicated

---

[132] [Lamicq], *Madero, por uno de sus íntimos,* 34.

99

that they would follow his lead.[133] And the choice was difficult indeed. Finally, after considering all aspects of the situation, practical as well as theoretical and idealistic, Madero put the weight of his influence behind Francisco Vázquez Gómez, Emilio's brother and personal physician to Díaz.[134] In taking this action, Madero hoped to prevent the persecutions which he was convinced were soon to come. So it was that Madero went to the convention with a commitment to support Dr. Vázquez Gómez.

[133] For example, the Puebla group tended to favor Esquivel but made it clear that they would do nothing unless Madero agreed.

[134] [Lamicq], *Madero, por uno de sus íntimos*, 35; Estrada, *La revolución y Francisco I. Madero*, 175–76.

V

The Convention and the Election

MADERO AND HIS ADVISORS were particularly anxious to have representation from the other independent political parties, the Partido Democrático and the Partido Nacionalista Democrático, at the convention along with the delegates from the various Antire-electionist clubs. To foster that idea, Estrada had been sent to Guadalajara in early April; but the Guadalajara independents, who were affiliated with the Democráticos, ultimately refused to co-operate. The Mexico City organization of the Partido Democrático also refused to participate, even though Madero made a strong last-minute plea for their aid. The Partido Nacionalista Democrático, on the other hand, was of slightly more independent bent and was willing to join with the Antire-electionists after the rumored return of Bernardo Reyes failed to materialize.[1] The Nacionalistas therefore selected their delegates on the same basis as that used by the Antire-electionists, but their small number[2] had little actual influence on the outcome of the convention. Nevertheless, the mere fact that the Nacionalistas were willing to co-operate was a healthy sign for the hopes of the Antire-electionists.

When the various Antire-electionist clubs began to select their convention delegates, a number of problems arose. Not only was there official intervention in many areas but within the clubs themselves there was disagreement and jealousy. Puebla may be taken as an example. There Aquiles Serdán, a shoemaker by trade, had taken the lead in organizing the opposition and in September, 1909, had been imprisoned for his political activities.[3] Undaunted by such treatment, he continued

[1] Estrada, *La revolución y Francisco I. Madero*, 194–95; Beltrán to Corral, January 5, 1910, *LP*, November 7, 1937, p. 7. Beltrán, an agent paid by Corral, insinuated himself into the confidence of the Antire-electionists.

[2] Fifteen; see the minutes of the convention, Estrada, *La revolución y Francisco I. Madero*, 199 ff.

[3] José C. Valadés, "La primera presa de la revolución," *LO*, March 11, 1934, p. 1.

his activities in behalf of the Antire-electionist cause and by 1910 was the leader of one segment of the party in Puebla. As the convention date neared and as the party became more popular, a rival group appeared under the leadership of a representative of the more "cultured" class, a follower of the Vázquez Gómez thesis concerning the re-election of Díaz. Serdán was a firm believer in antire-election and had supported Madero's nomination long before the convention met; friction consequently developed between the two groups. Through the intervention of other members the breach was partially healed, but in early April there was still a noticeable cleavage.[4] Serdán, who as president of his club had done a great deal to foster a democratic spirit in Puebla and the neighboring state of Tlaxcala, felt that he was justified in claiming the Antire-electionist leadership in his state. The meeting to choose the delegates to the national convention was characterized by long and acrimonious debate, but Serdán was able to carry the day for his choices.[5] At this point a very serious problem, one which confronted all the clubs, presented itself: the delegates lacked the resources to cover the expenses incidental to attending the convention, and the club itself was almost devoid of funds. In order to meet the need, each of the thousand or more members was assessed a small amount.[6] In spite of the difficulties which all small clubs encountered, by mid-April there was a general and growing enthusiasm for the convention and the principles for which the meetings of delegates stood.

By April 13, two days before the opening of the convention, the delegates began to arrive in Mexico City, and for the next week the party headquarters and the convention hall were filled with excited men who were embarking on a new experiment in Mexican politics.[7] When the first session convened, it was found that 120 delegates, 15 of whom represented the Nacionalistas and the remainder the Antire-electionists, had come from every state and territory but four.[8] Representatives from other clubs continued to arrive during the next few days, until the number reached approximately 200. A few failed to arrive at all be-

[4] Arenas to Madero, March 1, 1910, *ibid.*, p. 2.
[5] J. López Portillo to Chief of Puebla Police, March 20, 1910, *ibid.*, February 6, 1938, p. 1; Serdán to Madero, March 15, 1910, *ibid.*, March 11, 1934, p. 2.
[6] López P. to Chief of Puebla Police, March 27, 1910, *ibid.*, February 6, 1938, p. 1.
[7] Estrada, *La revolución y Francisco I. Madero*, 198.
[8] Minutes of the convention, *ibid.*, 199. Estrada was secretary. The states and territories not represented were Campeche, Tabasco, Nayarit, and Quintana Roo.

Madero and advisors at Bustillos in March, 1911, shortly after the battle of Casas Grandes
Pascual Orozco, Francisco I. Madero, José Garibaldi, and Raúl Madero

Revolutionary leaders during the truce meetings at Ciudad Juárez
Seated: Venustiano Carranza, Francisco Vázquez Gómez, Francisco I. Madero, Abraham González, José Maytorena, Alberto Fuentes D., and Pascual Orozco; standing: Francisco Villa, Gustavo Madero, Don Francisco Madero, José Garibaldi, Federico González Garza, José de la Luz Blanco, Juan Sánchez Azcona, and Alfonso Madero

cause they were either arrested on the road or detained immediately before departure.[9]

The mildly repressive measures of the past having been unsuccessful in preventing the growth of the Antire-electionist party, Corral decided that more direct means would have to be employed. Consequently, he ordered Madero's apprehension on the eve of the convention.[10] Madero was charged with having been responsible for the theft of a quantity of guayule from an hacienda bordering on his property. According to the plaintiff, workers for a company of which Madero was manager had cut the guayule, and Madero, having failed to make restitution, was therefore responsible for the criminal act.[11] Before the arrest could be made, Madero received information concerning the order and sought refuge in the home of a political friend.[12] The attempt to arrest Madero did not dampen the spirits or determination of the delegates; the meetings were held on schedule, and the order of business remained unaltered.

As soon as the delegates were accredited, the officers for the convention were chosen: Pino Suárez as president; Jesús L. González, Abraham González, and Alfredo Robles Domínguez the vice-presidents; and Roque Estrada the first secretary.[13] Immediately after the installation of officers, the meeting was thrown into momentary confusion by the entrance of Toribio Esquivel Obregón, who had no official status but, as a candidate for nomination, insisted on the right to speak.[14] Being granted that right, he vehemently opposed some portions of the regulations governing the convention and then insisted on his right to vote when the matter was put to the question. Inasmuch as he was not an official delegate, the right to vote was denied him by the convention itself in open vote, but he was given the right to speak on all subsequent questions.[15] The episode, disagreeable at the time, was soon forgotten, and the convention moved on to the business of selecting candidates.

Madero's name was placed in nomination by Roque Estrada. In spite of Madero's obvious popularity with the delegates, there were some who did not support him, and both Esquivel Obregón and

[9] *Ibid.,* 196, 205.
[10] Madero to Pino Suárez, April 16, 1910, *LO,* March 18, 1934, p. 1.
[11] [Lamicq], *Madero, por uno de sus íntimos,* 37.
[12] Madero to Pino Suárez, April 16, 1910, *LO,* March 18, 1934, p. 1.
[13] Estrada, *La revolución y Francisco I. Madero,* 199.
[14] [Lamicq], *Madero, por uno de sus íntimos,* 35.
[15] Estrada, *La revolución y Francisco I. Madero,* 200–201.

Iglesias Calderón were also nominated.[16] After long discussion from the floor, the balloting was overwhelmingly in Madero's favor, and he was officially designated as the candidate of both the Partido Nacionalista Democrático and the Partido Nacional Antirreeleccionista.

Before selecting a vice-presidential candidate, the convention undertook to formulate a set of principles within the framework of which the candidate was to work. In addition to the well-known principles of constitutional reform and political freedom, the general basis of the campaign was to include alleviation of the condition of the laborers, betterment of public instruction, creation of agricultural banks, and improvement of foreign relations.[17]

In the meantime, while still in hiding, Madero took steps to bring about a compromise with the government. Although he opposed the re-election of Díaz on principle, his greatest desire was to bring about a peaceful solution of the political stagnation confronting the nation. He therefore arranged an interview with Díaz, through the good offices of a "highly respected" friend, for April 15.[18] When he arrived at the presidential office at the appointed hour, he was told that Díaz would see him on the morrow at the same time. But before seeing Díaz and after having been unofficially notified of his nomination for the presidency, he informed the convention of his plans to bring about a compromise if possible. While he did not give the details of his plan, he said that if the terms were acceptable to Díaz, Madero would renounce his own candidacy. At the same time he interjected a note of warning that the public would "no longer allow [those rights] to be mocked in the fashion customary during the administration of General Díaz."[19]

In addition to advising the convention of his proposed action, Madero also made two suggestions. A directive committee to co-ordinate the general campaign was soon to be appointed,[20] and Madero wanted the powers of that commission broadened to include the naming of new candidates in case either of those nominated was eliminated through action by the government. He then suggested that the vice-presidential candidate should be a man of courage and trust who could take over the direction of the campaign in the event of Madero's im-

[16] *Ibid.*, 202. [17] *Ibid.*, 202–203.
[18] Madero did not name his friend, but he was Teodoro Dehesa.
[19] Madero to Pino Suárez, April 16, 1910, *LO,* March 18, 1934, p. 1. The letter was read to the delegates at Madero's request.
[20] Estrada, *La revolución y Francisco I. Madero,* 207.

104

prisonment. He stressed the necessity of this step, for, he said, "everything indicates that I will soon lose my liberty."[21]

On the second day the vice-presidential nominee had to be selected. Estrada, again acting as the spokesman for the Madero forces, nominated Dr. Francisco Vázquez Gómez. A number of other nominations were made, with Esquivel Obregón and Pino Suárez being serious contenders; but Dr. Vázquez Gómez received a clear though small majority on the first ballot and was declared the candidate of both parties.[22]

The following day, April 17, the two candidates appeared before the convention and accepted the nominations which had been tendered them.[23] Madero, who considered it "indecorous" for him to remain in hiding after he had received the nomination, still feared arrest, but his fears were unwarranted.[24] Demonstrations during much of April 17 and 18 showed that Madero had strong support in the capital, and it would have been a grave error to attempt to carry out the order for his arrest. Either because of political expediency, or, as was rumored at the time, because of a difference between Ramón Corral and Inspector of Police Félix Díaz, the charge was dropped or held in abeyance, for it was never mentioned again.[25]

In the meantime Madero had seen Díaz on April 16 and had been promised that the opposition party would be free to carry on the campaign and could be assured of a free and fair election.[26] What else was discussed is not clear, for the interview was held in private and neither of the protagonists ever amplified the bare outline of what was known. Popular belief held that Díaz had requested the interview[27] and that Madero had said he would withdraw from the campaign, leaving the presidency uncontested, if Díaz would guarantee fair elections for the vice-presidency, congressional posts, and municipal offices, in addition to a replacement of many of the state governors.[28] There seems to be

[21] Madero to Pino Suárez, April 16, 1910, *LO,* March 18, 1934, p. 1.
[22] Estrada, *La revolución y Francisco I. Madero,* 205.
[23] Transcribed copy of Madero's address, April 17, 1910, VC.
[24] Madero to Pino Suárez, April 16, 1910, *LO,* March 18, 1934, p. 1.
[25] [Lamicq], *Madero, por uno de sus íntimos,* 37–38; Estrada, *La revolución y Francisco I. Madero,* 197–98.
[26] Madero to Díaz, May 26, 1910, *LO,* February 18, 1934, pp. 1, 8.
[27] E.g., see Estrada, *La revolución y Francisco I. Madero,* 209–10; and Ferrer, *Vida de Francisco I. Madero,* 67–68.
[28] Madero reasserted these points in a message to the Antire-electionists on April 25, 1910.

good reason to deny, however, that the interview was requested by Díaz. Díaz, who had not yet taken the Antire-electionists seriously, made no move to meet Madero halfway. His innocuous promise must have convinced Madero that little but repression could be expected from the government.

Madero has been criticized often and bitterly for his willingness, or even desire, for a compromise with the government. His attempt to trade concession for concession has been attacked as an indication of fundamental weakness, as proof of his vacillating character, and as evidence that he was willing to sacrifice principles for personal gain. But principle itself, not a weakening of his basic beliefs, dictated his move toward compromise. He was torn between antithetical principles: that of the institution of democratic practices and that of the maintenance of peace at all costs. Normally, of course, these principles were not in opposition, but under the circumstances of 1910 the complete fruition of both was impossible. Madero was not so naïve as to assume that the dictator would abide by his promise of a completely free election, nor was he optimistic enough to believe that public opinion would force that position on the President. As a matter of practical politics it would have been advantageous to arrange some compromise, even at the cost of postponing a complete solution.

With the compromise effort a failure, Madero and his advisors began the formulation of plans and policies which would attract the greatest number of supporters. Among other things, it was vital to popularize Dr. Francisco Vázquez Gómez, for he was relatively unknown outside of Mexico City, and there his political connections had previously been with the Reyes group rather than the Antire-electionists. Madero felt that Vázquez Gómez' experience and background would be attractive to the intellectuals and the higher social and economic set, since he would be a conservative influence and would counteract criticism engendered by the more radical members.[29] The most important task now was to convince the rank and file of the candidate's qualifications.

Madero himself undertook to lead the way in portraying the strength which Vázquez Gómez brought to the party slate. In an anonymous article published in various independent newspapers, Madero ex-

[29] F. Vázquez Gómez to Madero, August 22, 1910, *LO,* January 14, 1934, p. 1. Vázquez Gómez reminded Madero of his earlier attitude.

106

plained that in their anxiety to select a man who had no political connections with the Díaz regime, the delegates had felt it necessary to choose a man who was politically unknown.[30] The interest which the doctor had previously shown in public affairs, particularly when he wrote on the question of public education,[31] was carefully pointed out, and the public was assured that the candidate had all the requisite qualifications—courage, integrity, judgment, patriotism, and civic responsibility. Madero did not mention that he himself had been primarily responsible for Vázquez Gómez' nomination.

Within a few days after the adjournment of the convention, the two candidates drafted a set of principles for consideration by the directive committee, and the committee then prepared a platform including the best features of both.[32] The platform as finally published was not revolutionary in either style or concept, being merely an enlargement and amplification of earlier general statements. The moral, material, and economic uplift of the masses was to receive special attention; Indian tribes were to be integrated into the pattern of national life; and there was to be improvement and expansion of public instruction. Agriculture was to be encouraged, and both small and large landholders were to benefit from the government program; irrigation and reclamation particularly were advocated. Finally, the tax burden was to be distributed equitably, and a system of universal military training was to be introduced.[33]

In addition to the platform drafted by the committee, Madero amplified his own position with regard to a number of ideas. Written as a message to the convention, even though that body had now adjourned, his statement indicated that he still hoped some compromise could be made, but stated categorically that if General Díaz permitted fraud and attempted "to support that fraud with force, then . . . I am convinced that force will be repelled with force by a public which is now resolved to make its sovereignty respected." Madero would renounce his candidacy, he said, as soon as victory was achieved if a revolution developed as a result of government persecution, for he had no desire

---

[30] Un Antirreeleccionista [Madero], "El Sr. Dr. Dn. Francisco Vázquez Gómez," *ibid.*, January 7, 1934, p. 2.

[31] *La enseñanza secundaria en el Distrito Federal,* published in 1907.

[32] Estrada, *La revolución y Francisco I. Madero,* 218.

[33] For complete statement, see Taracena, *Madero,* 253–55; or Estrada, *La revolución y Francisco I. Madero,* 218–22.

107

to come to the presidency through armed force, and he wanted to bring to an end the practice of having the "presidential chair . . . occupied by the soldier [who had been] victorious in fratricidal strife."[34]

In the program itself there were few essential differences from that already propounded by the committee. Madero favored the retention of the status quo with regard to the Laws of Reform until they could be revised by Congress to meet the public desires; while he did not say that he favored revision toward leniency, the implication was clear. He also favored combating any form of monopoly and wished to have foreign capital receive the same treatment as domestic investment. As for relations with the United States, he suggested not only friendly, but fraternal associations.[35]

The latter days of April and early May saw many pro-Madero public demonstrations in Mexico City. The government made some threatening gestures, one of the rallies being dispersed by the police, but in general the activities of the Antire-electionists in Mexico City met with little interference.[36] Madero soon resumed his speaking tour, going first to Guadalajara, where two successful demonstrations were held on May 8 without interruption from the local officials.[37] He then returned to Mexico in preparation for a tour of the eastern states.

The government's abstention from intervening to that point was encouraging to the Antire-electionists, and even Don Francisco was moved to observe that "without doubt . . . the lack of molestation is the result of the influence of Díaz, who truly wants the public spirit awakened." Don Francisco was probably voicing a hope rather than a belief, however, for he also gave proper thanks for the fact that Madero had been able to hold the Guadalajara meetings without suffering imprisonment and hoped he would always be so forutnate in the "unequal struggle."[38] The freedom continued for a time; Madero was not restrained from going to Puebla, where, as a result of the efforts of Aquiles Serdán, approximately thirty thousand people paraded through the streets in a demonstration for Madero.[39] The success of the Puebla meeting, hard on the heels of the Guadalajara and Mexico City demonstrations, encouraged Madero's family, who now became ac-

---

[34] For the complete address, see Taracena, *Madero,* 239 ff.
[35] *Ibid.*
[36] Casasola, *Historia gráfica,* I, 146.
[37] Estrada, *La revolución y Francisco I. Madero,* 223–24.
[38] Don F. Madero to Madero, May 9, 1910, *LO,* February 25, 1934, p. 2.
[39] Valadés, "La primera presa de la revolución," *ibid.,* March 11, 1934, p. 1; G. Madero to Madero, May 17, 1910, *ibid.,* February 25, 1934, p. 2.

tively interested in the campaign. Don Francisco again congratulated his son, and even Gustavo, practical man of business, believed it would be possible to win the election. Gustavo, in fact, was so optimistic even before the Puebla meeting that he had bought a newspaper plant to aid the campaign.[40]

But the honeymoon was almost over. Madero had hardly left Puebla for Jalapa and other points east when the persecutions began. He was not molested, but the local Puebla officials started closing in on the more active party members, badgering Serdán, subjecting his family to many galling restrictions, and confining most of the club officers to prison on one pretext or another.[41]

Madero himself was partly responsible for the increasing severity of governmental action. His statements were becoming consistently more direct and his attacks more virile and personal. Jalapa, Veracruz, and Orizaba held great demonstrations in the week following Madero's departure from Puebla on May 17. In each city Madero raised the public to a high pitch of excitement by reference to such practices as the brutal manner in which the strikers had been subdued at Río Blanco.[42] Estrada characterized the Orizaba speech as one which would incite to rebellion: it was not a coldly analytical condemnation of the government, but an appeal presented with emotion.[43] Madero was not deliberately fomenting revolution, but his own emotions frequently aroused passions to the boiling point.

By the time Madero returned to Mexico from his Orizaba tour, the repressive measures taken by various local officials had become so evident that the Central Committee feared a premature rebellion in reaction to the treatment. In order to forestall such a disaster, in the name of the party Emilio Vázquez Gómez sent a letter to every organized club in the country asking the officials in each to stress to all their members the paramount importance of patience and peace in the face of repression. All state governors were sent copies of the circular and asked to prevent persecution.[44]

[40] Don F. Madero to Madero, May 23, 1910, *ibid.*, February 25, 1934, pp. 2, 8; G. Madero to Madero, April 18 and May 23, 1910, *ibid.*, pp. 1, 2.
[41] Valadés, "La primera presa de la revolución," *ibid.*, March 11, 1934, p. 1; Madero to Díaz, May 26, 1910, *ibid.*, February 18, 1934, pp. 1, 8.
[42] Taracena, *Madero*, 277.
[43] Estrada, *La revolución y Francisco I. Madero*, 228–29.
[44] Circular letter signed by E. Vázquez Gómez, May 25, 1910, *El Diario del Hogar*, September 5, 1910, p. 1. Copies sent to the governors were dated June 2, 1910.

Madero appealed directly to Díaz, reminding the President of the promises which had been made and then pointing out the breaches of those promises. In Coahuila all Maderista demonstrations had been banned and all Antire-electionist publicity prevented. In San Luis Potosí, Aguascalientes, and Nuevo León the same situation prevailed. In Sonora, independent newspapermen had been jailed on flimsy pretexts, and in Cananea all officers of the Antire-electionist club had been imprisoned. Hundreds of men had been confined to prison in Puebla, Tlaxcala, and Atlixco. Madero warned Díaz of impending rebellion if the repressions continued, and declined to take responsibility if his supporters took "justice into their own hands" and destroyed the peace.[45]

Madero himself had not yet been molested, and he did not allow the threat of personal inconvenience or harm to deter him from fulfilling his political commitments. On June 3 he and Roque Estrada departed for the northern states, which Madero had not visited since the preceding summer. A large crowd met the train in San Luis Potosí, allowing both Madero and Roque Estrada to speak without police interference. At the Saltillo station the police attempted to disperse the crowd which gathered to hear the speakers, but the temper of the crowd forced the police to retire without carrying out their threat of arresting the candidate.[46]

Before Madero's departure from Mexico it was known that he was to stop in Monterrey, and the officials there made preparation. General Gerónimo Treviño assured his superiors that he and Governor Mier had been successful in nullifying every move made by the Antire-electionists.[47] The municipal president notified Corral that the local authorities had control of the situation, but advised stern action against all opposition in order to demonstrate the omnipotence of the government. Madero's supporters, even though they had been prevented from holding any demonstrations, circulated the pertinent information concerning the planned rally and invited all men of independent political thought to greet the candidate at the station when the train arrived.[48] Of the thousands who gathered, only a few were able to get into the station and greet the travelers because the authorities refused to allow

---

[45] Madero to Díaz, May 26, 1910, *LO,* February 18, 1934, pp. 1, 8.

[46] Estrada, *La revolución y Francisco I. Madero,* 236, 237; Madero manifesto, June 14, 1910, in Taracena, *Madero,* 290–94.

[47] Treviño to Corral, June 1, 1910, *LO,* October 10, 1937, p. 1.

[48] I. Zambrano to Corral, June 4, 1910, *LP,* January 23, 1938, p. 1. For the announcement, see *LP,* January 23, 1938, p. 1.

any but railroad ticket holders into the area.[49] The crowd which attempted to escort Madero to his father's home was effectively dispersed by the police, and only a small group appeared at the destination to hear the candidate deliver a short address. During Estrada's speech immediately following that of Madero, the chief of police ordered Estrada to refrain from speaking. The speaker's refusal to comply with the order brought on a heated exchange between the two men, and, according to the police, Estrada was "disrespectful" to the officials.[50] This alleged disrespect led to an attempt to arrest Estrada on the following day as he was leaving the house with Madero. Madero intervened to examine the credentials of the arresting officers, who were dressed in plain clothes, and 'in the ensuing confusion Estrada escaped.[51] Madero continued to the railroad station, for his train was waiting to take him to San Pedro;[52] but soon after he went aboard, the local police forced the train to remain in the station while a thorough search was made for Estrada. When he could not be found, Madero was arrested for having aided him in his escape.[53]

In the meantime, events in Yucatán completely unconnected with the Madero movement had their effect on Madero. Noticeable unrest in the peninsular state had become more vociferous with the arrest of Delio Moreno Cantón in late 1909; and when an uprising started in Valladolid on June 4, 1910, the immediate supposition was that the rebellion was coupled with both Moreno Cantón and Madero. Actually it was independent of both, being a result of purely local conditions, but the government, lacking specific and accurate information concerning the motivation for the rebellion, concluded that Madero was responsible and ordered his arrest.[54] His incarceration was a foregone conclusion, even had Yucatán remained peaceful. General Treviño later applauded the arrest because Madero was fomenting unrest; Yucatán was not mentioned.[55] It was an accident that the Monterrey

[49] Subsequently, while Madero was in jail, he wrote a description of the events leading up to his arrest, with the intent of having the account published, but it did not reach the press. See *LO,* August 15, 1937, p. 1.
[50] Estrada, *La revolución y Francisco I. Madero,* 238, 239.
[51] Madero manifesto, June 14, 1910, in Taracena, *Madero,* 290–94.
[52] Estrada (*La revolución y Francisco I. Madero,* 240) said that Madero was going to Victoria, but Madero, in his account, said he was going to San Pedro.— *LO,* August 15, 1937, p. 1.
[53] See Madero's account, *LO,* August 15, 1937, p. 1.
[54] Menéndez, *La primera chispa de la revolución,* 41, 51–54, 61; Mier to Corral, June 10, 1910, *LO,* October 17, 1937, p. 2.
[55] Treviño to Corral, June 6, 1910, *LO,* October 10, 1937, p. 2.

episode coincided with the Yucatán movement in time, but it was quite clear that Madero could not be held indefinitely on either charge. The original intent was to charge the candidate with inciting to rebellion in Monterrey, but the local federal judge was doubtful about the legality of the charge since Madero had made practically no statements in that region. General Mier accordingly instructed Juan R. Orcí, one of Corral's secretaries, to charge Madero with having made inflammatory statements in San Luis Potosí.[56] Fearing that her husband would be the victim of the *ley fuga* when he was arrested, in somewhat the same fashion as Gabriel Leyva was shortly thereafter eliminated,[57] Señora Sara Pérez de Madero requested and received permission to accompany him to jail; she remained at his side until permission was withdrawn in the latter part of the month.[58]

Even though his arrest was not particularly displeasing, for it made his cause more popular,[59] Madero roundly denounced Díaz for not fulfilling his promises. Mexican law, Madero said, "although observed by my supporters, has been frequently violated by yours who occupy public posts, and although you . . . denied that the Federation could intervene in the states in order to guarantee individual liberties, . . . [the federal authorities] have intervened to support the stifling acts committed by the local authorities." He charged Díaz with consistent dishonesty in allowing political repression. The public, he said, was determined to have a constitutional, and not a "paternal," form of government. He concluded with this warning:

But if you and Señor Corral insist on having yourselves re-elected in spite of the national will, and if you continue the offenses committed . . . in order to have the official candidates triumph, and if you try to employ fraud again . . . in the next elections, then, General Díaz, you will be responsible to the nation, to the world, and even to history if there is a breach of the peace as a result.[60]

Madero urged his supporters not to be discouraged because he was in jail or to allow the circumstances attendant upon his imprisonment

[56] Mier to Corral, June 10, 1910, *ibid.*, October 17, 1937, p. 2; Estrada, *La revolución y Francisco I. Madero*, 236.
[57] Taracena, *En el vértigo de la revolución mexicana,* 66.
[58] See Madero's account, *LO,* August 15, 1937, p. 1.
[59] Madero to M. Urquidi, June 11, 1910, in Casasola, *Historia gráfica,* I, 152.
[60] Madero to Díaz, June 15, 1910, in Taracena, *Madero,* 285–90.

to dampen their ardor; the very fact that he was in jail made it all the more important to bend every effort to gain victory at the polls.[61]

Although Madero's arrest may not have been surprising to him, and although he considered it to have certain advantages, it tended to make some of the party members more circumspect. Francisco Vázquez Gómez, fearful of further persecutions and pessimistic over the future, was therefore willing to listen when a group of anti-Corral Porfiristas proposed the election of Díaz and Teodoro Dehesa as a compromise with the Antire-electionists.[62] Since Dehesa, whose star was in the ascendancy,[63] was not only one of the most popular governors for his effective and just administration but was also considered to be a violent anti-Científico, favorable to the principle of no re-election, Vázquez Gómez strongly recommended supporting his candidacy.[64] Madero's immediate response was that it would be "indecorous and inexpedient to enter into any arrangements" so long as he was a prisoner because any compromise now would make it appear that he had been intimidated, which would in turn alienate supporters.[65] Vázquez Gómez, believing that a failure to take advantage of the political conditions favoring the compromise would preclude any hope of political reform, was disappointed at Madero's stand.[66]

In the meantime both the Círculo Nacional Porfirista and the Partido Democrático had announced their support of Dehesa for the vice-presidency and had drawn some support away from the Antire-electionists. Francisco Vázquez Gómez, to whom Madero had sent both the June 15 letter to Díaz and the June 14 manifesto for purposes of publication, decided it would be "inopportune" to have either appear under existing conditions.[67] Madero then practically ordered the vice-presidential candidate to publish both items, saying that he considered them of prime importance; but Vázquez still demurred on the

---

[61] Madero manifesto, June 14, 1910, *ibid.*, 290–94. He wrote the manifesto while in prison in Monterrey, but it was not published at the time.

[62] F. Vázquez Gómez to Madero, June 15, 1910, *MP*, 48–50.

[63] See Carillo to Corral, June 25, 1910; González Mena to Corral, June 23, 1910; González Mena to Sentíes, June 23, 1910; Sentíes to González Mena, June 23, 1910, *LO*, January 30, 1938, p. 2. Also, series of letters from J. Martínez Baca to Corral, dated June 26, 27, 28, 30, and July 1, 1910, *LP*, January 9, 1938, pp. 1, 7.

[64] F. Vázquez Gómez to Madero, June 15, 1910, *MP*, 48–50.

[65] Madero to F. Vázquez Gómez, June 21, 1910, *ibid.*, 50–51.

[66] F. Vázquez Gómez to Madero, June 23, 1910, *LO*, January 7, 1934, p. 2.

[67] Taracena, *En el vértigo de la revolución mexicana*, 64; F. Vázquez Gómez to Madero, June 23, 1910, *LO*, January 7, 1934, p. 2.

grounds that he could find no one willing to publish them and that their publication would make a settlement more difficult. The doctor favored further action only if Corral were elected; if Díaz finally selected Dehesa, he was determined to take no action at all.[68]

There now began to appear a fundamental difference between Vázquez Gómez and Madero on questions of policy. The primary election was held on June 26 amid scenes of indisputable fraud,[69] even though peace had generally prevailed.[70] To Madero the question of a compromise was now a dead issue, for any attempt to come to an agreement would give tacit consent to the fraudulent elections, and this he could not bring himself to do.[71] Francisco Vázquez Gómez, on the other hand, strongly favored any arrangement which would keep Corral out of the vice-presidency, regardless of the manner in which a compromise had to be carried out. Even after the primary elections Dr. Vázquez Gómez was optimistic over Dehesa's chances; but the electoral college, following instructions from Díaz, announced on July 10 that Díaz and Corral had received the majority of votes in the primary election.[72] Congress still had to act officially to name the successful candidates, and both the Vázquez Gómez brothers believed that Díaz could be prevailed upon to order Congress to declare Dehesa the successful candidate.[73]

In the latter part of the summer, with the Dehesa question still unsettled, a group of Científicos who cordially hated Dehesa and feared that Díaz might, after all, select him, proposed informally to Francisco Vázquez Gómez that he himself could expect their support in case it appeared that Díaz was going to select Dehesa. Dr. Vázquez then asked Madero to propose such a compromise to the government.[74] Madero, however, was irrevocably committed to oppose any attempt at

[68] Madero to F. Vázquez Gómez, June 24, 1910, *LO,* January 7, 1934, p. 2; F. Vázquez Gómez to Madero, June 27, 1910, *ibid.*

[69] Comité Ejecutivo Electoral Antirreeleccionista, *Memorial presentada a la Cámara de Diputados, pidiendo la nulidad de las elecciones,* passim. An inventory of the materials presented in the memorial was published in *El Diario del Hogar,* September 4, 1910, p. 1.

[70] *Times* (London), June 28, 1910, p. 5.

[71] Madero statement, August 15, 1910, *El Diario del Hogar,* August 17, 1910, p. 1.

[72] F. Vázquez Gómez to Madero, July 6, 1910, *LO,* January 7, 1934, p. 2; Taracena, *En el vértigo de la revolución mexicana,* 66.

[73] Taracena, *Madero,* 304.

[74] F. Vázquez Gómez to Madero, August 22, 1910, *LO,* January 14, 1934, p. 1.

compromise and therefore refused even to suggest the solution proposed, his final answer being a sharp reminder that continuing attempts at compromise were in bad taste and should cease immediately.[75] The maneuvering of his running mate only heightened Madero's misgivings concerning Vázquez Gómez' loyalty, and his suspicions were bolstered by the findings of Francisco Cosío Robelo. Cosío Robelo was convinced, along with Heriberto Frías, that the Vázquez Gómez brothers were traitors to the party and to Madero, being interested only in personal advancement. He urged Madero to act immediately to prevent the complete disintegration of the party, which even then, lacking Madero's leadership, showed signs of advanced deterioration.[76] But the popular candidate, now free on bail[77] though legally restricted to San Luis Potosí, was in no position to spark a resurgence of party activity.

The party fortunes were indeed at a low ebb. Francisco Vázquez Gómez insisted on maintaining his status as a political moderate, particularly since that very moderateness had been a strong factor in his selection as a candidate, despite accusations by the "intransigents" that the "moderates were traitors to the party."[78] His brother Emilio, too, was advocating compromise, combating critical commentaries against the government as both unwise and inexpedient. In addition, he feigned to see personal ambition rather than principle in Madero's adamant stand against compromise, and decried the greedy desire for office which many of Madero's more ardent followers seemed to display.[79] As he phrased it, he favored an "independent" rather than an "oppositionist" position. To Madero these were synonymous terms in 1910.

At least one portion of the party was active, nevertheless, in spite of the adverse conditions; the Executive Committee worked all summer collecting material to prove fraud at the polls in the primary election, and this even though some of the committee had been forced into exile or hiding. Under the able direction of Federico González Garza, Antire-electionist committees in nineteen states and territories compiled

[75] F. Vázquez Gómez to Madero, August 24, 1910, *ibid.*, p. 2. The doctor here lamented Madero's attitude and justified his own.
[76] Cosío to Madero, undated, *ibid.*
[77] He was freed on July 22.
[78] F. Vázquez Gómez to Madero, August 27, 1910, *LO*, January 14, 1934, p. 2.
[79] E. Vázquez Gómez to unknown addressee, undated, *ibid.* This is a fragment only; the text places the approximate date.

115

137 documents, including affidavits, patently fraudulent ballots, and other such materials, to present to Congress in support of the demand for nullifying the election. The memorial closed with these words:

The public has complied with its duty; the government now should comply with its duties, and the most immediate of these is justice. But if . . . [the government] fails to recognize this obligation . . . the responsibility for having broken the harmony between the government and the governed will not fall on the public.[80]

On the whole, however, the stand taken by the Executive Committee was a cry in the wilderness. Gustavo Madero rather aptly summed up the situation in late August when he plaintively said that the elections were over and so everyone was willing to forget the methods used and to accept the status quo.[81]

In the meantime Madero's status changed and his opinions underwent a profound transformation. After Juan Orcí had charged Madero and Estrada (who had surrendered the day after Madero's arrest) with inciting to rebellion in San Luis Potosí, they were transferred to that city on June 21. The transfer interrupted plans for an escape which were being perfected by Gustavo with the compliance of the warden.[82] In San Luis there was no effort to bring them to trial quickly since the principal reason for the arrest had been to remove Madero from the political scene until after the elections. The prisoners were hailed into court often, but it was not until early July that there was any evidence of action concerning Madero; it was then rumored that he would be given his freedom if he would leave the country for Europe.[83] If the offer was ever made, it was not publicized; and Madero never mentioned it. After the secondary elections had been authenticated, the first steps were taken to release the men on bail. On July 22 both Madero and Estrada were released on bond, but they were constrained to remain within the confines of the city of San Luis Potosí.[84]

---

[80] Comité Ejecutivo Electoral Antirreeleccionista, *Memorial presentada a la Cámara de Diputados*. The committee presented the memorial to Congress on September 1.

[81] G. Madero to Madero, August 27, 1910, *LO,* March 11, 1934, p. 2.

[82] Estrada, *La revolución y Francisco I. Madero,* 244, 255; Taracena, *En el vértigo de la revolución mexicana,* 64.

[83] F. Vázquez Gómez to Madero, July 6, 1910, *LO,* January 7, 1934, p. 2.

[84] Madero to Urquidi, July 13, 1910, in Casasola, *Historia gráfica,* I, 154; court order signed by Tomás Ortiz and Julio Betancourt, July 22, 1910, *El Universal,* August 28, 1941.

Even before they were freed on bail, the two prisoners had been discussing with Gustavo and Rafael Cepeda the possibility of revolution. July 14 had been set tentatively as the date to begin, but all concerned soon realized that insufficient planning had been done and the project was accordingly abandoned.[85] The next two months were filled with many indications of increasing tension and impending trouble. Army officers in Mexico City were reportedly collecting arms and ammunition for a pro-Madero revolution.[86] A small uprising of Huastec Indians in San Luis Potosí was erroneously interpreted to be Madero-inspired.[87] Minor movements in Sonora and Sinaloa amounted to nothing, but a rebellion fostered by the Flores Magón group in Veracruz was of greater import although easily subdued.[88] Persecution and repression were commonplace in Yucatán, and a number of Antireelectionists, including such men as Juan Sánchez Azcona, Enrique Bordes Mangel, and Aquiles Serdán, had quit the country and were in San Antonio, Texas, awaiting leadership and a favorable opportunity to rebel.[89]

While these events were transpiring, Madero was undecided as to his course of action. He was under almost constant surveillance and could do little, but more important was his desire to have recourse to arms only as a last resort. Until Congress had officially and irrevocably declared Díaz and Corral elected, there was a chance, though slight, that the administration would reconsider its position and allow a new election. On September 27 the Deputies finally took action; the Antireelectionist request for a nullification of the election was declared to be unjustified, and Díaz and Corral were named president and vice-president for the following term. One course only was now open to Madero: he must begin the insurrection, and in order to lead it he must be free.

After considering various means of escaping the surveillance of the government, Madero and Rafael Cepeda concluded that the best route by which to leave the country would be the railroad to Nuevo Laredo. On the night of October 5 the final plans were agreed upon; the next

[85] Estrada, *La revolución y Francisco I. Madero,* 263–66.
[86] Beltrán to Corral, August 3, 1910, *LO,* November 21, 1937, p. 1.
[87] *El Diario del Hogar,* August 12, 1910, p. 1.
[88] M. Iriarte to A. Vega, July 3, 1910, *LP,* October 3, 1937, p. 7; Casasola, *Historia gráfica,* I, 160.
[89] Pino Suárez to Madero, July 25, 1910, *LO,* March 18, 1934, p. 1; Pino Suárez to Madero, September 15, 1910, *ibid.,* p. 2; Sánchez Azcona to Madero, September 21, 1910, *ibid.,* March 11, 1934, p. 2.

117

morning Madero, dressed as a mechanic, secretly boarded the northbound train which was to carry him to freedom, and the next day Estrada and Rafael Cepeda followed by the same route.[90] It was now clear, even to Díaz, that Madero planned to rebel.

[90] For a description of the planning and the escape, see Estrada, *La revolución y Francisco I. Madero,* 287–93.

Madero and the cabinet of the provisional government

Madero (seated) ; José María Pino Suárez, *Public Instruction;* Dr. Francisco Vázquez Gómez, *Foreign Relations;* Venustiano Carranza, *War and Marine;* Federico González Garza, *Gobernación;* and Manuel Bonilla, *Communications*

Madero entering Mexico City, June 7, 1911

VI

The Revolution

WHEN MADERO ARRIVED in San Antonio, Texas, he found himself in a compromising position. From the beginning of his political career he had consistently decried the evils of revolution, constantly warning his compatriots of his repugnance toward the use of force.[1] He had bent his efforts to prevent revolutionary activity in his behalf immediately before and after his arrest;[2] but now all other means had been exhausted and he felt impelled, as the leader of a persecuted group, to take action in support of his principles. Having excoriated Reyes for his lethargy in the face of the arrest and exile of many Reyistas, Madero now could hardly be satisfied with inaction in view of the trials and tribulations to which his own supporters had been subjected. In addition, he was firmly convinced that the majority of the Mexicans viewed their government with discontent and disgust, that their dissatisfaction demanded a change. With the election of Ramón Corral to the vice-presidency all hope of reform was lost, for nothing in the past pointed to a diminution of absolutism or to greater political freedom once Corral took over the presidency.

That the public demanded a change can be of little doubt. Not all the malcontents wished to have Madero as president, to be sure, but much resentment was engendered by the arrest and imprisonment of the one independent candidate who had had the courage to face the government. One unknown writer admirably reflected this sentiment when he said to Corral, "I repeat to you that as far as we are concerned it could be Madero or anyone else; what we do not want is a continuation of the present state of affairs."[3] The resentment and bit-

---

[1] Madero, *La sucesión presidencial en 1910,* 56; Madero to Pino Suárez, August 15, 1909, *LO,* March 18, 1934, p. 1.

[2] Madero to Díaz, May 26, 1910, *LO,* February 18, 1934, pp. 1, 7; and June 15, 1910, in Taracena, *Madero,* 285–90.

[3] Anonymous letter to Corral, July 8, 1910, *LO,* February 6, 1938, p. 2.

terness needed leadership; and since Madero had been responsible for the crystallization of that feeling, it was incumbent upon him to assume direction of events.

Shortly after his arrival, Madero was publicly proclaimed president of a revolutionary junta to lead an insurrection, dispelling any supposition that he had left Mexico merely to obtain his freedom.[4] He then addressed himself to the American people, asking only for the "hospitality which all free peoples have always accorded to those from other lands who strive for liberty." He was, he said, the representative of the democratic desires of the Mexicans, appealing not for help but for understanding. His only mission in the United States was to organize a revolution against the dictatorial government, an insurrection which was to be carried on by Mexicans without foreign aid. He neither expected nor desired material assistance from the United States or its people. His only hope was that "the American public will be able to appreciate my conduct and will understand . . . [the justification of] my ambition to reconquer for my beloved land that happiness which it deserves."[5]

Giving aid to Madero in the formulation of revolutionary plans were many of those who had been most active in the prosecution of the electoral campaign. In addition to his brothers Julio, Raúl, and Alfonso, the exiles included Juan Sánchez Azcona, Roque Estrada, Rafael Cepeda, Federico González Garza, Aquiles Serdán, and Enrique Bordes Mangel, as well as numerous men whose names were not nationally known. On the other hand, neither of the Vázquez Gómez brothers was in the United States, nor was Madero's own brother Gustavo. Madero invited Francisco Vázquez Gómez to join the group and help draft the revolutionary plan, but the erstwhile vice-presidential candidate wished to dissociate himself completely from the movement and left Mexico only because he was "not disposed to suffer the consequences of acts" for which he was not responsible, fearing that he would be persecuted if he remained in Mexico City. On November 2 he and Emilio departed for San Antonio, seeking that city as a haven of refuge and not as a center of revolutionary activity.[6]

The government, in the meantime, arrested Gustavo Madero, probably in the hope of forestalling any action by his elder brother. But Ma-

[4] *FR*, 1911, p. 350.
[5] Madero, "To the American People," October 9, 1910, *San Antonio Express*, October 11, 1910.
[6] Madero to F. Vázquez Gómez, October 17, 1910, in Taracena, *Madero*, 335–37; F. Vázquez Gómez, *Memorias políticas*, 59.

dero, considering it his duty to consult the interests of the nation before those of his family, continued his planning, and Gustavo was soon released and the charges dropped.[7] It may well be that Gustavo was freed, as his father claimed, because the government wished to minimize the appearance of danger posed by the impending revolution.[8]

During October the revolutionary plan, ultimately published as the Plan de San Luis Potosí, was in the process of formulation. Madero completed the rough draft of the plan in late October and then submitted it for revision to a board consisting of Estrada, González Garza, Sánchez Azcona, Bordes Mangel, and Ernesto Fernández. The final wording was settled in early November.[9]

In order to prevent, if possible, international repercussions, the plan was given the date of October 5, the last night Madero had been in San Luis Potosí. The program itself was relatively simple in wording and concept.[10] The recent elections were declared null and void, and the government officials were not recognized as legally holding office.[11] Madero assumed the title of provisional president, with the power to declare war on the Díaz government, but with the stipulation that as soon as the capital was occupied by "the forces of the public" and at least half the states were in the hands of the insurgents, a presidential election would be held.[12] Strict military discipline was to be exercised by the revolutionary forces, and the armies were to operate within the framework of the recognized laws of war.[13] In case the federal troops engaged in activities which were contrary to the laws of war, the officials responsible for the orders culminating in those actions were to be given a summary trial as soon as captured. General Díaz and his ministers were to be exempt from this provision only to the extent that they would be tried by a civil rather than a military court.[14]

The provisional president was empowered to appoint provisional governors of the states, but in case he could not make such appointments, for any reason, the principal revolutionary leaders of the area

[7] Madero to F. Vázquez Gómez, October 17, 1910, in Taracena, *Madero*, 335–37.
[8] As quoted in *Regeneración*, November 5, 1910, p. 1.
[9] Estrada, *La revolución y Francisco I. Madero*, 308–309.
[10] The Plan may be found in various places, including Naranjo, *Diccionario biográfico revolucionario*, 264–68, and in English translation in *Investigation of Mexican Affairs*, 66 Cong., 2 sess., *Sen. Doc. 285*, II, 2631–33.
[11] Articles 1 and 2.   [12] Article 5.
[13] Transitory article, section B; Article 8.
[14] Transitory article, section C.

121

were to make the designation; each provisional governor was to hold elections for all posts as soon as possible.[15] At the triumph of the revolution there was to be a general revision of all laws and decrees which had gone into effect during the Díaz regime, with immediate abrogation of those considered to be in conflict with the principles of the revolution. All public officials were also to have their work reviewed, and those guilty of fraud, peculation, or corruption in office were to be held responsible for their acts.[16] Illegal acquisitions of land were also to be subject to review, with a provision for the restitution of the lands or payment for them, depending on the circumstances of the case.[17] A stipulation against the re-election of high government officials, including the president, vice-president, state governors, and municipal presidents, was also included.[18]

The revolutionary plan was not imposing as a political document, nor was it intended to be. It had little of political philosophy or socioeconomic doctrine, the greater part of the provisions dealing with the administrative aspects of the movement. The Plan de San Luis Potosí was not intended to be a program of reform to be put into effect at the conclusion of the insurrection; it was merely a guide for the disaffected to follow in the ensuing campaigns, a means by which the government was to be changed. The plan was a reflection of Madero's consistent belief that political reform must precede social and economic reform, that it was futile to speak of improving the general condition of the Mexican people until changes had been wrought in the political structure.

Accompanying the Plan de San Luis Potosí was an appeal to the army, for "the mission of the Army is to defend the institutions, and not to sustain tyranny."[19] Since the triumph of the revolution, Madero insisted, was "inevitable," the army would determine the length, not the success, of the revolution. Nevertheless, no large segment of the military ever joined the revolutionary forces.

In early November, copies of the plan were distributed in various parts of Mexico, the messengers of the junta keeping the local leaders informed of the plans being made.[20] No well co-ordinated movement

---

[15] Article 10.   [16] Article 3.
[17] *Ibid.* This provision has been subject to much discussion and misinterpretation and will be discussed at length in Chapter 10.
[18] Article 4.
[19] "Manifiesto al ejército mexicano," October 5, 1910, VC.
[20] Vasconcelos, *Ulises criollo,* 414–15.

was outlined. Leaders were assigned for specific areas, in which small uprisings were presumably to be followed by a general conflagration; and available funds were distributed among the local leaders for the purchase of arms and ammunition.[21] Provisional governors were appointed for those states which seemed likely to fall to the revolutionists within a relatively short time.[22] Madero himself was to lead the forces in the northern states after entering Mexico at Ciudad Porfirio Díaz.[23]

In the meantime the picture was obscured and complicated by events having no connection with Madero. The latent anti-American feeling which had become obvious to the United States ambassador by the autumn of 1910 flared into open hostility when Antonio Rodríguez was lynched by burning at Rock Springs, Texas, on November 4, 1910. A mob in Mexico City trampled an American flag, stoned the building of the American-owned *Mexican Herald,* and created other disturbances. In Guadalajara and other centers, similar manifestations of animosity occurred. In the midst of the demonstrations in Mexico City, which lasted for several days after the lynching, government agents discovered arms, ammunition, and some commissions signed by Madero in the possession of Francisco Cosío Robelo. Díaz immediately assumed that the anti-American demonstrations, fostered by the Madero protagonists, were a "convenient cloak" under which the revolutionists could operate.[24] In reality the riots were the result of deep-rooted hostility toward foreigners in general and Americans in particular, not the result of any anti-American propaganda disseminated by Madero or his supporters. Madero, always careful not to offend the United States, made no attempt to take advantage of a situation on which he could have capitalized with success. Inevitably, some of the men who joined the Madero movement did so because of hostility toward the foreigners who were reaping profits and advantages from the Díaz regime, but the movement against Díaz was never characterized by antiforeign sentiment.

[21] Estrada, *La revolución y Francisco I. Madero,* 319–20. Financing the revolution was a major problem. Madero had little cash on hand, most of the principals were men of moderate means, and money could not be borrowed to finance such an uncertain venture.

[22] Estrada, *La revolución y Francisco I. Madero,* 331–32; Casasola, *Historia gráfica,* I, 225.

[23] Rafael Aguilar, *Madero sín máscara,* 20.

[24] Wilson to State Department, October 31 and November 10 and 14, 1910, *FR,* 1911, pp. 353, 354–55, 358–59; Wilson to Creel, November 9 and 12, 1910, *ibid.,* 355, 357; Wilson memorandum, November 14, 1910, *ibid.,* 361.

The embarrassment to the government growing out of the riots may have given temporary aid and comfort to the revolutionists, but the rioting also led to the arrest of Cosío Robelo, and his apprehension led in turn to others. The ever widening circle brought evidence, by November 16, of the date scheduled for the uprising, as well as information leading to wholesale arrests and seizure of munitions of war within the next two days. In the meantime, the activities of Madero in San Antonio being well known to Díaz, the Mexican government was requesting preventive steps by the United States.[25]

In Puebla, where he had armed and equipped over five hundred men, Aquiles Serdán was impatiently waiting for November 20, the date he was scheduled to begin the movement in his state. Obtaining advance information concerning a police raid projected for November 18, however, Serdán determined to begin the insurrection by resisting the search.[26] A plan for concerted action failed, and Serdán and most of his family were killed, making this, the first action in Madero's behalf, a dismal failure even though a heavy toll had been taken of the attacking government forces.[27]

The Puebla disaster had no immediate effect on the over-all revolutionary plans, however, for most of the small contingents of revolutionaries were already on the move before the news was circulated. Madero, after sending Gustavo to Washington as his confidential agent,[28] left San Antonio for Ciudad Porfirio Díaz, which he considered would be easily captured. But the campaign against the border city was from the beginning a comedy of errors. After successfully negotiating the crossing of the river on the night of November 19,[29] Madero found to his disappointment that the small army which was to have met him for the attack had failed to materialize and the arms and ammunition for which he had already paid had not been delivered. In the absence of men and munitions, no attack could be made; without firing a shot, Madero retraced his steps into American territory. He was profoundly discouraged and heartsick, all his cherished beliefs and plans appearing to be but dreams; but he refused to admit defeat and consequently de-

[25] F. L. de la Barra (Mexican ambassador) to State Department, November 16 and 17, 1910, *ibid.*, 362; Wilson to State Department, November 14, 15, and 18, 1910, *ibid.*, 359, 363–64.

[26] Valadés, "La primera presa de la revolución," *LO*, March 11, 1934, p. 1.

[27] Casasola, *Historia gráfica*, I, 204–206; Vasconcelos, *Ulises criollo*, 415.

[28] Estrada, *La revolución y Francisco I. Madero*, 335.

[29] Consul Ellsworth (C. Porfirio Díaz) to State Department, November 20, 1910, *FR*, 1911, p. 365.

The Revolution

cided to use New Orleans as a point of departure for one of the Mexican Gulf coast cities.[30] The New Orleans venture, too, was doomed to fail. The limited financial resources then at the command of the revolutionaries had been exhausted, the family wealth in Mexico was unavailable and threatened with confiscation, and the members of the San Antonio junta were destitute, often eating no more than one meal a day.[31] Gustavo's efforts in New York and Washington were to no avail in view of the reported eight-million-peso debt the family owed to various Mexican banks[32] and the failure of the revolution to attract a strong following. To all appearances, the revolution had foundered before it began.

Meanwhile the various assaults in the interior of Mexico were not total failures. Pascual Orozco, who had agreed to co-operate with Abraham González in Chihuahua,[33] captured Guerrero in late November while Doroteo Arango, better known as Francisco Villa, began his long revolutionary career by capturing San Andrés.[34] José María Maytorena in Sonora began a movement which soon grew until the state was infested with small revolutionary bands.[35] Jesús Agustín Castro's capture of Gómez Palacio, Durango, availed nought, for the palace was immediately recaptured.[36] Zacatecas was the scene of serious, but unorganized, movements; and those attempts to foster revolution along the Texas-Mexican border met with little success.[37] Parral, Coahuila, was momentarily threatened but was eventually saved by government reinforcements.[38]

In spite of these outbreaks, however, the revolution appeared to be a colossal failure, justifying the United States Ambassador's speaking, before the end of the month, of the "recent disturbances" and "at-

[30] Aguilar, *Madero sin máscara,* 22–23; Estrada, *La revolución y Francisco I. Madero,* 350–51.

[31] *Times* (London), November 25, 1910, p. 5; Estrada, *La revolución y Francisco I. Madero,* 355–57. Estrada speaks at length of the pangs of hunger endured by the group.

[32] W. F. McCaleb, testimony to Senate Subcommittee on Foreign Relations, November 18, 1919, *Investigation of Mexican Affairs,* I, 735.

[33] "20 de noviembre de 1910," an announcement of the movements beginning that day; this single sheet, found in the Biblioteca Hacienda, was circulated in Mexico City at the time.

[34] Casasola, *Historia gráfica,* I, 210–11, 213–15.

[35] Vasconcelos, *Ulises criollo,* 416.

[36] "20 de noviembre de 1910," in Biblioteca Hacienda.

[37] *Times* (London), November 22, 1910, p. 5; Commanding General, Department of Texas, to Adjutant General, November 23, 1910, *FR,* 1911, p. 365.

[38] "20 de noviembre de 1910," in Biblioteca Hacienda.

tempted revolution." Still there were noticeable evidences of unrest and dissatisfaction, for the movement had been "remarkable for its intensity and bitterness," the majority of the population in Mexico City being openly sympathetic toward the revolution and condemnatory toward the government.[39] One newspaper editor was jailed for speaking of the "heroic" efforts of the revolutionaries. Other newspapers were either suppressed or threatened with suppression for speaking too freely of the situation.[40] Most qualified observers agreed that the government was safe and the revolution dead, but that some changes would be necessary in the administration in order to insure the peace.

But the revolution was not even moribund; it was merely catching its breath after the first shock of defeat. Even though the new year showed little evidence of a major revolution in the making, the continued resistance of Orozco, Villa, José de la Luz Blanco, and other leaders in the north stimulated movements in other regions. Far to the south, conferences between Emiliano Zapata, Gabriel Tepepa, and Pablo Torres Burgos in Morelos culminated in sending Torres Burgos to San Antonio to discuss plans for co-operation with the Madero followers; and in the other southern states a number of small groups were beginning to operate.[41]

In the meantime Madero's own fortunes were at a low ebb. When he left San Antonio for New Orleans after the Ciudad Porfirio Díaz fiasco, he had designated his brother Alfonso and Federico González Garza as the directors of the revolutionary junta; but a combination of general discouragement and intense dissension among the revolutionaries prevented any effective work, and when Madero returned to San Antonio in late December to resume active direction of affairs, he found little to encourage him.[42] The dejection of the revolutionists was soon intensified when in late January, Madero was forced, by fear of arrest by American authorities, to seek refuge with family friends in Dallas,[43] where he remained until he was ready to return to the border.

While Madero was thus on the move, the Mexican government was attempting to induce the American government to take steps to circumscribe his activities and to prevent the spread of the revolution,

[39] Wilson to State Department, November 26, 1910, *FR*, 1911, pp. 367–68.
[40] *Times* (London), November 28 and December 1, 1910, p. 5.
[41] Gildardo Magaña, *Emiliano Zapata*, I, 108; Casasola, *Historia gráfica*, I, 223–26.
[42] Estrada, *La revolución y Francisco I. Madero*, 358–61, 368.
[43] Angela Madero de Treviño to C. C. Cumberland, June 17, 1947, in interview in Monterrey, Mexico.

preferably by effecting Madero's arrest. Continual protests and vo-
luminous correspondence elicited the information from the United
States government that since no state of war existed there could be no
breach of international law governing neutrality in time of war or
armed rebellion, and that proof of an overt act would be necessary to
prosecute under the so-called neutrality statutes of the northern country. Oral and written statements did not constitute punishable acts
under the existing statutes, but the Mexican government was requested
to furnish evidence in its possession of the commission of any punishable acts by either Madero or his supporters.[44] Although the United
States attorney for the district of El Paso was of the opinion that evidence to consummate Madero's arrest was lacking, it is now clear that
Madero was guilty of infractions of the American statutes.[45]

Desultory fighting between the revolutionaries and the government
forces was increasingly common in late December and in January, thus
leading Díaz to renew his protests, but again no proof was forthcoming
from Mexico. There was considerable confusion and uncertainty concerning the true state of affairs, with the Mexican officials apparently
repeating as fact any rumor of armed movements. This uncertainty,
which gave material aid to Madero, is clearly illustrated by a report of
the Mexican consul in El Paso, who reported to the United States
deputy marshal that a large number of armed men were banding together at a nearby Texas ranch for the purpose of attacking Mexico.[46]
Investigation by American officials ascertained that the men in question were unarmed wood choppers plying their trade, with neither intention nor desire to raid any Díaz outpost.[47] The consul also reported
the presence of Praxedis Guerrero in El Paso in late December, while
in fact Guerrero had been killed on December 10 during an attack on
Janos.[48]

Reports such as these, easily demonstrable as false, merely served to
obscure the actual conditions along the border, where sporadic attacks
were becoming a nuisance and the crossing and recrossing of the border
by Maderistas was commonplace. By late January the situation had
become so obvious that cavalry troops were sent to Brownsville, La-

[44] Secretary of State Knox to De la Barra, December 1, 1910, *FR*, 1911, pp.
370–71; Knox to Attorney General Wickersham, December 2, 1910, *ibid.*, 371–72.
[45] Wickersham to State Department, December 2, 1910, *ibid.*, 371.
[46] Lomelí to Hillebrand, December 24, 1910, *ibid.*, 389–90.
[47] Nolte to Wickersham, December 31, 1910, *ibid.*, 388–89.
[48] Lomelí to Hillebrand, December 24, 1910, *ibid.*, 389–90; J. C. León to
Editor of *La Opinión*, January 12, 1930, VC.

127

redo, Eagle Pass, and Del Rio, with orders to patrol the border but not to cross into Mexico under any provocation.[49] By late January, too, the patience of the American officials had worn thin at repeated charges and protests unsubstantiated by evidence. The government to the north had no desire to accept the entire responsibility for patrolling the border to prevent the passage of men, arms, and ammunition to the revolutionary forces.

This places the burden wholly upon the wrong side. It seems entirely clear that such matters [are no violation of our statutes] . . . and they must therefore, if they are illegal on the Mexican side of the border, be there met and overcome. You will . . . take no action which will . . . appear to shift the responsibility of maintaining peace on the Mexican side of the border from the Mexican Government, where it belongs, to this Government, where it does not belong.[50]

Regardless of the American officials' reluctance, however, there can be no doubt that Madero was guilty of frequent infractions of the federal statutes providing punishment for any person beginning or setting on foot from United States soil a military expedition against a friendly power. Madero obviously had set on foot operations against the Mexican government, and the failure of the United States to take action against him was noted by the members of the San Antonio junta, who drew the obvious inference. The government of the United States was demonstrating "an attitude of sympathy . . . in favor of the insurrectional cause in Mexico."[51] Finally, in February, after Madero had been in the United States for four months, Washington acceded to the oft-repeated requests from Díaz; federal officials in Texas were instructed to issue and execute a warrant for Madero's arrest.[52] Governor O. B. Colquitt of Texas even suggested going into Mexico, if need be, to arrest Madero and bring an end to the revolution.[53]

In the meantime, a general concentration of Chihuahua revolutionary forces in the vicinity of Ciudad Juárez made it appear as though the border city would fall to the insurgents in late January or early February. Since the capture of the city would mark an auspicious oc-

[49] Adjutant General to Commanding General, Department of Texas, January 24, 1911, *FR*, 1911, p. 395.
[50] W. J. Carr to Ellsworth, January 25, 1911, *ibid.*, 398–400.
[51] Estrada, *La revolución y Francisco I. Madero*, 377.
[52] Knox to Mexican Chargé d'Affaires, February 4, 1911, *FR*, 1911, p. 401.
[53] Colquitt to President Taft, February 23, 1911, *ibid.*, 410.

casion in the fortunes of the revolution, Abraham González notified Madero of the impending victory and recommended his joining the forces soon thereafter.[54] With February 5 set as the date of his triumphal return to his own country, Madero readied himself for the momentous event only to be the victim of another bitter disappointment; the timely arrival of government reinforcements enabled the defending forces to beat off and defeat the attackers under Pascual Orozco.[55]

The defeat and withdrawal of Orozco put Madero in a most peculiar position, since he preferred to postpone his re-entry until there was positive evidence of incipient success; but at the same time there were critics who insisted that the leader of the revolution should be with his men.[56] Confronted by this dilemma, Madero's first action was to apologize to Orozco's men for his absence, saying the "imperious necessities" in connection with the revolution prevented his joining the army.[57] His decision, reached over the vigorous protests of some of his advisors, was to remain in Texas for a more auspicious moment; but the order for his arrest forced him to make another change of plans, and on February 14 he quietly crossed the border to the west of El Paso.[58]

Soon after joining the revolutionary forces, Madero had a serious difference of opinion with some of his officers concerning the position occupied by José Garibaldi (grandson of the famous Giusseppe), who had joined Madero and whom Madero had designated as a member of his staff. Protesting the appointment on the basis of both principle and personality, the officers objected to the tacit authority which had been granted the foreigner. In an answer which was conspicuously undiplomatic and did little to heal wounded sensibilities, Madero insisted that he alone was the best judge of Garibaldi's competence, that the Italian's authority was not tacit but absolute, and that the function of the army officer was to execute, not to question, the orders of higher authority.[59] Garibaldi continued to serve the revolutionary forces until

---

[54] Aguilar, *Madero sín máscara*, 38.

[55] *Ibid.*, 38–39.

[56] It was not fear that made Madero hesitate; he believed it would be better psychologically to return on the crest of success.

[57] Madero, "A los soldados del ejército libertador de Chihuahua," February 18, 1911, in Taracena, *Madero*, 346–48.

[58] Aguilar, *Madero sín máscara*, 39; Estrada, *La revolución y Francisco I. Madero*, 395–96.

[59] Madero to his staff, February 28, 1911, in Taracena, *Madero*, 352–54.

the overthrow of Díaz, but his presence was a constant source of irritation to a number of the Mexicans.

Again in Mexico and at the head of a revolutionary force, Madero made a bid for belligerent status. Before leaving the United States, he had appointed Dr. Francisco Vázquez Gómez to serve as confidential agent and diplomatic representative to Washington in behalf of the provisional government, although the doctor had steadfastly refused to associate himself with the San Antonio junta.[60] Vázquez Gómez reluctantly accepted now only because the revolutionary activities seemed to presage eventual success;[61] but whether he went willingly or hesitantly, Madero had a diplomatic representative in Washington, and through him a request for recognition was made. Since, according to the note delivered by Vázquez Gómez to the Department of State, the provisional government had given ample evidence of its ability to protect foreigners, prosecute a war, and abide by the recognized rules of warfare, that government had earned and deserved recognition as a belligerent. Madero further agreed to accept the foreign commitments made by the Díaz government previous to November 20, 1910, and to accept full responsibility for damages sustained, to either person or property, by the nationals of those countries according recognition.[62]

The United States made no reply, nor should one have been made, for Madero hardly deserved belligerent status. The revolutionary force was largely concentrated in a small segment of Chihuahua, and even there no cities had been captured.[63] Not a single port of entry was yet in the hands of the rebels, the army had been unable to inflict a real defeat on the government forces, and at best the revolutionaries were employing guerrilla tactics. Madero needed an important victory; the time had come to put all hesitation behind and to inaugurate a strong offensive.

Before his return to Mexico, he and his advisors had drafted a plan of campaign which envisaged the capture of some of the smaller towns

[60] F. Vázquez Gómez, *Memorias políticas,* 60, 72.

[61] Toribio Esquivel Obregón, *Democracia y personalismo,* 23–24. Esquivel was not merely expressing an opinion here; according to him, Vázquez Gómez said as much to him in April, 1911.

[62] Provisional President of Mexico (Madero) to State Department, February 15, 1911, *FR,* 1911, pp. 437–38. This note, drafted before Madero left Texas, was presented March 27.

[63] The isolated movements in other areas were neither integrated nor cohesive, nor directly supervised by Madero.

in northern Chihuahua, the isolation and defeat of small units of the federal army, destruction of communications between the state capital and Ciudad Juárez, and the ultimate capture of the border city.[64] Leaving Orozco to his own devices in operations in the immediate vicinity of Ciudad Juárez, Madero began the implementation of the plan by taking personal command of a segment of the army and drawing near Casas Grandes, chosen as the first point of attack.

While Madero was maneuvering for a favorable position in northern Chihuahua, members of his family were attempting negotiations to bring the revolution to an end. The Madero family was feeling the pressure being applied by both governmental and financial forces during February. Not only were the Mexican banks insisting on payment of debts but the French bankers with whom the family habitually did a heavy business refused to give aid, and it was almost impossible to sell any produce or investments. To complicate matters, Gustavo was threatened with arrest and extradition as a result of a series of questionable financial transactions by which he had obtained funds for the revolution.[65] From the standpoint of family fortunes, the revolution was disastrous. Goaded by this realization, Ernesto Madero, Evaristo Madero y Hernández (brother of Ernesto and uncle of Francisco), and Rafael Hernández arrived in Corpus Christi to discuss the basis of peace with Don Francisco and Alfonso Madero, hoping to arrive at some informal understanding which could be presented to Díaz. Even though Ernesto later denied the allegation, there is evidence to show that a representative of the Mexican government was also scheduled to take part in the conversations.[66] The attempted negotiations came to nought, however, when Dr. Vázquez Gómez insisted that telegraphic communications with Madero would be mandatory and that, if necessary in order to establish such a line of communication, a Mexican city would have to be evacuated.[67] Since the government was unwilling to make such a concession, nothing was accomplished.

While these negotiations were in progress, Madero continued the im-

---

[64] See plan of campaign in Taracena, *Madero,* 348–50.

[65] E. Madero to A. Madero, February 6, 1911, *LP,* January 16, 1938, p. 7.

[66] E. Madero to J. A. Robertson, March 11, 1911, in Estrada, *La revolución y Francisco I. Madero,* 409–10; F. Vázquez Gómez to A. Madero, February 25, 1911, BN 2100. Vázquez Gómez makes pointed reference to such an envoy.

[67] F. Vázquez Gómez to A. Madero, February 25, 1911, BN 2100. Vázquez Gómez remained in Washington but would have come to Corpus Christi had the negotiations continued.

131

plementation of his battle plans. Drawing near to Casas Grandes, which was reported to have a very small garrison, Madero gave the order to attack on March 6, 1911, even though his force consisted of only about five hundred men and was woefully deficient in artillery and other munitions of war. The federal garrison proved to be stronger than was expected, making the success of the venture doubtful, and when an unexpected reinforcement arrived during the midst of the battle, the outcome was no longer questioned. Madero was forced to retire with severe losses, including fifty-one killed, twelve captured, and the abandonment of most of the baggage and equipment.[68] In the final stages of the battle Madero was slightly wounded; and although the defeated force withdrew in confusion, the government troops failed to press home the attack and Madero was soon able to gather and regroup his men.[69]

Madero's defeat at the hands of government troops not only gave rise to a wide variety of pernicious rumors concerning the revolutionary chieftain[70] but it also was damaging to the morale of some of the troops who took part in the campaign, since it tended to undermine confidence in the commander. One of the immediate results of this loss of confidence was the withdrawal of Rafael Aguilar—who was the only trained army officer in the Madero force and was sharply critical of the poor state of discipline—over a question of tactics and strategy.[71] Part of the loss in confidence, at least in so far as the integrity and courage of the commander were concerned, was regained by Madero when he personally was responsible for the arrest of an officer who had refused to follow orders during the battle.[72]

In spite of the temporary reverse sustained in the Casas Grandes affair, the ultimate effect of the incident was to strengthen the revolutionary cause by encouraging revolutionary bands in other sections to renewed vigor. But even more important to the revolutionists was an action taken by the United States on the very day the battle was fought. On March 6, President Taft ordered a concentration of army forces along the Mexican border, with a full division at San Antonio, a brigade at Galveston, and another brigade in southern California,

---

[68] Aguilar, *Madero sín máscara*, 67, 70, 73. A report by Joaquín Terrazas, March 9, 1911 (BN 2007), lists these specific losses.

[69] Aguilar, *Madero sín máscara*, 74.

[70] Estrada, *La revolución y Francisco I. Madero*, 405.

[71] Aguilar, *Madero sín máscara*, 77.

[72] R. Fernández Güell, *El moderno Juárez*, 12. Espinosa's announced intention to fight rather than submit to arrest had made the mission dangerous.

ostensibly to carry out routine maneuvers.[73] Even though the United States attempted to dispel the belief that an intervention was contemplated, the action was a clear indication that the northern government seriously doubted Díaz' ability to protect American nationals and their property; and the implications were alarming to the Mexican government. The distress was amplified by a United States Navy announcement that part of the Pacific Fleet was to hold maneuvers off the west coast of Mexico; to the Mexican government the two announcements were not a coincidence and constituted a gratuitous insult.[74]

The Mexican government was correct in its assumption that the orders reflected a loss of confidence in Mexico's ability to restrain the revolutionary forces and maintain peace. The "maneuvers" grew out of a conference between President Taft and Ambassador Henry Lane Wilson, in which the Ambassador indicated his belief that the collapse of the Díaz government was in its incipient stage, and pointed to the dangers to American property and lives incident to the collapse and the inevitable "explosion" which would follow.[75] The President's orders, then, were purely preventive. He had no desire to give aid and comfort to the revolution; on the contrary, he hoped by his actions to eliminate the passage of arms and men across the border, and by so doing to aid Mexico to return to a condition of tranquillity—"a result devoutly to be wished."[76] Lest there be some misunderstanding of the situation, President Taft made his position clear but not public:

It seems my duty as Commander in Chief to place troops in sufficient number where, if Congress shall direct that they enter Mexico to save American lives and property, an effective movement may be made. . . . My determined purpose . . . is to be in a position so that when danger to American lives and property in Mexico threatens and the existing Government is rendered helpless by the insurrection I can promptly execute congressional orders to protect them.[77]

The official position concerning the purpose of the concentration of military and naval forces was reiterated by Washington, but Madero could not fail to see the advantages to his cause which would accrue

[73] Huntington Wilson, Acting Secretary of State, to Henry Lane Wilson, March 7, 1911, *FR,* 1911, p. 415.

[74] De la Barra to State Department, March 12, 1911, *ibid.,* 422.

[75] Annual Message of the President of the United States, December 7, 1911, *ibid., xi.*

[76] President Taft to Chief of Staff, March 15, 1911, *ibid., xii.*

[77] *Ibid.* This letter was "to be regarded as confidential."

from the action, and the Mexican government could hardly note the situation with equanimity. Even José Ives Limantour, who arrived in New York en route from Paris shortly after the announcement, unconsciously reflected the disturbed state of mind in Mexico when he said, with reference to the movements of warships off the Mexican coast, "It does not appear to me how these ships can co-operate with the troops in the general manoeuvres at so great a distance from the natural base."[78]

The effects of the battle at Casas Grandes and of the American action could soon be noted. Goaded by fear occasioned by its own failure to destroy the revolution, on March 17 the Díaz government suspended constitutional guarantees, providing for summary action against persons interfering with railroads, telegraph lines, power plants, or hacienda property.[79] When the United States demanded exemptions for foreigners,[80] the Mexican government countered by insisting on its right to apply the decree to persons of any nationality; a concession was made, nevertheless, by instructing the local officials to exercise "prudence" in the application of the order.[81]

While Díaz was taking belated and inconclusive steps to contain and defeat the revolutionists, unofficial but serious peace discussions were held in New York. Soon after Limantour's arrival there, he was engaged in conferences with Don Francisco, Gustavo, and Dr. Vázquez Gómez, who had been called from Washington by the Maderos in order to prevent charges of nepotism and to make it quite clear that any decision reached would be in the name of the revolution and not of the family.[82] From the beginning Limantour refused to consider the surrender of a border city to Madero in order to establish a line of communications, nor would he countenance any discussion concerning the resignation of Díaz.[83] The negotiations, then, revolved around general considerations only, since Vázquez Gómez, who was inclined to make concessions in behalf of peace, insisted on neither provision.[84]

[78] As quoted in the *Times* (London), March 13, 1911, p. 5.
[79] Chargé d'Affaires to State Department, March 17, 1911, *FR,* 1911, p. 427. The inclusion of hacienda property is interesting.
[80] Huntington Wilson to Chargé d'Affaires, March 16, 1911, *ibid.,* 425. The demand was made before the decree became official.
[81] Creel to Henry Lane Wilson, March 24, 1911, *ibid.,* 439.
[82] G. Madero to Madero, April 18, 1911, in Taracena, *Madero,* 395 ff.
[83] F. Vázquez Gómez to Madero, March 20, 1911, *ibid.,* 374 ff.
[84] F. Vázquez Gómez to Madero, March 24, 1911, *Nueva Era,* September 30, 1911, p. 1.

During two days of almost constant haggling, the conferees agreed on twelve bases for further discussion, with the clear understanding that neither party was to be irrevocably bound or to have any guarantee that any of the clauses would become a part of the final settlement. The provisions included stipulations for the resignation of Corral, a general amnesty, resignation of ten governors and appointment of Antire-electionists to fill the vacancies, reform of the constitution and electoral laws, and changes in the ministry to provide a capable cabinet of men not connected politically with the Díaz regime.[85]

During the conference Vázquez Gómez took the position that he and he alone was the representative of the revolutionary group, even though he made it clear that he could not speak definitively for Madero.[86] The doctor's attitude at the conference, in the face of his earlier refusal to support the revolution when it began, brought a bitter denunciation from Gustavo to Madero. To use the words of Gustavo, Dr. Vázquez had "comported himself in a very disagreeable manner."[87] But aside from Vázquez' determination to act as spokesman, the ideas he presented at the conference were in complete harmony with those he and his brother had previously advanced; his function, he insisted, was that of a peace delegate, a compromiser, a liaison between the more intransigent revolutionaries and the more conservative anti-Díaz elements.[88] He opposed a complete military triumph, for such a victory would mean a destruction of one party and the submergence of the interests of that group. He desired a compromise, for he believed that then both parties would be in a position to maintain themselves and to aid the free development of democratic practices.[89] Given the political conditions of the time, the doctor's reasoning is specious at best.

Promising his full co-operation in bringing the revolution to a close,[90] at the conclusion of the New York conferences Limantour left for Mexico City, where he was given an enthusiastic reception as the harbinger of peace. The American Ambassador felt that Limantour was the last hope of saving the government, and there were many who

[85] F. Vázquez Gómez to G. Madero, March 20, 1911, *MP*, 98–100.
[86] G. Madero to Madero, April 18, 1911, in Taracena, *Madero*, 395 ff.; F. Vázquez Gómez to Madero, March 20, 1911, *ibid.*, 374 ff.
[87] G. Madero to Madero, April 18, 1911, *ibid.*, 395 ff.
[88] F. Vázquez Gómez to Madero, March 24, 1911, *Nueva Era,* September 30, 1911, p. 1.
[89] *Ibid.* A change from this position, in expression if not in thought, will be noted in the summer of 1911.
[90] Edward I. Bell, *The Political Shame of Mexico,* 61–62.

shared that view. Business was stagnated, the populace in Mexico City was discontented, the revolutionists were increasing in number and activities, and every day some new incident deepened the gloom.[91] Limantour, fresh from Europe after an absence of some months and sensitive to the changed conditions and atmosphere, recognized the need for reform as a weapon against the revolution. But his task of saving the government was made more arduous by some of his friends, who insisted that he take over the government, and by Díaz, who was not only inactive but refused to delegate power to anyone else.[92] The dictator still had not recognized the gravity of the moment, nor could he believe that the revolution was of such serious proportions as to demand either maximum military effort or reform in government. But pressure was applied on the aged President from all quarters, with public discussion and Limantour's constant urging having their effect; in late March the cabinet, with the exception of Limantour and Manuel González Cosío,[93] resigned en masse and a new cabinet was announced on the same day. The new ministers were not men who were noted for their liberal philosophy, but they were able and honest men who had occupied important nonpolitical administrative posts and whose inclusion in the cabinet gave hope for reform. The best-known of the new cabinet members was Francisco León de la Barra, who had recently returned to Mexico from his post as ambassador to Washington.[94]

The cabinet change was followed immediately by a regular session of Congress beginning on April 1. In his message to Congress, Díaz reflected the government's anxiety when he almost completely succumbed to the demands of the reform group and outlined a program of far-reaching implications, including provisions for the correction of local political and judicial abuses, electoral reform and no re-election, and judicial reform through careful selection of judges and a lengthening of the term of office. By far the most startling of the proposals, however, concerned the issue of land; Díaz not only recognized the existence of an agrarian problem but proposed to discover a means by which some distribution of lands could be made.[95] His proposals, in spite of his

[91] Wilson to State Department, March 20, 1911, *FR,* 1911, pp. 430–31.
[92] Wilson to State Department, March 22, 1911, *ibid.,* 431–32.
[93] As Minister of Finance and Minister of War and Marine, respectively.
[94] A list of the cabinet members is available in most newspapers of that date; specifically see the *Times* (London), March 28, 1911, p. 5.
[95] Message of President Díaz to Twenty-fifth Congress, second session, April 1, 1911, *FR,* 1911, pp. 445–47.

efforts to cloak the message in honeyed terms,[96] were in actuality an indictment of the practices of his own administration, for they admitted political corruption, maladministration, and economic inefficiency, as well as all manner of electoral irregularities. More than a mere criticism of the past administration, the program showed the government's inability to cope with the revolution. It was an admission of weakness; rather than attracting support to Díaz, the tenor of the message encouraged the revolutionists to new efforts and demands. This was the last of a series of political blunders made by the aging President, but in all justice it must be recognized that he was forced into that position by his advisors. Madero's answer, indicative of the general opinion, was terse and to the point: nothing less than the resignatic of Díaz would be satisfactory.[97]

The revolutionaries could afford to be demanding, for every day there were new signs of eventual success. Armed activity accelerated in March, and within less than two months the Madero forces occupied a respectable portion of the national territory, including many cities. Chilapa, in the state of Guerrero, fell to the Figueroa brothers on March 25; and on April 15, Acapulco was captured.[98] Zapata, who rebelled in Morelos on March 10, had become a power there before the month was out.[99] Durango, Jalapa, Tehuacán, Saltillo, Torreón, and Culiacán were in danger of capture by the revolutionaries during March and early April; rebels were on the move in Veracruz; Luis Moya in Zacatecas was meeting some success; federal forces in Sonora were threatened with isolation; and revolutionaries were operating almost within sight of Mexico City.[100] In the north Madero organized a provisional government at Bustillos, which he used as his headquarters in March and early April; there he was both civil and military leader of the revolutionary forces.[101] Abraham González had established himself, with Madero's aid, as the provisional governor of Chihuahua; tentative plans for the invasion of Coahuila and Tamaulipas from the north were formulated; and in every sector unrest was growing.[102] Even

[96] For example, he attempted to put the responsibility on Congress for many of the abuses of the period.
[97] Wilson to State Department, April 13, 1911, *FR,* 1911, p. 444.
[98] Casasola, *Historia gráfica,* I, 278.
[99] Magaña, *Emiliano Zapata,* I, 109–13.
[100] Casasola, *Historia gráfica,* I, 276–78.
[101] Numerous documents in BN attest to this fact.
[102] General Orders from A. González, March 20, 1911, BN 806; G. Madero to Madero, April 18, 1911, in Taracena, *Madero,* 395 ff.

Mexico City was the stage for an attempt against the government; the so-called Complot de Tacubaya of March 27 was a total failure, but it was indicative of the unrest among younger army officers.[103]

The financial and material resources of the revolutionary forces were still scanty and so remained until the movement's end, but the human resources were daily increasing. Transportation and communication difficulties made central direction over the various chieftains impossible, but the vast majority of the men bearing arms were doing so under the aegis of the Plan de San Luis Potosí and were followers of Madero.

Giving the details of all the small movements against the government would be both difficult and unnecessary, but the actions at Agua Prieta and Ciudad Juárez were of such import that they warrant some attention. On April 13, Agua Prieta, across the international boundary from Douglas, Arizona, was captured by the rebels after a battle in which fire from the contestants fell in the Arizona city. Two Americans were killed and eleven wounded, creating a serious problem in international relations.[104] Investigation by authorities from the United States indicated that the bullets crossing the boundary had been from the guns of the Díaz forces, who had been attacked from the direction of the border.[105] A renewal of the battle on April 17, when again Americans were wounded on American soil,[106] brought a heated protest from Washington. The federal troops seemed "disposed to keep their agreement not to fire into Douglas,"[107] but the positions of the contending forces made a recurrence certain if there were any further fighting. For a short time it was feared that the United States would resort to the occupation of Agua Prieta, but on April 18, President Taft denied any intention of intervention except as a last resort.[108] While Washington was considering the problem, however, the situation was resolved by the rebels, who exhausted their supply of ammunition

[103] Statement by H. Garza and A. B. Arsiniaga, June 6, 1911, BN 745.
[104] Huntington Wilson to Wilson, April 14, 1911, *FR,* 1911, p. 456. For details of the damages, see *Claims Growing out of Insurrection in Mexico,* 62 Cong., 3 sess., *House Doc. 1168.*
[105] U.S. Attorney at Bisbee, Arizona, to Attorney General, April 14, 1911, *FR,* 1911, p. 458.
[106] Governor R. E. Sloan (Arizona) to President Taft, April 17, 1911, *ibid.,* 459.
[107] *Ibid.*
[108] President Taft to Governor Sloan, April 18, 1911, *ibid.,* 460.

and withdrew from the border city.[109] The contest for Agua Prieta was of scant military importance inasmuch as the town was not used by the revolutionaries as a port of entry; but the international repercussions, as slight as they were, had a marked effect on Madero's decisions when he was ready to attack Ciudad Juárez a few days later.

After the battle of Casas Grandes the revolutionary forces in Chihuahua and eastern Sonora gathered at Bustillos, the provisional capital which Madero had established, and for some weeks they devoted themselves to regrouping and replenishing their supplies. In late March an army of three thousand, with both Pascual Orozco and Villa directly under Madero's command, was reported to be advancing on Chihuahua City.[110] Although the information available to the government was inaccurate because the revolutionary bands had been successful in disrupting lines of communication, Díaz ordered Chihuahua City reinforced with any troops which were available in the state. In conformity with that order, troops were withdrawn from Ciudad Juárez. But the advance against Chihuahua was merely a feint to encourage the weakening of the border city; and as soon as the garrison had been diminished, Madero fell on the city unexpectedly. On April 19 he demanded surrender from General Juan Navarro, but the federal officer refused to capitulate.[111]

Madero was now confronted with a grave decision. Peace negotiations had begun,[112] and a repetition of Agua Prieta would almost surely create a dangerous international situation. On the other hand, the state of revolutionary finances was critical, there was a serious shortage of arms and ammunition, and a port of entry was essential.[113] Considering all factors, Madero believed he could accomplish all his desires and obviate the dangers by negotiation; he was therefore quite willing to arrange a truce for one day when he was approached by an unofficial representative of the government on April 20. Even though a majority of his officers and men favored an immediate attack, Madero agreed to a six-day armistice to begin at noon on April 22 and to apply to a limited area in northern Chihuahua only. At the expiration of this pe-

[109] G. Madero to Madero, April 18, 1911, in Taracena, *Madero*, 395 ff.
[110] Wilson to State Department, March 23, 1911, *FR*, 1911, p. 432.
[111] Fernández Güell, *El moderno Juárez*, 10; Casasola, *Historia gráfica*, I, 257.
[112] See pp. 145 ff. below.
[113] G. Madero to Madero, April 18, 1911, in Taracena, *Madero*, 395 ff. Vasconcelos to F. González Garza, April 26, 1911, *ibid.*, 410–14.

riod, nothing having been accomplished, the armistice was extended for five more days; and then on May 2 an additional extension of three days was granted, in spite of the growing restiveness of the revolutionary forces.[114]

On May 7, because of the sterility of the negotiations and because he feared international complications in the event of an attack, Madero announced the abandonment of the siege of Ciudad Juárez in order to prosecute the campaign against cities in the interior.[115] As a part of this plan he sent Garibaldi and his men to Sonora to organize the many small groups into a disciplined army which could act as a cohesive striking force.[116] The decision to abandon the attack on Ciudad Juárez was unpopular with the majority of the insurgents, who believed that the capture of the city would be accomplished easily because of the weakness of the garrison. Even after the announcement of his intentions, Madero was reluctant to withdraw. The following day he designated Roque González Garza as his agent to discuss "the delicate situation in which both forces" found themselves,[117] and arranged for a reopening of the negotiations with the understanding that he would "agree to the immediate suspension of hostilities in the vicinity of Ciudad Juárez until an armistice by the delegates of both parties has been arranged."[118] The government representative understood this to mean an armistice effective as of that moment, while Madero considered the suspension to be provisional only.[119]

The attack on, and capture of, Ciudad Juárez have been the subject of much disagreement, for the exact manner in which the battle began is not clear. During the critical period in which a renewal of the armistice was being discussed, firing began between the advanced outposts of the insurgents and the federal troops. Madero attempted to bring an end to the firing by sending an officer with a white flag into the immediate area, but the officer's horse was killed under him either by federal or by rebel bullets.[120] Madero then notified General Navarro that the suspension of hostilities was at an end, after which he ordered a full-

114 Esquivel and Braniff to Limantour, April 20, 22, 26, and 28 and May 2, 1911, *DP*, p. 33 and Appendix items 7, 9, 13, 25.
115 Madero manifesto, May 7, 1911, BN 1282.
116 Madero to Garibaldi, May 7, 1911, BN 742.
117 Madero to General Navarro, May 8, 1911, BN 870.
118 Madero to Esquivel and Braniff, May 8, 1911, BN 562.
119 Esquivel and Braniff to Limantour, May 9, 1911, *DP*, 68–70; Madero to Orozco, May 8, 1911, BN 1570.
120 Esquivel and Braniff to Limantour, May 9, 1911, *DP*, 68–70.

scale attack.[121] Whether Madero could have stopped the attack once it started is a moot point. He may, as he insisted,[122] have decided to take advantage of a peculiar situation which was to his advantage, or he may have ordered a general attack only as a means of maintaining a semblance of leadership; it was reported that Orozco had determined to press an attack rather than retire, regardless of any decision which Madero might make.[123]

Once the frontal assault began, it was only a question of time before Ciudad Juárez would fall; on May 10 the city was captured. Although a number of persons were killed or injured in El Paso, the United States took no steps to intervene.[124] Madero's fears of international difficulties proved to be groundless, and the capture of a port of entry made possible the legal importation of arms and ammunition.[125] In addition, there were banks in Ciudad Juárez from which money could be borrowed, under pressure if necessary, and bankers in the United States were now more inclined to lend money to the revolutionary leaders.[126] Even more important than the material gains, however, was the psychological effect; for the improvement of morale among the revolutionaries in other sections and the loss of confidence among the federal troops resulted in the uncontested occupation of Agua Prieta and Casas Grandes, even before the final capture of Ciudad Juárez was consummated.[127] The general movement supporting the revolution received a sharp impetus during the following days.

Almost before there was time to appreciate the prize, however, an incident in Ciudad Juárez almost disrupted the revolutionary party. The membership of the new cabinet[128] which Madero appointed for the provisional government was unsatisfactory to Pascual Orozco, who thought his service to the cause should have warranted his appoint-

---

[121] Statement by Madero, undated, BN 1283; Madero to Esquivel and Braniff, May 9, 1911, *DP,* 70–71.
[122] Statement by Madero, undated, BN 1283.
[123] Esquivel, *Democracia y personalismo,* 60.
[124] See *Claims Growing out of Insurrection in Mexico* for an investigation and report of the damages.
[125] S. G. Hopkins to G. Madero, May 12, 1911, BN 1305. Hopkins was Madero's legal representative in Washington.
[126] Hopkins to G. Madero, May 12, 1911, BN 1305. Numerous letters demanding loans from banks in Ciudad Juárez may be found in BN.
[127] Lomelí to Madero, May 10, 1911, BN 1111; report by L. B. Ponce, May 10, 1911, BN 1676.
[128] See letters of appointment to F. Vázquez Gómez, Gustavo Madero, Federico González Garza, J. M. Pino Suárez, and Venustiano Carranza, all dated May 11, 1911, BN.

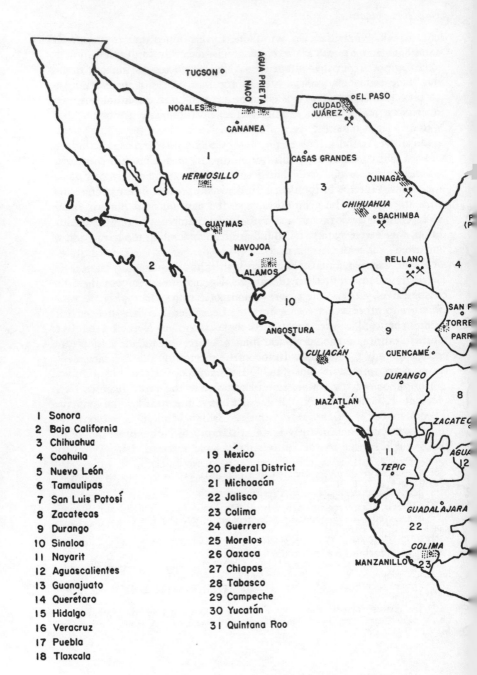

TUCSON ○

AGUA PRIETA

NACO

NOGALES

CANANEA

CASAS GRANDES

1

HERMOSILLO

GUAYMAS

NAVOJOA

ALAMOS

2

10

ANGOSTURA

CULIACÁN

MAZATLÁN

○EL PASO

CIUDAD
JUÁREZ

3

OJINAGA

CHIHUAHUA
○BACHIMBA

RELLANO

SAN F

TORRE

PARR

4

CUENCAMÉ ○

DURANGO

9

8

ZACATEC

AGUA

12

11

TEPIC

GUADALAJARA

22

COLIMA

MANZANILLO ○

23

P
(P

1 Sonora
2 Baja California
3 Chihuahua
4 Coahuila
5 Nuevo León
6 Tamaulipas
7 San Luis Potosí
8 Zacatecas
9 Durango
10 Sinaloa
11 Nayarit
12 Aguascalientes
13 Guanajuato
14 Querétaro
15 Hidalgo
16 Veracruz
17 Puebla
18 Tlaxcala

19 México
20 Federal District
21 Michoacán
22 Jalisco
23 Colima
24 Guerrero
25 Morelos
26 Oaxaca
27 Chiapas
28 Tabasco
29 Campeche
30 Yucatán
31 Quintana Roo

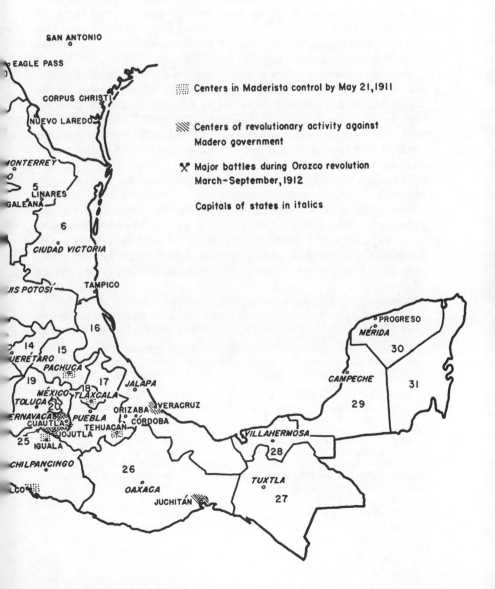

MEXICO

SAN ANTONIO

EAGLE PASS

CORPUS CHRISTI

NUEVO LAREDO

MONTERREY

5
LINARES
GALEANA

6

CIUDAD VICTORIA

IS POTOSI

TAMPICO

16

14   15
QUERÉTARO
PACHUCA

19   18 17   JALAPA
MÉXICO TLAXCALA
TOLUCA 20   ORIZABA VERACRUZ
ERNAVACA PUEBLA CÓRDOBA
CUAUTLA TEHUACÁN
JOJUTLA
25   IGUALA

CHILPANCINGO   26

LCO   OAXACA   JUCHITÁN

PROGRESO
MÉRIDA
30

CAMPECHE   31

29

VILLAHERMOSA

28

TUXTLA
27

▒ Centers in Maderista control by May 21,1911

▨ Centers of revolutionary activity against
Madero government

✗ Major battles during Orozco revolution
March–September, 1912

Capitals of states in italics

ment as Minister of War. In addition, while both Orozco and Villa desired the execution of the captive General Navarro, Madero insisted on according him his rights as a prisoner of war.[129] Discontented over the general situation and probably inflamed by men not in sympathy with the revolution,[130] on May 13, Orozco and Villa attempted to arrest Madero in order to force him to re-form the cabinet. Madero, whose personal and moral courage was never doubted, even by his bitterest enemies, refused to submit to the demands and after some anxious moments convinced the insubordinate generals that they had overstepped their authority.[131] An immediate exchange of *abrazos* and a later exchange of letters between Madero and Orozco ostensibly brought the incident to a close.[132]

But the incipient rebellion of two of the best-known Madero generals did not pass unnoticed. S. G. Hopkins, an agent for Madero in the United States, was seriously disturbed at the implications; and Limantour, hoping the episode could be used to advantage by the administration, was anxious to know more of the details.[133] Nevertheless, the storm abated as rapidly as it had risen. Madero refused to discuss the incident further, though he did escort Navarro across the Rio Grande in order to prevent a recurrence of the demand for the General's execution.[134]

The progress of the revolution following the capture of Ciudad Juárez was nothing short of amazing. As soon as Madero established his headquarters with facilities for communication, the reports began flooding in. Hundreds of small groups were under arms in every state; from innumerable *jefes*, representing thousands of men, came requests

[129] Esquivel and Braniff to Limantour, May 13, 1911, *DP*, 78.

[130] Madero made that charge against Toribio Esquivel Obregón. See Esquivel to Madero, May 14, 1911, *DP*, 81; and Madero to Esquivel, May 16, 1911, in Taracena, *Madero,* 421–23.

[131] Madero's statement, May 13, 1911, in Taracena, *Madero,* 417–18.

[132] Madero to Orozco, May 15, 1911; Orozco to Madero, May 15, 1911. These letters were published as handbills and distributed among the troops. Copies in VC.

[133] Hopkins to F. Vázquez Gómez, May 13, 1911, BN 2102; E. Fernández to Madero, May 13, 1911, BN 587; Esquivel, *Democracia y personalismo,* 78.

[134] Madero's statement, May 13, 1911, in Taracena, *Madero,* 417–19. It is curious to note the reactions of various people to the incident. The ardent Maderistas interpret it as a complete victory for Madero, indicative of his courage and his leadership. His detractors point to the incident as illustrative of his fundamental weakness and insist that Madero was forced to make a grave compromise with Orozco. Madero also denied that Orozco or any of his men demanded Navarro's execution, but there is evidence that they did.

144

for information and instruction.[135] By May 24 a large number of towns and cities were in revolutionary hands; the following partial tabulation will illustrate this point.[136]

State	Cities or Towns Held by Insurgents
Chihuahua	Ciudad Juárez, Casas Grandes
Coahuila	Torreón, Saltillo
Colima	Colima
Hidalgo	Pachuca
Guerrero	Acapulco, Iguala, Chilpancingo
Puebla	Tehuacán, San Juan de los Llanos
Sonora	Nogales, Agua Prieta, Hermosillo, Guaymas, Alamos, Naco
Tlaxcala	Tlaxcala
Morelos	Cuautla, Cuernavaca, Jonacatepec
Sinaloa	Culiacán

In addition, there were important revolutionary activities in many other states. Oaxaca was a center of southern activity;[137] and serious assaults were under way in Jalisco, Querétaro, Nuevo León, Zacatecas, Veracruz, Chiapas, and Yucatán. The Figueroa brothers in Guerrero were reported to have twelve thousand men under their command, Emilio Madero had approximately thirty-five hundred in the Torreón region, and other large forces were operating.[138] With thousands of men in open rebellion against him, and with implements of war available to the rebels, Díaz was doomed. The purely military aspects of the revolution had become overwhelmingly important. Even though Madero was not aware of the tremendous growth of the revolutionary armies, the advisors surrounding the dictator recognized the increase and knew their cause was lost.[139]

In the meantime, for months past there had been intermittent negotiations for peace. After the March conversations between Liman-

[135] Communiqués, mostly telegrams, in BN attest to this fact.
[136] This list was compiled from various sources.
[137] *Times* (London), May 10, 1911, p. 10.
[138] Vasconcelos to Madero, May 14, 1911, in Taracena, *Madero*, 423–26; Emilio Madero to Madero, May 26, 1911, BN 1210. It has been impossible to ascertain the exact number of men under arms, but the Minister of Gobernación under the ad interim government reported that there had been approximately seventy thousand.
[139] A study of the correspondence and actions make both these points abundantly clear.

tour and representatives of the revolution, Don Francisco Madero went to El Paso to talk to his son in the hope that some satisfactory arrangement could be made for peace.[140] In Mexico City, at approximately the same time, Toribio Esquivel Obregón and Oscar Braniff requested permission from Limantour to serve as unofficial and unprejudiced mediators between the government and the insurgents in order to establish points of reference for an official peace conference.[141] Granted their request, the two unofficial commissioners journeyed to Washington in early April to talk to Dr. Vázquez Gómez, who was then engaged in informal conversations with the Mexican ambassador; but the doctor refused to see either Braniff or Esquivel, for he had no desire to negotiate with unofficial agents.[142] Esquivel and Braniff, after notifying Limantour of the failure of their mission to Washington, went to El Paso to seek out Madero.[143] In the meantime two others were also seeking Madero with overtures for peace: Federico Moye, nonpartisan, unprejudiced, and unofficial, hoped to arrange a settlement, as did Rafael Hernández, who was "semiofficially representing the Mexican Government."[144] On April 20, with Madero threatening Ciudad Juárez, a galaxy of peace envoys including Don Francisco Madero, Ernesto Madero, Alfonso Madero, Rafael Hernández, Federico Moye, Esquivel, and Braniff were ready to enter into negotiations with the revolutionary leader.[145] It is therefore not surprising that Madero was willing to agree to an armistice when he was approached on that day.

Madero, supported by Gustavo and Pino Suárez, had no desire to begin negotiations on any basis other than the resignation of Díaz, but Limantour was unwilling to concede such a basis, and Braniff echoed

[140] Esquivel, *Democracia y personalismo*, 22.

[141] *Ibid.*, 22. Esquivel's attitude and position are curious. Even after he had disagreed with Madero in early 1910, he considered himself as a candidate for the Antirreeleccionista nomination until definitely eliminated by the convention. His ostensible reason for not taking a more active part in the early campaign in Guanajuato was that a revolution would be the only way to bring about a change in government, and that he would support any armed movement. Yet when the insurrection began, Esquivel was conspicuously absent from the ranks. Now, when it was apparent that the revolution had some chance for success, he appeared as a "disinterested" patriot whose only desire was to serve his country. Esquivel was also later the Minister of Finance under Huerta.

[142] Vázquez Gómez, *Memorias políticas*, 118–23; Esquivel, *Democracia y personalismo*, 25–27.

[143] Esquivel to Limantour, April 12, 1911, *DP*, Appendix item 2.

[144] *Times* (London), April 13, 1911, p. 9; April 19, 1911, p. 8.

[145] Braniff and Esquivel to Limantour, April 20, 1911, *DP*, 33.

the official position.[146] Apparently an impasse had been reached even before negotiations began. Further conversations on April 22, however, resulted in the six-day armistice and a set of principles to be used as a basis for further discussions. Madero abandoned his demand for Díaz' resignation but included changes in the cabinet and state gubernatorial posts, electoral reform, pardon for political prisoners, evacuation of the northern states by the federal forces, recognition by the government of some military grades among the revolutionary officers, the immediate resignation of Ramón Corral, and appointment of a new Minister of Foreign Affairs only with prior agreement by the insurgent provisional government.[147] This last provision was of paramount importance, for the man occupying that post would succeed to the presidency in case of Díaz' death or resignation after the resignation of Corral.

The continuation of the negotiations was threatened by a variety of factors, among which the advance of Colonel Rábago from Chihuahua, the material condition of the insurgent troops who were demanding food and clothing, and the absence of a bona fide government representative were the most important.[148] To forestall the insurgents from taking by force what they needed, Braniff on his own authority advanced 2,500 pesos to Madero for supplies, and Ernesto and Don Francisco Madero each advanced a like amount.[149] This was sufficient for the first week of the armistice, and as the negotiations were prolonged the government reluctantly advanced other sums;[150] but the lack of supplies was a constant source of irritation and discontent. After the beginning of negotiations, another source of difficulty was discovered; each party so distrusted the other that little could be done.[151] Limantour particularly objected to the suspicious attitude of the insurgent commissioners, but in view of the repressions to which the Antire-electionists had been subjected such suspicion was natural.[152]

---

[146] G. Madero to Madero, April 18, 1911, in Taracena, *Madero*, 395 ff.; Pino Suárez to Madero, undated, *ibid.*, 391–93; Esquivel, *Democracia y personalismo*, 32; Limantour to Braniff and Esquivel, April 21, 1911, *DP*, Appendix item 4; public declaration by Oscar Braniff, April 21, 1911, *ibid.*, Appendix item 5.

[147] Braniff and Esquivel to Limantour, April 22, 1911, *ibid.*, p. 38.

[148] Braniff and Esquivel to Limantour, April 22 and 26, 1911, *ibid.*, Appendix items 6, 9. Rábago was leading a federal force to relieve Ciudad Juárez.

[149] Braniff to Limantour, May 1 and 4, 1911, *ibid.*, Appendix items 29, 33.

[150] Limantour to Braniff, May 6, 1911, *ibid.*, Appendix item 36.

[151] The correspondence of Braniff and Esquivel is filled with demands by the insurgents for guarantees.

[152] Limantour to Braniff and Esquivel, May 1, 1911, *DP*, Appendix item 24.

Mexican Revolution

Immediately after the first armistice was arranged, Madero asked Abraham González to come from Guerrero (Chihuahua), Dr. Vázquez Gómez from Washington, Pino Suárez from New Orleans, and Guadalupe González from Ojinaga in order to advise him concerning the peace overtures; but he made no formal designation of peace commissioners until May 2.[153] The government, in the meantime, agreed to name an official representative on April 26; the following day Francisco Carbajal of the Supreme Court was selected "to discuss and to treat" with the Madero envoys.[154] After Carbajal entrained for the northern area, Madero appointed Don Francisco Madero, Dr. Vázquez Gómez, and José María Pino Suárez as his representatives, and the armistice was extended to May 3.[155] Limantour objected to Ciudad Juárez as the site for the negotiations, but on Madero's insistence it was finally agreed to hold the discussions in that vicinity.[156]

Immediately after Carbajal arrived, the discussions started, with the insurgents now demanding Díaz' immediate resignation. Díaz refused to make any commitment which would make it appear that he was resigning under pressure, and Carbajal was instructed not to discuss the question of the President's resignation; Madero insisted that Díaz was a usurper and there could be no peace until he resigned.[157] Under those conditions the negotiations ceased, and the armistice came to an end on May 6.

The government was wavering, however, and after a long cabinet session on May 7, the President announced his intention to retire from office "when his conscience tells him that on retiring he will not deliver the country to anarchy."[158] Although this did not constitute a direct commitment, Madero was willing to renew the negotiations even after he had ordered the abandonment of the siege of Ciudad Juárez. Before

[153] Madero to M. G. de Madero, April 25, 1911, in Taracena, *Madero*, 408–10.
[154] Limantour to Braniff, April 26, 1911, *DP,* Appendix item 10; Limantour to Francisco Carbajal, April 27, 1911, in Casasola, *Historia gráfica,* I, 261.
[155] Limantour to Braniff and Esquivel, April 30, 1911, *DP,* Appendix item 20; Madero to Don F. Madero, May 2, 1911, in Casasola, *Historia gráfica,* I, 262; Braniff and Esquivel to Limantour, April 28, 1911, *DP,* Appendix item 13.
[156] Limantour to Braniff and Esquivel, April 29 and 30, 1911, *DP,* p. 44 and Appendix item 20; Braniff and Esquivel to Limantour, April 29, 1911, *ibid.,* Appendix item 18.
[157] Limantour to Braniff and Esquivel, May 6, 1911, *ibid.,* Appendix item 28; *Times* (London), May 6, 1911, p. 10; Esquivel, *Democracia y personalismo,* 55.
[158] Wilson to State Department, May 8, 1911, *FR,* 1911, p. 478; Díaz manifesto, May 7, 1911, in Casasola, *Historia gráfica,* I, 267.

any further peace conversations had taken place, the attack began and the city was captured.[159]

With Ciudad Juárez in their hands, the insurgents found themselves in a much more advantageous position to negotiate. The excellent order prevailing in the captured city,[160] now the provisional capital, gave Madero's government international prestige, while the port of entry assured a flow of war materials. The success of the revolution was practically certain. When negotiations were renewed, Limantour requested a categorical statement concerning Madero's minimum demands for a conclusion of peace.[161] The demands were essentially the same: Díaz must go, and there must be a guarantee that he would leave office soon.[162] The government, not yet completely convinced of the success of the revolution, and encouraged by the Orozco defection, used delaying tactics, although Rafael Hernández, still an unofficial agent of the government, advised settlement on the basis of the New York conversations plus Díaz' ultimate resignation.[163] On May 16, Oscar Braniff recommended peace as soon as possible, for the increasing revolutionary successes throughout the country would encourage the insurgents to make greater demands with each passing day.[164] Díaz was adamant concerning his resignation, but suddenly on May 17 he succumbed to the inevitable and agreed to resign before the end of the month, promising that Corral would also leave office within that time.[165]

The Cabinet Council at which President Diaz's resignation was announced was most pathetic. The aged President lay in bed in an anteroom, with swollen face, suffering great pain from an ulcerated jaw. Senor Limantour, Minister of Finance, was the only member of the Cabinet who entered the sick room. President Diaz spoke the fewest possible words.[166]

Madero immediately conveyed his congratulations to Díaz and arranged a general armistice.[167] Even though the peace treaty was not signed for four days, the revolution was at an end.

---

[159] See pp. 138–39 above.   [160] *Times* (London), May 12, 1911, p. 5.
[161] Limantour to Braniff, May 10, 1911, *DP*, Appendix item 40.
[162] Braniff and Esquivel to Limantour, May 11, 1911, *ibid.*, Appendix item 41.
[163] Rafael Hernández to Limantour, May 12, 1911, VC.
[164] Braniff to Limantour, May 16, 1911, *DP*, Appendix item 44.
[165] *Times* (London), May 18, 1911, p. 8.
[166] *Ibid.*, May 19, 1911, p. 5.
[167] Madero to Díaz, May 17, 1911, BN 513.

A ten o'clock on the night of May 21, the official instrument concluding the insurrection was signed.[168] The treaty itself was a simple document, reflecting none of the tortuous negotiations which had been in progress informally and formally for over two months. Six basic conditions were stipulated: Díaz and Corral were to resign before the end of the month; Francisco León de la Barra was to be the ad interim president and hold the presidential election; "public opinion in the states" was to be satisfied; indemnification was to be made for destruction directly attributable to the revolution; and a general amnesty was to be proclaimed.[169]

The official document made no mention of change of ministers, of new state governors, of ranks for revolutionary officers, of electoral reform, or of new members to Congress, although these demands had been consistently made from the beginning of the peace efforts. The failure to mention these points did not mean that they had been abandoned by Madero and his advisors; each and every one, with the exception of new members to Congress, was agreed to verbally, and the ad interim government was charged with the duty of complying with them.

Díaz resigned on May 25, leaving the government in the hands of De la Barra. The fall of the old president was met with jubilation in every part of the country; not a voice was raised in protest at his going.[170] One enthusiastic Maderista wired: "Today I believe in God. Blessed are you, our Liberators."[171] There were many, nevertheless, who felt that disaster had struck Mexico with the triumph of the revolution; they would have cried out had the time been propitious. But the time for their actions was not yet; they could wait, and wait they did, for an opportune moment to strike out at the new regime. The Díaz government, its thought and its psychology, its beliefs and its philosophy, had not been destroyed by the Madero armies. Two-thirds of the country had been conquered by men bearing the Antire-electionist banner, but only a few of the Díaz supporters had been definitely eliminated. Díaz and Corral, Limantour, Pineda, and a few more of the best-known were gone, but the rank and file were still in Mexico and still dangerous to progress.

[168] Wilson to State Department, May 22, 1911, *FR*, 1911, p. 489.
[169] Tratados de Ciudad Juárez, May 21, 1911, BN 1290.
[170] R. Amieva to F. Vázquez Gómez, May 25, 1911, *MP*, 276; *Times* (London), May 23, 1911, p. 8.
[171] Inocencio Arriola to Madero, May 25, 1911, BN 117.

The Revolution

Within the ranks of the Madero followers, too, there were dangerous elements and sullen dissatisfactions. Every man who had taken up arms had done so in pursuit of an idea, an idea which generally was close to him personally. To some it had been nothing more than personal aggrandizement and the opportunity to take advantage of a situation which would improve their own well-being. To others the idea was broader, affecting the political and economic structure of the nation. But there had been no central idea, other than the elimination of the dictator, and no basis on which to build a strong, peaceful government. That was the task confronting Madero and the new president. It was a task of gigantic proportions and one which the Mexican public was ill suited to undertake.

It is reported that Díaz, just before boarding the ship which was to carry him into exile, remarked to one of his companions: "Madero has unleashed a tiger; let us see if he can control him."

VII

The Ad Interim Government

IN THE CAPTURE of Ciudad Juárez and the subsequent collapse of the dictatorship, Madero saw a great victory for the principles which he had espoused, a revindication of his belief that Mexico demanded political change. Even though Madero's primary concern for months past had been the destruction of the Díaz government, victory did not lessen his responsibilities or bring him respite. The hundreds of leaders of small bands now needed instructions and advice concerning the disposition of their troops. A condition of semibanditry prevailed in many sections, and Madero was expected to restore normalcy. Provisional governors for the states were needed, and for every position there were innumerable candidates. New cabinet members had to be appointed, in which task the ad interim government asked Madero's co-operation. In addition to these pressing and immediate problems, thousands of other details so sapped Madero's energies and consumed his time that he had no opportunity to consider the ultimate function of the revolutionary government. His first message to the nation was, therefore, merely an admonition to support the De la Barra government, a brief explanation of the factors involved in the Ciudad Juárez settlement, and a renunciation of the provisional presidency which he had assumed the previous November.[1]

In the selection of cabinet members Madero was confronted with a major decision.[2] Very few of the men in his confidence were of cabinet stature, lacking both the necessary experience and prestige to undertake the enormous task confronting them. The only true revolutionary whom Madero considered to be worthy of such a post was Manuel Bonilla of Sinaloa, who was named Minister of Communications.[3]

---

[1] Madero, "Manifiesto a la nación," May 26, 1911, VC.
[2] Although not a treaty stipulation, it was understood that the revolutionaries were to have representation in the ad interim government.
[3] Casasola, *Historia gráfica,* I, 297.

Ad Interim Government

Emilio Vázquez Gómez, who considered himself and his brother to be truly representative of the revolutionary ideals, received the post of Gobernación while Francisco Vázquez Gómez, who had shown an interest in public education, was made Minister of Public Instruction and Fine Arts.[4] Rafael Hernández, Madero's cousin whose conservative political philosophy Madero deplored but whose honesty and integrity were valuable attributes, was designated Minister of Justice over the objections of Emilio Vázquez, who considered Hernández to represent ideas contrary to those of the revolution.[5] Another conservative kinsman, Ernesto Madero, was made Minister of Hacienda at Madero's direct request, largely because of his long experience as the financial manager of the Madero enterprises.[6] The other cabinet posts were filled by men who were not representative of the revolutionary doctrines but whose appointments were acceptable to Madero.[7]

Madero offered the important post of governor of the Federal District to Gabriel Robles Domínguez; but when that active partisan of the revolution refused, Alberto García Granados, who had taken a minor part in opposition to Díaz, was named.[8] David de la Fuente, Antire-electionist and insurgent, was appointed Inspector General of Police.[9] In summary, it may be noted that of the important positions filled in the early days of the ad interim government, four were filled with loyal revolutionaries, three with men who had had no connection with the Díaz regime though of conservative bent, and only two by men who had been leagued with the erstwhile dictatorship. The cabinet was largely representative of the new, rather than the old, order.

One of the first actions of the new government concerned Gustavo Madero and subjected Francisco Madero to a great deal of criticism, even though he was in no way responsible. A decree on May 31 au-

---

[4] F. Vázquez Gómez, *Memorias políticas*, 283. As an indication of the background of these men for their posts, see Emilio Vázquez Gómez, *El pensamiento de la revolución*, and Francisco Vázquez Gómez, *La enseñanza secundaria en el Distrito Federal*. The sincerity of their revolutionary ideals may be seriously questioned, but there seems to be little doubt of their ambition.

[5] Madero to Hernández, May 24, 1911, BN 976; E. Vázquez Gómez to Madero, May 31, 1911, BN 2088.

[6] E. Madero to Madero, May 22, 1911, BN 1240.

[7] Manuel Calero, Fomento; Eugenio Rascón, War and Marine; no Minister of Foreign Relations was appointed. Madero to Jorge Vera Estañol, May 27, 1911, BN 528. Vera Estañol was then Minister of Gobernación.

[8] E. Vázquez Gómez to Madero, June 4, 1911, BN 2095; Casasola, *Historia gráfica*, I, 298.

[9] Casasola, *Historia gráfica*, I, 298.

thorized the government to make use of a six-million-peso emergency fund to pay the expenses of the auxiliary forces and the cost of war, only a few days after Manuel Calero had sponsored a resolution to liquidate the financial obligations resulting from the revolution.[10] Gustavo, who had largely financed the revolution with funds which he had embezzled for that purpose, soon presented a bill for some 700,000 pesos and asked for an immediate payment.[11] His itemized account was approved on July 3 by Emilio Vázquez Gómez, Minister of Gobernación, and shortly thereafter Gustavo received the money. Even though the expenditures made by Gustavo, as shown by his statement,[12] were legitimate, the fact that this settlement was made before any other claim was paid, and that the general public was not cognizant of an unexecuted warrant for Gustavo's arrest as a result of his embezzlement, made both Madero and his brother natural targets for charges of corruption and self-interest. The resultant unpopularity had a material effect on the failure of the regime.

One of the immediate and pressing problems confronting Madero was the appointment of provisional state governors, since it was essential to have the state organizations favorably inclined to the ideals of the revolution. The designation of these governors proved to be a monumental task. In some states there were rivals for the post, while in others no qualified men were available. In still others the legislatures, which according to the various constitutions were responsible for the final approval, and which were made up of Díaz' appointees, were unco-operative and insisted on naming men known to be opposed to Madero.

In Aguascalientes the legislature, immediately after Díaz' fall and without consulting Madero's wishes, named a governor whose appointment was displeasing to Madero.[13] The appointee was relatively unknown, and Madero felt that men of national prestige were needed.[14] At Madero's insistence the governor was not allowed to take office and Alberto Fuentes D., well known to be sympathetic to reform, was ap-

---

[10] Report by the Minister of Hacienda, October 13, 1911, *El País*, October 14, 1911, p. 1; Casasola, *Historia gráfica*, I, 296.

[11] See *Investigation of Mexican Affairs*, II, 2634–40, for the details of this embezzlement.

[12] Report of the Minister of Hacienda, October 13, 1911, *El País*, October 14, 1911, p. 1. Gustavo's itemized account there appears in full.

[13] Felipe Ruiz Chávez to Madero, May 28, 1911, BN 1832.

[14] Madero to E. Vázquez Gómez, May 31, 1911, BN 2087.

pointed.[15] Fuentes, carried away by his zeal, felt constrained to disregard the state constitution and to intervene in the election for constitutional governor. Madero rebuked him sharply for his activities, reminding him that his function as provisional governor was to provide honest elections, not to try to prevent election of the popular choice.[16]

In Chihuahua the situation was even more dangerous, for not only was the legislature recalcitrant in approving Abraham González but a federal force under General Villar continued to campaign in the state, attacking Cuchillo Parado on May 27, six days after the treaty had been signed.[17] It was not until early June that González was secure in his office and the state capital cleared of Villar's troops.[18]

Venustiano Carranza was selected by Madero and the revolutionary leaders to occupy the provisional post in Coahuila, but on May 26 the legislature approved a rival with Díaz sympathies.[19] Immediate objection by Madero and a threat of force by Francisco Vázquez Gómez brought about a change in attitude on the part of the legislature and resulted in the approval of Carranza on May 27.[20] Until the end of May the situation was critical in Durango, the state officials refusing to recognize revolutionary authority and denying the army the right to enter the capital.[21] In view of the delicate situation, Madero commissioned his brother Emilio, who had three thousand troops under his command at Torreón, to investigate and attempt a pacific solution.[22] By May 30 the situation was so explosive that the consul general of the United States at Monterrey requested Madero's direct intervention to prevent "unnecessary fighting" in Durango, and Madero ordered Emilio to "pacify" the state capital.[23] The immediate danger was brought to an abrupt end when Emilio occupied the city peacefully on May 31.[24]

---

[15] Casasola, *Historia gráfica*, I, 298.
[16] Madero to Alberto Fuentes D., June 18, 1911, BN 650.
[17] Madero to De la Barra, May 27 and 31, 1911, BN 153, 174.
[18] Madero to E. Madero, June 2, 1911, BN 1266.
[19] Salvador Madero to Madero, May 26, 1911, BN 1325.
[20] American Consul at Saltillo to State Department, May 27, 1911, *FR*, 1911, p. 495; F. Vázquez Gómez to President of Coahuila State Legislature, May 27, 1911, *MP*, 277; Vázquez Gómez, *Memorias políticas*, 278–79.
[21] Emilio Madero to Madero, May 27, 1911, BN 1212.
[22] Madero to Emilio Madero, May 28, 1911, BN 1214.
[23] M. E. Hanna to Madero, May 30, 1911, BN 938; Madero to Hanna, May 31, 1911, BN 939.
[24] Emilio Madero to Madero, May 31, 1911, BN 1222.

In Guerrero a crisis developed soon after the treaty had been signed. Francisco Figueroa was named provisional governor with Madero's approval, but his authority was contested by a political hopeful, Castillo Calderón, who promptly began appointing local provisional authorities.[25] As soon as this news reached Madero, he reaffirmed the appointment of Figueroa as the civil leader and Ambrosio Figueroa as the principal military chieftain and ordered Ambrosio to force Castillo Calderón to submit to proper authority.[26] Confronted with this show of force, Castillo recognized Madero's choice and thereby averted a serious clash.[27]

In other states the determination of the local authorities to maintain their power regardless of the central government's orders led to confusion and instability. In Jalisco the Díaz appointees demonstrated their ire by ordering the *rurales* to attack a popular victory demonstration; but when De la Barra ordered Governor Ahumada to cease resistance and the government was surrendered to Madero's choice for provisional governor, peace returned to Guadalajara and to Jalisco.[28] In San Luis Potosí the confusion was partly the result of conflicting orders from Madero and Francisco Vázquez Gómez: one ordered the local military leader to withdraw and the other told him to remain to establish order.[29] But the condition was soon clarified with the appointment of Rafael Cepeda, the most outstanding of the local Antireelectionists, as provisional governor.[30]

In Sinaloa, the incumbent governor's refusal to resign in spite of orders brought on armed conflict; the battle for Culiacán began on May 30 and ended on June 3 with the capitulation of the governor.[31] In Sonora the general problem was complicated by a lack of revolutionary finances, necessitating forced loans, and by the demands for redress by the militant and belligerent Yaquis.[32] By early June, however,

[25] Madero to A. Figueroa, May 24, 1911, BN 610; Figueroa to Madero, May 28, 1911, BN 611.

[26] Madero to Figueroa, May 29 and 30, 1911, BN 613, 615.

[27] Figueroa to Madero, May 31, 1911, BN 609.

[28] A. Arch to Madero, May 24, 25, and 26, 1911, BN 95–97; A. Ulloa to Madero, May 24, 1911, BN 2057; De la Barra to Madero, May 27, 1911, BN 155.

[29] Madero to Cándido Navarro, May 28, 1911, BN 1497; Navarro to Madero, May 29, 1911, BN 1498.

[30] Casasola, *Historia gráfica*, I, 299.

[31] Madero to Diego Redo, May 28, 1911, BN 1722; Madero to De la Barra, May 30, 1911, BN 170; M. Bonilla to Madero, June 4, 1911, BN 238.

[32] President of Cámara de Comercio of Hermosillo to Madero, May 23, 1911, BN 282; Bonilla to Madero, May 25, 1911, BN 233.

financial arrangements had been made to sustain the revolutionary troops, and the Yaquis agreed to return to their lands to await final consideration of their demands.[33] In the remaining states some difficulties arose, but they proved to be fleeting and easy of solution except in Morelos, where Emiliano Zapata was the recognized leader not only of the revolutionary forces but of the Indians as well. Since the complexity of the problem there defied solution by either the ad interim government or Madero during his tenure, a discussion of Zapata and Morelos will be reserved for a later chapter.

As soon as apparent peace had been restored by a partial solution of the more pressing matters, Madero began his journey to the capital. His trip to Mexico City was a veritable tour of triumph, with immense crowds gathering at every stop to cheer the new national hero. An estimated 100,000 persons lined the streets to welcome him to Mexico City when he arrived on June 7, with the normal crowds swollen by numerous revolutionary leaders and their staffs, some of whom had come hundreds of miles to be present on the memorable occasion.[34] Among those who had come to Mexico, and among the first to greet Madero as he alighted from the train, was Emiliano Zapata, for the Morelos insurgent had a number of grave issues to discuss with his chief. After a short stay in the city, Madero and his entourage began a trip through Morelos and Guerrero in compliance with a promise made to Zapata shortly after his arrival in Mexico.[35] During the rapid four-day tour Madero met and conferred with most of the revolutionary leaders and many of those having vested interests in the state, both groups attempting to impress him with the justice of their particular demands. In Cuernavaca he reviewed four thousand of Zapata's troops,[36] who wished to demonstrate both their loyalty and their strength. In most of the towns and cities he was received with enthusiasm, but in Tlaquiltenango he made himself unpopular by justifying the summary execution of Gabriel Tepepa by order of Ambrosio Figueroa.[37]

Back in Mexico City by June 16, Madero began seriously to consider

[33] E. H. Gayou to Madero, June 10, 1911, BN 785.
[34] Casasola, *Historia gráfica*, I, 305–306.
[35] Magaña, *Emiliano Zapata*, I, 158, 161–62.
[36] *Ibid.*, 164. According to Rosa King (*Tempest over Mexico*, 68), there were not so many under arms, but other sources seem to indicate approximately that number.
[37] Magaña, *Emiliano Zapata*, I, 165–66. Gabriel Tepepa was a colorful insurgent, very popular with his people; some of his activities bordered on ban-

the future of the revolutionary cause, for there was much planning necessary and much work to be done. Even then the forces of reaction had begun to re-emerge, and the revolutionary party showed signs of disintegration. Madero was bitterly castigated by the anti-Reyistas for allowing Bernardo Reyes to return immediately after the end of the revolution.[38] Another segment of the populace criticized him for allowing the federal army to remain unchanged while insisting on the discharge of revolutionary forces as rapidly as possible. The appointment of some conservatives and half-revolutionaries to the cabinet subjected him to other attacks; and within a month of the collapse of the Díaz regime there were indications that Madero had lost much of his popularity, even among some of those who had been previously very close to him. Roque Estrada said that he and many others considered Madero "only the apostle and the leader, but never the governor."[39] These events, coupled with other disturbing signs, impelled Madero to issue a public manifesto in late June, his first since the one following Díaz' resignation.

In this pronouncement, Madero reaffirmed his faith in the people's capacity to govern themselves "with serenity and wisdom" while he gave hope to the general public with his promise to do all he could for the alleviation of suffering of the lower social and economic orders. He made it clear, however, that economic improvement could not be obtained "by means of decrees or laws, but [only] by the constant and laborious efforts of all social classes." He made no promise to give better salaries, but he did promise an opportunity to obtain better salaries and an improved social condition by dint of hard work.

Pointedly promising unprejudiced justice and treatment, Madero warned the vested interests that they could no longer "count on the impunity which those privileged by fortune enjoyed in times past, when for them the laws were so lenient, and for the unfortunates so strict."[40] He promised justice according to law, not dependent on influence, and planned to give concessions to the privileged class only if those concessions were compatible with the public interest. To the colonial-minded

---

ditry. As a means of preventing a spread of rapine and pillage, Figueroa ordered his execution.

[38] Casasola, *Historia gráfica*, I, 308–309.
[39] Estrada to Madero, June 26, 1911, *MP*, 292–94.
[40] Madero, "Manifiesto a la nación," June 24, 1911, in Taracena, *Madero*, 437–43.

group fresh from the blessings of the Díaz period, Madero's statement must have been alarming. But the general aura of his statement was conciliatory, designed to be reassuring to those who feared a regime of radicalism while giving hope to those who sought reform. Far from meeting the desired end, however, the manifesto frightened the adherents of the old regime with its reforming tendencies at the same time that it convinced the more radical of the Antire-electionists of Madero's basic conservatism. The Vázquez Gómez brothers particularly decried his tendency to co-operate with those recently dispossessed of office and his failure to follow their own recommendations. Emilio Vázquez, impelled in part by a violent quarrel with President de la Barra and fearful of his own waning influence, proposed that the ad interim president resign immediately in order to allow Madero to assume the presidency. Objection on constitutional and political grounds, particularly by Ernesto Madero, insured the immediate failure of the proposal.[41]

Emilio, however, had enlisted the support of some of the revolutionary generals, who had pledged themselves and their men to use "all means at their command" to force compliance with the Plan of San Luis Potosí "in all its parts."[42] This compliance would mean Madero's elevation to the presidency at once and, incidentally, the recognition of these same revolutionaries as generals in the regular army. Madero was not unduly alarmed at the generals' statement, since he thought it would end there; but when these same generals demanded of De la Barra, on July 18, compliance with the Plan of San Luis Potosí, the expulsion of Científicos[43] from the cabinet, retention of Emilio Vázquez in the cabinet,[44] and appointment of revolutionary generals to regular status, the affair presented a different aspect.[45] Military leaders dictating to civilian officials being completely foreign to his concept of government, Madero warned the generals that he would not countenance their political interference. It is not surprising that when he em-

---

[41] F. Vázquez Gómez, *Memorias políticas,* 288, 303–304.

[42] Statement signed by Juan Andreu Almazán, Cándido Navarro, Gabriel M. Hernández, and others, July 11, 1911, Taracena, *Madero,* 494–95. Emilio had in his possession a copy of the demands made by Almazán *et al.;* see F. Vázquez Gómez, *Memorias políticas,* 303–304.

[43] Which would presumably include Ernesto Madero.

[44] Emilio was scheduled to leave the cabinet soon, since Francisco was a candidate for office.

[45] F. Vázquez Gómez, *Memorias políticas,* 306; G. M. Hernández and others to F. Vázquez Gómez, July 22, 1911, in Magaña, *Emiliano Zapata,* I, 227.

phasized his viewpoint to Francisco Vázquez Gómez the latter upheld the generals' actions, since their position was favorable to his brother.[46]

Since Vázquez Gómez had not reacted favorably, Madero called on Gustavo Madero to act as his intermediary.[47] Gustavo was instructed to tell the recalcitrant generals that if they wished to take part in politics they would have to sever their connections with the revolutionary army, and that if they continued in their attitude they would "feel the force of the government and the immense majority of the insurgent chiefs" still loyal to Madero's command.[48] Madero was now more than ever firmly committed to support the ad interim government and insisted on Emilio Vázquez Gómez' resignation.[49] In view of De la Barra's adamant refusal to consider their demands and Madero's trenchant stand on the question, a delegation of civilians and military men visited Madero in Tehuacán, Puebla, in an effort to force him to change his view. But he refused to submit to coercion; he was pleasant to the civilians, cold and haughty with the military men, and reaffirmed his decision to support the government.[50] The interview was acrid; some of the military made such seditious remarks as "We will renew the revolution" and "If another minister is put in the place of Emilio Vázquez Gómez, we will kick him out."[51] Emilio's resignation[52] on August 2 and the subsequent arrest of four generals when they returned from Tehuacán[53] brought an end to the affair but did nothing to heal the fundamental breach which had appeared in the revolutionary ranks. It was now obvious that Madero would not support Francisco Vázquez Gómez for the vice-presidency.

In the meantime another series of events had transpired which did much to convince a segment of the revolutionaries that Madero had been wooed and won by the reactionary camp. He was scheduled to appear in Puebla in mid-July, but some two weeks before that time he was warned of a plot against his life.[54] Although he was inclined to dis-

[46] Madero to F. Vázquez Gómez, July 23 and 25, 1911, *MP,* 355, 357; F. Vázquez Gómez, *Memorias políticas,* 355.

[47] Madero was then at Tehuacán, Puebla.

[48] Madero to G. Madero, July 25, 1911, *LO,* April 1, 1934, p. 2.

[49] Madero to E. Vázquez Gómez, July 26, 1911, *MP,* 364–65. A prior agreement had been made on this point, but now Emilio wished to remain.

[50] F. B. Serrano Ortiz to President of the Antire-electionist Club of Mexico, August 5, 1911, in Magaña, *Emiliano Zapata,* I, 239–43.

[51] Quoted in Casasola, *Historia gráfica,* I, 331.

[52] For the text, see *Nueva Era,* August 3, 1911, p. 3.

[53] *Times* (London), August 7, 1911, p. 3.

[54] Anonymous to Madero, June 29, 1911, BN 1673.

count the accuracy of the report, subsequent investigation convinced Rodolfo and Gildardo Magaña of the actual danger, and they in turn transmitted their fears to Gustavo and Emilio Vázquez Gómez in early July.[55] Madero was again warned, but again he refused to believe there was danger.[56] Nevertheless, Abraham Martínez, sent by Gustavo Madero to Puebla to investigate, was so firmly convinced of the authenticity of the reports that he arrested a number of prominent politicians, friends of the former Díaz governor, only to have the arrests disavowed by the President and to be subjected to arrest himself on the grounds of exceeding his authority.[57] As a final attempt to prevent harm from befalling Madero, a group of revolutionaries publicly threatened the old regime with drastic vengeance if Madero were made the object of an attack.[58]

On July 12, the day on which Madero was scheduled to appear in Puebla, a serious clash occurred between the federal troops and the revolutionaries in the city, apparently the result of deliberate action by the federal commander, General Blanquet.[59] Madero, having been delayed at Tlaxcala, arrived on the following day to be greeted with a highly colored account of revolutionary culpability, which convinced him the federal troops had taken proper action.[60] The sacking of the Covadonga textile mills, the day after his arrival, was added proof to him that malcontents masquerading as revolutionaries had been responsible for the disturbance. By attending a gala celebration given by the conservatives, even before the Maderista casualties had been interred, he further alienated his followers and made it appear that he had turned his back on his supporters and was allied with the old regime.[61] His handling of the entire situation, from the support he gave De la Barra in the arrest of Abraham Martínez to the public embrace he bestowed on General Blanquet for his "loyalty and valiancy," was totally inept, either because of misinformation or through a mistaken attempt to be conciliatory.[62] The mistake was costly; there

[55] Magaña, *Emiliano Zapata*, I, 209–10.
[56] Guillermo and Gustavo Gaona Salazar to F. Vázquez Gómez, November 7, 1930, *MP*, 314–33.   [57] Magaña, *Emiliano Zapata*, I, 213–14.
[58] Casasola, *Historia gráfica*, I, 323.
[59] Magaña, *Emiliano Zapata*, I, 215. The revolutionaries consistently reported that such a clash was to be the mask for an attack on Madero.
[60] F. Vázquez Gómez, *Memorias políticas*, 305, 313.
[61] Magaña, *Emiliano Zapata*, I, 217.
[62] As will be made clear during the course of this work, there seems to be no doubt that this action was an honest mistake on Madero's part and not the result of either self-interest or adherence to Porfirista ideas.

is little wonder that many revolutionaries were now skeptical and disappointed.

Contemporaneous with the prejudicial actions which Madero took with regard to the affair of the generals and the Puebla episode, a bitter internecine struggle developed over the formation of a new party. Feeling that the Antire-electionist party had served its turn and had disappeared, at least in name, Madero recommended to Francisco Vázquez Gómez, who was violently opposed to the idea, the establishment of the Partido Constitucional Progresista as a substitute for the old party.[63] Contending that a new party would appear to be an attempt to negate the principles for which the revolution was fought, the Vázquez Gómez brothers prophesied that a disintegration of the revolutionary front would result.[64] Even though Francisco Vázquez Gómez modestly said that he had no desire to be a candidate for the vice-presidency,[65] it seems clear that the real reason for his objection was the fear that he would no longer be considered the candidate if a new party were formed.

Disregarding Vázquez' objections, on July 9, Madero surrendered his titular leadership of the party, named a committee of well-known revolutionaries[66] to take command, and recommended the formation of the Partido Constitucional Progresista to uphold the constitution and bring to fruition the revolutionary ideals.[67] Vázquez Gómez charged that the committee were working against the interests of the revolution and were mere Madero puppets, but the inclusion of Roque Estrada, who was critical of Madero's recent actions, gave a rather hollow ring to the accusations.[68] Inasmuch as Madero recommended that the new party use the 1910 platform and the Plan of San Luis Potosí as the basis for its own platform, it was obvious that he envisioned a change in name and organization rather than in substance.[69]

One of the principal issues was, and continued to be, the vice-presi-

[63] Madero, "Manifiesto a la nación," July 9, 1911, *LO*, April 1, 1934, p. 1; F. Vázquez Gómez, *Memorias políticas*, 290.

[64] F. Vázquez Gómez to Madero, July 8, 1911, *MP*, 296–98.

[65] F. Vázquez Gómez, *Memorias políticas*, 287.

[66] Juan Sánchez Azcona, Gustavo Madero, José Vasconcelos, Alfredo Robles Domínguez, Roque Estrada, Enrique Bordes Mangel, Eduardo Hay, Miguel Díaz Lombardo, Heriberto Frías, and Roque González Garza. All these men had been connected with the movement longer than had Francisco Vázquez Gómez.

[67] Madero, "Manifiesto a la nación," July 9, 1911, *LO*, April 1, 1934, p. 1.

[68] F. Vázquez Gómez, *Memorias políticas*, 368; Estrada to Madero, June 26, 1911, *MP*, 292–94.

[69] Madero, "Manifiesto a la nación," July 9, 1911, *LO*, April 1, 1934, p. 1.

Ad Interim Government

dential candidacy. In early July, José María Pino Suárez of Yucatán was suggested as a candidate; Gustavo was bitterly opposed to Francisco Vázquez Gómez because of the New York meeting with Limantour; and Emilio Madero accused Emilio Vázquez of interfering in the politics of Durango.[70] Although Francisco Vázquez Gómez was assured that he was still the candidate in late July, he feared he was losing ground and therefore supported a group who constituted themselves as the Centro Antirreeleccionista de México, pretending to be the legitimate continuation of the old party and supporting the original nominees of 1910.[71] Vázquez Gómez' open affiliation with the Centro and the attacks which it in turn made on Madero convinced Madero of the need for a new candidate.[72] A final break was approached when Emilio, on leaving the cabinet, violently attacked De la Barra, and Madero replied by giving support to the government.[73]

The convention at which the new party was to select candidates and write a platform met in Mexico City on August 27; over fifteen hundred delegates, each representing at least a hundred voters, took part in the deliberations.[74] After renominating Madero by acclamation in the first session,[75] the convention undertook the more serious tasks of writing a platform and choosing a vice-presidential candidate. The platform presented no serious obstacles. In sessions sometimes "turbulent but generally well-conducted,"[76] each article was debated carefully and fully until agreement was reached on a basic set of principles which differed little from the 1910 document. The platform promised electoral and political reform, return to constitutional practices, a new constitutional article governing freedom of the press, increased facilities for public instruction along with general educational reform, "Mexicanization" of the railways,[77] redress to the Yaquis and Mayas particularly and improved Indian relations generally, encouragement

[70] Pino Suárez to F. Vázquez Gómez, July 13, 1911, *MP*, 359–60; Emilio Madero to Madero, July 14, 1911, BN 1231.
[71] Madero to F. Vázquez Gómez, July 22, 1911, *MP*, 353–55; F. Vázquez Gómez to Madero, July 29, 1911, *ibid.*, 366–72.
[72] Madero's speech in Veracruz, September 23, 1911, VC.
[73] See text of Emilio's resignation, *Nueva Era*, August 3, 1911, p. 3; Madero to De la Barra, August 2, 1911, *ibid.*, 1.
[74] Fred Morris Dearing (American chargé d'affaires) to State Department, September 4, 1911, *FR*, 1911, p. 516.
[75] Casasola, *Historia gráfica*, I, 341.
[76] Dearing to State Department, September 4, 1911, *FR*, 1911, p. 516.
[77] Meaning the installation of Mexicans in the responsible positions of the railroads, which now belonged to Mexico.

to the extent of financial assistance to the small agricultural enterprises, more equitable tax distribution, and, finally, strict enforcement of the Laws of Reform.[78] Since Madero believed that severe application of the Laws of Reform was unnecessary, the inclusion of this article indicates the freedom with which the convention deliberated.[79]

The only important struggle in the convention revolved around the selection of a vice-presidential candidate. Madero and the party's directive council supported Pino Suárez, but Vázquez Gómez still had a strong contingent and both Iglesias Calderón and Alfredo Robles Domínguez had their backers.[80] After long and choleric debates Pino Suárez was chosen by a clear majority. The hostility and fury of the defeated Vazquistas was so obvious that Antonio Díaz Soto y Gama recommended reconsideration of the action and proposed the popular Federico González Garza as a compromise candidate, but the convention declined.[81]

Dr. Vázquez Gómez, apparently forgetting the manner in which he had been selected in 1910, accused Madero of "imposing" Pino and of committing a breach of faith in supporting the *yucateco*. But from Madero's point of view his actions were completely justified. The special conditions which had dictated the nomination of Vázquez Gómez in the preceding year had disappeared, and a new set of circumstances, in which the more loyal Pino could be of greater help, had arisen. Pino Suárez was willing to accept Madero's leadership—this was vital for the stability of the regime. He had given distinguished service before, during, and after the revolution, and since he was decidedly progressive he could be counted upon to be a jealous guardian of the revolutionary ideas. Vázquez, on the other hand, had made it quite obvious that he would be more inclined to attempt to lead than to follow, had refused to give aid to the revolution until it was practically assured of success, and had certainly given little evidence of political liberalism. His one claim to the nomination was that he had been the candidate the year before.

Nevertheless, there were some murmurings of discontent with the choice. Madero felt constrained to enlist the aid of Governor Car-

---

[78] An English translation of the platform may be found in *FR*, 1911, pp. 515–16.

[79] Madero's speech to the convention, August 31, 1911, *Nueva Era,* September 1, 1911, p. 5.

[80] Madero's speech at Veracruz, September 23, 1911, VC.

[81] Casasola, *Historia gráfica,* I, 344.

ranza of Coahuila, to whom he lauded Pino and castigated Vázquez Gómez; and that of Abraham González of Chihuahua, to whom he wrote in the same vein, stressing the importance of unified action.[82] Pino Suárez himself made a conciliatory gesture to Vázquez Gómez, but Ernesto Madero reported in mid-September that the party leaders had been "encountering many difficulties" in persuading voters to support Pino.[83] Madero, then in Yucatán, promptly published a manifesto in which he condemned Vázquez and praised Pino for his devotion to the democratic cause and then, emphasizing the need for democracy, urged support for Pino because he was "the candidate of the convention," and it was "the duty of all the party members represented to accept his candidacy, since to do otherwise would make sterile the efforts of all those who fought for the triumph of democratic principles; therefore all those of like political beliefs are obligated to accept the decision of the convention."[84]

It was now obvious that Madero's original popularity was waning. The decline had begun with the hurried payment to Gustavo and continued with Pino's nomination, which had transpired in September. In order to take advantage of the trend, some of Madero's political opponents began a movement to have the election postponed.[85] Before detailing this maneuver, however, it will be necessary to trace other political developments during the summer, for by September Bernardo Reyes had again become a potent factor.

Shortly before the collapse of the Díaz regime, General Reyes had begun his return to Mexico but had stopped in Havana at Madero's insistence.[86] Once the success of the revolution was definitely assured, Heriberto Barrón took the lead in expressing strong sentiment for the return of the old warrior to allow him to lend his services in the monumental task of rebuilding the nation. Reyes and his supporters, according to Barrón, had no political ambitions or desires whatsoever.[87] The General's son reaffirmed Barrón's statements, thus convincing Ma-

[82] Madero to Carranza, September 7, 1911, *LO,* March 18, 1934, p. 2; Madero to González, September 7, 1911, *ibid.*

[83] Pino Suárez to F. Vázquez Gómez, September 8, 1911, *ibid.;* Ernesto Madero to Madero, September 11, 1911, *ibid.*

[84] Madero, "Manifiesto a la nación," September 12, 1911, *Nueva Era,* September 13, 1911, pp. 1, 8.

[85] Wilson to State Department, September 22, 1911, *FR,* 1911, pp. 518–19.

[86] Rodolfo Reyes, *De mi vida, memorias políticas,* I, 140–41.

[87] Barrón to Madero, May 20, 1911, *La Discusión* (Havana, Cuba), May 21, 1911.

dero; and on June 9, General Reyes was welcomed to Mexico City by large crowds in which there were a conspicuous number of army officers.[88] Within a few days Reyes renounced all political ambition, since, as he said, his candidacy would be an element of discord in an already delicate situation.[89]

Madero, hoping to take advantage of the General's undoubted popularity, and harboring the mistaken belief that Reyes would prove co-operative, tentatively offered him a post in the new cabinet, provided Madero proved successful in the presidential election.[90] Before the end of July, however, Madero changed his opinion considerably; he was now sure that Reyes was going to make a bid for the presidency, either by legal or by forceful means; and although he did not consider the old General's popularity sufficient to constitute a real threat to his own success or his government, he favored watching Reyes very closely.[91] True to form and expectation, Reyes "succumbed" to the supplications of his supporters and early in August asked Madero for "permission" to accede to the demands of his supporters and announce his candidacy. To be consistent with his stated political philosophy, Madero could do little but agree, but he took occasion to remind Reyes that there had never been any question of a promise not to run, and that requesting permission was unnecessary. Moreover, Madero promised Reyes perfect freedom in conducting his campaign in so far as he was able to make such a guarantee, while Reyes pledged to limit himself to purely democratic practices and to give his support to the victorious candidate regardless of the outcome.[92]

The agreement was short lived. Soon both candidates were exchanging recriminations, with each accusing the other of dishonesty and bad faith. While Madero was delivering a diatribe against Reyes in Cuautla, Morelos, the Maderistas were on the verge of riot in Mexico City as a result of Reyes' campaign of vilification.[93] In an effort to keep

[88] R. Reyes to Madero, May 30, 1911, BN 1731; Casasola, *Historia gráfica*, I, 308.
[89] "Manifiesto del Gral. Bernardo Reyes," June 12, 1911, Biblioteca Hacienda.
[90] Madero's statement concerning possible appointment of Reyes to Ministry of War and Marine, undated, BN 1728.
[91] Madero to F. González Garza, July 30, 1911, *LO,* April 8, 1934, p. 1.
[92] Madero to De la Barra, August 2, 1911, *LO,* March 25, 1934, p. 1. This letter, written by Madero and countersigned by Reyes, reported the results of the conference which the two men had held. The letter was published in *Nueva Era,* August 3, 1911.
[93] Madero's speech of August 18, 1911, *Nueva Era,* August 19, 1911; Casasola, *Historia gráfica*, I, 337.

the campaign within bounds, at Madero's suggestion two conferences between the candidates were held in late August, at which time Madero proposed the creation of a bipartisan electoral commission of six members to supervise and observe the campaign and election, the committee to meet in Monterrey, the capital of Reyes' home state, to insure freedom of action.[94] Even though such a commission, meeting in Nuevo León, would presumably be to his advantage, Reyes declined the offer.

A few days later a disgraceful attack on Reyes, in which the aged candidate was severely handled by a mob of enraged Madero partisans, completed the breach between the two. Although Madero was not responsible for the attack and publicly condemned those who had taken part, his waning popularity was still further reduced.[95] It was under these conditions that the Convención Reyista, at its opening session on September 12, petitioned Congress for a postponement of the election, arguing that to hold it then would be a "monstrous farce."[96] There had been some question, at the end of the revolution, concerning the date to be set for the general elections. At Madero's urging that a long delay would be dangerous, the general election date had been set for October 1, with the secondary balloting to be held on October 15.[97] In mid-September, with little more than two weeks remaining before the election and with Madero's power declining steadily, the Reyistas felt that a postponement would work to their advantage.

Even before the formal request had been made, Madero heard rumors that such a petition would be presented. He therefore telegraphed the president of the Chamber of Deputies, warning him that a postponement would be dangerous and might lead to a renewal of the conflict, since the people had learned "how to conquer their rights."[98] The message, couched in terms which smacked of coercion, was so strongly resented by many congressmen that some who had objected to postponement now supported delay.[99] Although a majority of the Chamber still opposed the petition, the margin was so slim that both Ernesto Madero and Manuel Calero urged Madero to clarify his previous state-

[94] Madero to Editor, *Nueva Era,* September 1, 1911, p. 1.
[95] *Nueva Era,* September 4, 1911, p. 1.
[96] Casasola, *Historia gráfica,* I, 349.
[97] Madero to Robles Domínguez, May 25, 1911, BN 1773; Madero to Calero, May 26, 1911, BN 265; *Times* (London), June 5, 1911, p. 5.
[98] Madero to President of the Chamber of Deputies, September 11, 1911, *LO,* March 25, 1934, p. 1.
[99] Calero to Madero, September 13, 1911, *ibid.*

ments in more diplomatic terms in order to placate Congress.[100] He complied immediately:

Permit me to call attention to the fact that no threat exists. . . . When I say that I will not be responsible for what happens, in spite of my desires, it is because the popular discontent would show itself in my name. . . . In case of a postponement of the elections . . . the public would think that the projects of Reyes were being favored and that the fruit of the revolution would be lost. You know I have grave responsibilities to the nation for having been one of the principal factors in the present state of affairs. . . . It is my intention to support the present government as much as my strength permits.[101]

The message served its purpose: after serious and extensive debates the petition for postponement was disallowed, four days before the election was to be held.[102] Reyes immediately withdrew from the race, charging Madero with coercion; then, exhorting his principal supporters to maintain the organization until such time as it would be opportune to return to occupy his "post," Reyes left the country.[103] Since many of his supporters had already gone to San Antonio, Texas, where they were freely predicting an outbreak of revolution as soon as he arrived, the atmosphere was heavy with impending civil war.[104]

On the eve of the election it was evident that Madero was still the popular choice for the presidency; but the outcome of the vice-presidential election was in doubt,[105] and it was principally with regard to that office that charges of coercion and fraud were mentioned. Reyes and Vázquez supporters were loud in their condemnation, insisting that the election would prove nothing except that Madero's policy of coercion was effective for the moment. In truth, there were some examples of political dishonesty throughout the country, with a particularly flagrant case of misuse of authority in Sinaloa, where the appointed provisional governor prevented the constitutionally elected governor from assuming office. Although Madero rebuked the governor for his actions, the fact remained that a Maderista was patently en-

[100] Ernesto Madero to Madero, September 13, 1911, *ibid.;* Calero to Madero, September 13, 1911, *ibid.*
[101] Madero to President of Chamber of Deputies, September 13, 1911, *ibid.*
[102] *Nueva Era,* September 26, 1911, p. 2.
[103] B. Reyes to José Peón del Valle and Samuel Espinosa de los Monteros, undated, in Casasola, *Historia gráfica,* I, 357.
[104] *El País,* October 4, 1911, p. 1.
[105] *Ibid.,* October 1, 1911, p. 1.

gaged in political malpractice and the odium reached to Madero himself.[106]

With regard to the probabilities of the election for vice-president, *El País,* although it supported Francisco León de la Barra, believed that Vázquez Gómez had the best chance to win and that Pino would run a poor third.[107] The Ambassador of the United States, on the other hand, was convinced that Pino would win.

> The intrigues of Francisco Vásquez [*sic*] Gómez and his brother . . . have come to naught. Gen. Reyes, who came into the country as the nominal savior of the old Díaz regime, seems to have become a byword and a jest in the arena of politics. . . . In my judgment, unless it should develop that there are combinations and arrangements governing the control of Congress and the naming of the Vice President, the elections will result in the complete triumph of the Maderista element.[108]

On election day a final appeal for orderly elections by the Executive Committee of the Partido Constitucional Progresista was apparently effective, for the American Ambassador reported that the polling places were peaceful, and De la Barra expressed his satisfaction that there had not been the "smallest disagreeable incident" in Mexico City that day.[109] As the first returns began to come in, it was obvious that Madero was winning by a large margin, and from the beginning the Reyes adherents charged fraud; but the Vázquez Gómez supporters withheld criticism until it was clear that Pino also was carrying the day. The October 1 election was merely for presidential electors, who then were charged with making the final selections on October 15, and toward the conversion of that group Vázquez bent his efforts. At Madero's behest the two antagonists met to discuss the situation, for Madero still hoped to obtain Vázquez' support for Pino; the conference, however, produced nothing but a public charge, which Madero categorically denied, that he had attempted to bribe Vázquez to support Pino Suárez.[110]

[106] Madero to Juan M. Banderas, September 20, 1911, in Taracena, *Madero,* 498.

[107] *El País,* October 1, 1911, p. 1. The ad interim president insisted that he was not a candidate and repeatedly said that he would refuse to take office even if elected. He tried to remain completely neutral in the struggle.

[108] Wilson to State Department, September 22, 1911, *FR,* 1911, p. 518.

[109] *El País,* October 1, 1911, p. 3; Wilson to State Department, October 27, 1911, *FR,* 1911, p. 519; Casasola, *Historia gráfica,* I, 361.

[110] *El País,* October 2, 8, 11, and 14, 1911, p. 1.

Immediately after the conference, Vázquez Gómez left for Guadalajara where, in spite of a previous commitment to support the party candidate, Roque Estrada was induced to throw his support to Vázquez.[111] But this maneuver, and others of the same type, availed the Vazquistas nought; for, aided by a summary prepared and published[112] by Gustavo Madero of the part played by Vázquez during the past year, the electors chose Pino Suárez by a comfortable majority. De la Barra was second, Vázquez a poor third, and a scattering of votes went to six other candidates.[113] In the presidential balloting, Madero received over 98 per cent of the votes.[114] That the election was the most nearly honest in the history of the Mexican nation admits of little doubt, but that Madero had alienated many groups was even less doubtful.

On November 6, 1911, Madero was sworn into office, De la Barra having decided, in view of the critical conditions in the country, to resign before the December 1 date on which Madero was scheduled for inauguration.[115] The government Madero was sworn to uphold was anything but stable and the country far from peaceful. Emilio Vázquez Gómez was in El Paso, Texas, sniping at Madero; Reyes was in San Antonio obviously plotting revolution; a former revolutionary was infuriated at Madero for a rebuke and was in open rebellion; Veracruz was on the verge of rebellion; two small revolutionary movements were in progress in Oaxaca; and, most serious of all, Emiliano Zapata had been in open rebellion for two months past in Morelos. To complicate further an already dangerous situation, many of Madero's followers had promised lands and better jobs to masses of people who were now demanding full compliance with those promises.

For Madero, who had insisted on the ad interim government in order to obviate criticism that he had seized power through a military operation, the period from May to November was disastrous. Without official status and therefore powerless and unwilling to determine government policy, he was nevertheless held responsible for every ill-judged action of the government. More important still, by his own actions he had lost popularity tremendously and now, when he needed the

[111] *Nueva Era,* October 6, 1911, p. 1; Madero to Estrada, October 8, 1911, *LO,* March 18, 1934, p. 2.
[112] In *Nueva Era,* October 16, 1911.
[113] For a tabulation of the votes see *ibid.,* October 24, 1911, p. 1.
[114] Gregorio Ponce de León, *El internato presidencial de 1911,* 196.
[115] Wilson to State Department, October 27, 1911, *FR,* 1911, pp. 519–20.

support of all elements of society, he found that a large proportion were either apathetic or openly hostile to him. One of the greatest factors of discord, one which has not yet been discussed, concerned Zapata in Morelos. The development of the Zapata rebellion should now be traced.

VIII

Zapata and Morelos

MORELOS, THE LAST BULWARK of the independent Indian communities where the villages were struggling with the encroaching haciendas, was on the verge of rebellion when Madero published his Plan de San Luis Potosí. The Indians of Anenecuilco, infuriated when a part of their village was taken by an *hacendado* in 1908, rebelled under the leadership of Emiliano Zapata, but the movement was quickly brought to an end. The "election" of Díaz-sponsored Pablo Escandón, by an adroit combination of fraud and force in 1909, further alienated the small landowner and villager in the state, but there was no attempt at rebellion then or immediately after Madero began his movement in 1910. It was not until December, 1910, that any real interest was shown in the Madero revolution. Pablo Torres Burgos was then sent to San Antonio, as an agent of Zapata and his friends, to discover means of co-operating with the Maderistas.[1] A quiet recruitment began at the turn of the year, and on February 7, before any information had come from Torres Burgos, Gabriel Tepepa attacked Tlaquiltenango to begin the revolution in Morelos. Within a month Zapata had assumed the leadership; by mid-April his forces were co-operating with those of the Maderista Ambrosio Figueroa of the neighboring state of Guerrero. This co-operation, in spite of friction and mutual mistrust, was so fruitful that by May 22 the Maderistas were in virtual control of both states.[2]

In the meantime, Zapata's natural suspicion of the motives of the relatively affluent Figueroa brothers was magnified when Ambrosio failed to comply with an agreement to attack Jojutla in April, and became conviction when Figueroa dispatched agents to discuss peace

[1] Magaña, *Emiliano Zapata,* I, 21, 105, 108.
[2] Gildardo Magaña, a member of Zapata's staff, consistently uses the term *maderista* with reference to his men in those months.

172

terms with Limantour in May.[3] Zapata did not then know that Figueroa was acting in concert with Madero, who was engaged in negotiations in Ciudad Juárez.[4] Nevertheless, the two southern leaders reached an accord on May 29 with regard to the future of Morelos, bringing that phase of the revolution to a close on a harmonious note.[5] A new factor fruitful of discord in the state was injected, however, when the ad interim government, apparently without consulting Zapata's wishes, appointed Juan C. Carreón as provisional governor.[6] Carreón, manager of the Bank of Morelos, favored the *hacendados* rather than the villagers.

After Madero arrived in Mexico City, Zapata had a long conference with him on June 8, at which time the Morelos revolutionary stressed his distrust of Figueroa, his fear that nothing progressive could be expected from the Carreón government, his desire not to demobilize his forces until the revolutionary gains had been consolidated, and a demand for land reform in Morelos.[7] In order to study the situation in person, Madero went to Cuernavaca, where on June 12 he conferred with the Zapatistas[8] and representatives of the *hacendados,* whose principal argument was that an immediate discharge of the revolutionary army was vital to peace in the state.[9] There could be little doubt concerning the desirability of an immediate discharge of most of Zapata's troops, for the maintenance of thousands of men under arms was a great expense. Since Zapata had no particular objection to a partial demobilization, Madero designated Gabriel Robles Domínguez to supervise the discharging operation in the Cuernavaca region and continued his journey through the remainder of the state and through Guerrero. Demobilization began immediately, with seven hundred men divested of their arms and returned to civilian life on the first day.[10] Depredations by other forces in the state, presumably Zapatistas, in-

[3] Magaña, *Emiliano Zapata,* I, 127–28, 158–59.
[4] *Times* (London), May 6, 1911, p. 10.
[5] Rodolfo Magaña to editors of Mexico City papers, May 29, 1911, in Magaña, *Emiliano Zapata,* I, 132–33.
[6] Magaña, *Emiliano Zapata,* I, 133.
[7] *Ibid.,* 158–61.
[8] Rosa E. King, *Tempest over Mexico,* 68. Mrs. King owned the hotel at which most of the party stayed while in Cuernavaca.
[9] Magaña, *Emiliano Zapata,* I, 162.
[10] Madero to E. Vázquez Gómez, June 13, 1911, BN 2096; Robles Domínguez to Madero, June 16, 1911, BN 1792. Each man was compensated, if an average payment of twenty pesos per man can be called compensation, for surrendering his arms and for his services to the cause.

tensified demands by the *hacendados* for an immediate disarming of all former revolutionaries and brought a demand from Madero to Zapata to punish those engaged in illegal activities.[11]

By the time Madero had completed his tour of inspection, he favored the continuation of demobilization until all Zapata's men had been discharged, but he also recommended to Carreón that former revolutionaries be brought from other states and put under Zapata's command to preserve order after that demobilization.[12] The prospect of retaining Zapata, under any consideration, as the commander of a military force was highly displeasing to those having property or financial interests in Morelos, and within a few days after Madero's return from that state these groups organized the "Sons of Morelos" to protect their interests.[13] Apparently at the instigation of the new group, *El Imparcial* published an exaggerated account of anarchy in Morelos, painting a picture of rape, rapine, pillage, and brigandage, with Cuernavaca a shambles and women fleeing from the horror.[14] The story was more than a mere exaggeration; it was almost wholly fabrication. Mrs. Rosa King and her daughter lived without fear in Cuernavaca, where Zapata maintained perfect order and where the citizens were protected from violence. The Zapatistas "lived among [them] peaceably for weeks. . . . Beneath their quite terrifying exteriors, [they] seemed . . . more like harmless and valiant children than anything else."[15] But the "Sons of Morelos" had access to the press, and their propaganda prevailed with the public.

Madero, convinced that conditions had not changed so drastically in the few days since he had left Morelos and anxious to invalidate the charge made by *El Imparcial* that Zapata was in rebellion, summoned the Indian leader to Mexico City for a conference. Zapata, who had implicit faith in Madero's honesty, immediately came to Mexico, conferred with Madero and Gustavo concerning the state of affairs in Morelos, and then returned to his state. While the general conditions there were stable and conducive to peaceful development, there was an unrest and impatience which led some villagers in Morelos and Puebla to seize lands which were legally or extralegally controlled by *hacen-*

---

[11] Association of Sugar and Alcohol Producers of Mexico to Madero, June 12, 1911, BN 121; Madero to Juan C. Carreón, June 15, 1911, BN 342.
[12] Edgcumb Pinchon, *Zapata, the Unconquerable,* 227.
[13] Magaña, *Emiliano Zapata,* I, 179.
[14] *El Imparcial,* June 19, 1911.
[15] King, *Tempest over Mexico,* 62–68, 76. Mrs. King describes in detail the situation in Cuernavaca under Zapata.

dados. Because of these actions, which could not be refuted, the propertied classes could hardly be expected to react favorably when Madero appealed to them to co-operate in "making those concessions which were compatible with an honest sense of justice."[16] They would make no concessions; the failure of the revolutionary ideal was vital to their interests, and Morelos was the first test. Here the reactionaries could experiment with methods of counterrevolution; here, too, could the more ardent social reformers experiment with complete revolution. Here the battle was fairly joined, and here the temporary triumph of the old regime was gained.

Neither Madero nor Zapata was fully cognizant of the force and power of the reaction, however, and demobilization in Morelos proceeded, with over three thousand men having been paid and returned to their homes before the end of July.[17] In spite of the demobilization, everyone conversant with the situation realized that some military force would be necessary to guarantee order after Zapata's army had disbanded; the obvious unrest precluded absolute order. Madero repeatedly recommended to Carreón that former revolutionaries from other states be brought to Morelos to serve as the garrison, and Carreón in turn repeatedly requested such troops from the government; but the request was consistently ignored by the Ministry of Gobernación under Emilio Vázquez Gómez.[18] The failure to supply troops for Morelos created an impossible situation in the state and justified Zapata's contention that complete demobilization would be dangerous. A slight increase in brigandage was further proof of his contention. At the same time this increase in depredations stimulated the vested-interest group in its determination to discredit the regime.

By late July the situation was so critical, in spite of an apparent peace and continued demobilization, that Madero requested Zapata to come to Tehuacán for an interview. Zapata, now completely wary, declined but at Madero's insistence sent his brother Eufemio and Jesús Morales as his agents. Zapata was convinced that De la Barra was giving aid to the machinations of the *hacendados,* and his agents so informed Madero; but Madero remained unconvinced.[19] Hardly had Eufemio and Morales returned to Morelos before it became obvious that De la Barra was not an advocate of the policy which Madero favored; on August

[16] Magaña, *Emiliano Zapata,* I, 199–200, 203. [17] *Ibid.,* 205–206.
[18] Madero to De la Barra, August 15, 1911, in Taracena, *Madero,* 453–56.
[19] Zapata to Madero, July 28, 1911, *LO,* April 15, 1934, p. 1; Madero to Zapata, August 7, 1911, *ibid.;* Magaña, *Emiliano Zapata,* I, 247.

Mexican Revolution

10, General Victoriano Huerta arrived in Cuernavaca in command of
a force of federal troops who were "to disarm the southerners if they
were opposed to being discharged."[20] In view of an attack which was
made on the federal force at Tres Marías,[21] between Mexico and Cuernavaca but in Morelos, Colonel Aureliano Blanquet was ordered to re-
inforce Huerta,[22] although it was recognized that large forces of federals in the state would probably precipitate open conflict. Zapata, still
hoping for a peaceful solution, notified Huerta that the responsibility
for a breach of the peace would rest with the government, but at the
same time he ceased discharging operations and notified his lieutenants
to be ready to fight.[23]

Madero, vitally concerned with the Morelos situation, decided to go
to Cuautla for a conference with Zapata in a last effort to avert a conflict. He arrived in Cuernavaca on August 13, the very day on which
De la Barra ordered Huerta to press the campaign to eliminate or disperse the Zapata forces. As a result of a telephone conversation with
Zapata, Madero strongly recommended to De la Barra that part of
Zapata's men be maintained as an effective force under the command
of a revolutionary from some other state.[24] To this suggestion De la
Barra replied that consideration of such a request could be given only
after the demobilization had been completed, and Huerta was ordered
to exercise his own discretion in the prosecution of the campaign but
to grant a truce if it appeared that a peaceful solution could be found.[25]
Zapata in his turn then demanded the resignation of Governor Carreón and the appointment of a man agreeable to the principal revolutionists, the withdrawal of the federal forces, and a guarantee of compliance with the revolutionary doctrine. Land reform was implicit in
this last demand.[26]

De la Barra was still unwilling to make concessions; he had a strong
antipathy to negotiating with Zapata, for he found it "truly disagree-

[20] Casasola, *Historia gráfica,* I, 332.
[21] Magaña, *Emiliano Zapata,* I, 248.
[22] Casasola, *Historia gráfica,* I, 332.
[23] *Ibid.,* 333; Huerta to De la Barra, August 12, 1911, *Nueva Era,* November
6, 1911, p. 1.
[24] De la Barra to Huerta, August 13, 1911, *Nueva Era,* November 6, 1911, p.
1; Madero to De la Barra, August 14, 1911, in Taracena, *Madero,* 451.
[25] De la Barra to Madero, August 14, 1911, *LO,* April 15, 1934, p. 2; José
González Salas to Huerta, August 14, 1911, *Nueva Era,* November 6, 1911, p. 2.
[26] Zapata to Madero, August 14, 1911, *Nueva Era,* August 16, 1911, p. 1.

176

able that an individual with antecedents such as his . . . [should be] permitted to maintain" such an independent attitude.[27] The President, imbued with the class consciousness and social philosophy of the Díaz regime, was amenable to supplication but not demands. Madero, on the other hand, was willing to make concessions to justified demands so long as the strength and prestige of the government did not suffer. He believed that naming Figueroa provisional governor, as De la Barra favored, would lead to bitterness and bloodshed which could be prevented by a more judicious choice. Moreover, he was convinced that the government was in error when it assumed that Zapata could be defeated easily.

I think it indispensable [he said to De la Barra] that it be resolved peacefully, for it would be dangerous to resort to arms. . . . Zapata now has over a thousand men ready and a large number could be raised and the revolution could then spread to Puebla. . . . Moreover, for these military operations the former revolutionaries [in the area] could not be counted on, since in no case will they fight against Zapata, but [will probably] make common cause with him.

For this reason I think it would be a very serious mistake to have recourse to arms, since this war would not be terminated in a few days and a great deal of blood would be spilled.[28]

Madero was now convinced that he could find a satisfactory solution to the impasse, but only if he had full authority to speak for the government. He exacted a promise from Huerta to refrain from offensive action for the nonce and then returned to Mexico on August 16, where he received the requested authorization.[29] The Council of Ministers recommended a suspension of hostilities for forty-eight hours, and Huerta was ordered to cease operations until further notice; but he had already begun an advance on Yautepec on the road to Cuautla,[30] which brought a bitter protest from Zapata. Zapata accused the government of deliberately fomenting conflict and charged Madero with

[27] De la Barra to Madero, August 15, 1911, *LO,* April 15, 1934, p. 2.
[28] Madero to De la Barra, August 15, 1911, in Taracena, *Madero,* 453–56.
[29] Madero to Huerta, October 31, 1911, *Nueva Era,* November 2, 1911, p. 1; Sánchez Azcona, "Madero, Huerta, el Gobierno y el Pueblo," *ibid.,* August 22, 1911, p. 1.
[30] González Salas to Huerta, August 17, 1911, *ibid.,* November 6, 1911, p. 2; Madero to Huerta, October 31, 1911, *ibid.,* November 2, 1911, p. 1.

177

Mexican Revolution

halfway measures in not having allowed the revolution to follow "its course until the full realization of its principles,"[31] but he then guaranteed the complete restoration of order within twenty-four hours provided the federal troops were withdrawn from the state.[32] Huerta, instead of complying with the orders to cease operations, informed the government that he was "consolidating" his forces on the road to Yautepec; he was again ordered to maintain his exact positions on August 18.[33]

In spite of Zapata's conviction that the government was responsible for the situation, he expressed his willingness to seek a peaceful solution, and for that reason Madero hurried to Cuautla even though he knew that his life would be in danger if his mission failed. Soon after his arrival on August 18 he spoke to the assembled Zapatistas, reaffirming his faith in the people and his belief in the justice of their demands while he blamed others for fomenting disorder in the state.[34] In the ensuing conferences Zapata and Madero quickly reached an agreement by the terms of which Eduardo Hay[35] was to be made provisional governor, Raúl Madero was to be given command of a revolutionary force to maintain order, the federal troops were to be concentrated in Cuernavaca and soon withdrawn, a garrison of former revolutionaries was to come from Hidalgo, and the demobilization of Zapata's men was to resume immediately.[36]

Although the agreement seemed to be satisfactory to both parties and Madero canceled a request for revolutionary troops from Guerrero,[37] a difference in interpretation developed at once, while Madero was still in Cuautla. Zapata insisted on the immediate withdrawal of federal troops, to be followed by complete demobilization, while De la Barra insisted on discharge first.[38] Zapata, still trusting in Madero's honesty

[31] Zapata to Madero, August 17, 1911, *LO,* April 15, 1934, p. 2. Zapata had reference to Madero's compromise in signing the Treaty of Ciudad Juárez.
[32] Zapata to De la Barra, August 17, 1911, in Magaña, *Emiliano Zapata,* I, 273.
[33] Huerta to González Salas, August 18, 1911, *Nueva Era,* November 6, 1911, p. 2; González Salas to Huerta, August 18, 1911, *ibid.*
[34] Zapata to Madero, August 17, 1911, *LO,* April 15, 1934, p. 2; Madero's address in Cuautla, August 18, 1911, *Nueva Era,* August 19, 1911, p. 2.
[35] Hay was one of Madero's most loyal lieutenants before the capitulation of Ciudad Juárez and had lost an eye in the campaign.
[36] Madero to De la Barra, August 18, 1911, *LO,* April 22, 1934, p. 1.
[37] Madero to Alberto García Granados, August 18, 1911, *ibid.* García Granados was then Minister of Gobernación.
[38] De la Barra to Madero, August 19, 1911, *LO,* April 22, 1934, p. 1.

Zapata and Morelos

and influence, agreed to the federal demand and began the slow discharge of his men before there was a concentration of government forces in Cuernavaca, but Huerta's almost simultaneous advance on Yautepec on August 19 brought the demobilization to a halt again.[39] Madero not only begged De la Barra to order Huerta to desist but also sent an urgent message to the commander of the advancing column asking him to refrain from offensive action until the situation could be clarified by orders from Mexico.[40] Madero was prepared to interfere personally after he received word that the mayor of Yautepec had been fired upon by the federal troops while carrying a white flag of truce, and on August 20 did go to Yautepec to see if he could remedy the situation.[41]

While Madero was desperately trying to convince the government of the efficacy of suspending hostilities, Governor Carreón was disseminating vivid accounts of Zapatista depredations in the state. Some of the men presumably engaged in these atrocities were actually conferring with Madero in Cuautla at the moment.[42] Confused by the conflicting reports, the Council of Ministers nevertheless agreed to order Huerta to suspend activities with the understanding that Zapata would evacuate Yautepec and concentrate his troops in Cuautla for demobilization, and that Cuautla would be garrisoned by Maderistas from Veracruz and Hidalgo as soon as demobilization had been completed.[43] Zapata was to be given forty-eight hours to complete discharging his men, during which time Huerta was ordered to cease offensive action but to remain in the state.[44] Zapata agreed to conform and withdrew from Yautepec on August 21.

In Cuautla the demobilization began anew under the direction of Raúl Madero and Gabriel Robles Domínguez,[45] while Madero and

[39] Madero to De la Barra, August 19, 1911, *ibid*. It is doubtful that Huerta actually ever suspended operations in compliance with the orders of August 17 and 18. It is certain that he was engaged in offensive action on the successive days August 14–21.
[40] Madero to De la Barra, August 19, 1911 (the second in a series of telegrams of that date), *ibid.;* Madero to Huerta, Blanquet, "or the chief of the federal forces advancing toward Yautepec," August 19, 1911, *ibid*.
[41] Madero to De la Barra, August 20, 1911, *ibid.*, 2; Madero to Robles Domínguez, August 20, 1911, *ibid.*, 8.
[42] Madero to De la Barra, August 20, 1911, *ibid.*, 2.
[43] De la Barra to Madero, August 20, 1911, *ibid.*, 8.
[44] De la Barra to Madero, August 20, 1911 (the second in the series of that date), *ibid*.
[45] Magaña, *Emiliano Zapata*, I, 307.

Zapata discussed the formulation of an agreement for bringing an end to the conflict. The new agreement was little changed from that of August 18, except for the stipulation, this time explicit, that federal troops were to remain in the state until the conclusion of demobilization and the understanding that free elections would be held for choosing a provisional governor.[46] At the same time, in the name of the government, Madero absolved Zapata and his men from any charge of rebellion for past activities, with the express provision that the absolution did not extend or give protection to anyone who "had committed any offense against the common order," since patriotic service, not brigandage, was to be protected.[47] But the agreement was never executed; the stage was already set for the final act of the drama which was to tear into shreds the carefully formulated settlement Madero had labored to complete.

Even though demobilization was proceeding, Governor Carreón's exaggerated accounts of chaos were used as an excuse for reinforcing the federal forces. At Carreón's insistence that Eufemio Zapata was contemplating an attack on Cuernavaca on the night of August 21, De la Barra immediately dispatched additional troops to the area, although in actual fact Eufemio was in Cuautla with a large federal force between him and Cuernavaca.[48] Madero vigorously protested, emphasizing the dangers of such a course, but to no avail.[49] Even Francisco Figueroa, whose brother Ambrosio was so hated by Zapata, strongly advised against the action in view of the jealousy with which Zapata guarded the sovereignty of the state.[50] To make the meaning of the reinforcement doubly clear, at the expiration of the forty-eight-hour truce Huerta began moving on Cuautla; in the light of the negotiations which had been in progress, this action can be interpreted only as a deliberate attempt to force the issue with Zapata, capture him if possible, and, incidentally, liquidate Madero, who would presumably be the victim of Zapata's vengeance.

Madero's first reaction was one of profound disbelief; he was convinced there had been a mistake in transmission of orders.[51] But there was no mistake; Raúl Madero was notified that "in view of the fact

[46] Zapata, "Al Pueblo de Morelos," August 27, 1911, *ibid.*, 323–25.
[47] Statement signed by Madero, August 22, 1911, *LO*, May 6, 1934, p. 1.
[48] De la Barra to Madero, August 21, 1911, *ibid.*, April 29, 1934, p. 1; Madero to De la Barra, August 20, 1911, *ibid.*, April 22, 1934, p. 2.
[49] Madero to De la Barra, August 21, 1911, *ibid.*, April 29, 1934, p. 1.
[50] F. Figueroa to Madero, August 22, 1911, *ibid.*, April 22, 1934, p. 1.
[51] Magaña, *Emiliano Zapata*, I, 311.

that the disarming has been a farce, the government has dictated the means conducive to guaranteeing the lives and haciendas in that state which has suffered so much."[52] In consequence of the aggression, Zapata demanded the return of his arms, but Raúl refused until he knew more of the circumstances; at the same time Cándido Aguilar, in command of the ex-revolutionaries who had just arrived to garrison Cuautla, withdrew when ordered to do so by the government.[53] Within a few days the Council of Ministers decreed full-scale war, Zapata demanded and received a return of a portion of his arms from Raúl, and Huerta arrived in Cuautla only to find that the Indian leader had escaped. To complete the ruin of Madero's hopes for peace, Ambrosio Figueroa, Zapata's bitter enemy who would neither ask nor give quarter and who could be depended upon to drive Zapata to open rebellion, was appointed provisional governor.[54] On August 30 a battle was fought between the Zapatistas and the federals at Chinameca; Morelos was now in rebellion.[55] The plaintive cry of the peasants was admirably expressed in prophetic terms by an old man who wanted those who had access to the press to "propose to the government the means for preventing those disasters which we are going to have with this fight to the death. Those who follow Zapata being so numerous, who knows but that these *hacendados* will have cause to regret tomorrow the ardent enmity which they display today."[56]

Madero was bitter over the failure of his mission and almost broke with the ad interim government. He considered Huerta, whose presence in Morelos he ascribed to Reyes' influence, primarily responsible for the renewal of the conflict. He decried as a major mistake the failure to appoint Hay, who had publicly stated that as provisional governor he would honor the wishes of the majority as expressed at the polls, even though the election should favor Zapata. Not a single one of the provisions of the agreement between Zapata and Madero had been fulfilled by the government, and Madero particularly resented the reflection on his own sincerity which this failure implied.[57]

---

[52] Raúl Madero to Robles Domínguez, August 25, 1911, *LO,* May 6, 1934, p. 1.
[53] R. Madero to Madero, August 25, 1911, *ibid.;* C. Aguilar to Madero, August 25, 1911, *ibid.*
[54] Magaña, *Emiliano Zapata,* I, 327–28, 329.
[55] Casasola, *Historia gráfica,* I, 371.
[56] Isaac Narváez to Juan Sarabia, September 5, 1911, in Magaña, *Emiliano Zapata,* I, 326.
[57] Madero to De la Barra, August 25, 1911, *LO,* May 6, 1934, p. 1.

During September and October the battle raged in Morelos. Huerta tried vainly to come to grips with the enemy, but the rapier-like guerrilla thrusts harassed the federals without allowing them to engage him in open battle. Even then, however, Zapata was apparently willing to come to terms; in late September he sent Juan Andreu Almazán to Mexico as his commissioner, but the Council of Ministers promised to absolve Zapata of the crime of rebellion only if he would surrender immediately. In any case, the southern leader would be held legally responsible for property and personal damages.[58] On those terms Zapata would not surrender, but again on October 8 he demonstrated his willingness to come to terms when he agreed to a fifteen-day truc   's-cuss the matter.[59] Nothing was accomplished, however, and within a few days after the expiration of the truce Zapata, who according to reports was encircled by the federal troops in southern Morelos, shocked and frightened the government by an audacious attack on Milpa Alta, within the Federal District and at the very doorway to the capital.[60]

The terrorizing attack precipitated an immediate cabinet crisis. Subsecretary and Acting Minister of War José González Salas resigned on October 27 as a result of criticism; Minister of Gobernación Alberto García Granados was forced from office by public pressure; and Francisco Vázquez Gómez also resigned.[61] At Madero's repeated urging, Huerta, whose campaign was an obvious failure, was replaced;[62] the public criticism which Madero leveled at the general laid the groundwork for the treachery of February 18, 1913.

Within a few days, on November 6, Madero was inaugurated. Zapata was in open rebellion and gaining strength, but he hoped on the strength of Madero's activities during the summer to be able to come to some agreement with the new president. Madero, in turn, was anxious to re-establish peace and dispatched Gabriel Robles Domínguez to Morelos as a negotiator, but the tempers on both sides were now so high and suspicion so rife that little could be done. Although Robles Domínguez was able to complete an understanding with Zapata on November 11 which did not differ materially from the August agreement,[63] the only concession which Madero would make was ab-

[58] Magaña, *Emiliano Zapata,* I, 330.
[59] *El País,* October 8, 1911, p. 1.
[60] Casasola, *Historia gráfica,* I, 372–73.
[61] *El País,* October 28, 1911, p. 1.
[62] Huerta to Madero, October 28, 1911, *ibid.,* October 29, 1911, p. 1.
[63] Robles Domínguez to Madero, November 11, 1911, in Magaña, *Emiliano*

Photograph Underwood & Underwood

Eufemio and Emiliano Zapata

Federal forces passing through Torreón going north to battle Orozco

solution from the charge of rebellion for all the rebels and protection to Zapata if he would surrender unconditionally and leave Morelos. "Tell him," said Madero, "that his rebellious attitude is causing great prejudice to my government, and I cannot tolerate the prolongation of such a situation for any reason; if he really wants to serve me, this is the only way he can do so."[64]

Zapata's answer was rebellion against the government—and the Plan de Ayala.[65] All during the Madero presidency the Zapata rebellion was in progress, a constant source of irritation and expense and uneasiness. As the months passed the battles were fought with increasing fury, the bitterness on each side mounted, and destruction of lives and property presented an appalling picture. The cruelty of the contestants knew no bounds: every peasant in Morelos was considered to be a potential rebel and was treated as such; every propertyholder in the state was regarded as an enemy of Zapata, who gave no quarter to his foes.

The beginning of the Zapata rebellion and the rebellion itself have all the elements of a Greek tragedy, with an inexorable progress toward a ghastly and destructive war. Morelos became a battleground between the old colonial ideas and the newborn progressive philosophies. Juan C. Carreón, Alberto García Granados, Huerta, De la Barra—these were the representatives of "stability" and the *gente decente*. Zapata, Raúl Madero, Otilio Montaño, Díaz Lombardo, the Magaña brothers, Robles Domínguez, Gabriel Hernández, and Francisco Madero believed in justice for people as opposed to special consideration for property; in equal justice for all, regardless of social and economic status. They could see the patent ills in Morelos and wished to see at least some of them rectified. Madero's failure to give lasting peace to the state was a catastrophe for his government, for the people of Morelos, and for the *hacendados* who had been largely responsible for his failure. Morelos with its problem was Madero's first test, one in which he failed, but partly because of circumstances beyond his control. The representatives of the old regime, of property and vested interests, had begun undermining the new regime as soon as Díaz was exiled; their work was tragically effective.

Zapata, II, 92. See "Bases para la rendición de las fuerzas del Gral. Emiliano Zapata," *ibid.*, 88–89.

[64] Madero to Robles Domínguez, November 12, 1911, *ibid.*, 92.

[65] Robles Domínguez to Madero, November 20, 1911, *ibid.*, 103–106. This revolutionary plan may be found in convenient form, *ibid.*, 126–31, or in Naranjo, *Diccionario biográfico revolucionario*, 272–74.

Mexican Revolution

The tragedy of Morelos should have been a warning to the reactionaries and counterrevolutionaries, those who wished a return to the fundamentals of the Díaz period and were determined to make meaningless the Madero victory. The *hacendados* had been victorious in their efforts to prevent popular government or agrarian reform, but during the course of the months following, they saw their homes burned, their animals stolen, their families killed, the cities razed, and desolation reigning where prosperity had existed. They saw the determination of the Zapatistas to obtain, by force if necessary, a rectification of the injustice of the past. They saw these things, but in their blindness and arrogance they could not see the danger to their country, and to their continued existence, inherent in their policies. The same attitude is clearly seen elsewhere during Madero's short term; the vested interests, in their anxiety to destroy the "dreamer" and the "idealist," continually fought and blocked the reform program presented by the government. Destroy him they did; but they could not destroy the ideas which had been liberated, and ultimately the destroyers were themselves destroyed.

IX

Rebellions Against the Madero Government

FROM THE VERY BEGINNING of his presidency Madero had to contend with revolutionary movements which kept the country in a continual state of turmoil, although none of them seriously threatened the continued existence of the government. He inherited, in addition to the Zapata rebellion, a large number of minor rebellions, and at no time during his short term was he in complete control of all portions of the nation. Chaotic as conditions were, however, they were never so serious as his opponents, including the American Ambassador, pictured them, and it was a *coup d'état,* not a revolution, which ultimately was responsible for his overthrow. Nevertheless, the revolutionary activities created grave problems of finance, prevented cohesive action for reform, and brought about conditions which made possible the Huerta *coup d'état.*

José F. "Che" Gómez was in rebellion against the state governor of Oaxaca when Madero took office on November 6, and within a few days not only had Juchitán been occupied by the rebels but Gómez declared he wished to elevate Emilio Vázquez Gómez to the presidency.[1] Since neither the state forces available to Governor Benito Juárez Maza nor a contingent of *rurales* under Gabriel Hernández and federals under Aureliano Blanquet were sufficient to suppress the movement, in late November, Madero sent Cándido Aguilar, of recognized loyalty and merit, to attempt a solution. In spite of Juárez Maza's strenuous objection that Madero's action was an abridgment of state sovereignty,[2] Aguilar was able to persuade Gómez to surrender to the state authorities under a guarantee of safe conduct. Unfortunately, the local officers in whose custody Gómez was placed subjected him to the

---

[1] Casasola, *Historia gráfica,* I, 403; *El País,* November 10, 1911, p. 1. This declaration was an obvious attempt to enlist the support of the Vazquistas.
[2] Juárez Maza had previously requested federal aid.

ley fuga, making it appear that Madero was guilty of the same tactics which had been employed by Díaz.[3]

In the meantime, in the same state another ambitious chieftain, Angel Barrios, attempted to profit by the Vazquista and Reyista propaganda. Charging that Madero was mentally incompetent and that Pino Suárez had been "imposed" by Madero, Barrios began an abortive revolution which came to a sudden end on November 16 when he was surprised and captured.[4] His movement was meaningless and useless, but galling. In Sinaloa the quarrel between Madero and one of his former lieutenants over the gubernatorial election culminated in a rebellion before Madero took office, but the state was pacified when the rebel surrended himself in Mexico City in early December.[5]

In addition to these minor troubles, as early as October, Ambassador Henry Lane Wilson reported that he had definite evidence, given to him in confidence, of a plot to seize the government before Madero could be inaugurated.[6] Huerta's retirement as a result of Zapata's attack in the Federal District brought an end to the immediate plans;[7] but the idea did not die, and two days after Madero's inauguration a plot for the violent overthrow of the government and the murder of Madero was discovered. In succeeding days large quantities of explosives were found and confiscated and a number of arrests were made, culminating in the apprehension of Generals Militón Hurtado and Higinio Aguilar in late December. When the two confessed, the ramifications and seriousness of the conspiracy were uncovered.[8]

These plots, rebellions, and conspiracies, however, were not particularly dangerous to the country, for the men were not highly placed and were not capable of attracting any widespread support. Contemporaneous with these developments, however, the Bernardo Reyes rebellion, which Madero had long predicted even while he prophesied its failure, became an actuality. Even though Reyes had become a "by-

[3] Casasola, *Historia gráfica,* I, 403; *El País,* November 29, 1911, p. 1. "Che" Gómez and a number of his men were killed "while attempting to escape" between Juchitán and Oaxaca. Who gave the order for the assassinations has not been ascertained.

[4] *El País,* November 17 and December 2, 1911, p. 1.

[5] See Madero to Juan M. Banderas, September 20, 1911, in Taracena, *Madero,* 497–98; *El País,* December 7, 1911, p. 1.

[6] Wilson to State Department, October 6, 1911, *FR,* 1911, p. 519.

[7] It was generally believed that Huerta was implicated in the plot.

[8] *El País,* November 8 and 9 and December 22 and 23, 1911, p. 1.

word and a jest in the arena of politics,"⁹ he was still considered to be a potent personality; and when he gathered his adherents at San Antonio to direct a counterrevolution, there was general apprehension.[10] Charging that Madero was harsh and tyrannical, guilty of persecuting any but his own supporters who had political aspirations, Reyes set December 1 as the date for the beginning of the revolution.[11] He could not be convinced of the folly of his ways by Luis de la Barra, who had been sent as an informal commissioner for his brother, the ad interim president, and for Madero.[12] A Reyista uprising in Tabasco which occurred before the commissioner's arrival strengthened Reyes in his determination, and he not only sent for his son Rodolfo, who arrived in San Antonio on November 11, but also openly began gathering material for his invasion.[13]

At this point the Mexican government, now in Madero's hands, requested the government of the United States to take precautions to prevent an armed movement from that territory; Washington complied by sending two companies of troops to the border to guard against any infraction of her neutrality statutes.[14] Mexican agents undertook to unearth evidence that "overt acts" which would constitute a breach of United States statutes were being committed, and in this search they were much more successful than the Díaz agents of 1910.[15] Among other things, the Mexicans discovered that the sheriff of Webb County, Texas, was giving the Reyistas aid; and this, coupled with evidence of river crossings, was sufficient, particularly in view of the unsympathetic attitude of the Texans generally toward the Reyes cause.[16] Reyes had previously been warned unofficially by Secretary Knox, but now American federal agents arrested him and his immediate staff, confis-

---

[9] Wilson to State Department, September 22, 1911, *FR*, 1911, p. 518.

[10] *El País*, October 4, 1911, p. 1.

[11] *El País*, October 8, 1911, p. 1. The former charge was made before Madero took office.

[12] Wilson to State Department, October 27, 1911, *FR*, 1911, pp. 519–20.

[13] *El País*, October 19, 1911, p. 1; statement by Rodolfo Reyes in *Proceso por rebelión contra el Lic. Rodolfo Reyes*, 19–20.

[14] Mexican Ambassador to State Department, November 10, 1911, *FR*, 1911, p. 520; *El País*, November 18, 1911, p. 1.

[15] The Mexican government had been notified in 1910 that mere purchase of arms and public statements did not constitute a breach of United States laws; certain overt acts only were liable. See Acting Secretary of State Adee to Wilson, November 19, 1910, *FR*, 1911, p. 364.

[16] Wilson to Taft, November 15, 1911, *FR*, 1911, p. 521; *El País*, November 18, 1911, p. 1.

cated arms and ammunition, and apprehended the guilty sheriff.[17] Reyes was given his freedom under bond but kept under surveillance, and the army was ordered to prevent him or any of his group from crossing the river under any pretense. Although Reyes pleaded with Senator LaFollette to intercede in his behalf, President Taft stated unofficially but categorically that he would not permit a revolutionary movement against the Mexican government from American soil.[18]

The vigorous action taken by the United States destroyed the original Reyes plan for a simultaneous invasion of Mexico from the Ciudad Juárez–Agua Prieta region and the Nuevo Laredo–Matamoros section,[19] and Reyes now had to depend on an uprising within Mexico itself. The pro-Reyes feeling in Chihuahua was neglible but evident, and some Reyes-inspired movements in the Cananea district of Sonora and San Luis Potosí had developed;[20] but the real danger of a serious uprising lay in Coahuila, Tamaulipas, and Nuevo León. Accordingly it was to General Gerónimo Treviño, commander of that military zone and personal and professional enemy of Reyes, that reinforcements were sent.[21]

Reyes was in a quandary. Fearful of the outcome of the approaching trial in the United States, and with his supremacy as the revolutionary leader threatened by José Peón del Valle, the doughty general slipped out of San Antonio on December 4 and crossed into Mexico above Eagle Pass some days later.[22] His disappearance created a sensation, for neither Mexican nor American officials knew his whereabouts. During the course of the two weeks following his escape he was variously and successively reported to be in New York, Laredo, Falfurrias (Texas), Galeana, El Paso, and Monterrey, but actually he was traveling through Coahuila and Nuevo León in a southerly direction. Although he had been joined by a group of about six hundred men immediately after crossing the Rio Grande, the populace did not rise to

[17] *El País,* November 20, 1911, p. 1; American Consul Garrett (Nuevo Laredo) to State Department, November 18, 1911, *FR,* 1911, p. 521.
[18] *El País,* November 19 and December 7, 1911, p. 1. Taft's statement (reported in *El País,* November 30, 1911, p. 1) was not intended for publication but had been published in *Le Matin* of Paris, from which source *El País* received it.
[19] Bernardo Reyes, *Defensa que por sí mismo produce el C. General de División Bernardo Reyes, acusado del delito de rebelión.*
[20] *El País,* December 1, 1911, p. 3; December 5, 1911, p. 1.
[21] *Ibid.,* December 7, 1911, p. 1.
[22] B. Reyes, *Defensa que por sí mismo.*

give him support; instead, in the plaintive words of the discouraged general:

The days passed and not even a single individual came to join me; I arrived at Laguna de los Indios, and the people, who appeared to be friends of mine, furtively put on foot, by means of the mails, telephone, and telegraph, a movement to give the civil and military authorities notice of my passing through there.[23]

By late December even the nucleus had disappeared, and Reyes was absolutely alone; his vaunted revolution was a dismal failure. Surrendering to the military commander at Linares on December 25,[24] he dispatched a telegram to General Treviño: "Since this act [his surrender] has been completed I ask, not only for myself but for all those who have compromised themselves in any form in supporting me, a full amnesty, which without doubt will do much to pacify the Republic."[25] A general amnesty was promised for the lesser individuals if they would surrender their arms, but to Reyes and his principal lieutenants no commitment was made; General Reyes was incarcerated in the military prison in Mexico City to await trial, and Rodolfo was jailed when he arrived in Mexico from the United States on January 3, 1912.[26] The government could not prove rebellion against Rodolfo, and he regained his freedom some months later;[27] but Bernardo was still in prison at the time of the 1913 barracks revolt.

The Reyes revolution, if the abortive "invasion" can be dignified by that term, was at the same time a source of strength and weakness for the government. An obvious refutation of the accusations and propaganda in which the Reyistas and Vazquistas were engaged, the disturbance nevertheless strained the financial equilibrium and dissipated the energies of the central government. The governors of the northern states, particularly Carranza in Coahuila, demanded reimbursement for the expenses incurred by the states in preparing to meet the emergency;[28] heavy concentration of military forces exhausted scanty revenues; and the members of the cabinet devoted much of their time for

[23] *Ibid.*
[24] Wilson to State Department, December 30, 1911, *FR,* 1911, p. 525.
[25] B. Reyes, *Defensa que por sí mismo.*
[26] *El País,* December 26, 1911, p. 1; Wilson to State Department, December 30, 1911, *FR,* 1911, p. 525; R. Reyes, *De mi vida, memorias políticas,* I, 177.
[27] *Proceso por rebelión contra el Lic. Rodolfo Reyes,* 80.
[28] Carranza to Madero, February 7, 1912, *LP,* March 13, 1938, p. 1.

a period of three months to discussing the problems of protection when they should have been considering reform.

Reyes is one of the most tragic figures in modern Mexican history. Arrogant, stubborn, and ambitious,[29] but having little moral or personal courage, he exemplified one segment of the population. He never admitted his mistake; he could not believe the thinking people of Mexico would prefer Madero to a famous divisional general. Hiding behind a façade of patriotism and reform, he plotted and schemed to make himself president, preferably by election but by force if necessary. Had he subordinated his political ambitions, he could have been a strong influence for stability; but his overweening desire to occupy the presidential post stimulated reaction, encouraged disloyalty, and led to dissension and revolt.

Emilio Vázquez Gómez, another victim of personal ambition who fled Mexico in baseless fear, co-operated with Reyes in October;[30] but he coveted the presidency and soon made a tentative bid for that position. On November 10, in a carefully worded circular which was ostensibly a report to the state governors of a proposition which had been made him and was not necessarily his own, Emilio denounced Madero for failure to comply with the Plan of San Luis Potosí, declared the national elections void, and hinted that he would accept the provisional presidency. The care with which the letter was prepared to prevent legal action is shown by the following excerpts:

The Chambers of Congress are declared dissolved, and it is said that, although I have always recommended peace, I am declared chief of the revolution, which is to elevate me to the presidency. . . . As may be seen, the object of the revolution is perfectly defined and, on the other hand, is not for vengeance or cruelty; it is solely for the salvation of the revolutionary principles in the exact moment when the former chief is wrecking them. I consider it my duty to give you this news for your information and guidance.[31]

Emilio lacked the courage to declare openly for revolution, even

[29] His *Defensa,* written in late 1912, shows these characteristics even more clearly than did his actions. He insisted that the Mexicans should have rallied to his support, but did not explain why they did not.
[30] *El País,* October 8, 1911, p. 1.
[31] E. Vázquez Gómez, circular letter to the governors of the Mexican states, November 10, 1911, *FR,* 1912, p. 711.

190

from the safety of the United States, but he was anxious to determine the attitude of the state governors. Within two weeks the so-called Plan de Tacubaya, obviously inspired by Emilio's letter, was announced to the public in a manifesto which declared that a revolution, not allied with the Reyes movement, would soon start.[32] On account of the coolness with which the announcement was received,[33] in late December, Emilio attempted to stimulate action by approving the plan without definitely committing himself other than to say that he would not "disown" his "partisans."[34] A month later he was still coy but admitted that he would accept the presidency if it were offered to him.[35] During January and February a number of feeble movements started in Emilio's behalf in Zacatecas, Sinaloa, and Chihuahua; but his adherents were making little headway when his revolution merged with, and was overshadowed by, the far more dangerous rebellion by Pascual Orozco.

Orozco felt that he had not been treated with proper consideration after Ciudad Juárez. He desired the governorship of Chihuahua and believed his popularity in the state would assure it to him, but he was overwhelmingly defeated in a free election by the popular and able Abraham González.[36] Again, when González took leave from his gubernatorial post to serve in Madero's first cabinet, Orozco was overlooked and another Maderista was designated to serve as the ad interim governor.[37] Orozco was requested by Madero to combat the Banderas rebellion in November, but after some hesitation he refused that commission.[38] In the meantime he was selected as the commander of *rurales* in Chihuahua, a post hardly commensurate with his political ambitions but one which suited his limited education and background; he had

---

[32] "Manifiesto a la nación," signed by Emilio Vázquez Gómez, Policarpo Rueda, Paulino Martínez, and others, *El País*, November 22, 1911, p. 1. Emilio later stated that his name had been "used" by the revolutionists when the plan was drawn up and that he had not authorized the action. However, he gave his approval.

[33] No revolutionary action was taken at all in Emilio's behalf; the state governors showed no inclination to rebel.

[34] E. Vázquez Gómez to Director, *El País*, January 2, 1912, p. 1. He wrote identical letters to the directors of all leading newspapers, most of whom published it on January 2.

[35] *El País*, February 3, 1912, p. 2. ·

[36] Ramón Puente, *Pascual Orozco y la revuelta de Chihuahua*, 39, 41–43.

[37] Casasola, *Historia gráfica*, I, 393; Puente, *Pascual Orozco*, 64–65.

[38] *El País*, November 14, 1911, p. 1.

191

neither the experience nor the breadth of vision to qualify for a cabinet position, nor did his military experience fit him for an army commission.

In late January, 1912, Orozco resigned as the commander of *rurales* on the plea that he wished to devote himself to business. His letter of resignation[39] had a patriotic ring and contained no hint of dissatisfaction, and yet it is now clear that even then he was toying with the idea of revolution. The Vázquez Gómez movement gave him the opportunity he sought, and he was wooed by the powerful landed families of Chihuahua, who feared the Madero government in general and Abraham González in particular.[40] Still, when mutinies in Chihuahua and Ciudad Juárez broke out in late January and early February, Orozco hastened to bring them to an end.[41] The situation was particularly dangerous in Ciudad Juárez because the governor of Texas and the citizens of El Paso were demanding intervention by Washington to bring an end to a reported carnage which actually never existed. Orozco, popular with the ranks, brought the mutiny to an immediate cessation when he reached Ciudad Juárez on February 3, and it appeared that peace had been regained.[42]

Contemporaneous with the solution of the Ciudad Juárez problem, however, in the interior of the state a new outbreak in behalf of Emilio Vázquez Gómez occurred under the leadership of Braulio Hernández, the secretary-general of the state and confidant of Orozco.[43] Within a matter of days, with the garrison at Casas Grandes and most of the troops in the city of Chihuahua supporting the revolution, Emilio assumed the title of provisional president in conformity with the revolutionary plan.[44] Before the month's end the main force of the rebel army demanded the surrender of Ciudad Juárez; Orozco, who was still in the city, ordered the loyal garrison to withdraw. On Eebruary 27 the insurgents occupied the important port of entry. Five days later, on March 3, Orozco joined the revolution; but Villa, one of his principal lieutenants, remained loyal to the government and immediately took

[39] Orozco to Madero, January 26, 1912, in Casasola, *Historia gráfica,* I, 413.
[40] Puente, *Pascual Orozco,* 71–72.
[41] The enlisted men reportedly mutinied when they received word that Orozco had resigned from the *rurales.*
[42] *El País,* February 3, 1912, pp. 1, 2; February 5, 1912, p. 1.
[43] *Ibid.,* February 6, 1912, p. 1; Casasola, *Historia gráfica,* I, 423.
[44] Wilson to State Department, February 18, 1912, *FR,* 1912, p. 721. Emilio remained in San Antonio.

the field against his former commander.[45] Villa's action did not prevent the loss of the city of Chihuahua, however; Abraham González, who had resigned his cabinet post in February to return to the state,[46] was forced to resign by the state legislature, which promptly surrendered the city to Braulio Hernández.

On March 4 the Plan de Tacubaya was promulgated anew, but a more important revolutionary plan, the Plan Orozquista,[47] was made public on March 6; Orozco was preparing to contest Emilio for the leadership but was not yet ready to make an open break. Orozco's plan made no specific charge against the Madero government and provided no reform program. According to the plan, Madero was generally incompetent and untrustworthy as was shown by his conduct of the revolution which had elevated him to the presidency. Madero was accused of having financed the original insurrection "with money from American millionaires," of allowing the Mexican flag to be profaned by "the sacrilegious hand of the Yankee," and of substituting the "vulture which devours Spanish-America" for the eagle-serpent design on the national banner. The Madero revolution had been born in dishonor and completed with treason, for the "principal elements [of the victory] were Yankee money and the phalanx of mercenaries who . . . assassinated" the Mexicans. It is strange indeed that after a lapse of nearly a year Orozco should suddenly discover that the revolution of which he was an admitted leader had been so subject to "Yankee" influence.

In addition to this evidence of Madero's perfidy, the Orozquistas charged that Madero had used "armed force in the elections which elevated him and José María Pino Suárez" to their posts,[48] had "violated the sovereignty of the states" by imposing "ad interim governors by force of arms," and had, "in a manner prejudicial and humiliating" made Mexico City merely a "dependency of the government in Washington." Not content with this listing of vague and baseless accusations against Madero, Orozco established a commission in New York to disseminate propaganda. His agent made additional charges against Ma-

---

[45] Casasola, *Historia gráfica,* I, 424; *El País,* February 28, 1912, p. 1; Consul Letcher (Chihuahua) to State Department, March 3, 1912, *FR,* 1912, p. 734.

[46] Casasola, *Historia gráfica,* I, 419.

[47] Naranjo, *Diccionario biográfico revolucionario,* 276–82.

[48] This is an obvious reference to Madero's message to Congress concerning the postponement of the national election. See Chapter 7.

dero,[49] but quite naturally did not mention Madero's presumed subservience to the United States. According to the propagandist, Madero was not giving protection to travelers in Mexico, he had not actually been elected by the Mexicans but had merely been accepted because no one else was available at the moment, and he had prevented the rise of a strong rival candidate by his opposition to postponement of the election. Not only was his government so profligate that it had dissipated the large treasury reserve left by Díaz, but Gustavo had virtually stolen over 700,000 pesos when he was paid that sum for "presumed expenses" of which he gave no accounting.

Each of these accusations was a monstrous distortion of a basic fact. Madero's "mercenaries" were few in number, but there were foreigners serving in his army. American financing of the revolution was nonexistent, but in 1912 some American oil concerns were suspected of having given aid. A casual reading of the diplomatic correspondence will make it perfectly obvious that Madero was not subservient to Washington, in spite of the efforts being made by Ambassador Wilson to achieve that goal. The "imposition" accredited to Madero, and the application of force, have already been discussed and need not be detailed again here. The treasury reserves had been exhausted in combating disloyal persons, among whom were Orozco and Emilio Vázquez Gómez. It was not safe for travelers in many parts of Mexico because the spiteful and personalistic rebellions encouraged banditry and vandalism; Orozco could hardly claim that his rebellion made for safety of travel in Chihuahua. Gustavo's claim for repayment had been approved by Emilio Vázquez Gómez himself; if chicanery was involved, Emilio was more at fault than Madero. An analysis of each and every one of the charges made against Madero by the Orozquistas shows that they were not justified.

In view of the illusory nature of the accusations, it is scarcely credible that Orozco, David de la Fuente, and Braulio Hernández believed what they wrote; nor was any concrete platform for reform stipulated. That Orozco was not leading a revolution for reform is fairly obvious; what he was attempting to do is not so clear. In order to ascertain the true meaning of the movement, it is necessary to search deeply for possible motives and to determine the positions of the people involved.

At that moment an Agrarian Commission engaged in the study of the land problem was making a report which indicated a possible line

[49] E.g., see *El País*, April 11, 1912, p. 1.

of action dangerous to the Chihuahua and Coahuila *hacendados* who dominated the economic landscape. In those states the land was more firmly in the grip of the *hacendados* than in any other area.[50] Any disturbance of the status quo would be disadvantageous to the Terrazas and Creel families; it was essential to them to prevent agrarian reform. In addition, Abraham González' evident desire to improve the lot of the submerged classes was an anathema to these same landowners.[51] The connection between Orozco and the Terrazas family is not clear, but Luis Terrazas paid part of the expenses of Orozco's revolution under the guise of export taxes when on one occasion in June he paid over 200,000 pesos. Further, Félix Terrazas served in Orozco's army.[52] Ramón Puente categorically stated that Orozco was suborned by the *hacendados,* who promised him power, position, and social prestige.[53] Orozco, ambitious and gullible, was easy prey for the machinations of the *hacendados,* while the rank and file had sublime faith in him and probably believed they were fighting against a tyrannical Madero.

Immediately after Orozco's defection, Minister of War José González Salas, in whom Madero had the utmost confidence, resigned from his cabinet post in order to take the field against the rebels. This action, coupled with a report that Emilio Vázquez Gómez was organizing a column of eight thousand men to march on the capital, induced a wave of hysteria in Mexico City.[54] The municipal council warned all "friends of order," native or foreign, to arm themselves for protection, and the governor of the Federal District began preparations for the defense of the city against the approaching Vázquez hordes, even though at least eight hundred miles separated the capital from the nonexistent army.[55] Caught up in the hysteria, American Ambassador Henry Lane Wilson sponsored a defense league of foreigners in the capital, requesting first a thousand rifles and a quarter-million rounds of ammunition and then a million rounds from the Department of State.[56] When notified of a defeat of the federals at Rellano,[57] Wilson demanded an addi-

[50] Tannenbaum, *The Mexican Agrarian Revolution,* 56, 97.
[51] Puente, *Pascual Orozco,* 71.
[52] *El País,* June 10, 1912, p. 1; Casasola, *Historia gráfica,* I, 455.
[53] Puente, *Pascual Orozco,* 72.　　　　[54] *El País,* March 5 and 7, 1912, p. 1.
[55] Wilson to State Department, March 6, 1912, *FR,* 1912, p. 739; *El País,* March 7, 1912, p. 1.
[56] Wilson to State Department, March 7 and 22, 1912, *FR,* 1912, pp. 739, 756, 757.
[57] On March 23; Rellano was north of Torreón, about six hundred miles from Mexico City.

Mexican Revolution

tional thousand rifles, one million rounds of ammunition, and the requisite service belts and equipment.[58]

In the meantime, Wilson constantly demanded that the Mexican government take steps to give protection to foreigners in the city; he insisted that he be given information concerning the number and disposition of troops in the vicinity and the number which the government considered necessary to give adequate protection.[59] The Foreign Office replied that the request for information concerning the disposition was improper and that the need and number would vary with conditions. Wilson, incensed because the Mexican government refused to bow to his wishes, insisted. But Foreign Minister Calero was adamant; his only comment was that Mexico City and the foreigners there would be safe.[60]

While Mexico City was never actually threatened, most of Chihuahua fell to the insurgents before the government could check their advance. The first major encounter, on March 23 at Rellano, between Torreón and Chihuahua City, was a crushing defeat for the federals under General González Salas, largely because supporting columns under Trucy Aubert and Aureliano Blanquet lost contact with the central force. His own train rammed by an explosive-filled insurgent train, González Salas was unable to rally his forces. Ashamed and humiliated at the defeat, the General took his own life during the retreat rather than face accusations of incompetency and disloyalty.[61] In the emergency, the cabinet insisted on recalling Victoriano Huerta to lead the government forces, despite the acrimonious exchange which had taken place between Huerta and Madero.[62] The choice was unfortunate, since it gave Huerta an opportunity to re-establish his reputation as a general and placed him in a position to make demands on the government. Far from conciliating the general, his recall merely amplified the smoldering bitterness he felt for Madero and stimulated him to complete long-cherished plans to discredit the Madero government when the occasion warranted.

A quiescent period followed. In early April, General Huerta arrived in Torreón, which, in spite of frequent reports to the contrary, was

[58] Wilson to State Department, March 25, 1912, *FR,* 1912, p. 758.
[59] Wilson to Calero (Minister of Foreign Relations), March 11, 1912, *ibid.,* 762.
[60] Calero to Wilson, March 13 and 19, 1912, *ibid.,* 763, 764.
[61] Casasola, *Historia gráfica,* I, 427, 428; Salvador Resendi, *La revolución actual,* 91–92.
[62] *El País,* March 26, 1912, p. 1.

still in government hands. In the succeeding month he devoted himself to organizing the defense while the rebels slowly but steadily advanced to the south. In early May, Orozco was prevented from taking Monclova, Coahuila, only by the herculean efforts of the state forces,[63] and he was not seriously checked until he was decisively defeated at the second battle of Rellano, on May 23.[64]

In the meantime the rebels were embroiled in dissension among themselves. Emilio Vázquez Gómez, who arrived in El Paso shortly after Orozco joined the revolution, was offered the presidency of the provisional revolutionary government by a representative who presumably came from Orozco.[65] On May 5 he arrived in Ciudad Juárez amidst the welcoming cheers of the revolutionists and immediately organized a government. Orozco, who had ideas of his own concerning the presidency, not only refused to recognize Emilio's right to the position but threatened him with arrest unless he resigned and left the country at once. When Emilio refused to comply with Orozco's demands, the General ordered his arrest and imprisonment, allowing him to go free only when Emilio agreed to resign and quit the country. From the safety of the United States the erstwhile Maderista then with calm impartiality condemned both Madero and Orozco for tyranny, breach of faith, and personal ambition.[66] Orozco not only showed his presidential ambitions by his action against Emilio but also eliminated one source of support for the revolution and thus inadvertently aided the government.

After the sound defeat which Huerta administered to him at Rellano, Orozco began a steady retreat to the north, always harassed and pressed by the federals, whose advance he delayed by a systematic destruction of the railroads. By July 1 the strength of the insurrection had waned to such a degree that Orozco began moving his government, which had been seated in Chihuahua City, to Ciudad Juárez.[67] Five days later the victory at Bachimba left the way to Chihuahua open for the federals; and on July 8, Huerta entered the state capital.[68] Orozco's

---

[63] Carranza to Madero, May 13, 1912, *LP,* March 13, 1938, p. 1. The battle for Monclova was the occasion for a bitter quarrel between Madero and Carranza, each of whom believed the other to be intervening in affairs over which he should have no control.

[64] *El País,* May 24, 1912, p. 1.

[65] Consul Edwards (Ciudad Juárez) to State Department, May 4, 1912, *FR,* 1912, p. 809.

[66] *El País,* May 5, 8, and 10 and June 22, 1912, p. 1.

[67] *Ibid.,* July 1, 1912, p. 1.   [68] Casasola, *Historia gráfica,* I, 454–55.

power had been broken. From that time forward the campaign was primarily one of mopping-up, with the volunteers bearing the brunt of the struggle, and with Huerta spending part of the time in Mexico City.[69] During August and September the dwindling revolutionary forces were continually pressed by government troops, who under General Rábago captured Ciudad Juárez in mid-August and then reduced the last stronghold, Ojinaga, in early September. Orozco fled to the United States, small bands were liquidated, loyal state officials returned to their posts, and by early October the revolution was over.

Madero's government had weathered a severe storm; it had been able to suppress a powerful insurrection led by a popular and resourceful man and supported by the majority of the *hacendado* class in the north. The rebellion created new situations boding ill for the future, and heavily taxed the scanty government resources. Rebel seizure of Ciudad Juárez had denied the government a source of income at the very moment when increased expenditures were necessary. Early in April a portion of the treasury reserve was allocated to the pacification fund.[70] Before the rebellion ended, the government borrowed an additional twenty million pesos, the loan being approved only after heated debate and bitter denunciation by the opposition parties.[71] A vast increase in military personnel was necessitated. With approximately forty thousand men in federal pay, the government requested an additional thirty thousand men in April; by mid-June the army of regulars, volunteers, and *rurales* reached fifty-four thousand.[72] The total authorized complement of seventy thousand had been recruited before Orozco was defeated.[73]

Madero's government was also the subject of attack over the question of constitutional guarantees; for, in view of conditions, Madero wished to suspend those guarantees in Chihuahua, in Sonora, in a part of Durango, in Morelos, in Tlaxcala, in some districts of Puebla and

[69] Letcher to State Department, October 16, 1912, *FR*, 1912, pp. 850–52; *El País*, July 29, 1912, p. 1.

[70] President's Message to Twenty-fifth Congress, April 1, 1912, *Diario oficial*, Vol. CXIX, No. 27 (April 1, 1912), 405–13.

[71] *El País*, October 4, 1912, p. 1.

[72] *Ibid.*, April 16 and June 19, 1912, p. 1.

[73] Not all this increase in money and personnel was devoted to the northern campaign, since other areas needed attention. Before the collapse of the Orozco rebellion, it was estimated that eighteen thousand men were under arms against the government.—*Times* (London), September 3, 1912, p. 3.

Henry Lane Wilson presents Huerta to the diplomatic corps; Félix Díaz on Wilson's left

Photograph Brown Brothers

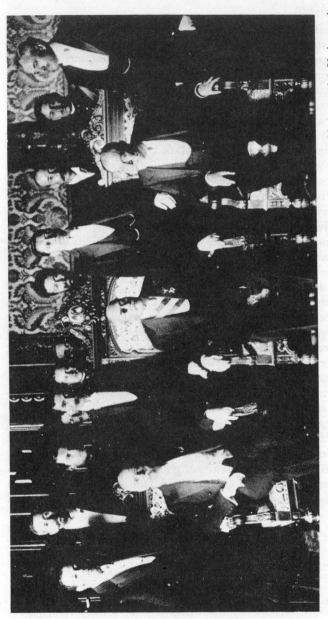

Huerta's cabinet
Rodolfo Reyes, *Justice*; Toribio Esquivel Obregón, *Finance*; Francisco de la Barra, *Foreign Relations*; Manuel Mondragón, *War and Marine*; Huerta; Jorge Vera Estañol, *Education*; Alberto García Granados, *Gobernación*; and Alberto Robles Gil, *Fomento*

México, and in one district of Coahuila. The proposal, made to the Council of Ministers in late July, brought caustic criticism from the opposition press.[74] Madero nevertheless requested the permanent congressional committee[75] to approve the suspension; this was done after some delay.[76] The suspension, even though it may have been justified, was intensely unpopular as a manifestation of tyranny seriously at variance with the fundamental philosophy of the revolution. Madero was accused of emulating the harshness of the Díaz government without maintaining the peace and stability the dictator had been able to impose, of showing all the weaknesses and none of the strengths of the past regime.

Even more important than these general criticisms were the government's relations with Huerta during the summer. Before he would agree to take command of the campaign, Huerta had demanded and received some concessions, one of which was that the President would not interfere with him in any way as long as the fighting was in progress.[77] Madero soon found himself unable to abide by his promise. Huerta condemned to death Francisco Villa, who was under his command, after a summary trial resulting from a minor infraction. Emilio and Raúl Madero, also with Huerta's army, asked their brother to intervene to prevent an unjustified execution.[78] Madero's order staying the execution until an investigation could be made, arrived just at the moment when Villa was standing before a firing squad.[79] Huerta resented the President's action, seeing here a classic example of administrative meddling in military affairs, and almost broke openly with the President. But the Villa episode was merely one of a number of irritating events during the campaign. Huerta wished to maintain peace in the recaptured areas by force and violence and therefore considered the government policy of conciliation to be indicative of weakness.[80] He particularly resented the cold snubbing to which he and his officers were subjected by the citizens of Chihuahua; in the words of the American consul:

---

[74] E.g., see *El País,* July 24, 1912, p. 1.
[75] Congress was not in session.   [76] *El País,* August 2 and 7, 1912, p. 1.
[77] Letcher to State Department, October 16, 1912, *FR,* 1912, pp. 850–52.
[78] Manuel Bonilla, *El régimen maderista,* 16. Villa had refused, despite Huerta's order, to return a horse he had appropriated from a rancher.
[79] A photograph of Villa in front of the firing squad, taken by the divisional surgeon, may be found in Casasola, *Historia gráfica,* I, 450.
[80] Letcher to State Department, October 16, 1912, *FR,* 1912, pp. 850–52.

199

[The] Federals have been almost ignored socially since their arrival here, and their position has not been very different from that of a conquering army in a conquered foreign territory. This ostracism is keenly felt by the officers, to whom such treatment is all the more embarrassing because of their realization that they are observing only a perfunctory loyalty to the Government and that only in compliance with a sense of duty and against their own inclinations. . . . The aristocracy, formerly Porfiristas and Orozquistas, at present almost to a man treat them with coldness.[81]

Probably the most important result of the unsettled conditions accruing from the Orozco rebellion, however, was the attitude which developed in the United States. Stimulated by exaggerated reports from Ambassador Wilson, who as a representative of American interests feared reform, the United States lost faith in the ability of the Madero government to give protection to Americans in Mexico. Wilson advised all Americans to leave areas threatened by revolution, couching the announcement in terms which made it appear as though Washington had advised the action and which precipitated a wave of hysteria; and at his insistence an American troop transport was sent to evacuate the "refugees" who were presumably crowding all Pacific ports. The Department of State believed that "a ship with a capacity for from five to six hundred persons would . . . be adequate for all needs."[82] A ship of that capacity was indeed adequate; for when the *Buford* arrived at the principal ports of Sinaloa, one of the states reported to be in the grip of anarchy, only eighteen persons took passage.[83] The correspondent for the London *Times* admirably summed up the cruise of the *Buford*:

The Washington Government, . . . alarmed at reports of impending anti-American outbreaks, recently sent a cruiser down the Pacific coast to collect refugees. The only refugees that have so far been collected seem, however, to be people who wanted a free passage to San Diego. Other stories of unrest have proved upon investigation to be equally exaggerated.[84]

[81] *Ibid.*
[82] Press release, March 2, 1912, quoted in Wilson to State Department, March 4, 1912, *ibid.*, 735; Knox to Wilson, April 26, 1912, *ibid.*, 803; Secretary of State to Secretary of War, April 25, 1912, *ibid.*, 802.
[83] *El País*, May 11, 1912, p. 1. The fact that *El País* published this notice indicating that Americans in Sinaloa were satisfied is interesting, since the Catholic daily had been stressing the supposed anarchy in Sinaloa for weeks past.
[84] May 13, 1912, p. 5.

Rebellions Against Madero

Nevertheless, Wilson, whose admiration for Díaz' method of granting concessions to Americans had been boundless, continued to report a dangerous anti-Americanism in Mexico. He insisted that Madero was "conducting a campaign against American interests in Mexico" and foresaw "confiscation, harassment, and dislodgment through suborned judicial decrees" unless Mexico was "taught in due season that every American and every American interest in Mexico" was an object of respect.[85] The Mexican Foreign Office was besieged with demands for protection for Americans and their interests; at one point the Department of State presumed to tell the Mexican government the place and size of garrisons needed to protect Americans.[86] Press reports and diplomatic correspondence indicated that no American was safe in Mexico, that the Madero government was responsible for innumerable American deaths, and that American property was subject to seizure by the government on any or no pretext. And yet, when the American Ambassador presented the government with a harsh note concerning Mexican failure to punish perpetrators of crimes against Americans, he could name only three Americans who had been murdered during the year and only five more who had lost their lives since the fall of Díaz.[87]

The Mexican Foreign Office investigation showed, however, that the perpetrators in three cases were serving prison sentences, in two cases the accused had been released for want of evidence, and in two the investigation by police had been barren of results. One victim had been killed by a husband protecting his wife from undesired attentions, three had been executed by federal troops when captured in a filibustering expedition, and others had been killed in mountain areas where law enforcement was difficult and investigation all but impossible.[88] This exchange of correspondence showed that not only were murders of Americans less frequent than generally believed, but also that the American Ambassador was not particularly well informed concerning the disposition of cases which had come to his attention. But there is no denying that anti-American feeling was growing; the increased tension was reflected and enhanced by Ambassador Wilson and other Ameri-

[85] Wilson to State Department, August 28, 1912, FR, 1912, pp. 828–32.
[86] Acting Secretary of State to Wilson, September 2, 1912, ibid., 833.
[87] Wilson to Minister of Foreign Relations, September 15, 1912, ibid., 842–46. A tabulation in Investigation of Mexican Affairs (I, 848–63) gives a much larger number of deaths, but many of these were unsubstantiated.
[88] Pedro Lascuráin to Wilson, November 22, 1912, FR, 1912, pp. 871–77.

can officials. The nationals of other countries were much less disturbed by conditions than were Americans.[89]

The defeat of Orozco did not bring peace to Mexico. Even before the last of the Orozquista groups was overcome, Félix Díaz rebelled in Veracruz. Personally ambitious, discontented with Madero's administration, and a staunch advocate of "firm" government, Don Porfirio's nephew used the general discontent as an opportunity to fulfill his own desires. Depending on his name and his prestige in military and conservative circles to bring him support, and expecting the federal army to come to his aid, Díaz made no plans beyond the capture of the port city. On October 10 he quietly left Veracruz,[90] where he was in command of a federal army, and less than one week later he captured the city without firing a shot when the garrison there refused to fire on his force from Orizaba and Oaxaca. He requested recognition of belligerent status from the United States, taking occasion to deny any personal ambition and promising national elections as soon as "national life shall be completely normalized."[91] He presented no plan of reform to the Mexicans; his principal reason for rebelling apparently was that the "honor" of the army had been "trampled on" by the Madero government.[92] His was obviously nothing more than a personal bid for power, merely one more attempt at making a special interest paramount.

Contrary to his expectations, no group outside Veracruz gave him military support, and he was soon isolated in the city, which was surrounded by a large force under General Joaquín Beltrán.[93] The small units of the Mexican navy remained loyal to the government, effectively blocking the sea as a means of escape or aid, and it was soon apparent that Díaz was in an untenable position. The only way to dislodge the rebel, however, was to undertake a full-scale attack, which presented grave difficulties in view of the extensive foreign holdings and the number of foreigners resident in the city. The Madero government could ill afford any action which would increase antipathy by foreign governments, particularly the United States, for destruction of American property could well have had serious consequences. Madero was widely

[89] Calero to Wilson, March 19, 1912, *ibid.*, 765.
[90] *El País*, October 13, 1912, p. 1.
[91] Félix Díaz to Knox, October 19, 1912, *FR*, 1912, p. 856.
[92] F. Díaz to Editor, *Mexican Herald*, October 17, 1912; see also "Plan Felicista," in Casasola, *Historia gráfica*, I, 469.
[93] General Beltrán had previously agreed to support Díaz, but at the last moment declined to do so.

202

criticized for his inaction during the early days of the rebellion,[94] but the dispatch of the American cruiser *Des Moines* to Veracruz and the importunities of American diplomatic officials made it appear that American intervention would follow any attempt by the federal forces to capture the city.[95] Verbal and written negotiations between General Beltrán and W. W. Canada, the American consul and dean of foreign representatives, finally cleared the way for an assault which began on October 22.[96]

Advantageous positions having been occupied by the federals on October 22, the city was captured with surprising ease on the morning of October 23 after a short engagement.[97] The unexpected collapse of the Díaz rebellion was shocking to some of the government's more irreconcilable opponents, who were surprised and disappointed at the show of strength. Among those evidently most disappointed was the American chargé d'affaires who, in relating the capture of Díaz, said: "This collapse of his revolt greatly complicates the general situation. Temporary success will only result in prolonging trouble. . . . [The] Madero administration is absolutely impotent to bring about even a semblance of peace and order."[98]

Consul Canada at Veracruz, in an attempt to explain the surprising success, attributed Díaz' failure to an act of treachery by Beltrán, whose agents reportedly advanced under a flag of truce, disarmed the rebel general's personal guard, and then arrested him.[99] Even the bitterly anti-Madero José Fernández Rojas did not make that charge, though he did accuse Beltrán of treachery when the latter refused to support the rebellion.[100] The kernel of the matter was that the officers and men under Díaz lost heart for the fight when the remainder of the army failed to come to their aid; they had no stomach for a fight with the numerically superior loyal forces.

[94] E.g., the London *Times* (October 22, 1912, p. 5) said: "The Madero Government . . . has adopted the usual ostrich-like attitude of official optimism, but the fact remains that General Díaz still occupies Vera Cruz."
[95] Acting Secretary of State to Secretary of Navy, October 17, 1912, *FR*, 1912, pp. 853–54; Acting Secretary of State to American Chargé d'Affaires, October 19, 1912, *ibid.*, 857.
[96] Canada to State Department, October 23, 1912, *ibid.*, 860. For details of these negotiations see *ibid.*, 858–66.
[97] *El País*, October 24, 1912, p. 1.
[98] Chargé Schuyler to State Department, October 23, 1912, *FR*, 1912, p. 860.
[99] Canada to State Department, November 27, 1912, *ibid.*, 870.
[100] Fernández Rojas, *La revolución mexicana*.

The general public reaction to the affair seemed to be one of high pleasure at the government success. Many state and municipal officers expressed their delight at the outcome, and some of the conservatives congratulated the government on its show of strength. *El País,* which was strongly anti-Madero, was also critical of Díaz and expressed pleasure at the failure of his movement.[101] Even with the added prestige of the rapid victory over Díaz, however, the government was still plagued with rebellious movements, some of a serious nature.[102]

The aftermath of the Díaz rebellion constituted a greater danger to the government than had the rebellion itself. Díaz was taken prisoner on October 23; a military court was convened on October 24; he was tried and convicted of rebellion on October 25; and his execution, along with twenty-six of his leading lieutenants, was ordered for the dawn of October 26.[103] This precipitous action, coupled with Madero's refusal to intercede to prevent the execution, gave credence to the impression that the decision had been dictated in advance by the President. The sentence was without precedent, at wide variance with the treatment accorded Reyes, the Sinaloa rebel, and the Orozco generals who had been captured, and a public clamor ensued. Friends of Félix Díaz in the Chamber of Deputies attempted to pass a hasty resolution ordering a stay of execution, but a number of government deputies prevented action by refusing to attend the session and so a quorum was lacking.[104] A delegation of women asked Madero to intervene for the sake of the wives and children of the condemned men, but the President brusquely reminded them that the soldiers who had lost their lives fighting Díaz were also husbands and fathers; the ladies then circulated the rumor that Madero had been rude and insulting.[105] Their personal condemnation of Madero added fuel to the flame of hatred and dissatisfaction already engendered by his stubborn refusal to intervene.

In the meantime, an extraordinary meeting of the Supreme Court, taking cognizance of the peculiar legal circumstances involved, rendered a decision that Díaz was not subject to a military court.[106] The

---

[101] See issues of *El País,* October 17–31, 1912.

[102] In November, Chargé Schuyler noted the additional strength accruing to Madero. (Schuyler to State Department, November 27, 1912, *FR,* 1912, p. 870.) He also noted, with evident distaste, that Madero was openly delighted because Woodrow Wilson had been elected.

[103] *El País,* October 26, 1912, p. 1.   [104] *Ibid.,* October 27, 1912, p. 1.

[105] Alfonso Taracena, *Francisco Madero y la verdad,* 7, 8.

[106] For a discussion of the legal aspects of the case, see *Breve estudio sobre la incompetencia del tribunal militar que juzgó al Sr. ingeniero don Félix Díaz y*

Rebellions Against Madero

Chief Justice ordered postponement of any action until further study could be made.[107] Within a short time the government saw the broader implications of the case, and cooler counsel prevailed; in late November, Mexico City announced that there would be no request for the death penalty when Díaz came to trial. Nevertheless, the entire episode caused immense ill-feeling and distrust.

In spite of the temporary prestige—tempered somewhat by the trial —which Madero had gained as a result of the defeat handed Díaz, the government was weak; of that there could be no doubt. Zapata was still in arms in the south, with an alternately expanding and receding sphere of influence which made difficult an accurate estimate of his strength at any moment. The efforts to destroy him were unavailing, even though a succession of federal generals were able to contain his forces with some degree of effectiveness.

But more disturbing and more wearing on the government resources and the public patience were the hundreds of independent bands, usually quite small, which were constantly appearing and disappearing. A vast number of men at one time or another indicated their dissatisfaction and unrest by an appeal to arms, but there was never any coalescing of the groups because of the divergence of desires. Some were bandits pure and simple, interested only in the loot they were able to seize at the moment. Others were demanding land, even taking it at the point of a gun and working it with rifles in their hands. Some were encouraged by extreme radicals, who convinced them that Madero was unfaithful to the revolution; others were stimulated by the reactionaries and Porfiristas, who hoped to consummate Madero's fall. Revolution begat revolution; disturbances forced the government to divert its energies from constructive work to the task of pacification; and needed reforms were postponed. Madero could not cope properly with the problem, largely because he could not obtain the co-operation of those elements in society which should have given strength to the regime. Instead of giving aid to the regeneration of the country through political and economic reform, the opposition was purely destructive, having no concrete plans or programs for the salvation of the government or the nation. But not even the most avid enemies of the regime

los demás señores aprehendidos con motivo del sublevación ocurrida en Vera Cruz el 16 del presente mes. The title indicates the line of argument: that Díaz was not in the army at the moment of insurrection and therefore was subject to civilian rather than military courts.
[107] *El País,* October 27, 1912, p. 1.

could agree on the nature of the ills confronting the public; in their desire to weaken Madero and bring about his destruction, they were guilty of making the antithetical accusations that his government was a "vicious despotism" and that it was flaccid, vacillating, and completely inept.

With all its weakness, Madero's government had hidden springs of strength when confronted by a major crisis, as the Félix Díaz defeat showed. Congress was loyal but not subservient, the major portion of the army supported the Madero government, and most of the state administrations were willing to follow his lead. Nonetheless, in the face of the evident unrest, the failure to bring peace and stability, and the many unsolved problems confronting the regime, it is curious that no leader was able to overthrow the government through armed revolution.[108] The inescapable conclusion is that not only was the opposition unable to unite but the majority of the people—or rather of that portion of the population which normally took an interest in the government—still maintained faith in Madero and were not infected with the dissatisfaction so evident in particular cases. The opponents were vociferous in their agitation and propaganda, maliciously spreading and swelling every damaging rumor,[109] while those who were satisfied made no effort to give support unless a major crisis was at hand. While brigandage and pillage were common, most of the sections were relatively peaceful.

Nor were business and commerce severely affected. "The disturbances . . . interfered less with business than might have been expected, and the Customs duties for the last half of 1912 showed an actual increase as compared with 1911."[110] The Minister of Finance reported that the customs dues collected during September were over a million dollars more than those for the same month the preceding year and half a million more than those for September, 1910.[111] More indicative of business conditions was the general trend of import and export totals for the period: imports remained steady with little variation from 1909 until 1913, while exports showed a steady increase during the same period, with a four and one-half million pound sterling increment

---

[108] It must be remembered that a *coup d'état*, not a revolution, was finally responsible for Madero's downfall.

[109] One myth still current is that Madero regularly communed with the spirits of Washington, Jefferson, and other outstanding Americans.

[110] *Annual Register, 1913*, 482.

[111] *Times* (London), November 16, 1912, p. 18.

for 1912–13 over 1909–10, which was a year of presumed prosperity.[112] Even the banks were not adversely affected, gaining in assets to some extent.[113] The indications are, therefore, that, in spite of lurid reports of bandit raids and destitution of economic life, the vast majority of enterprises maintained a fairly steady business with no adverse effect on total production. A comparison of production figures will show little variation from preceding years.

Again, however, it must be emphasized that the general concept, among Mexicans and foreigners alike, was that the Madero government was totally unable to stabilize or pacify the nation. Vast government expenditures with no apparent results and constant reports of bandit raids, property destruction, and revolutionary activity created an atmosphere of distrust. The greatest danger to Madero was not the attacks of the thousands of men who occasionally took to arms, but the reaction to the exaggerated accounts of these attacks. In answer to Madero's insistence that conditions were not so chaotic as reported by the press, the opposition accused him of being "ostrichlike" and ridiculously idealistic, unable to effect promised reforms. He was not given credit for the reforms he did institute, meager though they were; and as the year ended, conditions were conducive to a *coup d'état.*

[112] See *Commercial Relations of the United States, 1910,* 41–42; *1911,* 70–72; *1912,* 106–10; *Statesman's Yearbook, 1914,* 1083.
[113] *Investigation of Mexican Affairs,* I, 735.

X

Agrarian and Labor Reform

WHEN THE DIAZ GOVERNMENT fell, in May, 1911,
the triumphant revolutionists were ill prepared to cope with the problem of agrarian and labor reform. The revolution had been begun and
fought as a movement for the renovation of Mexico and, as such, was
dedicated to economic and social, as well as political, reform. But
among the victors there were few whose ideas concerning reform had
advanced beyond an elementary stage; most of the leaders were convinced of the need, but they had no concrete plans for the future. Madero himself, before his revolution began, had concluded that economic
and social stability depended upon access to arable land by the rural
masses and had supported labor's demands; but his ideas were poorly
formed and nebulous.[1] Other men close to the revolutionists were in
somewhat the same condition, with only Ricardo Flores Magón having
proposed a concrete plan for reform,[2] and he was not admitted to the
councils of the victorious group.

That the landless Indian's way of life needed improvement was abundantly clear to all but the adherents of the old regime, and even among
the Díaz group there were some who admitted that a serious situation
had developed. But the nature of the ill, and the method through which
amelioration would come, were subject to wide divergence of opinion.
Madero believed strongly in the development of small holdings as a
means of combating the economic and social degradation so evident in
the rural areas; but when he was campaigning for the presidency, he
still did not realize that the Indian had not developed a concept of private land ownership. His ideas, therefore, were basically concerned
with encouraging a class of small landowners patterned on the French.

[1] Madero to Esquivel, December 2, 1909, *LO,* January 28, 1934, p. 1; Madero
to Sentíes, January 19, 1907, *ibid.,* November 26, 1933, p. 1.
[2] Programa del Partido Liberal, July 1, 1906, VC.

208

Agrarian and Labor Reform

When he accepted the Antire-electionist nomination, he had little to offer as a reform platform other than a recommendation for the founding of agricultural and mortgage banks to finance dam construction, well-drilling, and reclamation of wastelands to encourage small holdings.[3] Neither Madero nor his chief advisors had given much thought to the future of the *ejidos,* and it was a question of elementary justice, not fundamental economic and social concept, which dictated the inclusion of the oft-cited third article in the Plan de San Luis Potosí which heralded the outbreak of revolution.

In abuse of the law on public lands numerous proprietors of small holdings, in their greater part Indians, have been dispossessed of their lands by rulings of the Department of Public Improvement [Fomento] or by decisions of the tribunals of the Republic. As it is just to restore to their former owners the lands of which they were dispossessed in such an arbitrary manner, such rulings and decisions are declared subject to revision, and those who have acquired them in such an immoral manner, or their heirs, will be required to restore them to their former owners, to whom they shall also pay an indemnity for the damages suffered. Solely in case those lands have passed to third persons before the promulgation of this plan shall the former owners receive an indemnity from those in whose favor the dispossession was made.[4]

In spite of the inferences later drawn by opponents from the wording of the article, the provision was simple and straightforward, consistent with Madero's concept of peasant holdings.[5] It was the disappearance of the ranchos, not the elimination of the *ejidos,* that disturbed Madero in 1910, and it was the small private holdings to which the revolutionary plan referred. Even after Díaz had fallen, Madero hardly considered the larger problem involved in aiding millions of landless peons; in his first two public manifestos, of May 26 and June 24, 1911, after the dictatorship had been destroyed, he made no reference at all to the subject.[6] Nor was Madero alone among the revolutionaries in overlooking the implications and the immediacy of land reform. Party

[3] Madero address, April 25, 1910, in Taracena, *Madero,* 239 ff.

[4] Plan de San Luis Potosí, Article 3, as translated in *Investigation of Mexican Affairs,* II, 2631–33.

[5] Those who wished to discredit the administration and those who wished to force Madero to make rapid reform insisted that the revolutionary plan had promised both a restoration of the *ejidos* and a general redistribution of land.

[6] Madero, "Manifiesto a la nación," May 26, 1911, VC; "Manifiesto a la nación," June 24, 1911, in Taracena, *Madero,* 437–43.

councils did not discuss either the extent of dissatisfaction or plans for reform. None of the leaders mentioned the possibility of expropriation or general redistribution. The general consensus seemed to be that there was no immediate necessity for action and that understanding and encouragement, plus a just administration, would rectify the situation; even Pino Suárez, considered by some to be a radical socialist, emphasized co-operation rather than government leadership or action.[7]

In spite of this indifference on the part of the leaders, demands for agrarian reform were increasing. One independent investigator saw the national importance of the situation and recommended a partition of the largest estates.[8] Zapata, in his first interview with Madero, demanded restoration of village lands; and the provisional governor of Aguascalientes promised general land redistribution for his state.[9] By late June some peasants were seizing property in Oaxaca, Puebla, and Morelos, while Madero urged the *hacendados* of those states to alleviate the suffering voluntarily.[10] Some reformers, conversant with the need for relief, were convinced that the conservative landowners not only objected to any type of reform but also desired to perpetuate public ignorance about the nature of the issue.[11] González Roa summarized the conflict of opinions:

On the one hand, there were those who wanted to attack the problem and resolve it by energetic means. On the other hand, those who accused the revolution of being a force which disturbed the national well-being pretended to take halfway measures which would in no way disturb the tranquility and the productive monopoly which the *hacendados* enjoyed.[12]

With the passage of time after Díaz' defeat, the interest in reform increased. Madero arranged a settlement with Zapata in August which included a provision for ultimate improvement, but these efforts came to nought because of De la Barra's failure to approve them.[13] At approximately the same time, Andrés Molina Enríquez, irked by official

[7] Pino Suárez, "Manifiesto," June 24, 1911, VC.

[8] Carlos Basave del Castillo Negrete, as quoted by González Roa, *El aspecto agrario de la revolución mexicana,* 208.

[9] Magaña, *Emiliano Zapata,* I, 159–60; Madero to Alberto Fuentes D., June 18, 1911, BN 650.

[10] Magaña, *Emiliano Zapata,* I, 203, 204.

[11] González Roa, *El aspecto agrario,* 211.

[12] *Ibid.,* 210.

[13] Pp. 178–80 above. See specific provisions of the settlement in Madero to De la Barra, August 18, 1911, *LO,* April 22, 1934, p. 1.

inactivity, denounced the ad interim government in his Plan de Texcoco, proposing expropriation of large estates and general distribution to landless peasants.[14] The abortive nature of this "revolution" which attracted almost no adherents lent credence to the conservative opinion that reform was unnecessary and therefore discouraged rather than stimulated revision.

That Madero was not yet vitally concerned with agrarian improvement is shown by his failure to make more than cursory reference to the question when he addressed the Constitutional Progressive party convention on September 1, 1911.[15] To him agrarian reform was to be a process of evolution rather than revolution; speaking to a group in Veracruz shortly before the election, he said:

> I well realize that the situation of the Mexican worker from the economic and social standpoint has not materially changed with the revolution. . . . The triumph of the revolution has returned political rights and liberties to every citizen; from that point of view the change has been radical and rapid. But from the economic and social point of view the change cannot be so rapid; it cannot be brought about by a revolution, nor by laws, nor by decrees.[16]

But even an evolutionary process must have a starting point, and Madero persuaded De la Barra to appoint a national commission to study the agrarian needs. The commission, consisting of three engineers, two lawyers, and four landowners and men of public affairs under the presidency of Minister of Fomento Rafael Hernández, represented the conservative rather than the reform group.[17] Even Hernández, who was Madero's cousin, recognized the existence of an agricultural illness and "in general had a liberal spirit," but was not, "by political and personal antecedents and by conviction, in any condition to dictate means of a radical order."[18] The most influential man on the committee, Oscar Braniff, was nominally independent and unprejudiced, but he owned large estates and was satisfied with the status quo. Even though the

---

[14] Plan de Texcoco, August 23, 1911, in Casasola, *Historia gráfica*, I, 338.
[15] Address to the convention, *Nueva Era*, September 1, 1911, p. 5.
[16] Madero's speech at Veracruz, September 23, 1911, VC. Even though he had reference primarily to the day laborer in the textile mills and other industrial concerns, his remarks were characteristic of his general ideas concerning social reform.
[17] *Nueva Era*, September 28, 1911, p. 8.
[18] González Roa, *El aspecto agrario*, 213.

211

commission took its work seriously and held meetings twice weekly, its membership assured recommendations in the Díaz tradition.

Madero had hardly begun his tenure as constitutional president before Zapata proclaimed his Plan de Ayala, advocating immediate seizure of those lands which had been taken from the villages, the expropriation of one-third of the lands held by *hacendados* who did not obstruct the revolution's course, and complete expropriation of lands held by men who "directly or indirectly" opposed the plan.[19] As the Zapata movement gained in strength and as large parts of Morelos and contiguous states came under his sway, the land provisions of the Plan de Ayala were largely activated in the regions subject to his control. There the peons seized the land from the *hacendados* and worked it as though it were their own, in spite of the fact that only a small part of the area was ever sufficiently under Zapata's control to allow even a semblance of peaceful occupation and cultivation.

Zapata's demand for land reform was not echoed in other sections; his program was the outgrowth of a concerted attempt, during the recent past, to despoil the Indians of their lands and did not reflect the general attitude among Mexico's landless. Only in isolated areas was there any attempt to occupy the land by force, even though some discontent was noted among the agrarians. The peons of Cuencamé, Durango, pleaded for a restitution of their lost lands, but their action was confined to requests.[20] A small uprising in Tamazunchale, San Luis Potosí, in which the town was captured by discontented agricultural workers, was engendered by a desire for unpaid wages, not free land.[21] The experiences of these areas were repeated with variations in other sectors.

In the meantime Madero's new government was taking hesitant steps in the direction of reform. Rafael Hernández, who as Minister of Fomento was responsible for the development of a program, believed the solution to consist of two basic parts: augmentation of production and limited redistribution of lands. The small agricultural production, according to Hernández, was the result of a fundamental lack of natural resources and improper utilization of those available,

---

[19] Articles 6, 7, and 8 of the Plan de Ayala, in Magaña, *Emiliano Zapata*, II, 115–31. The exact intent of the drafters of Articles 7 and 8 is obscure. Simpson (*The Ejido—Mexico's Way Out*, 51) translates Article 7 to mean that one-third of the value of the land would be paid to the owners, but the text of the two articles seems to imply the meaning given here.

[20] *Nueva Era*, December 11, 1911, p. 1.

[21] *El País*, December 16, 1911, p. 1.

and in order to make the most of the limited assets a program of conservation and education would have to be undertaken; the consummation of such a program would require funds in abundance. At the same time, Hernández recognized the need for a more equitable distribution of the land, tending toward the creation of a small planter class alongside the *hacendados;* this he hoped to accomplish through the sale of small plots of national lands and through colonization projects.[22]

Consistent with this idea, in late November, Hernández introduced a bill for the construction of dams, reclamation of waste lands, construction of irrigation systems, and purchase of private lands for resale in small plots on favorable terms. A new bond issue was to be floated to finance the program.[23] Congress approved the bill with an amendment which prevented resale at less than cost and further safeguarded the treasury by providing that lands were not to be purchased at exorbitant prices.[24] On December 18, 1911, the bill became law.[25]

In early February, 1912, the National Agrarian Commission made its preliminary report, which included consideration of conservation of national forests and water resources, partition of large estates and intensification of farming practices, agricultural education, importation and manufacture of modern farming equipment, agricultural credit, and an integrated agricultural industry. The question of ejidal holdings had been considered by the commission, but no concrete proposal could yet be made; it was clear, however, that the members favored the partitioning of extant *ejidos* among the members of the communities, with the provision that the lands thus granted would be inalienable for twenty years.[26] In its recommendations, the commission limited its discussion to the land itself, with the proposed program to center around reclamation of wasteland, purchase of private property, and delimitation of national lands, all these then to be sold in small plots on easy terms. The basic philosophy was that land should be made available to those who had the resources and the ambition to work it and make it pay; there were to be no gifts, nor was the government to sustain a financial loss from the program. The only real service the government

[22] González Roa, *El aspecto agrario,* 213, 214.

[23] The proposed law may be found in its entirety in *Diario de los debates,* Cámara de Diputados, December 1, 1911, pp. 13–15.

[24] *El País,* December 12, 1911, p. 1.

[25] President's message to Twenty-fifth Congress, April 1, 1912, *Diario oficial,* April 1, 1912, pp. 405–13.

[26] This report of the National Agrarian Commission was published in full in *El País,* February 9 and 10, 1912.

was to render, other than to make the land available, was to establish a corps of trained agronomists to give education and aid to the new landowners; this at least was recognition of government responsibility for the development of a sound agricultural economy.

The report and recommendations reflected the conservative nature of the commission's members, anxious to safeguard the sanctity of private property and doubtful of the abilities of the average landless peon to make use of the lands if he had them. The plan was not one which would be advantageous to the destitute; a small amount of capital at the very least would be essential, for even though the proposed schedule for payments was unusually liberal, there was no provision for financing the beginning of the enterprises. At the same time, the commission was careful to develop a plan which would prevent land speculation or the concentration of large holdings. Considering the social, economic, and political background of most of the commission members, this last was a great concession.

It was quite obvious, moreover, that the majority of official opinion favored private rather than corporate ownership. When the report was presented to the Minister of Fomento, and then by him to the Council of Ministers, there was general agreement with the proposals, including the partitioning of the *ejidos*.[27] The problem of ejidal parceling was discussed at length, with the result that on February 17, 1912, Hernández dispatched a circular letter to all governors, recommending immediate delimitation of the existing ejidal holdings and an allotment of the lands to the community members.[28] The new owners were to be protected against loss of their lands through legal or extralegal means. A week later the government by executive decree ordered the survey and sale of national lands, with the stipulation that no individual could purchase, rent, or lease more than two hundred hectares of arable land or five thousand hectares of pasture land.[29] Villages contiguous to available national lands were to have sections set aside for them if they did not have *ejidos*,[30] and some lands were to be given to agricultural colonies to encourage small-scale farming in isolated areas. Hernández also requested that all state governors give particular atten-

[27] *El País*, February 14, 1912, p. 1.
[28] President's message to Twenty-fifth Congress, April 1, 1912, *Diario oficial*, April 1, 1912, pp. 405–13.
[29] "Decreto sobre terrenos baldíos y nacionales," February 24, 1912, in Julio Cuadras Caldas, *Catecismo agrario*, 195–99.
[30] The evident intent was to allow the villages to purchase the land necessary and then to divide it among the inhabitants.

tion to the restitution of ejidal lands to the villages so that distribution could be made.[31]

These actions indicated that reform was in the making, even though the reforms suggested barely touched the surface and were hardly revolutionary. Not even this conservative approach, however, was acceptable to the great landholders, many of whom feared a gradual but real encroachment on their privileges and were anxious to prevent such a development. The Chihuahua legislature, dominated by the *hacendados,* refused to extend the leave earlier granted to Governor Abraham González to serve in the federal cabinet, indicating their desire to bring to a halt any further consideration of land reform.[32] Pascual Orozco's rebellion within a matter of days after the presidential decrees was not a mere coincidence; it was a deliberate attempt to prevent any semblance of reform in Chihuahua, where the government estimated there were nearly two million acres of national lands and where nearly 60 per cent of all the rural population was attached to the haciendas.[33] In their turn the *hacendados* realized that ultimately some reform or simulated reform would be necessary to gain sufficient adherents to contest the government; this explains the rather innocuous provision of the Plan Orozquista, which proposed a program not unlike that being considered by the government, but which had additional safeguards for private property and for indemnification in case of expropriation.[34] The honesty of Orozco's intentions may be judged from his hasty acceptance of the Huerta government after Madero's fall; not even the most naïve believed that Huerta would institute far-reaching agrarian reforms.

While the Orozco rebellion effectually prevented surveys in Chihuahua, the delineation of national lands in other areas was quickly begun. Madero informed Congress in April, 1912, that thirteen surveying commissions were either at work or preparing to operate in as many states. By late May the government announced that seventy thousand hectares had been surveyed and were ready for distribution, in two-hundred-hectare plots, in Durango; no transactions were to be made through agents or intermediaries for fear of speculation.[35] By early

[31] *El País,* February 22, 1912, p. 1.   [32] *Ibid.,* February 18, 1912, p. 1.
[33] Article 6, "Decreto sobre terrenos baldíos y nacionales," February 24, 1912, in Cuadras Caldas, *Catecismo agrario,* 197; Tannenbaum, *The Mexican Agrarian Revolution,* Appendix B, Table V, p. 466.
[34] Article 35, Plan Orozquista, the text of which may be found in Naranjo, *Diccionario biográfico revolucionario,* 276–82.
[35] *El País,* May 21 and 31, 1912, p. 1.

summer the surveys in those regions accessible to the government were practically completed,[36] but the sale of the surveyed plots went slowly. Most of the Indians desiring property wished to remain in their own neighborhoods, where their families had practiced agriculture for generations, and in most cases land was not available in those areas. In addition, it was generally believed that the available land was not suitable for cultivation, even though some investigations showed that it would be excellent for small-scale farming.[37] The program for the purchase and resale of private land was no more successful, largely because the *hacendados* wanted exorbitant sums for their properties; they were quite willing to sell, but at such fantastically high prices that the government could not make the purchases under the provisions of the law.[38] Some agrarian colonies were established and a number of trained agronomists were put in the field to give training and aid, but the program met with only moderate success.[39] As a consequence, little additional land was in the hands of the small proprietor by the year's end, although Madero announced that over twenty million hectares were available for sale.[40]

Faced with the failure of the program developed during the year, Madero presented the problem of agrarian reform to the incoming Twenty-sixth Congress, the first elected since the revolution and generally sympathetic to reform. In one of his first statements to the congressmen, Madero stressed the importance of land and social reform; but he soon made it clear that he still favored an evolutionary development, and his plea was for patience and understanding. He believed that if Mexico could solve her agrarian problem within twenty years she could well be proud of the achievement.[41]

But the demands for action were constantly more articulate, and the

[36] *Ibid.,* June 28, 1912, p. 1.
[37] González Roa, *El aspecto agrario,* 215; statement by Máximo Alcalá in *El País,* October 3, 1912, p. 1.
[38] González Roa, *El aspecto agrario,* 215.
[39] See the reports concerning these activities, in the 1912 issues of *Boletín de la Dirección General de Agricultura.*
[40] Madero, *Informe leído por el C. Presidente de la República al abrirse el primer período de sesiones del 26° Congreso de la Unión.* These figures were probably exaggerated, and certainly included lands unsuited to the Indian's needs.
[41] *Comentarios al brillante discurso del Sr. Presidente de la República, aplicados a la situación actual, por el Prof. José Rumbia;* Madero manifesto, *El País,* November 3, 1912, p. 5.

peon could not wait twenty years. A cabinet crisis in the latter part of November seemed to augur well for the long-heralded reform; for, as a consequence of resignations and shifts, a man of liberal views took over the portfolio of Fomento. The crisis was precipitated when Madero wished to shift Jesús Flores Magón, a man of real ability and pronounced views but politically ambitious, from the powerful post of Gobernación to the less powerful position of Fomento, where his reform ideas would be of real value.[42] Instead of accepting the new post, Flores Magón accused Madero of political chicanery and resigned from the government.[43] Still desiring to have a man of advanced ideas in the cabinet position which had jurisdiction over agrarian questions, Madero considered offering the post to Luis Cabrera, who was recognized as a practical liberal, but objections by Rafael Hernández and Ernesto Madero blocked the appointment.[44] Madero then selected Manuel Bonilla, whom Flores Magón characterized as a perfectly balanced liberal patriot, to fill the post of Fomento; Hernández was shifted to Gobernación; and Jaime Gurza was brought into the cabinet to fill the post of Communications, which Bonilla had previously occupied.[45]

Within a short time the new atmosphere was reflected in Congress, where Luis Cabrera, supported by Roque González Garza, Adrián Aguirre Benavides, José Macías, and fifty-nine others, introduced a bill for the restoration of the *ejidos* on a communal basis. Restitution was to be made where such action was possible; but in case return of the original ejidal lands to the village was impracticable, the government was to resort to expropriation. Since the Constitution of 1857 and subsequent legislation prohibited the villages from holding lands, the bill proposed that the government retain ownership and allow the villagers to work the land without charge.[46] There were objections, of course. Hernández agreed with the principle of the proposal, but he believed

---

[42] *El País,* November 26, 1912, p. 1.
[43] See text of his resignation in *Boletín oficial de la Secretaría de Relaciones Exteriores,* November, 1912, p. 2.
[44] González Roa, *El aspecto agrario,* 223. González was Acting Minister of Gobernación after Flores' resignation, and was therefore conversant with the cabinet situation.
[45] *El País,* December 1, 1912, p. 7; see *Boletín oficial de la Secretaría de Relaciones Exteriores,* November, 1912, pp. 8, 9, 11, for text of appointments.
[46] "Proyecto de Ley," *Diario de los debates,* Cámara de Diputados, December 3, 1912, pp. 1, 3.

217

the problem to be so complex that the details would be almost impossible to arrange.[47] Madero entertained grave doubts concerning the efficacy of the proposal,[48] and Bonilla feared that the cost of any attempt at wholesale restoration would be prohibitive. He estimated that there were six thousand villages which needed ejidal lands, with each *ejido* consisting of at least twenty-five hundred hectares; at the price at which the government could acquire lands the cost would be staggering.[49] Nevertheless, consideration of the bill continued until the beginning of the Huerta barracks revolt in February.

Meanwhile, Bonilla was preparing himself for a frontal assault on the land problem. Inasmuch as the National Agrarian Commission had done little to effect a solution, Bonilla decided to ignore that group and depend on reports, investigations, and recommendations from individuals whom he could trust. Accordingly, he commissioned Lauro Viadas, José Covarrubias, and Carlos Basave del Castillo Negrete to make independent studies. Viadas and Covarrubias co-operated on their report, being in basic agreement on the nature of the problem and its solution. They believed the prices for agricultural produce to be entirely too high because of poor production, tariff protection, and high transport rates. In order to reduce the cost of food, land should be expropriated to develop small holdings, new transportation and communication lines should be constructed, transport rates reduced, tariffs lowered, import of needed material encouraged, and general aid and protection given to the small landowners.[50] The investigators believed that the incorporation of these reforms would mean an increase in agricultural production through proper utilization of the land, a drain of indigent labor away from the cities, and immeasurable improvement in the general condition of the near-destitute. Even while recommending expropriation, however, Covarrubias and Viadas were careful to stipulate that a fair price should be paid for the land taken.

Basave differed in detail with respect to the problem and the need. He contended that the basic ill was land speculation on the one hand and the differential between wages paid foreigners and those paid natives on the other. Prevention of land speculation, equalization of wages, and a campaign to raise the moral, physical, and economic

[47] *El País,* December 5, 1912, p. 1.
[48] Luis Cabrera, as quoted in *El Hombre Libre,* February 8, 1931.
[49] González Roa, *El aspecto agrario,* 232.
[50] *Ibid.,* 227–28. The author has been unable to unearth any copy of the original report and must therefore depend on González Roa.

218

standards of the peons were the actions he suggested. At the same time he recommended the establishment of agricultural colonies to encourage small proprietors.[51] At the time Madero was overthrown, Bonilla was studying the proposals made by his three investigators, and his later record would indicate that had he remained in office he would have been able to accomplish some notable reforms.

"The concrete net results of Madero's halfhearted attempts to deal with the agrarian problem were exactly nothing," reports one investigator.[52] In terms of acres distributed, haciendas broken up, and of new farms established, this evaluation is justified; but the establishment of an idea, of a concept, is as concrete as the distribution of land plots, and in the development of the fundamental concepts of ejidal restoration and expropriation as a technique for land reform, the Madero period made a great contribution to the progress of the revolution. Whereas only the most radical reformers had earlier spoken of expropriation, and then only with extreme hesitation and many qualifications, the end of the Madero regime found men of public affairs freely discussing the possibilities and probabilities of expropriation. Ejidal restoration had not been considered seriously before the last months of the Madero period; the provision of the Plan of San Luis Potosí did not envisage a complete reinstitution of communal land practice, but only a restitution of lands which had been illegally seized from individuals, and this proved to be impossible under existing legal conditions. But by late 1912 the restoration program was receiving serious consideration from Congress and the Council of Ministers. These developments marked long strides forward in the direction finally taken by succeeding governments.

The development of concepts, however, does not satisfy the untutored masses, and in retrospect it is not difficult to see that Madero should have taken more deliberate and drastic steps to solve the problem; but it must also be remembered that when Madero came to office the idea of wholesale agrarian reform was new and untried, and unpopular among the "important" classes of society. Even Emilio Vázquez Gómez, who considered himself to be a paragon of agrarian reform and whose doctrines were thought by many to embody the panacea, proposed nothing more advanced or liberal than the program actually attempted by the government. He opposed expropriation and favored the purchase and resale of uncultivated lands, the construction

---

[51] *Ibid.*, 228, 229.   [52] Simpson, *The Ejido—Mexico's Way Out,* 49.

of dams, and the establishment of grange schools; that was the extent of reform proposed by one of Madero's bitterest critics.[53] With the exception of the cases of Zapata and Molina Enríquez, land reform was not a factor in any of the various revolutionary movements which troubled the Madero government. The landless peons were dissatisfied; but their unrest was ephemeral, vague, and inarticulate, manifesting itself in banditry rather than land seizures, giving no indication that immediate agrarian reform was a vital necessity. Francisco León de la Barra, even after witnessing the titanic struggle which ended in Obregón's final victory, was the spokesman for his economic and social class when he said that Mexico had no land problem.[54] An American long resident in Mexico said in 1920: "I never heard of any land question . . . in Mexico. Amongst the many Indian villages that I have visited I have always found them in possession of their community fields, with which, so far as ever came to my knowledge, they seemed to be perfectly contented."[55] The majority of the Mexicans of influence, including Madero, simply did not recognize the emergency nature of the problem.

Misunderstanding concerning Madero's attitude was probably even more important, as a factor in his overthrow, than his failure to recognize the need for drastic and immediate reform. Nelson O'Shaughnessy, on the staff of the American Embassy in Mexico, was patently wrong, but nevertheless reflected one strong segment of opinion, when he said that Madero "wanted a division of a good many of the large estates, and he wanted to do it in a summary manner. At least, that is what he wanted to do in the beginning. Of course, there was a national organized opposition to any such action."[56]

Luis Cabrera, among others, insisted[57] that Madero had pledged a general and complete restoration of the *ejidos,* and Madero's failure to carry out such a program was considered by that group to be a negation of one of the fundamental reasons for having fought the revolution. This misunderstanding regarding Madero's promises and ideas about land reform had an adverse effect on his position, for it tended to

[53] E. Vázquez Gómez, *El pensamiento de la revolución,* 5–8.

[54] González Roa, *El aspecto agrario,* 210.

[55] Eder Cole Byam, testimony before the Subcommittee of the Senate Committee on Foreign Relations, May 1, 1920, in *Investigation of Mexican Affairs,* II, 2688.

[56] Testimony, *ibid.,* 2706.

[57] In a speech to Congress, December 3, 1912, in support of his bill for the restoration of the *ejidos.* See *Diario de los debates,* Cámara de Diputados, December 3, 1912, p. 4.

alienate both the conservatives and the radicals—the conservatives because they feared reform which would entail the destruction of the
haciendas, and the radicals because they considered Madero to be a
traitor to the revolution since he did not comply with his promises.[58]
Madero's efforts to clarify his position and his promises were to no
avail; the misconception persisted, and each attempt at explanation
was made the subject of a new attack.[59]

So the situation stood just before the end of the Madero period. In
spite of all the internal disturbances—including the revolution led by
Reyes, the eternal heckling of Emilio Vázquez Gómez, the Orozco rebellion, the Félix Díaz uprising, the inherited Zapata troubles, and the
huge number of bandit raids—the Madero government found the time,
energy, and finances to make a vast survey of government lands and
was well on the way to the establishment of real agrarian reform. Had
the Madero government continued, reform would certainly have been
instituted, though probably at a slower rate and with a different focus
from that which ultimately developed. But the changes would have
come without the violence and slaughter which characterized the struggle after 1913.

The attitude of Madero and his government toward labor was somewhat the same as it was toward the landless peon. Although he was an
interested spectator of the labor troubles after 1900, labor reform was
not one of the items which he stressed in his campaign for the presidency. The Plan of San Luis Potosí contained no reference to labor,
nor did any other public pronouncement until he issued the manifesto
of June 24, 1911; and then he promised no more than an opportunity:

[From] the political point of view your situation has changed radically
since you have passed from the role of a miserable pariah and slave to
the august height of a citizen, [but] . . . do not hope that your economic
and social situation will become better so rapidly, since this cannot be
done by means of decrees or by laws, but only by the constant and laborious efforts of all members of society.[60]

Madero was sympathetic to the desires of labor, however, and had
no intention of leaving the workers to the mercy of the industrialists;

---

[58] Many persons in Mexico insist today that Madero promised complete and
total redistribution of lands.
[59] E.g., Madero manifesto, *El País,* November 3, 1912, p. 1.
[60] Madero, "Manifiesto a la nación," June 24, 1911, in Taracena, *Madero,*
437–43.

he favored organization and realized that the laborers would have to obtain government protection before they could take the steps to help themselves. In order to gain economic freedom, he said, "it is necessary for the workers to unite and it will be our task, that of the government officials, to protect them so that they may unite. . . . Now the situation will be different, justice will be with the deserving, and the culpable will be punished regardless of his station. . . . [We] are going to protect the worker in the formation of his unions."[61]

The period of the De la Barra ad interim government was marked, in labor as in most other fields, by inaction, a failure either to suppress or to abet labor organization. In October the government announced that an Oficina General de Trabajo to survey labor conditions and report to the government would be formed, but the office was never actually established.[62] Later in the month, Madero again made it quite clear that he favored labor organization when he spoke to the railroad workers at Gómez Palacio; and all during the period numerous groups were taking advantage of the promised protection by organizing into trade unions.[63]

As should have been expected, but apparently was not, the new freedom and the absence of fear of government reprisals engendered a wave of strikes by groups who were thoroughly dissatisfied with conditions and could see no hope of improvement except through their own militant actions.[64] The most serious strike in the waning days of 1911 was one in Torreón, which assumed all the characteristics of a general strike before the final settlement in favor of the strikers.[65] One of the most interesting aspects of the situation was the order which prevailed; unlike the Cananea and Río Blanco strikes, in Torreón there was no attempt to molest the management or property.

The nature and depth of labor unrest was slow to penetrate into the consciousness of the public and the government. Instead of recognizing the strikes as symptomatic of a fundamental malady, Madero accused his political opponents of fomenting them in order to weaken the government, and there were persistent rumors to the effect that the Tor-

[61] Madero's address at Veracruz, September 23, 1911, VC.
[62] El País, October 5, 1911, p. 1.
[63] Clark, Organized Labor in Mexico, 18–19. The speech, made on October 31, was published in its entirety in Nueva Era, November 1, 1911, p. 1.
[64] Madero was obviously surprised and displeased at the incidence of strikes.
[65] See Nueva Era for November 14, 15, and 17 for the development of the strike to general proportions.

reón strikers received funds from General Reyes.[66] The London *Times* correspondent stated that the industrial troubles could not "be considered intrinsically serious."[67] But the evident unrest and clamor for reform dictated the necessity for some official recognition and action; accordingly, a Department of Labor was established as a part of the Ministry of Fomento on December 13, 1911. The new department was to serve as a bureau of information concerning labor conditions, was to act as a mediator in labor difficulties if the contesting parties requested mediation, was to act as an employment office, and was generally to promote proper and healthy labor-management relations.[68]

The establishment of a labor office did not still the demands for labor reform, however. By early January the situation was reaching such proportions that the Council of Ministers held a special meeting to discuss the question; but their deliberations consisted primarily of a discussion of the need for raising the moral, intellectual, and social standards of the workers. The only concrete recommendation coming from the session was that the *pulquerías* should be closed earlier to prevent the wage earner from drinking to excess.[69] But the workers were demanding more than the uplift of their morals; they wanted more pay and less work, along with better working conditions and less tyranny by the management. In Manzanillo a strike was successful, but a series of strikes in Jalisco, involving over a thousand workers, met with only partial success.[70]

The primary scene of labor difficulties, however, was the area comprising the Federal District and the states of Tlaxcala, Puebla, and Veracruz, where the workers in the textile mills took the lead by going on strike for a ten-hour day and an increase in wages. With most of the mills in the area closed by the strike, Madero sponsored a meeting between the industrialists and representatives of labor, the invitations actually being issued by the Minister of Gobernación. It was hoped that the conference would result in some standardization of wages and hours throughout the country.[71] The laborers, still suspicious of management and not completely trusting the government, not only refused

[66] See Madero's speech in Cuautla, August 18, 1911, *LO*, April 15, 1934, p. 2. *Nueva Era*, November 17, 1911, p. 1.
[67] November 21, 1911, p. 5.
[68] Decree of December 13, 1911, *Diario oficial*, December 18, 1911, p. 629.
[69] *El País*, January 4, 1912, p. 1.
[70] *Ibid.*, January 5 and 8, 1912, p. 5.
[71] *Boletín del Departamento de Trabajo*, July, 1913, p. 18.

223

to resume work on the basis of a promise of a new wage-and-hour scale to go into effect the following month but also insisted that Madero himself take part in the deliberations of the forthcoming conference.[72] Since Madero found it impossible to attend the meetings, he delegated Gustavo to act as chairman and his personal representative.

On January 20, 1912, forty-eight industrialists met at the Ministry of Gobernación to discuss the possibility of establishing uniform wages and hours throughout the nation.[73] It was soon obvious that varying conditions precluded uniformity; the best that could be hoped for would be a uniform raising of wages and reduction of hours.[74] Eventually a compromise was reached which was satisfactory to all parties: a maximum of ten hours of work per day was set as the standard, and all factories then using a longer workday were to reduce the length of day immediately, without granting any increase in wages. Those factories already on a ten-hour day were to grant a wage increase.[75] One other basic problem was discussed, but with little or no concrete result: Gustavo insisted that some provision be made to care for the children working in the factories; he asked specifically a shorter day and proper precautions to prevent accidents. Some of the employers agreed not to hire "extremely young" children, but since there was no agreement concerning specific ages, the promise was illusory.[76]

Within a few days after the announcement of the agreements reached, the majority of the strikers returned to their jobs, not completely satisfied but now becoming conscious of their power and of the support which they could expect from the government for any legitimate demand. The workers had learned something further from the conference: they would have to form strong and well-disciplined unions if they were to attain success, for since the disastrous Río Blanco strike five years before, in which the Círculo de Obreros Libres had been destroyed, the textile workers had not organized into a cohesive union.[77] And yet it was clear that if there had been a strong organization, it would not have been necessary to accept the rather meager concessions made by the industrialists. The government, too, recognized this need, and in February the laborers were strongly encouraged by

[72] *El País,* January 11 and 18, 1912, p. 1.
[73] *Boletín del Departamento de Trabajo,* July, 1913, pp. 19–20.
[74] Circular of August 4, 1912, *ibid.,* 35.
[75] Circular of January 25, 1912, *ibid.,* August, 1913, p. 109.
[76] See *Boletín del Departamento de Trabajo,* July, 1913, pp. 20–32; and August, 1913, pp. 107–10, for a general discussion of the conference.
[77] Clark, *Organized Labor in Mexico,* 14.

Agrarian and Labor Reform

the government to form their unions.[78] From that time forward there was increased activity among those organizing groups into unions.

The agreements reached in the January conference were recognized to be a temporary expedient to meet the problems of the moment and not to bring about a solution to all the questions which might arise between management and labor. During the course of the next few months numerous strikes began, particularly in the textile mills, which made it all too clear that some permanent agreement would have to be reached in order to assure even a semblance of industrial peace. Again the government took the lead, and in July another conference was called under the auspices of the national government, with Minister of Fomento Hernández presiding.[79] The government promulgated the regulations to be in force during the conference, stipulating the order of business and the method of voting.[80] In addition, as a basis for discussion the Department of Labor presented a program consisting of ten basic points, outlining the duties, rights, and responsibilities of both workers and managers. The provisions, which of course would not have had the force of law even if accepted by all parties, were generally conservative by present standards, but they did provide a basis of understanding and a method for correcting existing abuses.[81] Sitting for nearly a month, the conferees thoroughly discussed the proposals and ended the sessions by liberalizing the proposals to some extent in favor of labor, but not without a considerable amount of heated discussion and debate between the representatives of labor and those of the mills.[82] The laborers gained additional concessions because they had organized a central negotiating committee since the January meeting and were therefore in a more favorable bargaining position.

The final agreement was prefaced with a commitment to institute a general increase in wages, and therefore there was no mention of a wage increase in the body of the understanding other than a provision for a minimum wage of one peso and twenty-five centavos a day.[83] The laborers obtained some decided advantages in the other stipulations, particularly in that well-defined rights, privileges, and obligations were set forth. A maximum of ten hours of daylight work and nine hours of

[78] Circular of February 24, 1912, *Boletín del Departamento de Trabajo,* July, 1913, pp. 33–34.   [79] Circular of August 4, 1912, *ibid.,* July, 1913, p. 35.
[80] "Proyecto de reglamento," June 29, 1912, *ibid.,* October, 1913, pp. 304–306.
[81] *El País,* July 5, 1912, p. 7.
[82] For the proceedings of the convention, see *Boletín del Departamento de Trabajo,* October, 1913; November, 1913; December, 1913; January, 1914; and February, 1914.   [83] Circular of August 4, 1912, *ibid.,* July, 1913, p. 37.

night work was set, with time and a half for overtime in general but with only a 20 per cent increase over base pay for stipulated types of work. On paydays, which were to be once each week, there were to be only nine hours of work. The foremen could not demand money from the employees on any pretext, nor could they accept gifts from men under them; they were also enjoined not to treat their men harshly or to use insulting or derogatory language.[84] Fifteen days during the year were to be legal holidays on which no demands could be made upon the time of the workers. The companies surrendered the practice of assessing fines for infractions of rules or for any other reason. But for poor work which was his own responsibility, and not that of machine or material, the worker could be forced to pay an indemnity; he could, if he chose, however, leave the job instead of paying for the damage. Company stores, long the bane of the worker's existence, were prohibited, as was payment of wages or loans in anything except national money.[85] Hiring children under fourteen years of age was prohibited, free medical service and medicine were to be provided, and the factory owners were to encourage education among their employees. Any claim presented against the management by an employee was to receive action within ten days. All moving of heavy equipment or material was to be done by professional movers, and not by the men working in the factories. And finally, if the shop closed or a man was discharged without just cause, the company was to pay for a full week's work regardless of the day on which the separation occurred.

A careful study of these provisions in the light of acutal conditions will reveal a number of decided benefits for the workers. Complete compliance with all these provisions would not, of course, have placed the Mexican laborer on a parity with his counterpart in the United States; but the most vicious of the labor practices—company stores, payment in company money, release without cause, long overtime hours, negation of wages through assessment of fines, unsanitary working conditions, and general maltreatment of the workers by the foremen—were obviated. This was in a sense the charter of freedom for the Mexican laborer.

These concessions to the laborers were not granted without cost, however, for the industrialists received some guarantees and benefits as

---

[84] This provision leads one to wonder about the presumed apathy and docility of the Indian workman.

[85] A favorite practice had been to pay in company-printed scrip, which was good only for purchases in company stores.

well. Each worker was obligated to remain at his place of work during the hours of labor, he was not to disrupt or disturb the work of others for any reason, and he must pay for damage resulting from his negligence; his obligations to the employer also included working a full week and working overtime to repair machinery in case of necessity. Finally, all provisions of the agreements were to be considered as integral parts of the labor contract, and the acceptance of a job was in itself the acceptance of all provisions relative to the conduct of the men while on the job.[86]

Before the conclusion of the convention, the labor representative from the Puebla-Orizaba area requested that the announcement of the new contract be suspended until the new wage schedule went into effect, for he feared a hostile reaction in view of the fact that no mention was made of wages in the agreement itself. Since many strikes had been averted only because the conference was being held, and since one of the major reasons for demanding a strike was higher wages, there was real danger that a wave of strikes could paralyze the industry unless the full implications of the agreement were thoroughly understood. But the industrialists accused labor of bad faith and refused to accede to the request. Within a matter of days, twenty-three mills in the Orizaba and Puebla area were closed by strikes, and it was necessary to withdraw the regulations for study by the employees. The workers were soon convinced of the advantages in the agreement and returned to their posts.[87]

The greatest weakness of the agreement resulting from the July convention was the absence of machinery for effective enforcement. The unions, with government encouragement and aid, established a central Permanent Workers' Committee, with headquarters in Mexico and branches in the textile centers, to investigate infringements of the agreement and to act as labor's representative in disputes.[88] But the committee had only partial success; generally poor observance moved the government, in December, to pass a tax law which gave distinct advantages to the concerns which fulfilled all their obligations under the agreement.[89]

The agreement and tax law, however, were only stopgap measures,

---

[86] These provisions may be found in *El País*, July 5, 15, and 18, 1912.
[87] *Ibid.*, August 2, 6, and 9, 1912, p. 1.
[88] Clark, *Organized Labor in Mexico*, 20.
[89] Decree of December 18, 1912, *Boletín del Departamento de Trabajo*, September, 1913, p. 214.

still giving the laborer little or no legal protection; furthermore, only the textile industry was involved, and it was essential to draft a legal labor code which would meet the needs of industrial labor in general. The Department of Labor therefore undertook to study the full problem of labor legislation and in the latter days of the Madero regime was engaged in preparing a projected law for presentation to Congress.[90] The proposal was never presented because Madero was overthrown by Huerta, who held a deep antipathy for organized labor.

Probably even if Madero had not been overthrown, there would not have been any startling innovation in labor codes established in Mexico, but labor certainly would have been in a more advantageous position than it had ever been before. Madero believed that the proper function of government with respect to labor was to give the laborer an opportunity to improve his condition, to give him protection against exploitation by the employer, and to give him encouragement in his struggle to become a respected member of society. Luis Cabrera, an ardent agrarian reformer, felt that labor was getting more than its share of attention from the government,[91] which in itself is indicative of the interest that Madero and his advisors took in the labor problem.

The most important contribution which the Madero government made to the progress of Mexican labor, however, was the development of an attitude. Beginning with the manifesto of June 24, 1911, and progressing through the Veracruz and Gómez Palacio speeches to the government-sponsored meetings of January and July, 1912, the Mexican government came to be looked upon as the defender and protector of labor. The laborers themselves did what they could, in a halting and tentative fashion, to improve their own condition, but the formulation of contracts resulting from the July conference was due almost entirely to official intervention. The laborers looked to the government to aid them in getting organized, in finding meeting places, and in forcing or encouraging the industrialists to fulfill their contracts. The pattern for later developments was set. To a large degree the Mexican labor movement has been characterized by government paternalism; the government has led the laborer, rather than the laborer forcing governmental action. That attitude began during the Madero administration.

[90] Colina, *Madero y el Gral. Díaz,* 122.
[91] *Diario de los debates,* Cámara de Diputados, December 3, 1912, p. 4.

XI

The Huerta Coup d'Etat

As 1912 CAME TO AN END, there was just cause for optimism. While Orozco was again reported to be active in Chihuahua, and Carranza spoke of "rebels" in Coahuila, there were no serious armed movements against the government.[1] The American Ambassador, who was consistently pessimistic concerning Madero's government, reported: "Armed revolution against the Government has for the moment sensibly diminished, but one or more revolutionary movements may at any time be dangerous to the Government, already suffering from universal unpopularity. In the north the revolution exists only in the States of Durango and Chihuahua; violence elsewhere is simply brigandage."[2]

Not only was violence less in evidence than at any time since Madero's inauguration, but the government showed greater strength and activity than it had at any time during the past year. Manuel Bonilla and his aides working on the agrarian problem were sympathetic to reform; with the help of a militant group in Congress supporting the project for the restoration of the *ejidos,* the Minister of Fomento hoped to be able to carry out a positive program despite the *hacendados'* objections. The financial structure, which the Díaz government had left in a weakened condition in spite of a treasury surplus, and which had been further undermined by the numerous revolutions, was in the process of being strengthened through new foreign loans. Banking institutions were sounder than they had been in the latter days of the

[1] Wilson to State Department, January 7, 1913, *FR,* 1913, p. 692; Carranza to Madero, January 13, 1913, *LP,* March 13, 1938, p. 7. Emiliano Zapata was still in rebellion in Morelos, a constant source of irritation. He did not constitute a real danger to the administration, however, since he was not attempting to overthrow the government, but to improve conditions in Morelos.

[2] Wilson to State Department, January 7, 1913, *FR,* 1913, p. 692.

Díaz government.[3] Recent developments with respect to railways[4] had opened new jobs for many Mexican mechanics and white-collar workers and were a source of strong support to the government and to the general economic picture. Foreign trade was good, and business had suffered little from the revolutions.

A further source of real encouragement to Madero was the forthcoming inauguration of Woodrow Wilson to the presidency of the United States. Convinced that the new administration would demonstrate a more sympathetic attitude toward his government, Madero made no attempt to mask his outright pleasure at Wilson's election.[5] To indicate his optimism, and incidentally to give the lie to the current supposition that his brother was responsible for official policy, Madero commissioned Gustavo to undertake a mission as a special ambassador of good will to Japan; Gustavo was scheduled to leave in January.[6] Since the younger Madero had been the target of much antiadministration propaganda, accused of a wide variety of illegal and extralegal activities including the creation of La Porra, a band of ruffians presumably hired to maul political opponents,[7] wisdom dictated his absence for a short period. Inasmuch as Gustavo was his elder brother's devoted aide, completely loyal and capable, the decision to send him to Japan was a gesture of real faith in the future.

But the situation was far from static, and peace had not returned to Mexico. Unrest and brigandage threatened foreign interests to such a degree—and under prevailing attitudes danger to the interests of a world power might easily mean intervention—that Madero took the "unusual and, from a political point of view, possibly dangerous course of asking all priests in Mexico to offer a mass simultaneously for the restoration of order."[8] The press was generally anxious to discredit the administration; and Henry Lane Wilson, who Madero hoped would be recalled by Woodrow Wilson immediately upon Wilson's inauguration,

---

[3] *Investigation of Mexican Affairs,* I, 735. [4] Pp. 250–51 below.
[5] Chargé d'Affaires Schuyler to State Department, November 27, 1912, *FR,* 1912, p. 870. Madero believed that the Taft administration neither understood nor agreed with the program which he hoped to follow; Woodrow Wilson's record and campaign speeches, on the other hand, convinced him that Wilson would do both. [6] José C. Valadés, in *LO,* February 20, 1938, p. 1.
[7] The existence of such an organization is doubtful, and Gustavo's connection is even more doubtful. There is no doubt, however, that ruffians under the leadership of administration supporters did occasionally handle political opponents rather violently. [8] *Times* (London), December 21, 1912, p. 5.

was increasingly violent in his fulminations against the Madero government.[9]

Damaging rumors, the product of clever propagandists opposed to the administration, persistently undermined and discomfited the government, keeping both officials and general public in a nervous state, and made every government action the object of suspicion. Supported by the press, the opponents of the administration could often cloak their illegal activities quite effectively by starting a rumor, which many papers would report as fact, accusing the government of planning some questionable action.

One demonstration of this technique occurred shortly after the beginning of the new year, when a group of the friends of Félix Díaz, still in prison in Veracruz as a result of the October rebellion, planned a *cuartelazo,* or "barracks revolt," to free the prisoner. The government uncovered the plot; and in order to protect themselves the conspirators immediately charged that the government was planning a sham uprising in Veracruz, during the course of which members of La Porra were to assassinate Félix Díaz.[10] Within a short time the accusation came to the ears of the American consul, who considered the information as having come from "reliable sources," and by him was reported immediately to the Department of State.[11] The officials of the State Department, shocked by the callousness of the reported plan, instructed Ambassador Wilson to warn the Mexican government against any such tactics.[12] In taking this officious action, the United States was unknowingly serving as the agent of a group conspiring to overthrow the Mexican government.

The Mexico City press, which became more violently anti-Madero with each passing day, was a source of constant danger to the administration. The government, committed to a policy of constitutional guarantees, hesitated to close any of the papers or to attempt censorship, and accordingly the papers were unrestrained in their criticism. With the exception of the small *Nueva Era* and a few other newspapers of even less importance, Mexico City newspapers were solidly opposed to

[9] As an example, see Wilson to State Department, February 4, 1913, *FR,* 1913, pp. 696–99. Wilson accused Madero's government of being inept, capricious, dishonest, tyrannical, intolerant, and hypocritical.

[10] Emigdio Paniagua, *El combate de la Ciudadela narrado por un extranjero,* 9. Paniagua, violently anti-Madero and pro-Huerta, was proud of this maneuver.

[11] Canada to State Department, January 14, 1913, *FR,* 1913, pp. 693–94.

[12] Knox to Wilson, January 16, 1913, *ibid.,* 694.

231

the administration. Francisco Bulnes has well summarized the influence and tactics of the opposition press, led by *El País* and *El Imparcial:*[13]

> Those who read these newspapers, whose flaming words were intended to electrify the masses and arouse their basest passions, whose route of circulation was marked by a fiery trail, whose incendiary opinions were everywhere discussed, will be my witnesses that the doctrine preached by this anarchistic press was regicide. . . .
>
> All these monsters [revolutionaries and bandits fighting the government] were declared to be good, capable of governing, the true democrats for whom the country had been sighing, the enlightened guides who were to conduct the people along the road of duty and constitutionalism. Madero alone was evil. He was a reptile which, according to the advice of *El Heraldo,* ought to be stepped upon. He should be overthrown, said *La Tribuna;* cast out at once, said *El Mañana.* It was a savage campaign in the interest of regicide.[14]

With a background of public opinion inflamed by a press which could not distinguish between liberty and license, vicious and defamatory rumors circulating concerning members of Madero's cabinet, vague and unfounded accusations of fraud and corruption in government circles, and unrest brought on by Madero's failure to solve the outstanding problems confronting his administration, another attempt to displace the government was inevitable. But the events of the past year had demonstrated conclusively that there could be no hope of overthrowing the government by a revolution beginning in an outlying area and then converging on the capital; only a *cuartelazo* could be successful, and the elements for a *cuartelazo* were concentrated in Mexico City in early February, 1913. General Bernardo Reyes, anxious to regain his freedom so that he might lead another attack, was in the military prison in Mexico awaiting trial for his abortive 1911 revolution. Generals Manuel Mondragón and Gregorio Ruiz, bitter and resentful over Madero's insistence that civil government should be in the hands of civilians, were stationed in the capital and anxious to restore the army's "honor." And finally Félix Díaz, who had lost none of his arrogance or his ambition as a consequence of his defeat at Veracruz,

---

[13] *El País* had supported Francisco León de la Barra for the presidency, and resented Madero's failure to repeal the Laws of Reform. *El Imparcial* had received a generous subsidy from the Díaz government, and the Madero government had not continued the gift.

[14] Francisco Bulnes, *The Whole Truth about Mexico,* 186–87.

232

was transferred to prison in Mexico City when the government erroneously concluded that an attempt would be made to free him in Veracruz.[15] These were the principal leaders of the group which conspired to take control. Outside the immediate circle of their friends they had little prestige and no following; ambitious and selfish, they had no program and no common bond other than resentment against the government.

Rumors of the revolt reached Gustavo shortly before he was to embark for Japan, and he therefore postponed his trip in order to help his brother if necessary.[16] By February 8, evidence of the impending attempt was so strong that some of the suborned army units were transferred to other barracks;[17] but none of the leaders were suspected of their activities. Even though the transfer of some troops upon which they were depending was a blow to the conspirators, they decided to carry out the original plans which called for an uprising on the morning of February 9. At that time, according to the plan, Reyes and Díaz were to be released by force from their respective prisons, the troops of the Ciudadela and the students of the National Preparatory School were to rebel, and the National Palace was to be seized by the troops stationed there on guard duty. Reyes and Díaz were scheduled to appear at the National Palace after it was in friendly hands.

On the morning of February 9, 1913, the plan went according to schedule in the early phases. Reyes and Díaz were released, the National Palace was captured, and the rebellious troops, now led by Reyes and Díaz, marched to the center of the government. In the meantime Gustavo Madero, warned of the plot, rushed to the National Palace and assisted loyal troops to recapture the edifice. Very shortly thereafter General Lauro Villar, commandant of the Mexico City garrison, arrived on the scene to direct the defense against imminent attack. When Reyes and Díaz, leading their columns, appeared before the National Palace, they found it well defended by loyal troops rather than in the control of their fellow-rebels. Momentarily nonplussed by this development, Reyes nevertheless decided that he could capture the government even under the changed conditions. He quite evidently did not believe that Villar, an old companion-at-arms, would give the order

---

[15] Victor José Velásquez, *Apuntes para la historia de la revolución felicista,* 8–9. A deliberate rumor to that effect had been started by a group of conspirators who wished to have Félix Díaz transferred to Mexico City, where it would be easy to free him.   [16] José C. Valadés in *LO,* February 20, 1938, p. 1.
[17] Gonzalo Espinosa, *La decena roja,* 14.

to fire on him. When Reyes refused to halt his column, Villar's troops opened fire and after a short but sharp battle drove the rebels from the field; General Reyes and nearly two hundred of his men were killed in the engagement. The government's losses were fewer in number but more telling, for among the wounded was General Villar, one of the few high-ranking officers of unquestioned loyalty to the government and with the ability to quell the uprising.[18]

The loss of Villar, whose wound incapacitated him, was a blow to the government; Madero and his advisors were now confronted with the difficult task of selecting a successor to direct the battle. After long hesitation, and in spite of Villar's protests, Madero commissioned Victoriano Huerta even though the general's honesty and loyalty were open to serious question.[19] With Huerta's appointment Madero signed his own death warrant.

With Félix Díaz fortified in the Ciudadela, General Huerta situated in the National Palace, and the populace milling through the streets in confusion, there began the bloody struggle commonly referred to as *la decena trágica,* or "the Tragic Ten Days."[20] From its inception the battle for Mexico City was a brutal travesty on decency, justice, and honesty. The conspirators, soon to include Huerta,[21] brought death and destruction to the capital as a part of a deliberate plan to sicken the populace to the point of demanding Madero's overthrow to put an end to the carnage. The basic motif of the battle was an aimless artillery duel between the rebel batteries in the Ciudadela and the government batteries stationed near the National Palace. Shells fell in all parts of the city except the areas under bombardment; battery commanders in both camps were careful not to destroy the batteries of the opponents. The result was ruin in some residential and commercial districts, death for thousands of noncombatants, comparative safety for the troops, and no ascertainable damage to the Ciudadela or other areas where military forces were concentrated.[22] Not all the officers and their men were

---

[18] It was reported that Porfirio Díaz, just before leaving Mexico, had warned Madero through Robles Domínguez not to trust the army. He had said, further, that in case of emergency General Villar was the only high-ranking officer who would remain absolutely loyal to the government.

[19] Wilson to State Department, February 10, 1913, *FR,* 1913, p. 701.

[20] Wilson to State Department, February 9 (2:00 P.M.), 1913, *ibid.,* 699–700.

[21] Taracena (*Madero,* 587) says that Huerta conferred with Félix Díaz almost immediately after Huerta's appointment as commandant. Jesús Urueta claimed that he saw Huerta and Díaz in conference on the initial day.

[22] Manuel Márquez Sterling, *Los últimos días del Presidente Madero,* 414.

party to the deception; the majority of them were loyal, but they were subject to the orders of a disloyal commander. Soon after the battle began, Madero rushed to Cuernavaca to urge General Felipe Angeles to transport his trusted troops to Mexico City,[23] the President's hurried journey immediately giving rise to rumors that he had deserted his capital and left its defense to Huerta.[24] Within a few days Angeles arrived with two thousand men, who, instead of being used to dislodge the four or five hundred rebels holding the Ciudadela, were promptly consigned by Huerta to the needless task of guarding the city against a wholly mythical attack by Zapata.[25] No attempt was made to impose an effective blockade on Díaz, although isolation of the Ciudadela could have been accomplished with ease. Huerta led Madero to believe that the ring was tightly drawn, but in actuality men and supplies moved in and out of the fort with no interruption from federal forces.[26] The only frontal assault on the rebel stronghold was criminal in its conception and its execution: a large force of Maderista irregulars in close formation and without cover was thrown against the bastion, the attack coming from an exposed area which precluded success and guaranteed virtual annihilation for the government troops.[27] Huerta assured the President that the rebels would be forced to submit at any moment. But for ten days the battle raged; for ten days business in the city was at a standstill while the bodies of civilians, forced into the danger zone by their search for food, lay in the streets where they had fallen, victims of the battle.

Immediately after the insurrection began, Félix Díaz demanded Madero's resignation, requesting the American Ambassador to serve as his messenger, but for the moment Wilson declined to play the part. Henry Lane Wilson, ardent admirer of Porfirio Díaz and "strong government," desired above all else Madero's resignation and the negation of all Madero's policies. He feared reform, since reform would inevitably mean a lessening of American influence and fewer special advantages for American interests; he bitterly resented Madero's refusal to be guided by the "advice" freely rendered by the Embassy; he looked on Madero at first with amused tolerance and then with utter contempt

[23] Manuel Valderrama, "Apuntes biográficos," in *Corona funebre en memoria del inmortal Francisco I. Madero*, 5–6. This is a collection of accounts and essays concerning Madero.   [24] *Times* (London), February 12, 1913, p. 5.

[25] Luis Lara Pardo, *Madero*, 322. There was no real reason to believe that Zapata would support Díaz.

[26] Márquez Sterling, *Los últimos días del Presidente Madero*, 425–26.

[27] José Vasconcelos, *Ulises criollo*, 515.

and finally with a burning personal hatred; and he believed whole-heartedly that the Mexicans were fit only for dictatorship and direction by a great power. It was not principle, therefore, which prevented Wilson from acting as Díaz' emissary; he merely considered that the time was not auspicious for such a move, and so contented himself with a demand for ample protection for foreigners from both Madero and Díaz. He also asked Washington to dispatch war vessels to Mexican waters to impress upon the Madero government the gravity of the situation—and incidentally to force the government's capitulation to rebel demands.[28]

As the fighting continued and the losses mounted, pleas for intervention reached Washington. Governor O. B. Colquitt of Texas was particularly insistent, demanding intervention because it was the "obligation of the United States . . . under the Monroe Doctrine."[29] Ambassador Wilson did not favor intervention at that time, but he strongly urged his government to send Madero "firm, drastic instructions, perhaps of a menacing character," to bring the battle to an end; he did not bother to indicate the source of authority by which the government of the United States could instruct the President of the sovereign state of Mexico. When the United States dispatched warships and marines to Mexican waters, Wilson requested that he be given complete authority over the naval forces so that he might have full discretion in using them as a threat to the Mexican government.[30] Officials in Washington, however, were more concerned than the Ambassador with questions of propriety and protocol; Secretary of State Knox failed to see the necessity for granting Wilson either plenary powers or authority over the armed forces, and consistently counseled against intervention except in case of vital necessity to protect American lives. Knox fully recognized the possible dangers to American nationals in the city, but he further recognized the right of the Mexican government to protect itself against the rebels; he recommended removal of Americans into safer zones if imminent danger threatened.[31]

After a week of battle, during which Díaz persisted in demanding Madero's resignation and in urging that his own belligerent status be

[28] Wilson to State Department, February 9 (7:00 P.M.) and 10, 1913, *FR,* 1913, pp. 700, 701.
[29] Governor Colquitt to President Taft, February 12, 1913, *ibid.,* 705. This is a peculiarly distorted interpretation of the Monroe Doctrine.
[30] Wilson to State Department, February 11 and 14, 1913, *ibid.,* 704, 708.
[31] Knox to Wilson, February 14 and 15, 1913, *ibid.,* 709, 710.

recognized by the world powers, the pall began to have its effect. At Wilson's suggestion and with the agreement of representatives of England and Germany, on February 15 the Spanish minister requested Madero's resignation. Madero, indignant at the breach of diplomatic etiquette inherent in the action, denied that the representatives of foreign powers had any right to make such a request; he stated categorically that he would die at his post rather than be subject to foreign pressure.[32] Even though Madero's attitude did much to convince Wilson that under any circumstance the President would have to be displaced, most of the members of the diplomatic corps agreed with the beleaguered President.[33] In commenting on the situation, the Cuban minister to Mexico said:

The intervention of the United States or the underhanded overthrow of Madero would explain the tortuous conduct and obscure words of the Ambassador. The revolution was no longer in the Ciudadela, but in the spirit of Mr. Wilson. Madero did not have to fear Félix Díaz, but the representative of President Taft.[34]

Shortly after this attempt at quasi intervention, a delegation of senators demanded that Madero resign for the safety of Mexico City, but the President refused to see or speak to them concerning the topic.[35] Every suggestion made to Madero that he resign or make any concession to the rebels was coldly scorned as discussion unbefitting a President. It became perfectly obvious that public pressure, stimulated by the frightful conditions for which Díaz and Huerta were responsible, was not sufficient to force Madero to resign. Confronted with his adamant refusal to leave office, Díaz and Huerta determined to remove him by force; they were convinced that the public was so sickened by the battle that it would view with indifference a *coup d'état*. By February 17 the plans were perfected and the American Ambassador, whose interest was obvious and whose sympathies were unmistakable, was notified to expect Madero's removal at any moment.[36] The following afternoon Huerta executed the coup with little difficulty. Gustavo was first eliminated by rank treachery;[37] and then Madero, Pino Suárez,

[32] Chargé d'Affaires to State Department, February 15, 1913, *ibid.*, 710.
[33] Márquez Sterling, *Los últimos días del Presidente Madero,* 405.
[34] *Ibid.*
[35] Wilson to State Department, February 15, 1913, *FR,* 1913, p. 711.
[36] Wilson to State Department, February 17, 1913, *ibid.*, 718.
[37] Huerta invited Gustavo to lunch with him and during the course of the

237

the cabinet members, and two high-ranking officers were arrested by General Blanquet after a brief altercation in which Madero's guards killed two of the arresting officers.[38] Ambassador Wilson, who had wired Washington at noon, before the actual arrest, that the government had fallen, was immediately notified officially by Huerta and asked to serve as the spokesman for the new regime to the remainder of the diplomatic corps.[39] Wilson gladly complied, for Madero's fall was the consummation of his wishes and policy.

The American Ambassador, not content merely to watch developments, then took an active part in determining the course of events. Since, he said, he was "apprehensive of what might ensue" in case of a contest for power between Huerta and Díaz, he "invited" the two generals to the Embassy to consider means for preserving order in the city.[40] From that meeting resulted the instrument, signed by Díaz and Huerta, known as the "Pacto de la Ciudadela"[41] (or more commonly among Mexicans as the Pact of the Embassy), outlining the course to be followed by Díaz and Huerta for the restoration of peace. The agreement recognized Huerta's right to succeed to the provisional presidency, stipulated the names of the cabinet members to serve under him, and included a solemn promise by both Huerta and Díaz that they would do anything necessary to prevent the restoration of the Madero regime. Díaz, aided and advised by Rodolfo Reyes, was primarily responsible for choosing the cabinet.[42] When the agreement was signed, Wilson congratulated himself and the Department of State for the "happy outcome of events, which have been directly or indirectly the result of instructions"; he was pleased with the part he had played,

---

meal excused himself for a moment. Gustavo was then arrested by Huerta's men, turned over to Félix Díaz, and killed in a most brutal fashion. His body was never recovered, the generally accepted version being that he was burned to ashes in the plaza of the Ciudadela. For details, see Vasconcelos, *Ulises criollo,* 516–18; Miguel Alessio Robles, *Historia política de la revolución,* 39, 44; Taracena, *Madero,* 595–600.

[38] Taracena, *Francisco I. Madero y la verdad,* 16–17. Blanquet, one of Huerta's old army friends, had been ordered to Mexico City with his men to support the government.

[39] Gruening, *Mexico and Its Heritage,* 567; Wilson to State Department, February 18 (5:00 P.M.), 1913, *FR,* 1913, p. 720.

[40] Wilson to State Department, February 18 (midnight), 1913, *FR,* 1913, pp. 720–21.

[41] A copy of the pact may be found in Manuel Bonilla, *El régimen maderista,* 86–87, or in English translation in *FR,* 1913, pp. 722–23, n. 1.

[42] R. Reyes, *De mi vida, memorias políticas,* II, 61.

even though his action had put the stamp of approval on a man whom he had already characterized as being of doubtful honesty.[43]

The first step taken by the successful generals in consolidating their power was to force Madero and Pino Suárez to resign. Then, in order to assure at least a façade of constitutionality for the new regime, all the cabinet members with the exception of Foreign Minister Pedro Lascuráin were forced to resign while under arrest. Upon Lascuráin devolved the presidency; and as soon as he had been vested with presidential authority, he in turn named Huerta to the post of Gobernación. Lascuráin then resigned, and Huerta became constitutional president in conformity with the provision governing presidential succession. The new cabinet, which included Francisco León de la Barra, Rodolfo Reyes, Toribio Esquivel Obregón, and Manuel Mondragón, was named immediately.[44]

The most urgent problem confronting the new government was the disposition to be made of the deposed president, vice-president, ministers, and generals who were in custody. At Wilson's insistence[45] the cabinet members were released, but Madero, Pino Suárez, and two generals who had refused to recognize the new government were retained in custody. Apparently Madero and Pino Suárez were doomed to assassination from the beginning. The new government's attitude toward the deposed president and vice-president was succinctly expressed later by a Huerta propagandist: "Let us be clear: nobody wanted to leave these dangerous propagandists of violence and anarchy alive, and their deaths were considered . . . a national necessity."[46] Still, since Madero was a popular and sympathetic figure to many Mexicans, Huerta had to exercise care in handling the situation. Anxious to retain the support of the American Ambassador and hesitant to take any action which might be condemned by the Embassy, Huerta sought Wilson's

[43] Wilson to State Department, February 10 and 18 (midnight), 1913, *FR,* 1913, pp. 718, 720–21. According to reports of those who were there when Wilson announced the settlement to the diplomatic corps, Wilson was in a jovial and expansive mood, obviously quite content with the outcome.

[44] See *Boletín oficial de la Secretaría de Relaciones Exteriores,* February 28, 1913, pp. 68, 71, for the texts of the resignations and appointments. The full cabinet was as follows: De la Barra, Foreign Relations; Alberto García Granados, Gobernación; Jorge Vera Estañol, Education; Rodolfo Reyes, Justice; Alberto Robles Gil, Fomento; Toribio Esquivel Obregón, Finance; and Manuel Mondragón, War and Marine.

[45] Wilson to State Department, February 19 (5:00 P.M.), 1913, *FR,* 1913, pp. 722–23.

[46] Carlos Toro, *La caída de Madero por la revolución felicista,* 59.

advice by asking whether it would be better to commit Madero to an insane asylum or to exile him. Wilson, who until that time had been consistently attempting to force his will on the Mexican government, now developed a strange reluctance to intervene in internal affairs; he merely told Huerta that he should "do what was best for the peace of the country,"[47] and thereafter insisted that he could do nothing in the former president's behalf. Wilson certainly must have known that Madero's life hung in the balance. Madero himself was convinced that he would never leave Mexico alive. His wife was consumed with fear for his safety, and the Cuban minister recognized the danger and reported that danger to Wilson. It was common knowledge that Gustavo and at least one other strong Maderista had been assassinated. Furthermore, Wilson realized that his opinion would carry great weight with Huerta; his innocuous statement, therefore, was tacit consent to Madero's death, and was so interpreted by Huerta.

Preparatory to the assassinations, the government announced that Madero and Pino Suárez would be sent into exile, and a train was made ready to convey the prisoners to Veracruz. At the last moment, however, Huerta announced that he had learned that the commandant of the Veracruz garrison was a Madero sympathizer and planned a movement in support of Madero's return to power as soon as the former president arrived in the port; on that excuse the government postponed the journey into exile.[48] Since their arrest, Madero and Pino Suárez had been held in the National Palace; but in view of the postponed exile, according to the official announcement later, it was decided to move them to the federal prison in the city. On the night of February 21, at an hour approaching midnight, the transfer was begun, but the two deposed officials were killed at the prison gates. According to the government's version, which was accepted by the American Ambassador and all others who wished to uphold Huerta, Madero and Pino Suárez were killed during an exchange of shots between their guards and a group attempting to free the prisoners.[49] In actuality,

[47] Wilson to State Department, February 19 (10:00 P.M.), 1913, *FR*, 1913, pp. 723–24.

[48] Alessio Robles, *Historia política de la revolución*, 48–50.

[49] Wilson to State Department, February 24, 1913, *FR*, 1913, p. 736. In this message Wilson said that he was "disposed to accept the government's version of the affair and consider it a closed incident, in spite of all the current rumors." He repeated this belief in mid-March (Wilson to State Department, March 12, 1913, *ibid.*, 768–76).

For a detailed account of the official version and the investigation concerning

they were the victims of a variation of the *ley fuga,* deliberately killed by two officers acting under Huerta's orders.[50]

In the meantime the state governors were hesitant to make their positions clear with regard to recognition of the new government. Carranza and the Coahuila legislature immediately took exception to the *coup d'état* and declared that the state would consider itself independent of the central government, but the remainder of the states either adhered to Huerta or made no statement at all.[51] Within a few days Carranza appeared to be on the verge of reversing his original position, Ambassador Wilson was urging all consular officers to request the states' co-operation with Huerta, and most foreign governments were ready to extend recognition.[52] By February 21, it appeared that the change of governments would be generally accepted, but at that point the brutal assassination of Madero and Pino Suárez occurred and destroyed any chance the Huerta government might have had for survival. Madero's friends were shocked into opposition, while even many of his enemies considered the deaths unnecessary and the action bestial.

Ambassador Wilson, however, reported that the event had had no ill effect on the temper of the people and that there would be an immediate restoration of peace and prosperity.[53] But American consular

---

the deaths, see the documents in *LP,* September 4, 11, 18, 25; October 2, 9, 23, 30; November 6, 13, 20, all in 1938. Nearly all the documents support the official account, but in addition there are some statements concerning Madero's attitude and actions during his last days that do not bear out this account.

.[50] For a good short account of the assassinations, see Alessio Robles, *Historia política de la revolución,* 65–69. For a more lengthy account, see Calixto Maldonado R., *Los asesinatos de los señores Madero y Pino Suárez.* There are many accounts which give this version, all in substantial agreement on the basic facts. Some of the investigators have concluded that the cabinet discussed the question of disposing of the prisoners and finally decided upon the execution, but this accusation has not been substantiated sufficiently to warrant serious consideration.

[51] Proclamation of the Governor of Coahuila, February 19, 1913, *FR,* 1913, p. 721; Carranza to Coahuila Legislature, February 19, 1913, in Alfredo Breceda, *México revolucionario,* I, 145.

[52] Consul P. E. Holland to State Department, February 21, 1913, *FR,* 1913, pp. 727–28. Wilson to State Department, February 23, 1913, enclosing dispatch to all consular officers in Mexico, *ibid.,* 732.

[53] Wilson to State Department, February 24, 1913, *ibid.,* 734. Most Mexican writers of the period accuse Wilson of direct complicity in the assassinations; e.g., see Alessio Robles, *Historia política de la revolución,* 57–58. There seems to be no reason to believe either that Wilson was specifically informed prior to the act or that he counseled the move; but there can be no doubt that he did not look on the murders as a national catastrophe since he believed or feigned to believe that Madero was a man of "disordered intellect" who "developed all the

officials were less sanguine than the ambassador; at Hermosillo, Nogales, Cananea, Monterrey, Ciudad Porfirio Díaz, and Ciudad Juárez they saw signs of an impending revolution of serious proportions even while Wilson was urging them to recommend state recognition for Huerta.[54] Within a matter of days it was obvious that Coahuila and Sonora would not support the usurper; and large segments of the population in Chihuahua (where Governor Abraham González was assassinated by Huerta officials only a few days after Madero's murder), Campeche, Durango, Guerrero, Chiapas, and other states were soon in opposition. Madero's overthrow and death, which heralded a return to the Díaz philosophy and tradition, destroyed the last hope of the reformers for social and economic improvement through constitutional and peaceful methods. Lest there be some misunderstanding concerning the meaning of the Huerta coup, the American publisher of the *Mexican Herald* announced in boldface type: "Viva Díaz! Viva Huerta! . . . After a year of anarchy, a military dictator looks good to Mexico."[55] Henry Lane Wilson, who had been such a bitter and implacable foe of the Madero government, quite unconsciously foretold the coming revolution with all its brutality and its destruction when he characterized Huerta as "pre-eminently a soldier, a man of iron mold, of absolute courage, who knows what he wants and how to get it, and he is not . . . overly particular as to methods. He is a firm believer in the policy of General Porfirio Díaz and believes in the cultivation of the closest and most friendly relations with the United States."[56]

The Ambassador could not recognize the changed conditions; he ardently desired a return to the Díaz system and failed to take into account the fact that there could be no return to such a system in Mexico; the somnolent population had been awakened. It is ironic that the one thing for which Wilson labored, the restoration of a government which

---

characteristics of that dangerous form of lunacy of which the best example in ancient times is a Nero and in modern times a Castro" (Wilson to State Department, March 12, 1913, *FR,* 1913, pp. 768–76). In this letter Wilson justified his actions and insisted that he had no reason to fear for Madero's life.

[54] Hostetter to State Department, February 28, 1913, *FR,* 1913, p. 747; Bowman to State Department, February 24, 1913, *ibid.,* 735; Simpich to State Department, February 27, 1913, *ibid.,* 744; Simpich to State Department, February 28, 1913, *ibid.,* 746; Hanna to State Department, February 24, 1913, *ibid.,* 736; Ellsworth to State Department, February 27, 1913, *ibid.,* 743; Edwards to State Department, March 2, 1913, *ibid.,* 752; Wilson to Hostetter, February 26, 1913, enclosed in Hostetter to State Department, March 1, 1913, *ibid.,* 751.

[55] February 19, 1913, p. 1.

[56] Wilson to State Department, March 12, 1913, *FR,* 1913, pp. 768–76.

would be subservient to the American Embassy and would intervene in behalf of American interests, was almost completely lost as a result of his attitude toward the Madero government. There can be no doubt that he encouraged, deliberately or accidentally, the conditions which were in large part responsible for Madero's failure. For the death and destruction which followed the Huerta coup, and for the violent anti-Americanism which characterized Mexican policy for years to come, Wilson must bear a large share of the responsibility.[57]

[57] Manuel Márquez Sterling, Cuban Minister to Mexico (*Los últimos días del Presidente Madero*), believed that the country would have been pacified almost immediately had the February revolt been defeated. He considered Wilson to have been largely responsible for the success of the *coup d'état*.

XII

An Evaluation

EVALUATING MADERO'S IMPORTANCE in the development
of the Mexican Revolution presents grave problems, for material progress was small and most of the gains effectuated were changes in spirit
and outlook rather than practice. Attempting to explain categorically
the reasons for his failure to introduce and maintain a strong, democratic regime capable of reform is also difficult because of the complex
design. In any evaluation, moreover, a number of basic conditions,
over which Madero had little or no control, must be considered.

Foremost was the lack of a complete victory over the protagonists
of the Porfirista idea concerning the function of government. Although
Díaz was defeated on the battlefield, the capitulation was conditional,
a compromise which left most of the old elements firmly entrenched in
the governmental and economic life of the nation. As a result of the
compromise, made necessary in a democratic concept, Madero never
gained full control of the government; the Senate always contained a
majority of Díaz personnel, and not until the summer election of 1912,
for the congressional term beginning in September, could the government muster a majority in the Chamber. Even this majority, inexperienced in parliamentary tactics, was never able to make its full
weight felt in the development of a reform program. The older members, those representing the old way of life, were always able by clever
maneuvering to maintain control, or at least to block and postpone actions desired by the reformers. The inexperience of the government
party and the variety of interests led to serious fallacies in the attempt
to introduce and maintain an effective parliamentary system. Congress
was not a cohesive unit with well-defined objectives and an integrated
program. There had been no unanimity during the revolutionary period, other than the hatred for Díaz; and now that the government was
ostensibly in the hands of the group which had been responsible for the
change, there was still no singleness of purpose, and many disturbing

244

and distracting petty differences arose within the legislative chambers. Each representative had his particular desire and his project but was unwilling to subordinate himself and his program to the well-being of the whole. Madero, partially because of his conviction and partially because he lacked the essential characteristic needed in a strong parliamentary leader, was unable to force either restraint or action; and any attempt to do either most certainly would have made him subject to accusations of tyranny.

The same situation prevailed within the ranks of the various cabinets, but here the basic ill was aggravated by the open and public disagreements between the members, conveying the impression of fundamental factional cleavage and administrative chaos. All of Madero's cabinets were heterogeneous, a reflection of his desire to attract to his government the ablest men of every class. By their own lights they were honest men all, but some of them on occasion used their official posts to apply pressure in electoral contests and in so doing lent credence to the widely spread charges of administrative hypocrisy concerning the revolutionary principle of effective suffrage. The actions and words of the ministers encouraged the circulation of rumors of graft and corruption, largely unjustified,[1] and precluded public confidence in the government. Too late Madero recognized that his method of selecting ministers was faulty and that he was depending too much on men not in sympathy with the ideals of the revolution. This was borne home to him particularly during the early moments of the Tragic Ten Days, when a majority of the ministers suggested that he resign; as a consequence of this evidence of timidity and disloyalty, Madero planned to re-form his cabinet to represent the younger and more determined liberals.[2] Whether there actually would have been a reconstitution of the cabinet is a moot point, but some of the American diplomats saw increasing evidence of the practical politician in Madero before the end of his regime.[3]

Another element of supreme importance, a strong factor in formulation of public opinion in Mexico and in foreign countries, was the attitude of the Mexican press. Throughout the Díaz period the press had

---

[1] See Bonilla, *El régimen maderista,* 123, for a tabular comparison of pre- and postrevolutionary financial status of various important personages.

[2] Vasconcelos, *Ulises criollo,* 514.

[3] Testimony of Nelson O'Shaughnessy to Subcommittee of the Senate Committee on Foreign Relations, May 3, 1920, *Investigation of Mexican Affairs,* II, 2707.

been subjected to rigorous censorship of one kind or another, with governmental persecution certain to follow any inadvertent criticism of the Díaz policies. When Madero lifted the ban and encouraged constructive criticism by responsible members of the press, the newspapers for the first time felt free to express any opinion and to report any incident. But editorial responsibility, that fine shade of civic consciousness which prevents a degeneration from liberty to license, was almost completely lacking among newsmen, and the result was disastrous. The government made no attempt to subsidize any newspaper and was therefore dependent upon the small and relatively poor *Nueva Era* for distribution of favorable information, while the opposition, after the first few months of Madero's term, could depend on the larger, well-established publications for the dissemination of vituperation and destructive rumors.

The accusation has been made that both the publisher of the *Mexican Herald* and the management of *El País* offered to support the government in return for substantial grants and then turned against Madero when he refused to comply with the request.[4] The imputation has not been proved, but the enmity of the two publications before the end of the regime was obvious, untempered by good taste or respect for truth. Rumors of the government's weakness or failure were given the widest possible publicity as though actual facts were being reported, but at the same time those news items which tended to show the strength of the administration were either not published or relegated to the back pages. Fact and fiction were mixed with abandon, without discrimination. A hostile and prejudiced press, more interested in serving the selfish ends of the management than in serving the public, made the administrative program more difficult than it would have been under normal conditions. Many of the administration's supporters considered the feasibility of restricting the freedom of publication, but any hint of such action was so roundly denounced as dictatorial and repressive that no real effort was made to force the press to be more discriminating in the choice of material presented to the public.[5] The

[4] C. Maldonado R., "Apuntes biográficos del patriota de Gustavo A. Madero," *Pro-Madero: Reseña de las ceremonias conmemoritiva,* 168.

[5] The *Mexican Herald,* along with its Spanish-language counterpart, *El Heraldo Mexicano,* was closed for a short time in 1912 for refusing to comply with instructions concerning the publication of news of military value; the paper was American owned and managed. Trinidad Sánchez Santos of *El País* was imprisoned for libel and calumny, but his paper was not closed. In no case was a Mexican-owned paper closed.

246

lack of an efficient and honest press which would report and analyze the administration's problems and reform projects was certainly a severe handicap to the Madero government.

Another factor which had a marked effect on Madero's administration was the blindness of many of the intellectuals, American and Mexican, concerning the need for agrarian and other reforms. As late as 1920 an American who had, according to his own statement, spent the major part of his adult life in Mexico insisted that there was sufficient land for all who desired it, that it could be bought and leased on favorable terms, and that in essence there was no land problem.[6] At the same time, Nelson O'Shaughnessy, who was connected with the American Embassy all during the Madero regime, believed that the agrarian problem was "very much exaggerated," more being heard about it in the United States than in Mexico.[7] That failure to recognize the fundamental problems may be further illustrated by a statement of a representative of the conservative class, who wrote in 1920: "In Mexico . . . the land problem lacks the two essential conditions for existence: there is no population group which demands lands to cultivate, and there are no great obstacles to their acquisition. Therefore in Mexico the land problem does not exist."[8]

Not all the opposition to reform was the result of selfish interests, though selfishness played its part. Regardless of the reasons, however, the very fact that there existed no general recognition of the need for reform precluded co-operation from those who should have been leading the way. The same attitude held true with regard to education, labor, and other aspects of the needed socioeconomic program. In the face of such apathy and resolute opposition, only hesitant and completely inadequate steps could be taken with any assurance of fruition. The country would have had to be educated to recognize its needs before any real advances could be made, and for that educational task there was neither sufficient time nor adequate propagandizing agencies.

The greatest obstacle to fundamental reform was the chaotic conditions which Madero inherited and which he was never able to correct. As has already been indicated, most of the armed movements during his administration were dictated by political ambition and selfish

[6] Testimony of E. C. Byam to Subcommittee of Senate Committee on Foreign Relations, May 1, 1920, *Investigation of Mexican Affairs,* II, 2690–91.

[7] Testimony of Nelson O'Shaughnessy, *ibid.,* 2706.

[8] Emilio Rabasa, *L'Evolution historique du Mexique,* 306. See his Chapter 15 for an interesting exposition of his views.

interest; the Zapata movement was the only exception to the general pattern. The major revolutionary outbreaks followed one another with disheartening regularity, allowing the government no respite and dissipating its energies. Only a few days passed between the definite elimination of the original Reyes threat and the beginning of the Orozco rebellion. Orozco was followed by Félix Díaz, and peace had hardly been restored when Orozco again threatened in the north. During all the period of Madero's government Emilio Vázquez Gómez encouraged rebellion, using any or no excuse. Added to those were the perennial Zapata sorties and the myriad smaller movements. Not for a single day was the entire country at peace. Each group responsible for the chaos had an ostensible reason for recourse to arms, but an examination of the programs and demands of each shows clearly that their actions contradicted their presumed ideals. It would have been difficult, if not impossible, to inaugurate fundamental reform in Morelos, for example, since any careful investigation of the situation was precluded by the state of war. At the same time, the very existence of large armed bands made mandatory a vast increase in military expenditure, diverted numerous people from constructive enterprises, kept government personnel under constant tension, and tended to destroy public confidence in the administration's ability to carry on the routine business of government. The increased expenditures for military purposes precluded finances for schools and other badly needed public works, while the demands of the radical reformers destroyed the willingness of the administration to make any concession which would indicate weakness.

In summary, then, neither the psychology of the majority of the Mexicans nor actual conditions were conducive to reform or to efficiency in government. Baited and fought bitterly and viciously by groups who had destructive rather than constructive ideas, constantly confronted with emergencies, the Madero government served out its short sixteen months. Considering all factors, the wonder is not that so little was accomplished, but that anything at all was done and that Madero retained the presidency for slightly more than a year.

Nevertheless, a number of political advances were made. A new electoral law of 1912 went far in the direction of democratization even though it did not, and could not, correct all the abuses prevalent in elections. Pressures were still applied in local areas, and there were many accusations of unfair electoral practices, only a small part of which were justified. A tabulation of the members of the Chamber of Deputies of the Twenty-sixth Congress, the only one elected during the

An Evaluation

Madero period, shows that the imputation of governmental pressure was largely propagandistic, for only a bare majority of bona fide Maderistas were elected, and not all of them were members of the Constitutional Progressive party; a coalition of all other parties could have mustered a majority. Had repressive measures been used, such men as Querido Moheno, Tomás Braniff, Nemesio García Naranjo, and Francisco M. de Olaguibel would never have been allowed to take their seats in the Chamber. By the same token, if Madero, or particularly Gustavo, had been in control of the electoral machinery and had used it to his own ends, Francisco León de la Barra and his supporters would not have become members of the Senate. Political parties operated openly—and on occasion viciously—for the first time in fifty years. In the elections for the Twenty-sixth Congress there were eight well-defined parties in the lists, with three of the opposition parties[9] polling a relatively large vote. The elections held on June 30, 1912, were first reported by *El País* to have been successful, with a notable lack of pressure and chicanery: "For the first time in many years we are having an electoral struggle. This is a novelty for the younger generation, for those who grew up in an age in which liberty of suffrage was absolutely nonexistent."[10]

Even though the propriety of the electoral procedures at the time was generally recognized, the unsuccessful candidates accused the government of fraud as soon as the returns were completed, usually basing their accusations on the fact that only about 8 per cent of the eligible voters had cast their ballots. But even *El País,* violently opposed to Madero, had to admit that it was apathy and not pressure which had been responsible for the small vote, since absolute order and honesty had prevailed at most of the voting booths in Mexico City.[11] Nevertheless, and in spite of the fact that the electoral board in Michoacán nullified approximately seventeen times as many votes cast for the government party as for the opposition,[12] the Partido Católico loudly accused the state government of fraud. Regardless of general charges, however, and of specific instances of unfair tactics, it must be conceded that the election was the most nearly honest ever held in Mexico. Although there was not perfect electoral freedom, at least an approach was made,

[9] The Partido Católico, the Partido Liberal, and the Partido Antirreeleccionista, now supporting Vázquez Gómez.
[10] *El País,* June 30, 1912, p. 1.
[11] *Ibid.,* July 2, 1912, p. 3.
[12] See *ibid.,* August 23, 1912, for the exact numbers.

and it is to Madero's credit that he consistently decried official intervention in either the elections or the seating of elected members.

In the same general field of political advancement, the new freedom accorded to the judiciary must be mentioned. It was a freedom which brought much ill repute to Madero, particularly from foreign sources. Allowing complete independence of judicial action did not guarantee perfect justice, nor did it guarantee either efficiency or rapidity in making decisions. Court procedure was more deliberate under Madero than it had been under Díaz; no longer could the American Ambassador or the diplomatic representatives of any other foreign power demand immediate and favorable judicial action and have any assurance that his demands would be met. But the courts were free; reference need be made only to such cases as the complete acquittal of Rodolfo Reyes, the decision that Félix Díaz was not subject to a military court, or the failure of the court to hold Francisco Vázquez Gómez (for the complicity in the Emilio Vázquez Gómez rebellion) to indicate the nature and sincerity of that freedom. With direct elections, which had been instituted in April, 1912, relative political freedom, and an independent judiciary assured, a definite forward stride had been made.

In material advancement the successes of the Madero government were not marked. Revolutionary activities and bandit raids were not conducive to railway and highway construction, but some work was completed in an effort to develop an adequate and serviceable system of transportation. One of the greatest faults with the railway concessions as granted by Díaz had been that there was no plan for a network of railroads which could service all parts of the country; the development of connecting lines was a project of Madero's government. Many concessions for the construction of these lines were granted under terms favorable to the government, and a considerable portion of the projected construction had been completed before the debacle of February, 1913. The creation of the office of Inspector of Roads, Bridges, and Highways was another step in the improvement of the general transportation system, for the primary function of that office was the maintenance of existing roads and planning construction of others. As long as transportation was poor, there could be no full-scale development of the national economy, and the development of that economy was a prerequisite to political and social stability.

One other aspect of the general transportation scene, closely allied with the labor problem, needs mention because it not only showed the tendency of the government but indicated the difficulty involved in

250

transforming hopes into reality. The administration of the Mexican National Railways, in which the government had long since purchased a controlling interest, was almost completely manned by foreigners, principally Americans; most of the responsible operating posts were also held by citizens of the United States. As a means not only of encouraging the development of a class of administrators and technicians but also of gaining complete control of the railroads, "Mexicanization" of personnel had long been discussed. The replacement of American by Mexican personnel, however, would mean the displacement of considerable numbers of Americans in Mexico, and the American Ambassador was jealous of the rights and prerogatives of American citizens, even when it came to a question of their employment in a Mexican industry. Consequently there were many threats, couched in diplomatic but pointed terms, of the dire consequences which would result from the "mad" policy which Madero was determined to follow.[13] The President was able to carry his point, despite great inconvenience and some momentary disruption of service, and most of the railways were ultimately absorbed into the national pattern. The validity and usefulness of this step can hardly be doubted; the total fruition of the railroad program, including both the Mexicanization of the roads and the construction of new lines, was interrupted by Madero's fall.

In education relatively little was accomplished. The magnitude of the problem was appalling, so that anything done was a definite advance. But the sum total accomplished during Madero's administration was no more than a slight attack on the periphery; the core was never reached. A new philosophy or concept of education, of its place in the development of the nation, was not attained. A few special, night, and industrial schools were established in the Federal District; one or two grange schools to teach the techniques of dry farming were inaugurated in the northern states; and a large number of primary schools, *escuelas rudimentarias,* had either been completed or were in the process of construction before the end of the regime. Some twenty-nine public lunchrooms, serving nearly six thousand school children two meals daily, were in operation by mid-1912; clothing and shoes were distributed regularly—an estimated total of twenty thousand simple suits and twelve thousand pairs of shoes—among the poor children as a stimulus for attendance; and a national meeting of the primary teach-

[13] For the diplomatic correspondence concerning this question, see *FR,* 1912, pp. 911–24.

ers was held. Some steps were taken to improve salaries, general status, and quality of the teachers. These advances in public education were important and necessary, but the attack on fundamentals had not yet crystallized. Most of the activities were purely emergency measures which would have little long-range effect unless followed by a whole-hearted revolution in educational technique and philosophy. That revolution was long in coming.

Enough has already been said of the general agrarian and labor reforms undertaken by Madero, but in reviewing the accomplishments of his government certain fundamentals must be reiterated. As for land reform, it will be remembered that some distribution of national lands was under way, the government had been empowered to purchase lands for division and sale to small holders, a bank had been established for the purpose of improving and building irrigation works, and a program for the restoration of the *ejidos* was being discussed. Only a small portion of the program was actually carried out; the complexity of the problem prevented hasty action, and even among the most ardent revolutionaries there were sincere differences of opinion regarding the best means of developing a reform program. The question of the restoration of the *ejidos,* for example, was the subject of much debate; many felt that private ownership, properly supervised and protected, was essential for the ultimate development and well-being of the rural population. The conviction that the ejidal program was the panacea had not yet developed to any appreciable degree, but the idea of expropriation occurred to more and more responsible leaders, and both ideas were growing in popularity.

Recognition of the need for reform was growing, though still limited; but along with this recognition was also the realization that practical difficulties stood in the way of the immediate consummation of any thorough or worth-while program. With few exceptions, the consensus was that many years would be needed before concrete results could be seen; and it was on the basis of years, rather than months, that the problem was approached. Because of the nature of that approach, the results during the sixteen months of Madero's administration were almost negligible, but the foundation was being laid for a complete over-hauling of the agricultural economy. Madero was thinking in terms of twenty years for the ultimate solution of the agrarian problem; experience since Madero's death seems to indicate that the twenty-year goal, ridiculed by some of his opponents as being so far in the future as to be meaningless, was actually too optimistic.

An Evaluation

With respect to labor and social legislation the same generalizations hold true. At the time of Madero's death the newly created Labor Department was in the midst of a study of possible labor legislation to present to Congress; but aside from that, little action had been taken except of a purely emergency nature. A number of strikes had been settled, generally in a manner favorable to the laborers, as a result of official or semiofficial representations; but legally labor was in a position no more advantageous than it had been under Díaz. An attitude, not legislation, was Madero's greatest contribution to the Mexican laborer. Compared with recent developments in the labor field, Madero's ideas were far from advanced; but in comparison with attitudes of his contemporaries in other parts of America and in Europe, his ideas should not be subject to scorn. Madero was not responsible for the development of concepts of sickness benefits, guarantees of employment, and the host of other provisions which were later incorporated into the Mexican labor code; but few countries, even those highly industrialized, had then accepted the philosophy which fostered those concepts.

An evaluation of the contributions of the Madero regime shows a steady advancement of the idea of governmental responsibility for the well-being of the masses, a recognition and partial crystallization of the need for economic and social reform, and at least an attempt at democratization at the political level. No startling developments in any of these fields are discernible; it would be rank folly to credit the Madero administration with the formulation of all the ideas and ideals incorporated into the Constitution of 1917 and the legislation stemming from the charter. Conversely, complete denial of any beneficent influence could scarcely be justified. Unfortunately, the greatest contribution which Madero could have made was precluded by his destruction; his natural function was that of developing a transition from the semifeudalistic colonial concept, characteristic of the Díaz period, to a progressive, socially conscious administration which could carry out the vitally needed reforms. His background and his idealism admirably fitted him for that task, while neither his education, his natural proclivities, nor his intellect qualified him to undertake a revolutionary program. Had he received the co-operation of all elements, or even of all responsible elements, he could have fulfilled his appointed task. His failure to receive that co-operation all but halted the advancement of his program and eventuated in the overthrow of his government.

Many and varied have been the reasons advanced for Madero's failure to maintain his government. The ardent anti-Maderistas, which

253

would include the majority of American diplomatic representatives to Mexico as well as most of the interests which constituted the bulwark of the Díaz administration, give his weakness of character and his mystical idealism as the principal causes. Others would have us believe that a popular revulsion against the "despotic" and "tyrannical" activities of his administration was responsible. One school would credit the "imposition" of Pino Suárez with the debacle; another would insist that failure to comply with insincere and exaggerated promises brought Madero to an untimely end. The more charitable are convinced that the demobilization of the revolutionary army, which left him at the mercy of the federal forces, was his greatest error in judgment and policy. The fictitious Pirra-Purra, author of *El dolor mexicano,* simplifies the entire problem by saying that the injury sustained by Lauro Villar in the first shock of *la decena trágica* was the cause of Madero's downfall, since Villar's incapacitation gave Huerta his opportunity.[14]

Any and all of these explanations, however, suffer from oversimplification and a failure to consider the broader aspects of the extant philosophies and capabilities of the Mexican people. Madero's presumed weakness of character and mystical idealism were overemphasized; an explanation couched in those terms satisfies nothing. Weakness of character is relative, meaning nothing unless explained and analyzed, and no attempt at analysis has been made by the supporters of that thesis. Madero certainly showed strength of character, or at least physical and moral courage, throughout his public career. His highly publicized idealism has been attacked as though the acceptance of ideals were an indication of basic weakness. Madero was, to be sure, an idealist in one sense of the word: he believed, and strongly, that Mexico had a democratic future which, if properly developed, could go far toward establishing the country as a modern nation. He had faith in the abilities of the Mexican masses, but his idealism did not completely obscure his thinking. He recognized the limitations of his people and of his country. He saw the potentialities of a revolution against Díaz and was almost the only man in the nation who was convinced that the population in general was ready for a change. In view of the success of that revolution, in view of the strides which have since been made in the direction of democratization, in social reform, in educational advancement, and in the assimilation of the masses and the welding of a Mexican nation, who can deny that his idealism was justified?

[14] *La parra, la perra y la porra. El dolor mexicano,* 63–65.

An Evaluation

Madero was confused and vacillating, to be sure, and he placed his trust in untrustworthy men. His confusion was engendered by the magnitude of the problems confronting him, and his vacillating policy was the result of constant and strong forces exerted from every side. He was forced to confide in men unworthy of confidence, because of the very nature of the political degeneracy of the class which should have been of most help to him. It must not be forgotten that he also had faith in many men who truly justified that faith: José González Salas was a suicide because he felt he had failed the government; Abraham González was assassinated because of his support of Madero; and Felipe Angeles suffered long because of his loyalty. A host of lesser individuals, including Pastor Rouaix, made their contributions and paid their price at a later time.

The tyranny and the despotism of which Henry Lane Wilson accused Madero were largely figments of the peculiar imagination of the American Ambassador. A casual reading of the Mexico City newspapers will serve admirably to refute the charges of press censorship. The impunity with which enemies of the government made their vicious attacks, the personal and political freedom enjoyed by the most ardent oppositionists, the lack of political executions and assassinations —all these factors graphically and forcefully deny the existence of a despotic government. Félix Díaz and Bernardo Reyes, in spite of their declarations, were not attacking or attempting to destroy a dictatorial or tyrannical regime; nothing in the political or military background or experience of either of these generals, or of Huerta, would indicate that they were constitutionally opposed to the idea of a dictatorship.

The oft-cited "imposition" of Pino Suárez was not, by the broadest interpretation of the meaning of the term, an imposition at all; Madero frankly and freely gave his support to the candidate of his choice. Under the best democratic practices such is a recognized procedure.

The exaggerated promises presumably made by Madero were never actually made; some were put in his mouth by men anxious to discredit his regime and were therefore used as a tool against him, while other promises were read into his speeches by men who had at stake a particular interest. In fact, Madero's promises at all times were simple and direct: greater political freedom, a sympathetic attitude toward labor which would assure that group of an opportunity to bargain for better working conditions, impartial justice for all men, encouragement to small agricultural holdings, and the return of stolen lands to their owners. In his promises he was absolutely sincere, and in the main there

255

was compliance. Only with respect to the despoiled lands had nothing concrete been done, but here the legal complications were almost insurmountable.

The thesis that the demobilization of the revolutionary army was responsible for Madero's fall is untenable, for there was no assurance that an army of revolutionaries, of sufficient strength to combat the federal army and therefore serve to deter that group from any overt attack on the government, would have been loyal to the regime. Zapata's army was a revolutionary army, as was Orozco's, and yet both of them were active in rebellion against the government. This was true of Juan Andreu Almazán, Juan Banderas, Angel Barrios, "Che" Gómez, and many others. The mere fact that the leader of forces had made common cause with Madero for the overthrow of the Díaz dictatorship did not mean, per se, that he would be self-effacing or willing to co-operate with the new regime.

Finally, the serious wound sustained by Villar and the subsequent appointment of Huerta to the post of commandant can hardly be given full credit for the success of the *coup d'état*. The event did, of course, offer Huerta an opportunity to consummate his treachery, but the stage had already been set: Huerta was merely the instrument.

To what factor or factors, then, can the downfall of• Madero be credited? His personality was partly responsible; for, even though he was intelligent, generous, and well meaning, he was neither wise nor diplomatic. His habit of saying exactly what he thought alienated a great number of people. The Puebla episode and the affair of the revolutionary generals who wished to coerce him were both handled with a conspicuous lack of diplomacy which caused distrust and misgivings. His resentment of the failure of the De la Barra government to support him in Morelos fostered the harsh and undiplomatic attack on the ad interim president, thereby enraging both De la Barra and the Catholic party. His refusal to pander to the military men, both regular and irregular, made him unpopular with the majority of the army. His lack of obsequiousness in his relations with the American Ambassador convinced Wilson that Madero was anti-American and therefore dangerous. In one way or another, through unfortunate or hasty statements, Madero alienated a large number of influential people, powerful men and vindictive.

Madero's failure to attract and hold the co-operation of the influential elements was not in itself a factor; it was a symptom. He failed in this task because dissimulation was foreign to his nature; but had other factors not been operative, dissimulation would not have been necessary. Fear, suspicion, selfishness, inexperience, inability to grasp the significance of the changes in progress, ignorance of and unwillingness to understand the complexity of the problem of renovation—these were the basic factors. For the first time in their memory the Mexicans were free to express their opinions and their prejudices. They were free, many of them, from pressures to which they had been subjected all their lives. Not understanding the responsibilities of that freedom, but only the rights, the average citizen responded with selfish demanding. The nature of the political campaign preceding the revolution and the development of the insurrectionary movement precluded the growth of a cohesive political and social program which would assure co-operation. The entire complexion and atmosphere of the events between 1908 and 1911 had been destructive rather than constructive. Extirpation was the watchword during those years; elimination, not orderly progression, had received the emphasis. That same philosophy of destruction was carried over when the new government came into power. All classes and all groups were anxious to rid themselves of obnoxious or unpopular facets of the civilization under which they lived; every man knew what was wrong, but few had remedial proposals to offer. The major tragedy was that not even the opponents of the government could co-operate for the presentation of a concrete reform platform.

Each element in the society of Mexico must bear its share of the responsibility for Madero's failure, which was, in fact, the failure of the nation rather than of the man. Each group must accept at least a partial responsibility for the suffering of all during the long years following Madero's death. The landowning aristocracy refused to co-operate in any attempt to resolve the agrarian problem and paid for their recalcitrance; in a vain attempt to stem the tide of reform, they brought only ruin and desolation. The impatient peasants, weary of the impositions of the aristocracy, expectant of immediate change, and infuriated when that reform was not immediately forthcoming, used the only weapons at their command; in so doing they postponed for many years any hope of amelioration. The intellectuals, recognizing the shortcomings of the government, indulged in carping criticism instead of giving unstinting aid to Madero and his small group. The government of the United States, through Ambassador Henry Lane Wilson, was guilty of weakening the regime by constant objections in matters of policy and activity. That attitude served only to undermine confidence in Madero's government and thereby helped bring on the truly catastrophic events that followed.

As an illustration of the inefficacy of the Embassy's attitude, the Tragic Ten Days may be mentioned. The constant, pointed, and threatening protests emanating from the American Embassy, on the ground that there was absolutely no point of safety for American citizens and that the entire colony was threatened with destruction, were certainly an important element in the success of the coup. In the final analysis, however, amidst all the death and destruction wrought by the aimless bombardment and the vicious fighting, only four Americans were killed. These deaths could hardly compare with the eighteen killed at Santa Ysabel by Villa in 1916 or the sixteen killed at Cumbre Tunnel in 1914. Far from protecting American lives and property by giving aid and comfort to Madero's opponents, the American Ambassador helped pronounce sentence of death on literally hundreds of Americans who died in Mexico between 1913 and 1920.

A combination of these factors—American opposition,[15] reactionary fervor and hatred, intransigence, personal animosity and jealousy, selfish desires, political ambition, irresponsible freedom, misunderstandings, impatience, lack of cohesion, lack of a concrete social and economic program, and poor diplomacy—these were the reasons for Madero's failure. The problems presented would have taxed the ingenuity and wisdom of any statesman ever produced by Mexico. The explosive qualities which had been fermenting for many years finally burst forth; Madero was the victim.

The fall of the Madero government was a national disaster, regardless of the merits of the government itself. Those who were responsible, either through active opposition or lack of aid and encouragement, had no substitute which would be acceptable to the nation; nothing was gained by his overthrow. It may be argued, with some degree of force, that Madero forfeited his right to the presidency because he was unable to cope with the situation by which he was confronted, but no lucid argument may be presented which will justify the *cuartelazo* which displaced him. Regardless of actual conditions, the only justification for a

---

[15] While the attitude of the Washington government was not particularly hostile to Madero, Henry Lane Wilson as the official representative of the American government was exceedingly antagonistic. Since Wilson was given at least tacit support in his activities, it may be said that the American government was hostile.

revolution is improvement; within the framework of this criterion the Felicista rebellion and the Huerta coup must be evaluated. Huerta and Díaz gave no hope for an improvement of conditions, for the advancement of the democratic ideal, for economic betterment of the masses, or for making the Indian population an integral part of the Mexican nation. The only hope which the new regime held out was pacification, and the brutal murder of Madero and Pino precluded peace. The *coup d'état* settled nothing, proved nothing, solved nothing. The same basic ills from which the nation suffered during the Madero government continued during Huerta's regime, and to those ills were added many more. Huerta himself was a symbol of the times, representative of a powerful segment of opinion: Madero must be destroyed at any cost. The tiger which Madero had unleashed in 1910 was somnolent during his administration; it awakened to its full power for destruction with his death.

Bibliography

I. BIBLIOGRAPHIES, CATALOGUES, AND INDEXES

Bibliografía de la imprenta de la Cámara de Diputados, 1912. Mexico City, Departamento de Aprovisionamientos, 1918.

Bibliografía de la Secretaría de Hacienda y Crédito Público, 1821–1942. Mexico City, Imprenta del Gobierno Federal, 1943.

Castillo, Ignacio B. del. *Bibliografía de la revolución mexicana de 1910–1916.* Mexico City, Talleres Gráficos de la Secretaría de Comunicaciones y Obras Públicas, 1918.

Hasse, Adelaide R. *Index to United States Documents Relating to Foreign Affairs.* Washington, Carnegie Institution of Washington, 1919.

Iguínez, Juan B. *Bibliografía biográfica mexicana.* Mexico City, Imprenta de la Secretaría de Relaciones Exteriores, 1930.

"Indice de *La Opinión*," in *La Opinión* (Los Angeles, California), February 13, 1938.

"Indice de *La Prensa*," in *La Prensa* (San Antonio, Texas), February 13, 1938.

Ker, Anita M. *Mexican Government Publications.* Washington, U.S. Government Printing Office, 1940.

Lombardo Toledano, Vicente. *Bibliografía del trabajo y de la previsión social en México.* Mexico City, Imprenta de la Secretaría de Relaciones Exteriores, 1928.

Naranjo, Francisco. *Diccionario biográfico revolucionario.* Mexico City, Imprenta Editorial "Cosmos," 1935.

Pan American Union. *Bibliography on Labor and Social Welfare in Latin America.* Mimeographed. Washington, Pan American Union, Division of Labor and Social Information, 1940.

Ramos, Roberto. *Bibliografía de la revolución mexicana.* Vols. I and II. Mexico City, Imprenta de la Secretaría de Relaciones Exteriores,

261

1931, 1935. Vol. III. Mexico City, Imprenta de la Secretaría de Educación Pública, 1940.

Times (London) Index (cumulative).

United States Government, Department of Commerce. *General Censuses and Vital Statistics of the Americas.* Washington, U.S. Government Printing Office, 1943.

II. PRIMARY SOURCES

A. MANUSCRIPTS

Madero Archive, Biblioteca Nacional, Mexico City.
Valadés Collection, Mexico City.

B. PRINTED DOCUMENTS AND CORRESPONDENCE

Alvarez, Alfredo, ed. *Madero y su obra. Documentos inéditos.* Mexico City, Talleres Gráficos de la Nación, 1934.

———. *Madero y su obra. Documentos para la historia.* Mexico City, Talleres Gráficos de la Nación, 1935.

Aragón, Agustín. *Datos para la historia de un crimen con algunos comentarios y ciertas reflexiones.* Mexico City, Tipografía Económica, 1914.

Casasola, Agustín, ed. *Historia gráfica de la revolución mexicana,* Vols. I and II. Mexico City, Archivo Casasola, n.d.

Documentos de la revolución mexicana. Mexico City, Secretaría de Educación Pública, n.d.

Esquivel Obregón, Toribio. *Democracia y personalismo.* Mexico City, Imprenta de A. Carranza é Hijos, 1911.

Evans, Rosalie (*nee* Caden). *The Rosalie Evans Letters from Mexico.* Indianapolis, Bobbs-Merrill, 1926.

Madero, Francisco I. *El candidato Madero escribe al Presidente de la República.* Mexico City, 1910.

United States Government. Department of State. *Papers Relating to the Foreign Relations of the United States.* Washington, U.S. Government Printing Office, various publication dates.

Bibliography

Valadés, José C., ed. "Archivo de Carranza," in *La Prensa* (San Antonio, Texas), or *La Opinión* (Los Angeles, California), parts published weekly from March 6, 1938, to July 10, 1938.

―――. "Archivo de Corral," in *La Prensa* (San Antonio, Texas), or *La Opinión* (Los Angeles, California), parts published weekly from September 26, 1937, to February 6, 1938.

―――. "Archivo de Madero," in *La Prensa* (San Antonio, Texas), or *La Opinión* (Los Angeles, California), parts published weekly from October 15, 1933, to May 6, 1934.

―――. "Archivo de Villarreal," in *La Prensa* (San Antonio, Texas), or *La Opinión* (Los Angeles, California), parts published weekly from September 23, 1934, to December 30, 1934.

C. LAWS AND DECREES

Cuadros Caldas, Julio. *Catecismo agrario*. Puebla, La Enseñanza, 1932.

Decreto expedido por el Congreso de los Estados Unidos Mexicanos señalando la forma a que se sujetarán las próximas elecciones de diputados y senadores del Congreso de la Unión y de ministros de la Suprema Corte de Justicia de la Nación. Mexico City, Imprenta del Gobierno Federal, 1912.

Decretos y demás disposiciones del ejército constitucionalista: febrero 19 de 1913 a abril 30 de 1914. Chihuahua (City), Imprenta del Gobierno, 1914.

Dictamen proponiendo que no se aplacen las elecciones de presidente y vicepresidente de la República. Mexico City, Imprenta de Antonio Rodríguez, 1911.

Ley electoral de los Estados Unidos Mexicanos, señalando fechas para elecciones de poderes federales. Saltillo, Imprenta del Gobierno, 1912.

Recopilación de decretos y circulares expedidos durante el año de 1913. Mexico City, Talleres Gráficos de la Nación, 1925.

D. *MEMORIAS,* REPORTS, AND SPEECHES

Acevedo, Jesús, and others. *Breve estudio sobre la incompetencia del tribunal militar que juzgó al Sr. ingeniero don Félix Díaz y a los*

263

demás señores aprehendidos con motivo de la sublevación ocurrida en Vera Cruz el 16 del presente mes. Oaxaca (City), Imprenta de J. S. Soto [October, 1912?].

Affairs in Mexico. Washington, U.S. Government Printing Office, 1911.

Bonilla, Manuel. *Informe que rinde al caudillo Francisco I. Madero, sobre la comisión que le confió para la pacificación de Sinaloa.* Mexico City, Imprenta Popular, 1911.

Comisión de estudio de la campaña de 1910–1911. *Campaña de 1910 a 1911. Estudio en general de las operaciones.* Mexico City, Secretaría de Guerra y Marina, 1913.

Comité Ejecutivo Electoral Antirreeleccionista. *Memorial presentada a la Cámara de Diputados, pidiendo la nulidad de las elecciones.* Mexico City, Imprenta "Idea Libre," 1910.

Covarrubias, José. *Varios informes sobre tierras y colonización.* Mexico City, Imprenta y Fototipia de la Secretaría de Fomento, 1912.

Díaz, Porfirio. *Informe del ciudadano General Porfirio Díaz, Presidente de los Estados Unidos Mexicanos, a sus compatriotas acerca de los actos de su administración en el período constitucional comprendido entre el 1º de diciembre de 1900 a 30 de noviembre de 1904.* Mexico City, Imprenta del Gobierno Federal, 1904.

Madero, Francisco I. *Informe leído por el C. Presidente de la República al abrirse el primer período de sesiones del 26º Congreso de la Unión.* Mexico City, n.d.

———. *El Partido Antirreeleccionista y la próxima lucha electoral.* San Pedro, Coahuila, El Demócrata, [1909?].

———. *La sucesión presidencial en 1910.* San Pedro, Coahuila, 1908.

———, and Francisco Vázquez Gómez. *Programa de los ciudadanos Francisco I. Madero y Francisco Vázquez Gómez, candidatos de la gran convención nacional independiente, para la presidencia y vicepresidencia de la República Mexicana.* Mexico City, 1910.

Proceso por rebelión contra el Lic. Rodolfo Reyes. Mexico City, Imprenta de Inocencio Arriola, 1912.

Reyes, Bernardo. *Defensa que por sí mismo produce el C. General de División Bernardo Reyes, acusado del delito de rebelión.* Mexico City, Imprenta Lacaud, 1912.

Rumbia, José. *Breves comentarios al brillante discurso del Sr. Presidente de la República, aplicados a la situación actual.* Tlaxcala (City), Comité Central Ejecutivo del Partido Liberal Antirreeleccionista, 1912.

Bibliography

E. MEMOIRS, DIARIES, AND CONTEMPORARY
ACCOUNTS

Aguilar Olmos, Rafael. *Madero sín máscara.* Mexico City, Imprenta Popular, 1911.

Alcerreca, Félix M., comp. *Crónica histórica de los acontecimientos trágicos y políticos que tuvieron lugar en la ciudad de México del 9 al 19 de febrero de 1913.* Mexico City, Imprenta Mixta, 1913.

Amado, Enrique. *La revolución mexicana de 1913.* Valencia, Prometeo Sociedad Editorial, 1914.

Aragón, Alfredo. *El desarme del ejército federal por la revolución de 1913.* Paris, [Imprimeries Wellhoff et Roche], 1915.

Atristáin, Darío. *Notas de un ranchero.* Mexico City, Librería de la Viuda de Ch. Bouret, 1917.

Banco Central Mexicano. *Las sociedades anónimas de México.* Vol I. Mexico City, Tipografía de Bouligny y Schmidt, Sucesores, 1908.

Beltrán, Joaquín. *La toma de la plaza de H. Veracruz el 23 de octubre de 1912 y la intromisión yanqui.* Mexico City, Herrero Hermanos, Sucesores, 1930.

Blasco Ibáñez, Vicente. *Mexico in Revolution.* New York, E. P. Dutton, 1920.

Bonilla, Manuel, Jr. *Apuntes para el estudio del problema agraria.* Hermosillo, Imprenta del Gobierno del Estado, 1914.

———. *Diez años de guerra.* Mazatlán, Imprenta Avendaño, n.d.

———. *El régimen maderista.* Mexico City, Talleres Linotipográficos de El Universal, 1922.

Breceda, Alfredo. *México revolucionario, 1913–1917.* Madrid, Tipografía Artística Cervantes, 1920.

Cabrera, Luis. *Obras políticas del Lic. Blas Urrea.* Mexico City, Imprenta Nacional, 1921.

Cadena, Marín y Compañía. *Voto de confianza del comercio de la República al Sr. Gral. Porfirio Díaz.* Mexico City, privately printed, 1909.

Calero y Sierra, Manuel. *Cuestiones electorales,* Mexico City, 1900.

———. *Un decenio de política mexicana.* New York, privately printed, 1920.

———. *La nueva democracia.* Mexico City, Imprenta de Ignacio Escalante, 1901.

———. *El problema actual. La vice-presidencia de la República.* Mexico City, Tipografía Económica, 1903.

265

Castillo, José R. del. *Historia de la revolución social de México.* Mexico City, 1915.

Ceballos Dosamantes, Jesús. *Antinomia política de D. Francisco I. Madero. Profilaxia del cáncer clerical.* Mexico City, Imprenta de A. Carranza é Hijos, 1911.

————. *La gran mistificación maderista.* Mexico City, Imprenta de A. Carranza é Hijos, 1911.

Colina, Federico de la. *Madero y el Gral. Díaz.* Mexico City, Guerra y Vázquez, 1913.

Comité Ejecutivo de la Agrupación Pro-Madero. *Pro-Madero: Reseña de las ceremonias conmemorativas que tuvieron lugar en la República el día 22 de febrero de 1920.* n.p., n.d.

Corona fúnebre en memoria del inmortal apóstol Francisco I. Madero. Mexico City, Imprenta de A. Carranza é Hijos, 1915.

Didapp, Juan Pedro. *Los Estados Unidos y nuestros conflictos internos.* Mexico City, Tipografía "El Republicano," 1913.

Espinosa, Gonzalo N. *La decena roja. La revolución felixista, caída del gobierno maderista.* Mexico City, 1913.

Esquivel Obregón, Toribio. *Democracia y personalismo.* Mexico City, Imprenta de A. Carranza é Hijos, 1911.

————. *Mi labor en servicio de México.* Mexico City, Imprenta Linomex, 1934.

————. *El problema agrario en Mexico.* Mexico City, Librería de la Viuda de Ch. Bouret, 1912.

Estrada, Roque. *La revolución y Francisco I. Madero.* Guadalajara, Imprenta Americana, 1912.

Fernández Güell, Rogelio. *El moderno Juárez, estudio sobre la personalidad de D. Francisco I. Madero.* Mexico City, Tipografía "Artística," 1913.

Fernández Rojas, José. *De Porfirio Díaz a Victoriano Huerta, 1910–1913.* Mexico City, F. P. Rojas y Compañía, 1913.

————. *La revolución mexicana.* Mexico City, F. P. Rojas y Compañía, 1913.

Figueroa Domenech, J. *Veinte meses de anarquía.* Mexico City, 1913.

González, Antonio P., and J. Figueroa Domenech. *La revolución y sus héroes.* Mexico City, Herrero Hermanos, Sucesores, 1912.

González Garza, Federico. *La revolución mexicana. Mi contribución político-literaria.* Mexico City, A. del Bosque, 1936.

————. *El testamento político de Madero.* Mexico City, Imprenta Victoria, 1921.

266

Bibliography

González Garza, Roque, and others. *Memorandum que en el tercer aniversario de la muerte del Presidente de la República Mexicana Francisco I. Madero dirigen al C. Venustiano Carranza y personas que integran los elementos civil y militar de su gobierno de facto.* New York, 1916.

González Roa, Fernando. *El aspecto agrario de la revolución mexicana.* Mexico City, Departamento de Aprovisionamientos Generales, Dirección de Talleres Gráficos, 1919.

[Goribar, Benigno A.] *El maderismo en cueros. Apuntes íntimos escritos en el año de 1912 por un maderista decepcionado (léase avergonzado).* Havana, Imprenta del Advisador Comercial, 1913.

Guadardo, Tomás. *Efemérides del año de 1912.* Guadalajara, Tipografía "El Regional," 1913.

Hernández, Fortunato. *Mas allá del desastre.* Mexico City, 1913.

Hernández Chávez, Salvador. *La angustia nacional en 16 meses del gobierno de don Francisco I. Madero.* Mexico City, Imprenta de Alfonso López, 1913.

————, and A. López Ituarte. *Fracaso y desastre del gobierno del Sr. don Francisco I. Madero.* Mexico City, Imprenta de Alfonso López, 1913.

King, Rosa E. *Tempest over Mexico.* Boston, Little, Brown and Company, 1935.

Lamicq, Pedro. *Criollos, indios y mestizos.* Mexico City, Editorial Azteca, [1915?].

————. *Madero, por uno de sus íntimos.* Mexico City, Editorial Azteca, [1915?].

———— (pseud. Pirra-Purra). *La parra, la perra y la porra. El dolor mexicano.* Mexico City, Editorial Azteca, [1915?].

Lara Pardo, Luis. *De Porfirio Díaz a Francisco I. Madero.* New York, Polyglot Publishing and Commercial Company, 1912.

León Osorio, Adolfo. *Rastros de sangre.* Havana, Imprenta y Papelero "El Iris," de Gumersindo Martínez, 1913.

Lerdo de Tejada, C. Trejo. *Nuestra verdadera situación política y el Partido Democrático.* Mexico City, Talleres Tipográficos de "El Tiempo," 1910.

Luján, Manuel L. *Reconocimiento de la revolución mexicana de 1912, por el gobierno de Francisco I. Madero.* El Paso, Texas, 1913.

Madero, Francisco I. "Mis memorias," *Anales del Museo Nacional de Arqueología, Historia y Etnografía.* Mexico City, Museo Nacional, 1922.

267

Mexican Revolution

Maldonado R., Calixto. *Los asesinatos de los señores Madero y Pino Suárez.* Mexico City, 1922.

Manero, Antonio. *El antiguo régimen y la revolución.* Mexico City, Tipografía y Litografía "La Europa," 1911.

Márquez Sterling, Manuel. *Los últimos días del Presidente Madero.* Havana, Imprenta "El Siglo XX," 1917.

Martínez, Rafael, and E. Guerra. *Madero, su vida y su obra.* Monterrey, 1914.

Martínez, Rafael, and others. *La revolución y sus hombres.* Mexico City, Talleres Tipográficos de "El Tiempo," 1912.

Melgarejo Randolph, Antonio Damaso. *Los crímenes del zapatismo.* Mexico City, F. P. Rojas y Compañía, 1913.

O'Shaughnessy, Edith Louise. *Intimate Pages of Mexican History.* New York, George H. Doran and Company, 1920.

Palavicini, Félix Fulgencio. *Mi vida revolucionaria.* Mexico City, Ediciones Botas, 1937.

Paniagua, Emigdio. *El combate de la Ciudadela narrado por un extranjero.* Mexico City, Tipografía Artística, 1913.

Parra, Gonzalo de la. *De como se hizo revolucionario un hombre de buena fé.* Mexico City, 1915.

Ponce de León, Gregorio. *El interinato presidencial de 1911.* Mexico City, Secretaría de Fomento, 1912.

Prida, Ramón. *¡De la dictadura a la anarquía!* El Paso, Texas, Imprenta de "El Paso del Norte," 1914.

Resendi, Salvador F. *La revolución actual. Sus causas y tendencias. Sus triunfos y fracasos.* Mexico City, Librería de la Viuda de Ch. Bouret, 1912.

Reyes, Bernardo. *Manifiesto del Gral. Bernardo Reyes.* Mexico City, 1911.

Reyes, Rodolfo. *De mi vida, memorias políticas.* 2 vols. Madrid, Biblioteca Nueva, 1929.

Ribot, Héctor. *Félix Díaz en Vera Cruz. El movimiento revolucionario del 16 al 25 de octubre, 1912.* Mexico City, Imprenta 1ª Calle de Humboldt, 1912.

———. *Las últimas revoluciones. Grales. Díaz y Reyes, Madero, De la Barra, los Vázquez Gómez, Limantour, Corral, Pino Suárez.* Mexico City, Imprenta 1ª Calle de Humboldt, 1910–11.

Rivero, Gonzalo. *Hacia la verdad. Episodios de la revolución.* Mexico City, Compañía Editora Nacional, 1911.

268

Bibliography

Sentíes, Francisco de P. *La organización política de México.* Mexico City, Imprenta y Librería de Inocencio Arriola, 1908.

Serrano, T. F. *Episodios de la revolución en México (Estado de Chihuahua).* El Paso, Texas, Modern Printing Company, 1911.

Sierra, Santiago J. *Apuntes biográficos del C. Ramón Corral, candidato de la clase obrera a la vicepresidencia de la República en el próximo sexenio.* Mexico City, Talleres Tipográficos de Carlos E. Unda, 1910.

Taracena, Alfonso. *En el vértigo de la revolución mexicana.* Mexico City, Editorial "Bolivar," n.d.

————. *Mi vida en el vértigo de la revolución mexicana.* Mexico City, Ediciones Botas, 1936.

Toro, Carlos. *La caída de Madero por la revolución felicista.* Mexico City, F. García y Alva, Editorial, 1913.

Turner, John Kenneth. "Election Day in Mexico," *Regeneración* (Los Angeles, California), October 8, 1910.

————. *La intervención en México y sus nefandos factores.* Laredo, Texas, Laredo Publishing Company, 1915.

Vasconcelos, José. *Ulises criollo.* Mexico City, Ediciones Botas, 1936.

Vázquez Gómez, Emilio. *El pensamiento de la revolución,* n.p., n.d.

Vázquez Gómez, Francisco. *Memorias políticas (1909–1913).* Mexico City, Imprenta Mundial, 1933.

Velásquez, Victor José. *Apuntes para la historia de la revolución felicista.* Mexico City, Librería de la Viuda de Ch. Bouret, 1913.

Wilson, Henry Lane. *Diplomatic Episodes in Mexico, Belgium, and Chile.* Garden City, New York, Doubleday, Page and Company, 1927.

F. OFFICIAL PUBLICATIONS

1. BRITISH GOVERNMENT

The Annual Register. London, Longmans, Green and Company.

British Foreign Office. *British Foreign and State Papers.* London, His Majesty's Stationery Office, annual.

Keltie, J. Scott, ed. *The Statesman's Yearbook.* London, Macmillan and Company, Limited, annual.

2. MEXICAN GOVERNMENT

Comisión Monetaria. *Datos sobre rentas de fincas urbanas en la ciudad de México*. Mexico City, Tipografía de la Oficina Impresora de Estampillas, Palacio Nacional, 1903.

Congreso Constitucional. Cámara de Diputados. *Diario de los debates*. Mexico City, Imprenta del Gobierno Federal.

———. Cámara de Senadores. *Diario de los debates*. Mexico City, Imprenta del Gobierno Federal.

Ministerio de Fomento. Dirección General de Estadística. *Censo general de la República Mexicana*. Mexico City, Oficina Tipográfica de la Secretaría de Fomento, various years.

Secretaría de Estado y del Despacho de Fomento, Colonización é Industria. *Memoria presentada al Congreso de la Unión, 1907–08*. Mexico City, Imprenta y Fototipia de la Secretaría de Fomento, 1910.

Secretaría de Fomento, Colonización é Industria. *Anuario estadístico de la República Mexicana, 1906*. Mexico City, Imprenta y Fototipia de la Secretaría de Fomento, 1910.

———. *Boletín de agricultura, minería é industrias*. Mexico City, Secretaría de Fomento, various dates.

———. *Boletín del Departamento de Trabajo*. Mexico City, Secretaría de Fomento, various dates.

———. *Boletín de la Dirección General de Agricultura*. Mexico City, Secretaría de Fomento, various dates.

———. *Informes y documentos relativos a comercio interior y exterior*. Mexico City, Secretaría de Fomento, various dates.

Secretaría de Gobierno. *Diario oficial*. Mexico City, Imprenta del Gobierno Federal.

Secretaría de Industria, Comercio y Trabajo. *La industria, el comercio y el trabajo en México*. Vol. III. Mexico City, Secretaría de Industria, Comercio y Trabajo, 1928.

Secretaría de Relaciones Exteriores. *Boletín oficial*. Mexico City, Imprenta del Gobierno Federal, various dates.

3. UNITED STATES GOVERNMENT

Department of Commerce. *General Censuses and Vital Statistics of the Americas*. Washington, U.S. Government Printing Office, 1943.

Bibliography

Department of State. *Papers Relating to the Foreign Relations of the United States.* Washington, U.S. Government Printing Office, various dates.
Department of War. *Claims Growing out of the Insurrection in Mexico.* Washington, U.S. Government Printing Office, 1912.
Senate. *Investigation of Mexican Affairs.* 66 Cong., 2 sess. *Sen. Doc. 285.* 2 vols. Washington, U.S. Government Printing Office, 1919–20.
————. *Revolutions in Mexico.* 62 Cong., 2 sess. *Hearing* before a subcommittee of the Committee on Foreign Relations pursuant to *Sen. Res. 335.* Washington, U.S. Government Printing Office, 1913.

G. INTERVIEWS

Interview with Señora Angela Madero de Treviño, sister of Francisco I. Madero, in Monterrey, Nuevo León, Mexico.
Interview with General Emilio Madero, brother of Francisco I. Madero, in Mexico City.

III. NEWSPAPERS

El Anti-Reeleccionista (Mexico City), 1909.
El Constitucional (Mexico City), 1909–10.
El Diablito Bromista (Mexico City), 1903–1907.
El Diablito Rojo (Mexico City), 1906.
El Diario del Hogar (Mexico City), 1909–12.
El Dictamen (Veracruz), 1909.
Don Cucufate (Mexico City), 1906.
La Guacamaya (Mexico City), 1906.
El Imparcial (Mexico City), 1908–12.
Mexican Herald (Mexico City), 1911–12.
México Nuevo (Mexico City), 1909–10.
New York Herald, 1909–13.
New York Times, 1909–13.

271

Mexican Revolution

Nueva Era (Mexico City), 1910–12.
Ojo Parado (Mexico City), 1912.
La Opinión (Los Angeles, California), 1934–38.
El Padre Eterno (Mexico City), 1908.
El País (Mexico City), 1909–13.
Panchito (Mexico City), 1911.
La Porra (Mexico City), 1912.
La Prensa (San Antonio, Texas), 1913, 1934–38.
El Progreso Latino (Mexico City), 1911–13.
Regeneración (El Paso, Texas, and Los Angeles, California), 1906–11.
San Antonio Express (San Antonio, Texas), 1909–13.
Tilín-Tilín (Mexico City), 1911.
Times (London), 1909–13.
El Universal (Mexico City), 1911–12, 1941.

IV. SECONDARY SOURCES

A. ARTICLES FROM PERIODICALS

Basave y del Castillo Negrete, Carlos. "Notas sobre política nacional agraria," *El Economista Mexicano,* December 2, 1911, pp. 173–75.
———. "La revolución y el ministro de formento," *El Economista Mexicano,* November 4, 1911, pp. 94–97.
Rosales, Hermán. "La madre del presidente Madero habla de la infancia de su hijo," *El Universal,* May 17, 1927.
Valadés, José C. "La primera presa de la revolución," *La Opinión,* March 11, 1934, section 2, p. 1.

B. SPECIAL STUDIES

Alessio Robles, Miguel. *Ideales de la revolución.* Mexico City, Editorial "Cultura," 1935.
Alvarez, Alfredo. *El limantourismo de Francisco Madero.* Mexico City, Talleres Tipográficos de la Casa de Orientación para Varones, 1934.
Amaya, Juan Gualberto. *Madero y los auténticos revolucionarios de 1910.* 3 vols. Mexico City, privately printed, 1946.

272

Bibliography

————. *Síntesis social de la revolución mexicana y doctrinas universales.* Mexico City, privately printed, 1947.

Andrade, Luis. *México en España.* Madrid, Editorial Hispánica, 1919.

Araquistaín, Luis. *La revolución mejicana. Sus origenes. Sus hombres. Su obra.* Madrid, Renacimiento, 1929.

Baerlein, Henry. *Mexico, the Land of Unrest: Being Chiefly an Account of What Produced the Outbreak of 1910.* London, Herbert and Daniel, 1913.

Bell, Edward I. *The Political Shame of Mexico.* New York, McBride, Nast and Company, 1914.

Blumenkron, Fernando. *Porfirio Díaz en el destierro.* Mexico City, 1922.

Bulnes, Francisco. *El verdadero Díaz y la revolución.* Mexico City, E. Gómez de la Puente, 1920.

Carvajal, Angel. *Al margen de las resoluciones presidenciales sobre la cuestión agaria.* Mexico City, Talleres Gráficos de la Nación, 1929.

Clark, Marjorie Ruth. *Organized Labor in Mexico.* Chapel Hill, University of North Carolina Press, 1934.

Colina, Federico de la. *Porfirio Díaz. Su vida militar. Sus perfidias políticas.* Mexico City, Talleres del "Diario Republicano," 1911.

Creelman, James. *Díaz, Master of Mexico.* New York, D. Appleton and Company, 1911.

DeBekker, Leander Jan. *The Plot against Mexico.* New York, Alfred A. Knopf, 1919.

Díaz, Carlos Félix. *Génesis de la revolución mexicana.* La Paz, Bolivia, Litografía é Imprenta "Moderna," 1918.

El ejemplo de una vida. Porfirio Díaz y su obra para los niños, para los obreros, para el pueblo. Mexico City, 1908.

Esquivel Obregón, Toribio. *La influencia de España y los Estados Unidos sobre México.* Madrid, Casa Editorial Calleja, 1918.

Ferrer de M., Gabriel. *Vida de Francisco I. Madero.* Mexico City, Secretaría de Educación Pública, 1945.

García, Rubén. *El antiporfirismo.* Mexico City, Talleres Gráficos de la Nación, 1935.

García Granados, Ricardo. *Por qué y como cayó Porfirio Díaz.* Mexico City, A. Botas é Hijos, 1928.

Godoy, José Francisco. *Porfirio Díaz, President of Mexico: The Master Builder.* New York, G. P. Putnam's Sons, 1910.

González Blanco, Andrés. *Un déspota y un libertador.* Madrid, Imprenta Helénica, 1916.

González Blanco, Pedro. *De Porfirio Díaz a Carranza.* Madrid, Imprenta Helénica, 1916.

Hackett, Charles W. *The Mexican Revolution and the United States.* Boston, World Peace Foundation, 1926.

Hannay, David. *Díaz.* London, Constable and Company, 1917.

Lara Pardo, Luis. *Madero. Esbozo político.* Mexico City, Ediciones Botas, 1938.

Lemke, William. *The Crime against Mexico.* Minneapolis, Great-West Printing Company, 1915.

Leyva Velázquez, Gabriel. *Resonancias de la lucha. Ecos de la epopeya sinaloense.* Mexico City, Imprenta Mundial, 1931.

Lombardo Toledano, Vicente. *La libertad sindical en México.* Mexico City, "La Lucha," 1926.

López Portillo y Rojas, José. *Elevación y caída de Porfirio Díaz.* Mexico City, 1921.

McBride, George M. *The Land Systems of Mexico.* New York, American Geographical Society, 1923.

McCaleb, Walter Flavius. *Present and Past Banking in Mexico.* New York, Harper and Brothers, 1920.

Magaña, Gildardo. *Emiliano Zapata y el agrarismo en México.* Vol I. Mexico City, 1934. Vol. II. Mexico City, Edición de la Secretaría de Prensa y Propaganda del Partido Nacional Revolucionario, 1937.

Marquand, H. A., and others. *Organized Labor in Four Continents.* New York, Longmans, Green and Company, 1939.

Márquez, J. M. *El veintiuno. Hombres de la revolución y sus hechos.* Mexico City, 1916.

Mecham, John Lloyd. *Church and State in Latin America.* Chapel Hill, University of North Carolina Press, 1934.

Menéndez, Carlos R. *Historia del infame y vergonzoso comercio de indos vendidos a los esclavistos de Cuba por los políticos yucatecos desde 1848 hasta 1861.* Mérida, Yucatán, Talleres Gráficos de "La Revista de Yucatán," 1923.

——. *Noventa años de historia de Yucatán.* Mérida, Yucatán, Compañía Tipográfica Yucateca, 1937.

——. *La primera chispa de la revolución mexicana.* Mérida, Yucatán, Imprenta de "La Revista de Yucatán," 1919.

Molina Enríquez, Andrés. *Esbozo de la historia de los primeros dies años de la revolución agraria de México.* 5 vols. Mexico City, Talleres Gráficos del Museo Nacional de Arqueología, Historia y Etnografía, 1932–36.

274

————. *Los grandes problemas nacionales.* Mexico City, Imprenta de A. Carranza é Hijos, 1909.

Morales Hesse, José. *El general Pablo González. Datos para la historia, 1910–16.* Mexico City, 1916.

Orozco, Wistano Luis. *Legislación y jurisprudencia sobre terrenos baldíos.* 2 vols. Mexico City, Imprenta de "El Tiempo," 1895.

Ortega, Felipe de J. *La revolución y la patria.* Mexico City, 1911.

Ortiz Rubio, Pascual. *La revolución de 1910. Apuntes históricos.* Mexico City, Ediciones Botas, 1937.

Osborne, Julio. *El neroncete mejicano.* Buenos Aires, Editorial Venmar, 1927.

Oviedo Mota, Alberto. *Paso a la verdad. Causas de la revolución mexicana.* Mexico City, Secretaría de Gobernación, 1920.

Paz, Ireneo. *Porfirio Díaz.* 2 vols. Mexico City, Imprenta y Encuadernación de Ireneo Paz, 1911.

Pazuengo, Matís. *Historia de la revolución en Durango.* Cuernavaca, Tipografía del Gobierno del Estado, 1915.

Phipps, Helen. *Some Aspects of the Agrarian Question in Mexico.* University of Texas *Bulletin No. 2515.* Austin, Texas, April 15, 1925.

Pinchon, Edgcumb. *Zapata, the Unconquerable.* New York, Doubleday, Doran, 1941.

Puente, Ramón. *Pascual Orozco y la revuelta de Chihuahua.* Mexico City, E. Gómez de la Puente, 1912.

Ramos Pedrueza, Rafael. *La lucha de clases a través de la historia de México.* Mexico City, Talleres Gráficos de la Nación, 1941.

Retinger, J. H. *Morones de México. Historia del movimiento obrero en ese país.* Translated by Manuel Torres Cano. Mexico City, Biblioteca del "Grupo Acción," 1927

Rojas, Luis Manuel. *La culpa de Henry Lane Wilson en el gran desastre de México.* Mexico City, Compañía Editora "La Verdad," 1928.

————. *Epocas de Porfirio Díaz y Francisco I. Madero en el proceso histórico de nuestra nación.* Mexico City, Publicaciones de la revista "Irrigación de Mexico," 1931.

————. *México pide justicia. Yo acuso al embajador Henry Lane Wilson.* Mexico City, Tipografía Guerrero Hermanos, 1926.

Romero Flores, Jesús. *Anales históricos de la revolución mexicana.* Mexico City, Ediciones Encuadernables, El Nacional, 1939.

Rosales, Ramón M. *El 20 de noviembre de 1910 y el patriota ciuda-*

dano doctor Francisco Vázquez Gómez. San Antonio, Texas, Editorial Ramón M. Rosales, 1921.

Rouaix, Pastor. *La revolución maderista y constitucionalista en Durango.* Mexico City, Editorial "Cultura," 1931.

Serrano, T. F. *El crimen del 22 de febrero.* El Paso, Texas, 1913.

Simpson, Eyler Newton. *The Ejido—Mexico's Way Out.* Chapel Hill, University of North Carolina Press, 1937.

Starr, Frederick. *Mexico and the United States: A Story of Revolution, Intervention, and War.* Chicago, The Bible House, 1914.

Taracena, Alfonso. *Carranza contra Madero.* Mexico City, Editorial "Bolívar," 1934.

———. *Francisco I. Madero y la verdad.* Mexico City, Editorial "Bolívar," 1933.

———. *Madero. Vida del hombre y del político.* Mexico City, Ediciones Botas, 1937.

———. *La tragedia zapatista.* Mexico City, Editorial "Bolívar," 1931.

Torrea, Juan Manuel. *La decena trágica. Apuntes para la historia del ejército mexicano.* Mexico City, Ediciones Joloco, 1939.

Turner, John Kenneth. *Barbarous Mexico.* Chicago, C. H. Kerr and Company, 1911.

Valverde, Custodio. *Julián Blanco y la revolución en el estado de Guerrero.* Mexico City, Imprenta de J. Chávez é Hijos, 1916.

Valverde, Sergio. *Apuntes para la historia de la revolución y de la política en el estado de Morelos, desde la muerte del gobernador Alarcón, pronunciamientos de los Grales. Pablo Torres Burgos y Emiliano Zapata, martires, hasta la restauración de la reacción por Vicente Estrada Cajigal, impostor.* Mexico City, 1933.

Vázquez Gómez, Francisco. *La enseñanza secundaria en el Distrito Federal.* Mexico City, Talleres Gráficos de Editorial Aguirre, 1907.

C. GENERAL ACCOUNTS

Alessio Robles, Miguel. *Historia política de la revolución.* Mexico City, Ediciones Botas, 1938.

Beals, Carleton. *Porfirio Díaz: Dictator of Mexico.* Philadelphia, J. B. Lippincott Company, 1932.

Bemis, Samuel Flagg. *The Latin American Policy of the United States.* New York, Harcourt, Brace and Company, 1943.

Bibliography

Blakeslee, G. H., ed. *Mexico and the Caribbean.* Clark University Addresses. New York, G. E. Stechert and Company, 1920.

Bulnes, Francisco. *The Whole Truth about Mexico.* New York, M. Bulnes Book Company, 1916.

Callcott, Wilfrid Hardy. *Liberalism in Mexico.* Stanford University, California, Stanford University Press, 1931.

Case, Alden Buell. *Thirty Years with the Mexicans in Peace and Revolution.* New York, Fleming H. Revell Company, 1917.

Creel, George. *The People Next Door.* New York, John Day Company, Inc., 1926.

Gruening, Ernest. *Mexico and Its Heritage.* New York, The Century Company, 1928.

McCullagh, Francis. *Red Mexico: A Reign of Terror in America.* New York, L. Carrier and Company, 1928.

Plenn, Jaime H. *Mexico Marches.* Indianapolis, Bobbs-Merrill, 1939.

Pollard, Hugh B. C. *A Busy Time in Mexico.* New York, Duffield and Company, 1913.

Rabasa, Emilio. *L'Evolution historique du Mexique.* Paris, Librairie Félix Alcan, 1924.

Rippy, J. Fred. *The United States and Mexico.* New York, F. S. Crofts and Company, 1931.

———, José Vasconcelos, and Guy Stephens. *Mexico.* Chicago, University of Chicago Press, 1928.

Rosas y Reyes, Román. *Las imposturas de Vicente Blasco Ibáñez.* Barcelona, Sintes, 1922.

Ross, E. A. *The Social Revolution in Mexico.* New York, D. Appleton-Century Company, 1923.

Sáenz, Moisés, and Herbert Ingram Priestley. *Some Mexican Problems.* Chicago, University of Chicago Press, 1926.

Seoane, Luis F. *México y sus luchas internas.* Bilbao, Spain, Viuda é Hijos de Hernández, 1920.

Shipman, Margaret. *Mexico's Struggle toward Democracy: The Mexican Revolutions of 1857 and 1910.* New York, Margaret Shipman, 1926.

Silva Herzog, Jesús. *Un ensayo sobre la revolución mexicana.* Mexico City, Cuadernos Americanos, 1946.

Smith, Randolph Wellford. *Benighted Mexico.* New York, John Lane Company, 1916.

Tannenbaum, Frank. *The Mexican Agrarian Revolution.* New York, The Macmillan Company, 1929.

————. *Peace by Revolution*. New York, Columbia University Press, 1933.

Teja Zabre, Alfonso. *Guide to the History of Mexico*. Mexico City, Press of the Ministry of Foreign Affairs, 1935.

Vasconcelos, José. *Breve historia de México*. Mexico City, Ediciones Botas, 1937.

Weyl, Nathaniel and Sylvia. *The Reconquest of Mexico*. London, Oxford University Press, 1939.

Index

Acapulco, Guerrero: captured by revolutionaries, 137; occupied by revolutionaries, 145

Agrarian colonies: 216

Agrarian Commission: *see* National Agrarian Commission

Agrarian demands: 205

Agrarian reforms: demand for, 24, 173, 174–75, 210; proposed by Díaz, 136–37; feared by northern *hacendados*, 195; accomplished, 208 ff., 252; need for, 208–209, 247; ideas current on, 208–10; in Plan de San Luis Potosí, 209; absence of general demands for, 212; legislation on, 213; proposed by Agrarian Commission, 213–14; provisions for, in Plan Orozquista, 215; objections to, 215, 220; and Twenty-sixth Congress, 216 ff.; investigations made for, 218

Agricultural villages, conditions in, under Díaz: 23

Agua Prieta, Sonora, battle of: 138–39

Aguascalientes (city), Antire-electionists in: 97–98

Aguascalientes (state): Antire-electionist demonstrations banned in, 110; provisional governor selected, 154–55

Agüeros, Victoriano: 44, 56

Aguilar, Cándido: in Morelos, 181; in Oaxaca, 185

Aguilar Higinio: 186

Aguilar, Rafael: 132

Aguirre Benavides, Adrián: 217

Ahumada, Miguel: 79, 82, 91; disrupts Reyes meeting, 68–69; ordered to surrender Jalisco government, 156

Alamos, Sonora: 92, 93, 145

Almazán, Juan Andreu: 182, 256

American nationals: deaths in Mexico, 201, 258; danger to, in Federal District, 236; protection of rights of, 251

American property, protection of: 17, 133

Anarchy reported in Sinaloa: 200

Anenecuilco, Morelos, 1908 rebellion in: 172

Angeles, Felipe: 235, 255

Angostura, Sinaloa: 92

Anti-Americanism: 123, 193, 200–201, 256

Anti-Reeleccionista, El: 76; inauguration of, 79; becomes a daily, 80; function of, 80; closed by Díaz, 85–86

Antire-electionist convention: plans for, 77–78; date set, 89; attended by delegates of Partido Nacionalista Democrático, 101; problems in holding, 101–102; held, 101–106; delegates to, 102–103; nominates Madero for presidency, 103–104; platform drafted, 104; nominates Francisco Vázquez Gómez for vice-president, 105

Antire-electionist party: organized, 62–65; liquidated, 162

Antire-electionists: attempt to organize, 61–62; encounter difficulties in organizing, 61–62; organized, 62–65; co-operation with other parties, 63; party officers, 63; party organization, 63, 79; party platform, 63–

279

Index

Braniff, Oscar: as peace emissary, 146; refuses to discuss Díaz' resignation, 146–47; advises Limantour to settle peace negotiations quickly, 149; member of Agrarian Commission, 211–12

Braniff, Tomás: 27 n., 249

Brownsville, Texas, United States troops concentrated in: 127–28

Buford, U.S.S.: 200

Bulnes, Francisco: on Díaz, 3, 8; on wages under Díaz, 15; on Mexican press, 232

Business and commerce: under Díaz, 6–7, 9–10, 12–13, 15–16; under Madero, 206–207, 230

Bustillos, Chihuahua, provisional capital for Madero revolution: 137

Cabinet: members of ad interim government, 152–53, 153 n.; crisis in ad interim government, 182; crisis in 1912, 217; under Huerta, 239, 239 n.; character of, under Madero, 245

Cabrera, Luis: Antire-electionist, 62; introduces bill to restore *ejidos,* 217; on Madero and agrarian reform, 220–21

Caja de Préstamos para Obras de Irrigación y Fomento de Agricultura, chartered by Díaz: 13

Calderón Baca, Esteban: and Cananea strike, 16–17; sent to prison, 17

Calero y Sierra, Manuel: on Díaz, 8; on the Científicos, 10–11; in ad interim cabinet, 153 n.; proposes liquidation of revolutionary financial obligations, 154; urges Madero to clarify position on 1911 election, 167–68; answers Henry Lane Wilson, 196

Campeche (city): 73, 74, 75

Campeche (state), not represented at Antire-electionist convention: 102 n.

Canada, W. W.: 203

Cananea strike: 16–17

Carbajal, Francisco, Díaz peace negotiator: 148

Cárdenas, Miguel: 41, 42, 76; governor of Coahuila, 40; obtains central government support, 43; elected governor of Coahuila, 44

Carranza, Venustiano: candidate for governor of Coahuila, 76; member of revolutionary cabinet, 141 n.; provisional governor of Coahuila, 155; refuses to accept Huerta *coup d'état,* 241

Carreón, Juan C.: appointed provisional governor of Morelos, 173; requests irregular troops to garrison Morelos, 175; disseminates exaggerated accounts of disorder in Morelos, 179; representative of reaction, 183

Casas Grandes, Chihuahua: 145; Madero defeated at, 132; effects of battle of, 132

Castillo Calderón, Rafael del, contests Figueroa authority in Guerrero: 156

Castro, Jesús Agustín, begins revolution in Durango: 125

Censorship of press: 7, 246, 246 n.

Centro Antirreeleccionista de México: organized, 1909, 63; new party, 1911, 163

Centro Organizador del Partido Democrático: organization of, 51; Madero's reaction to, 51–52; membership of, 52–53; Reyista tendencies of, 56

Cepeda, Rafael: Antire-electionist leader in San Luis Potosí, 98; discusses plans for revolution with Madero, 117; flees to San Antonio, Texas, 118; helps draft revolutionary plan, 120; provisional governor of San Luis Potosí, 156

Chango, El: 25

Chiapas (state), revolutionary progress in: 145

Chihuahua (city): 94; Madero feint toward, 139; meeting, 192; cap-

Mexican Revolution

tured by Orozquistas, 193; reoccupied by federal troops, 197

Chihuahua (state): Antire-electionists in, 94; revolutionary progress in, 145; provisional governor selected, 155; Reyes support in, 188; rebellion in, 191 ff., 229; controlled by Orozquistas, 196; constitutional guarantees suspended by Madero government, 198–99; legislature objects to land reform, 215

Chilapa, Guerrero, captured by revolutionaries: 137

Child labor prohibited: 226

Chile Piquin, El: 25

Chilpancingo, Guerrero: 145

Chinameca, Morelos, scene of clash between Zapatistas and federals: 181

Chintatlahua, La: 25

Científicos: defined, 10; organized, 10; influence on Díaz, 10; and the Liberal Union, 10 n.; function of, 10–11; proponents of upper-class control, 11; political attitudes, 11–12; claims on economic development, 12; materialistic policies of, 34; continuation of control, 39; protest Díaz' intention to retire, 48; attitude toward Antire-electionists, 69; expulsion from ad interim cabinet demanded, 159

Círculo de Obreros Libres: 18, 224

Cities and towns held by Madero insurgents: 145

Ciudad Juárez, Chihuahua: 94; threatened by revolutionaries, 128–29; isolation planned by revolutionaries, 131; besieged by Madero forces, 139; lifting of siege announced, 140; battle of, 140–41; captured by Madero forces, 141; advantages to Maderistas, 149; Treaty of, 150, mutiny in, 192; occupied by Vazquistas, 192; reoccupied by federal forces, 198

Ciudad Porfirio Díaz, Coahuila: 76; objective of Madero revolution, 123; Madero attempts to capture, 124

Club Antirreeleccionista Benito Juárez de Chihuahua: 95

Club Antirreeleccionista de Obreros Benito Juárez: 65

Club Central Antirreeleccionista, organized: 62

Club Central Reyista: 83

Club Democrático Benito Juárez: 40

Coahuila (state): 88, 96; Antireelectionists in, 75; elections in, 75; Antire-electionist demonstrations banned, 110; plans to invade fail, 137; revolutionary progress in, 145; provisional governor selected, 155; reinforced to prevent Reyes revolution in 1911, 188

Colima (city): Antire-electionists in, 92; captured by Madero forces, 145

Colima (state), revolutionary progress in: 145

Colquitt, O. B. (governor of Texas): recommends Madero's arrest, 128; demands United States intervention, 192, 236

Commodity prices, under Díaz: 14

Company stores: 18, 18 n., 226

Congress: under Díaz, 7–8; during Madero administration, 244–45

Constitucional, El: 96

Constitutional amendments: concerning vice-presidency, 1904, 39; proposals for, 67

Constitutional guarantees: suspended by Díaz, 134; suspended under Madero, 198–99

Constitutional Progressive Party: *see* Partido Constitucional Progresista

Constitution of 1857, agrarian provisions of: 19

Convención Reyista, requests postponement of election of 1911: 167

Corral, Ramón: 42, 48, 74, 75, 78, 92; elected vice-president, 1904, 12, 39; supported by Científicos, 12; interest in Coahuila election, 1904–1905, 40–41; stimulates Reelectionists, 65; renominated for vice-presidency in 1909, 66; supported for vice-presidency, 68;

Index

news advance on Cuautla, 180; responsibility for Zapata rebellion, 180; recalled from Morelos, 182; representative of reaction, 183, 259; implicated in plot to seize Madero, 186; appointed to combat Orozco, 196; quarrels with Madero over Orozco campaign, 199; conspires to overthrow Madero, 234, 234 n.; appointed to combat Félix Díaz rebellion, 234–38; executes *coup d'état*, 237–38; makes agreement with Félix Díaz, 238; becomes president, 239; confers with American Ambassador on Madero's fate, 239–40; orders Madero's assassination, 241

Humboldt, Baron Alexander von, on wages: 14–15

Hurtado, Militón: 186

Iglesias Calderón, Fernando: 44, 61, 99; candidate for vice-presidential nomination, 164

Iguala, Guerrero: 145

Imparcial, El: publishes Creelman interview, 47; publishes anti-Zapata articles, 174

Inauguration of Madero, 1911: 170

Indians, treatment of, under Díaz: 6

Inspector of Roads, Bridges, and Highways: 250

Intellectuals: position of, under Díaz, 26–27; fail to support Madero, 247, 257

Interference with electoral campaigns: 90

International complications: resulting from battle of Agua Prieta, Sonora, 138; feared by Madero, 139; resulting from Ciudad Juárez riots, 192; resulting from Felicista revolution, 202–203

Intervention by central government under Díaz: 38–39, 40, 43–44, 73–74

Intervention in Mexico by United States: dangers of, 133–34; demanded by Texas governor, 192, 236; threatened during Tragic Ten Days, 236

Izábel, Rafael, governor of Sonora, 1906: 17 n.

Jalapa, Veracruz: Antire-electionists in, 109; threatened by revolutionaries, 137

Jalisco (state): Antire-electionists in, 79, 90–91; Reyes strength in, 81–82; revolutionary progress in, 145; trouble in, after revolution, 156; strike in, 223

Jiménez, Chihuahua: 94

Jonacatepec, Morelos: 145

Juárez Maza, Benito: 51, 185, 185 n.

Juchitán, Oaxaca, occupied by rebels: 185

Judiciary: under Díaz, 7, 26 n.; Supreme Court rules Félix Díaz not subject to military court, 204–205; during Madero administration, 250

Justice: reform proposed by Díaz, 136; reform proposed by Madero, 158

King, Rosa, reports peaceful conditions in Cuernavaca, Morelos: 174

Knox, Philander C.: 236

Labor: organization under Díaz, 16, 18; strikes and conflicts, 16–17, 18–19, 222–25; demands under Díaz, 18; agrarian, 24; publications, 25–26; organizations favored by Madero, 221–22; establishment of government labor office, 222; government department created, 223; organization of unions, 224–25; obligations under new contract, 226–27

287

Index

110; imprisoned at Monterrey, 111 n., 111–12; quarrel with Francisco Vázquez Gómez, 113–14; released on bond, 115, 116; decides on revolution, 117; escapes from San Luis Potosí, 117–18; leadership in revolution, 119 ff.; appeals to Americans for understanding, 120; appeals to army to support revolution, 122; returns to Mexico, 129; wounded in battle, 132; demands Díaz resignation as peace condition, 146; returns to Mexico City, 157; visits Morelos and Guerrero after revolution, 157; plan to assassinate, in Puebla, 160–62; and 1911 election, 162–70; nominated by Partido Constitucional Progresista, 163; supports De la Barra government, 163; supports Pino Suárez' candidacy, 164–65; opposes Reyes' candidacy, 166–68; attempts to pacify Morelos, 173 ff.; favors demobilization in Morelos, 174; appeals to Morelos *hacendados*, 175; reaches agreement with Zapata, 178–81; bitter over failure of the government to keep terms of agreement, 181; charges Huerta with responsibility for Morelos rebellion, 181; quarrels with ad interim government over Morelos policy, 181; urges replacement of Huerta in Morelos, 182; fails to re-establish peace in Morelos during his administration, 182–84; representative of reform, 183; charges against, by Orozco, 193–94; quarrels with Huerta over Orozco campaign, 199; accused of anti-Americanism by H. L. Wilson, 201; weakness of government, 205, 207; strength of government, 206, 229–30; ideas on land reform, 208–10, 211; contributions to labor benefits, 228; removed by *coup d'état*, 237–38; forced to resign, 239; assassinated, 239–41, 240 n., 241 n.; characteristics of administration, 244 ff.; reasons for fall, 253 ff.; character of, 254

Madero, Gustavo: 32, 33, 37, 41, 80; education of, 30–32; buys newspaper plant to aid campaign, 109; plans for Madero's escape from prison a failure, 116; discusses plans for revolution with Madero, 117; arrested in Mexico, 120–21; as revolutionary agent in Washington, 124; discusses peace proposals with Limantour, 134–35; quarrels with Francisco Vázquez Gómez, 135; member of revolutionary cabinet, 141 n.; demands Díaz' resignation as peace condition, 146; repaid for revolutionary expenditures, 153–54; warns generals against interference in government, 160; fears for Madero's life in Puebla, 161; director of Partido Constitucional Progresista, 162 n.; opposes Francisco Vázquez Gómez' candidacy, 1911, 163; accuses Francisco Vázquez Gómez of opportunism, 170; accused of graft by Orozco, 194; and labor, 224; mission to Japan, 230; postpones mission to Japan, 233; prevents *cuartelazo* led by Félix Díaz, 233; killed, 237–38, 237 n.

Madero, Julio, helps draft revolutionary plan: 120

Madero, Raúl: 37; helps draft revolutionary plan, 120; proposed as commander of forces in Morelos, 178; supervises demobilization in Morelos, 179–80; notified that Zapatistas to be forcibly disarmed, 180–81; representative of reform, 183

Madero family: background, 30; relationships, 36–37; enterprises, 36 n.; financial problems, 56; attempts to dissuade Madero, 88–89; encourages Madero, 108–109

Madero revolution: 119 ff.; and anti-foreign feeling, 123; finance of, 123, 123 n., 125, 138, 139, 141, 147, 153–54, 194; begins prematurely in Puebla, 124; character of beginning, 124; apparent early failure, 125–26; inaction in late 1910, 126; Díaz' confusion concerning, 127; dissension among leaders of, 129–30, 141–44, 144 n.; request for

289

Index

Naco, Sonora: 145

National Agrarian Commission: established by De la Barra, 211; report and recommendations of, 213–14; ineffectiveness of, 218

Nationalism, under Díaz: 26

National lands: survey of, ordered by Madero, 213; survey and sales of, under Madero, 215–16; distribution of, 252

Navarro, Juan: commands federal forces in Ciudad Juárez, 139; execution demanded by Orozco and Villa, 144, 144 n.; escorted to safety in United States, 144

Nayarit (territory), not represented at Antire-electionist convention: 102 n.

New Orleans, Louisiana, Madero in: 125

Nogales, Sonora: 145

Nueva Era: 231, 246

Nuevo León (state): Antire-electionists in, 74; reported free of political agitation, 96; Antire-electionist demonstrations banned in, 110; revolutionary progress in, 145; reinforced to prevent Reyes revolution, 1911, 188

Oaxaca (city), Antire-electionists in: 89

Oaxaca (state): anti-Madero movements in, 170; rebellion in, 185, 186; land seizures in, 210

Oficina General de Trabajo: 222

Olaguibel, Francisco M. de: 249

Opposition party, choice of Mexico City as place for organization of: 50

Opposition to Díaz: political clubs for, 38, 41–42; in local elections, 1904–1905, 40; in state elections, 40–44, 50, 75, 77; beginning of national organization of, 44; and Creelman interview, 48; evidence of, in Yucatán, 72–73; decline of,

due to repression, 86; evidence of, 119–20

Opposition to Madero: result of repayment to Gustavo Madero, 154; development of, during ad interim government, 158, 159, 165, 170–71; growth of, over quarrel with generals, 160; resulting from Puebla episode, 161–62; as result of party convention, 164–65; and Reyes' candidacy, 166–68; as result of Felicista revolt, 204; formed by diverse elements, 205–206; techniques of, 231–32

Orcí, Juan R., charges Madero with inciting to rebellion in San Luis Potosí: 112

Orizaba, Veracruz, Antire-electionists in: 109

Orozco, Pascual: 248, 256; begins revolution in Chihuahua, 125; and battle of Ciudad Juárez, 141; attempts to displace Madero, 141–44, 144 n.; commander of *rurales*, 191; resigns as *rurales* commander, 192; rebels, 192–93; motives for rebellion, 195; forces Emilio Vázquez Gómez to leave Mexico, 197; cost and importance of rebellion of, 198; flees to United States, 198; and agrarian reform, 215

Orozco, Wistano Luis: on need for improvement, 1895, 15–16; on need for reform, 1895, 24

O'Shaughnessy, Nelson, on Madero and agrarian reform: 220, 247

Pachuca, Hidalgo: 145

"Pacto de la Ciudadela": 238

Pact of the Embassy: 238

País, El: 81, 246, 246 n., 249; on anarchy in Sinaloa, 200 n.; on Felicista revolt, 204

Palavicini, Félix F.: secretary of Centro Antirreeleccionista, 63; begins propaganda tour, 65; accompanies Madero, 71 ff.; in Monterrey, Nuevo León, 74; accuses Díaz of

Index

Puebla (state): 77, 88; revolutionary progress in, 145; land seizures by villagers in, 174–75, 210; constitutional guarantees suspended in, by Madero government, 198–99; strikes in, 223

Puente, Ramón: 195

Querétaro (city), Antire-electionists in: 90

Querétaro (state), revolutionary progress in: 145

Quintana Roo (territory), not represented at Antire-electionist convention: 102 n.

Rábago, Jesús M.: 147, 147 n., 198

Radical revolutionaries, fear Madero conservatism: 158–59

Railways: 250–51

Rancheros: 20

Rascón, Eugenio, in ad interim cabinet: 153 n.

Reaction: 205, 210; evidence of, after Díaz' exile, 158; in Morelos, 174; power of, in Morelos, 175; in Chihuahua, 192, 195; in Coahuila, 195

Rebellion: in Oaxaca, 185, 186; in Sinaloa, 186, 190; Reyes', 186–90; in Tabasco, 187; in Zacatecas, 190; in Chihuahua, 191–98, 229; in Veracruz (city), 202–205; extent of, under Madero, 205; in Durango, 229; Reyes–Félix Díaz *cuartelazo*, 233 ff.; in opposition to Huerta, 242

Redo, Diego: 77

Re-electionists: 82, 83; organizing for a convention, 65; in Guadalajara, 83–84

Reform: urged under Díaz, 15–16; 17–18, 24; proposed by Díaz, 136–37; postponed by Madero, 205;

agrarian, 208 ff., 252; labor, 221–28, 253; obstacles to, 244–48; political, 248–50; judicial, 250; educational, 251–52

Reform laws: 20

Regeneración: 25, 44

Rellano, Chihuahua: federals defeated at, 195, 195 n., 196; federal victory in second battle of, 197

Renacimiento, El: 76

Restitution of ejidal lands: 214–15, 217, 219, 252

Revolution: planning for the future of, 158; obstacles to consolidation of, 244–48; *see also* Madero revolution

Revolutionaries in ad interim government: 153

Revolutionary forces, number of: 145, 145 n.

Revolutionary generals: attempt to intervene in politics, 159–60; threaten force, 160

Revolutionary leaders greet Madero in Mexico City: 157

Revolutionary movements against Madero: 185 ff.

Revolutionary party: shows signs of disintegration, 158; reorganized, 162

Reyes, Bernardo: 38, 48, 74, 75, 77, 78, 248; opposed to Científicos, 11; treatment of opposition, 38–39; responsible for suppression in Monterrey, 1903, 38–39; presidential ambitions of, 65–66; political maneuvering of, 66; supported for vice-presidency, 68; blocked by Corral, 68–69; popularity of, in Jalisco, 68–69, 81–82; political strength of, 81–82; candidate for vice-president, 81–85; refuses to commit himself, 82–83; returns to hacienda, 84; in seclusion during Monterrey flood, 84, 84 n.; goes to Europe on military mission, 85; threat to Díaz dissipated, 85; return to Mexico rumored, 101; returns to Mexico, 165–66; renounces political ambitions, 165–66; an-

293

nounces candidacy for presidency, 1911, 166; tentatively offered cabinet post, 166; beaten by mob, 167; accuses Madero of coercion, 168; leaves for San Antonio, Texas, to begin revolution, 168; rebels, 186–90; arrested in United States, 187–88; revolution fails, 189; imprisoned, 189; importance of rebellion, 189–90; plots new revolt against Madero, 232–33; killed in assault on National Palace, 234

Reyes, Rodolfo: 52, 238, 250, 255; supports father's revolution, 187; imprisoned and released, 189; in Huerta's cabinet, 239, 239 n.

Reyistas: 74

Río Blanco strike: 18–19, 36, 46, 109

Robles Domínguez, Alfredo: Antire-electionist, 62; vice-president of Antire-electionist convention, 103; director of Partido Constitucional Progresista, 162 n.; candidate for vice-presidential nomination, 164

Robles Domínguez, Gabriel: offered governorship of Federal District, 153; designated to supervise discharge of Zapata troops, 173; supervises demobilization in Morelos, 179–80; fails in final attempt at peaceful settlement in Morelos, 182–83; representative of reform, 183

Robles Gil, Alberto, in Huerta's cabinet: 239 n.

Rock Springs, Texas: 123

Rodríguez, Antonio, lynched in Texas: 123

Romero Rubio, Manuel (Díaz' father-in-law), Científico: 10

Rouaix, Pastor: 255

Ruiz, Gregorio: 232

Rurales: 185, 191, 198

Salaries: *see* wages

Saltillo, Coahuila: 76; threatened by revolutionaries, 137; captured by Madero forces, 145

San Antonio, Texas: gathering place of Madero revolutionaries, 117, 119; additional troops for, 132; Reyes goes to, 168; base for Reyes revolution, 187

Sánchez Azcona, Juan: 51, 56: Reyes supporter, 53, 61; proposes constitutional amendment, 67; flees to San Antonio, Texas, 117; helps draft revolutionary plan, 120, 121; director of Partido Constitucional Progresista, 162 n.

Sánchez Santos, Trinidad: 246 n.

San Juan de los Llanos, Puebla: 145

San Juan de Ulloa: 17

San Luis Potosí (city): Antire-electionists in, 98; reception of Madero in, 110; Madero and Estrada in prison in, 116

San Luis Potosí, Plan de: 121–23, 159, 209, 221

San Luis Potosí (state): Antire-electionist demonstrations banned in, 110; confusion in, after revolution, 156; Reyes support in, 188

San Pedro, Coahuila: 75

Santa Anna, Antonio López de: 19

Santa Ysabel massacre: 258

Schools: 251

Sentíes, Francisco de P.: 44, 51, 56; purported author of *La sucesión presidencial en 1910,* 57; Antire-electionist, 62

Serdán, Aquiles: imprisoned for political activity, 1909, 101; leader of Puebla Antire-electionists, 101–102; supports Madero's nomination, 102; sponsors Antire-electionist demonstration in Puebla, 108; flees to San Antonio, Texas, 117; helps draft revolutionary plan, 120; begins revolution in Puebla, 124; killed, 124

Sinaloa (state): 77, 78; Antire-electionists in, 92; fighting in, after revolution, 156–57; rebellion in, 186, 190; anarchy and anti-Americanism reported in, 200

Social reform, Madero's ideas on: 158

Index

Social stratification, under Díaz: 4 ff.

Sonora (state): Antire-electionists in, 92; newspapermen imprisoned in, 110; revolutionary success in, 145; trouble in, after treaty, 156–57; Reyes support in, 188; constitutional guarantees suspended in, by Madero government, 198–99

Sons of Morelos, organized to protect property in Morelos: 174

Spiritism, influence on Madero: 33–35

State governors, appointed after end of revolution: 154–57

Strikes: under Díaz, 16–17, 18–19; in 1911–12, 222–25

Sucesión presidencial en 1910, La: 54, 55 ff., 70; writing of, 55–56; family approval for publication of, 56–59; question of authorship of, 57–58; objections to, by Don Evaristo Madero, 58; published, 58–59; effect of, 59; volume of circulation of, 59; contents and character of, 59–61

Suertes: 21

Suspension of constitutional guarantees: under Díaz, 134; under Madero, 198–99

Syndicalism: 16, 25

Tabasco (state): not represented at Antire-electionist convention, 102 n.; pro-Reyes rebellion in, 187

Taft, William Howard: orders concentration of troops on Mexican border, 132; prepares for intervention, 133; declares intent to prevent revolutionary movements from the United States, 188

Tamaulipas (state): Antire-electionists in, 73–74; reported free from political agitation, 96; plans to invade fail, 137; reinforced to prevent Reyes revolution, 1911, 188

Tamazunchale, San Luis Potosí: 212

Tampico, Tamaulipas: 73, 74, 75

Tehuacán, Puebla: 86, 89, 145; threatened by revolutionaries, 137; Madero interview with dissident group in, 160; scene of conference between Madero and Eufemio Zapata, 175

Tepepa, Gabriel: plans revolution in Morelos, 126; executed, 157, 157 n.; inaugurates revolution in Morelos, 172

Terrazas, Félix: 195

Terrazas, Luis: 27 n., 195

Terrenos baldíos: 22

Terrenos de común repartimiento: 21

Texas, attitude toward Reyes rebellion in: 187

Tiempo, El: 56

Tienda de raya: defined, 18 n.; prohibited, 226

Times (London): on chaos in western Mexico, 200; on Felicista revolt, 203 n.; on labor troubles, 223

Tlaquiltenango, Morelos: 157

Tlaxcala (city), captured by Madero forces: 145

Tlaxcala (state): 102; constitutional guarantees suspended in, by Madero government, 198–99; strikes in, 223

Torreón, Coahuila: 76, 196; Antire-electionists in, 75, 76–77; threatened by revolutionaries, 137; captured by Madero forces, 145; general strike in, 222

Torres Burgos, Pablo: plans revolution in Morelos, 126; sent to Madero for co-operation by Morelos revolutionaries, 172

Tragic Ten Days: 234–38, 258

Transportation: 250–51

Tres Marías, Morelos, scene of clash between federals and Zapatistas: 176

Treviño, General Gerónimo: 86, 96, 99; appointed military commander to watch Reyes, 84; takes over administration in Monterrey, 84; criticizes Reyes, 84–85; assures Corral that Monterrey is safe

295

Mexican Revolution

against Antire-electionists, 110; reinforced to check Reyes revolution, 188

Tribuna, La: 232

Truce: at Ciudad Juárez 139–40; granted for Zapata to demobilize, 179; expires in Morelos, 180

Trucy Aubert, Fernando: 196

Twenty-sixth Congress: 216 ff., 248

Ugarte, Manuel: 98

United States: fails to act against Madero, 128; orders Madero's arrest, 128; concentrates troops on Mexican border, 132; reinforces border to hinder Reyes revolution, 187; changes attitude toward Madero government, 200; warns Madero government against political assassination, 231; opposition to Madero, 257, 258 n.

University of California at Berkeley: 31

Valladolid, Yucatán, rebellion in: 111

Vasconcelos, José: 70, 80, 85, 86; Antire-electionist, 62; secretary of Centro Antirreeleccionista, 63; director of Partido Constitucional Progresista, 162 n.

Vásquez Tagle, Manuel: 61

Vázquez Gómez, Emilio: 70, 78, 80, 86, 97, 99, 248, 250; interest in opposition party, 53; speaks for Antire-electionists, 62; president of Centro Antirreeleccionista, 63; influence on Antire-electionist manifesto, 64; proposes Díaz' re-election, 86, 96; quarrels with Esquivel Obregón, 95; urges caution, 109; advocates compromise, 115; flees Mexico, 120; in ad interim cabinet, 153; approves repayment to Gustavo Madero, 154; decries co-opera-

tion with Díaz supporters, 159; quarrels with De la Barra, 159; proposes that Madero assume presidency, 159; resignation from cabinet requested, 160, 160 n.; fears for Madero's life in Puebla, 161; objects to party reorganization, 162; criticizes De la Barra, 163; plans revolution, 170; ignores requests for irregular troops to garrison Morelos, 175; movement for, in Oaxaca, 185, 185 n.; co-operates with Reyes, 190; encourages revolution against Madero, 190–91; assumes title of provisional president, 192; involved in Orozco revolution, 192–93; breaks with Orozco, 197; and agrarian reform, 219–20

Vázquez Gómez, Francisco: interest in Antire-electionists, 62; Madero's choice for vice-presidential nomination, 99–100; nominated for vice-presidency, 105; attitude and function of, 106; qualifications for vice-presidency, 107; helps to draft platform, 107; supports Teodoro Dehesa for vice-presidency, 113; quarrels with Madero, 113–14; asks Madero to propose compromise with Díaz, 114–15; accused of disloyalty by Cosío Robelo and Frías, 115; refuses to join revolution, 120; flees Mexico, 120; as Madero's diplomatic representative, 130; discusses peace proposals with Limantour, 134–35; opposes complete military victory by revolutionaries, 135; quarrels with Gustavo Madero, 135; member of revolutionary cabinet, 141 n.; refuses to discuss peace with Esquivel Obregón, 146; Madero peace negotiator, 148; in ad interim cabinet, 153; threatens force in Coahuila, 155; decries co-operation with Díaz supporters, 159; supports revolutionary generals, 160; objects to party reorganization, 162; accuses Madero of dictatorial methods, 162, 164, 168; confers with Madero concerning 1911 election, 169; resigns from ad interim cabinet, 182; complicity of,

Index